THE MAMMOTH BOOK OF
Mountain Disasters

THE MAMMOTH BOOK OF

Mountain Disasters

True Accounts of Rescue from the Brink of Death

Edited by Hamish MacInnes

CARROLL & GRAF PUBLISHERS
New York

Carroll & Graf Publishers
An imprint of Avalon Publishing Group, Inc.
161 William Street
16th Floor
NY 10038–2607
www.carrollandgraf.com

First published in the UK by Robinson,
an imprint of Constable & Robinson Ltd 2003

First Carroll & Graf edition 2003

ISBN 0-7867-1239-2

8176

Printed and bound in the EU

Come hither, you that walk along the way;
See how the pilgrims fare that go astray:
They catched are in an entangled net,
'Cause they good counsel lightly did forget:
'Tis true they rescued were; but yet, you see,
They're scourged to boot. Let this your caution be.

John Bunyan

Contents

Introduction

This selection of mountain rescue epics is probably the most comprehensive ever produced under one cover. It spans the years when serious attempts were being made on unclimbed peaks and walls, when equipment design wasn't keeping pace with climbers' aspirations for ever harder and more dangerous routes. I have drawn on two of my earlier books, *High Drama* and *The Price of Adventure*, as an historical framework for they contain irreplaceable stories and many of the writers are no longer with us. Also I have added new chapters to plug gaps and to give a wider coverage; some illustrate the quantum leap in the evacuation of the injured.

These true rescue tales come from all corners of the globe. They substantiate the axiom that there's nothing stranger than truth. It is on the great expanses of the sea, polar regions and the mountains that you find this truth, especially when the odds are stacked up against you. It is also true that accidents often originate from poor organisation and lack of experience. However, nature can muscle in with its arsenal of bad weather and hazards which can shatter the best laid plans of even the best prepared. The most safety-conscious mountaineer can find himself caught in a rogue avalanche, a rockfall which seems to have descended from heaven or a sudden blizzard which shifts one into slow motion mode – the premed to a lingering death.

Some say those hitching a ride on this adrenalin roller-coaster get what they deserve; that's the price! However dicing with death isn't necessarily the goal of the addicts of verticality. The quest for adventure and the experience only found in high places and wide spaces lurks in our genes and it has been so since man first ventured from the security of his cave.

I have spent most of my life mountaineering and rescuing. This has had a spin-off in providing contacts with fellow rescuers internationally; from them has come this understated collection of events which otherwise may have been lost to posterity; rescuers are not vociferous about their exploits.

There's inherent danger in many outdoor sports, but if you have a combination of space beneath your boots, high altitude and bad weather, in conjunction with even a simple stumble, you were in the wrong place at the wrong time.

Even a minor injury in severe conditions can be compounded by such factors; multiply this by the trauma of evacuation, then the consequences can be catastrophic. As shown in the following pages some rescues can be measured in days, not hours.

Let's take an example which occurred, not on a Himalayan summit but on a hill walk, on a low heather-clad mountain on the fringe of Loch Etive.

A Dutchman, Antinias Peters, known as Ton, had been a dozen times to Scotland. On this visit he chose Beinn nan Aighenan for his summer hike, an innocent hill walk in an idyllic West Highland setting. He was fit, a veteran of twenty marathons. As he was looking down a gully he inadvertently stood on a clump of overhanging heather to get a better view and crash . . . he plunged into the rocky defile, still with his rucksack on, landing with a thud on the bouldery bed of the steep mountain torrent. It was obvious to him that his leg was either broken or badly injured, but he crawled to the edge of the channel and realised that in his present condition it would be impossible to climb out.

He gulped down some Panadol tablets he had in his first aid kit and resolved to stay where he was until his leg was sufficiently healed for him to move. As a mathematician he logically allocated his miniscule supply of food into various day lots and commenced to write up his soggy diary.

But next day monsoon-like rain triggered a flash flood which carried him down over several rocky pitches. At the bottom of these he managed to crawl about five metres in four hours to try and get out of the defile, but he was still in danger.

Twenty-four hours later he was again swept down the gully,

this time getting his injured leg jammed behind a submerged tree. His only hope was to extricate himself and attempt to climb a short rock wall which was both vertical and smooth.

Since his initial fall he had been swept down over 300 metres. His remaining food was now lost, leaving him with only some cold tea in a flask and an abundance of fresh water. Somehow he managed to scale that rock wall and gasped like a landed fish on top. From here he could see the floor of Glen Kinglass. Down this isolated glen runs a dirt track leading to an away-from-it-all hunting lodge. For six hours he called for help. Amazingly his calls were heard not by two men from a deer stalking party far below, but by the wife of one of them beyond, some distance down the slope. She assumed that it was her husband shouting. It was only when the three stalkers returned to Glen Kinglass Lodge, which they had hired for hunting, that she asked her husband why he had been making that frightful din. When he denied this, they put it down to the bleating of a sheep.

Next morning by the grace of God, Tim Healy, a gamekeeper employed to take the guests stalking, heard calls high on the hillside, from the very lip of the final impressive waterfall which free falls from Beinn nan Aighenan. He mentioned this to his companion, Alasdair Loder. They took out their telescopes – an essential appendage of all stalkers – and spotted Ton waving his anorak from the edge of the waterfall. The ordeal was over, a search and rescue helicopter was scrambled from HMS *Gannet* in Ayrshire and within an hour Ton was winched to safety.

Mountain rescue facilities vary. In some countries a slick instant pick-you-off-the-mountain service is in operation. In more out of the way mountain ranges it's often the old back-breaking trudge it's always been. Generally, the facility is free, with no cost to the victim, but insurance schemes are available offering more comprehensive cover for that disastrous mountain holiday.

The type of helicopter varies to the specific rescue requirement, some dictated perhaps by a joint military obligation, where the aircraft is primarily deployed for marine or ambulance work. For lofty mountain regions, helicopters with a high operational ceiling are a must.

Rescue teams are usually volunteers, but some are made up of professional mountain guides, instructors, military or park rangers. Usually the police are involved in varying degrees, for there's inevitable form-filling for both the living and the dead. All these rescue disciplines are synchronised to the common cause; locating, stabilising and evacuating the injured, or the dead. With this in mind they work closely as a unit, from the helicopter crew to team members and the search and rescue dog.

You may ask why they risk their lives for someone who, perhaps through an act of folly, gets injured or even killed. Well, the rescuers are usually climbers and may themselves have been rescued in the past – they are all aware that a twist of fate can trip even the most wary.

Glossary

abseil	descending a rock face by sliding down a rope
alpine-style	climbing at high altitude in one continuous push in the mountain without making intermediate camps
arête	a rock or snow ridge
belay	a method of safeguarding a climbing partner by tying oneself to a firm anchor from which one can pay out or take in the rope
bergschrund	the gap between a glacier and the upper face of a mountain
brèche	a gap in a ridge
cornice	a mass of snow overhanging the edge of a ridge
crampons	steel spiked frames fitted to boots for better grip on ice
crevasse	a crack in the glacier ice
dièdre	a corner feature in a rock wall
étrier	portable loop ladder used as a climbing aid
gendarme	a rock pinnacle protruding from a ridge
grades	systems of stating the degree of difficulty of a climb; the earliest UK examples included V Diff (Very Difficult) and VS (Very Severe).
jumar clamp	a friction device to aid climbers ascending fixed ropes
karabiners	metal snaplinks used to attach a rope to an anchor
layback	a strenuous crack-climbing technique
litter	stretcher (USA)

névé	snow ice
piton	a metal peg hammered into a rock crack to support a belay
prusiking	ascending a rope with the aid of prusic knots and foot loops
rappel	another name for abseil
rimaye	the gap between snow ice and a rock face
sérac	unstable ice pinnacle
sling	a loop of rope or tape used for belays or in abseiling
strop	nylon loop used for lifting a casualty in helicopter winching
voie normale	the most regularly climbed, usually easiest, route on a mountain

Rescue on the Droites

Blaise Agresti and Jamie Andrew

This is a sad tale, a story of two climbers at the height of their abilities, brought to a halt by the fickleness of fate. They had done nothing wrong, the difficult climb was well within their climbing experience; they were well equipped; the weather was fine. But nature always has the last say, it has that final card which can represent thumbs up in the elation of achievement or thumbs down with a terrible finality.

It is also a tale of the PGHM, a dedicated rescue group, the high mountain police of Chamonix. They went far beyond the boundaries of duty and risked their own lives in what is possibly the most remarkable helicopter rescue ever conducted in the Alps.

The history of mountain rescue goes back a long way in this region, in fact to 1786, and though they didn't have helicopters in those days, the motivation was just the same, the saving of human life – it's an old instinct.

The account of this incident from 1999 is told by the survivor, Jamie Andrew, and the rescue controller, Blaise Agresti. It's a moving story of the rescuer and the rescued and I think a lesson to us all in humility.

Blaise Agresti

"He's alive! I saw him making a hand signal."

Immediately, these words created a stir on the helipad at Les Bois. In a few minutes we gathered in a back room to escape the media throng and prying cameras. Philippe Pouts went on, "I saw one of them alive, that's definite, he gave us a hand signal. They are still at the Brèche des Droites!"

Around the table each person weighed the importance of this news. For two nights, we had been unable to get near the place where the two British climbers had been stuck since Tuesday, and now it was Sunday. Five nights out in the storm at 4,000 metres, trapped by a northerly wind blowing at more than 100 kilometres an hour. Even the strongest alpinists could not have resisted conditions like these. The pair had set out seven days before to climb the famous North Face of the Droites by the Corneau-Davaille route, an extremely difficult ice route. Jamie Andrew and Jamie Fisher were two experienced climbers, accustomed to serious routes, and, despite their youth, had climbed all over the world.

On Wednesday we had been alerted by the families who were concerned that the two were overdue. In Chamonix weather conditions were deplorable, snow and wind creating zero visibility. At the first clearance, on Friday, an attempt was made without success to assess the situation, but the wind was still too strong. Trousselier had been winched to within just a few metres of the climbers, but the helicopter couldn't be stabilised in order to position him to carry out the rescue. All the same, he was able to see that one of the climbers was still alive. On Saturday the north wind was even stronger, nearly 150 kilometres an hour. The temperature was around −15°C in the valley, while at 4,000 metres, we knew that it was not possible to survive for long. In the morning Daniel Poujol had made several reconnaissances to let the climbers and their families know that we were not abandoning them, although we were convinced that we could do nothing useful that day. On one of the flights, Daniel suggested taking me for a look. Right from take-off, the helicopter was buffeted by the storm and we climbed very quickly towards the summit of the Aiguille Verte but then were unable to make any headway against the wind, despite the skill of the pilot. Below us, vortices of spindrift swirled above the ridge which leads along to the Grande Rocheuse, the Col Armand Charlet and the summit of the Droites. The aircraft was thrown around like a nutshell by this wind coming straight from the northern Steppes. I hung on as best I could to the seats of the pilot and the mechanic. Returning to the helipad was difficult, but we finally got down unharmed. The consensus is clear: today we can do nothing.

Jamie Andrew

The storm-tossed helicopter, pitching and rolling on a sea of turbulence, is forced to pull out one more time. Swinging crazily at the end of the winch line, the blue-uniformed rescuer, whose outstretched hand we could for a moment almost touch, is jerked suddenly upwards, dangerously close to the rocks that flank the narrow brèche and then away to the open sky above the glacier. Then the curtain of clouds, which parted so recently, closes again around man and helicopter, objects of our salvation, and they are gone.

The show is over. We are alone on the mountain once more, left to suffer yet another night on this hopeless ledge of ice, scooped in desperation from the snowy crest of a knife-edge ridge, and Jamie Fisher and I begin to despair. It's Friday afternoon now. We've been stuck here since Tuesday, on the mountain since Sunday, and now it looks like we might never get down from this godforsaken spot.

We arrived in Chamonix on Saturday to find the resort enjoying a rare spell of settled winter weather – the sky was blue, the Chamonix Aiguilles sparkled in the sun, and the forecast was for more of the same. We had planned a week of skiing and snowboarding with the large group of friends, but it was too good a chance to miss and Jamie and I quickly decided to put skis and snowboards aside and go for a speedy ascent of the North Face of Les Droites. There would be time for fun on the pistes later in the week. So we hurriedly prepared our kit and on Sunday afternoon we took the last 'frique up to the Grands-Montets station and bivvied there till early the next morning, before crossing the Argentière Glacier to the foot of the vast sheer face that rises for over 1,000 metres to the serrated summit ridge of Les Droites.

It was another beautiful day, the climbing was great, and we made good progress up the face, knowing the route was well within our capabilities. We have been close friends for many years and climb well together as a team – strong and efficient.

We hoped to complete the route and be back down in the valley by Wednesday evening. But the winter days are short and we had to move fast to keep to our schedule. By nightfall we were about halfway up the face. We managed to dig out a couple of small ledges to sleep on and passed the night in relative comfort, considering the situation.

Tuesday morning once again dawned fine and we set to work at first light. Things were going well and we were at least three-quarters of the way up the face when out of nowhere snow began to fall. Before long clouds were rolling over the ridge above us and the snowfall had grown into a blizzard. We didn't panic however and kept on climbing, despite the snow which swept over us in waves of suffocating spindrift and piled onto our shoulders and rucksacks. But it was slow and dangerous climbing in those conditions and it was well after dark when we finally reached the Brèche des Droites, the narrow notch in the summit ridge from where the descent down the other side begins.

It was too late now, and the weather too ferocious to continue, so we dug in as best we could and spent the rest of the night shivering in our bags and praying for better weather. But in the morning the weather was if anything worse and we didn't debate long before deciding to continue to wait.

And now, three days later, we're still here, still waiting. The storm has raged and raged and there has never been a chance of making a descent. The food is long gone, water only a memory. We are fatigued with cold and stiffened with inactivity. Rescue has become our only hope. But that hope too has now been dashed. The Siberian wind rifles through our exposed stance and we huddle together and wait.

Blaise Agresti

In the afternoon I met the families of the two climbers, along with Anne Sauvy, the mountain writer, and her husband, John Wilkinson. I explained to them that we held out little hope. I drew a diagram on the board in the PGHM meeting room explaining the position of the two men and the difficulties which we were having in rescuing them. The press were also beginning to take an interest in the story of this rescue, drawing parallels with the tragedy of Vincendon and Henry forty-two years before.

However, today, Sunday, against all expectations, after a further night, one of the climbers is still alive.

At the helipad, amongst the helicopters, the faces are grim, each knowing that the two Jamies could not much longer survive the glacial cold of this month of January 1999. In the hut which is our shelter on the long days of duty Daniel Poujol, the pilot, was telling how he was thrown around in his machine, an Alouette III, in the turbulence on the Droites ridge during the reconnaissance. The day before, the impossible had been attempted, but nature had been too strong: the north wind, fast-flowing and bitter, forbade any rescue attempts. All the same, Daniel had agreed to take off to "have a look", despite the high risk involved.

This morning the rescuers who flew up know that life is hanging by a thread and depends on the speed of our action. Despite the emotional pressure engendered by the reconnaissance, we have to think about our preparations, weigh the risks, analyse the situation and choose an option. We must resist the temptation to act hastily, we must get the team to work safely. Each member puts forward plans, suggests an idea, then another, the older ones thinking of other, similar rescues, and step by step a scenario is worked out together.

The Alouette is not powerful enough for a rescue such as this and we have to call on Pascal Brun, a private pilot who owns a Lama, a very powerful helicopter which is particularly suited to high-altitude rescue missions. Pascal prefers to use his second pilot, Corrado Truchet, who is both an experienced pilot and a mountain guide. The only problem is that he has gone for the weekend to Courmayeur in the Val d'Aoste on the other side of Mont Blanc. Daniel Poujol suggests going to fetch him in the Alouette III in order to save time. The Alouette takes off straight away and Corrado is soon among us to finish our preparations. Now we have the best possible team for a successful rescue and we go over the plan a final time: the rescuers will be put down as close as possible to the climbers, by a strop carried below the helicopter on a rope, which will avoid the need for the helicopter to come too close to the mountainside where it would be more subject to the effects of turbulence. As well as the Lama, we decide to use the Alouette III in order to share the load-carrying and avoid delays: the Lama will evacuate the climbers from the Brèche des Droites to the Grands-Montets ski area, from where the Alouette will take them to hospital.

As soon as the methodology is decided, everyone sets about their preparations, the Lama soon lands and the strop is fitted, the rescuers check their sacks, put on their crampons, last adjustments, last looks around, the show is on the road, it is time. The characteristic whine of the turbines fills the air, the blades begin to turn, on the tarmac of the helipad everyone protects themselves against the rotor downwash and soon the helicopters claw their way off the ground and fly away towards the Brèche des Droites, 3,000 metres higher, behind the Drus and the Verte. The noise fades, in a few moments calm returns, the commotion of the preparations gives way to a tranquil silence. Now the operation is under way, faces are serious and ears tuned to the crackling of the radio which will bring us news of developments. Up on the Droites ridge, Iglesis Alain, experienced rescuer, devoted alpinist, is moving precisely, methodically. Put down a few cable lengths from the climbers, on an airy pinnacle, Julio, as he's known to his friends, sets up an abseil and goes down to the brèche.

Jamie Andrew

Saturday morning and we've survived the night. But the new day brings us little in the way of hope. The sky is blue this morning but the north wind is stronger than ever and great plumes of spindrift stream from the mountain peaks like vapour trails. There will be no helicopters flying today.

We wait. We talk, share our thoughts, share our warmth. But the energy is failing now. We can't hold out much longer. The hours drag by and finally daylight leaves us once again to the savage night.

Sometime in the night the battle for survival is lost. Comprehension evaporates into the darkness and confusion reigns. Jamie is shouting at me but I can't understand him. My fingers are frozen like pieces of meat. One of the bivvy bags disappears into the night. Finally Jamie stops shouting. He is lying face down in the snow now. I sit beside him, face into the wind, and wait for the end to come.

But death doesn't come and I wait and wait, staring straight ahead into the cold darkness. And the next thing I see is not death, but sunlight, touching the summits of the mountains all around, lighting them up like candles, and a small flame of life is rekindled deep within me. Then when the helicopter comes, swoops overhead with thundering blades, I manage to stir enough to raise an arm, wave my hand, rigid and lifeless as stone.

I watch with curious dispassion as a man is set down on the ridge above. He sets up a rope, struggling in the strong wind and abseils down into the brèche to join Jamie and me on the ledge which we have shared for so long.

Blaise Agresti

Iglesis' heart sinks when he sees the porcelain-white face of Jamie Fisher wrapped in a bivouac bag which is flapping in the wind. Beside him, the face of Jamie Andrew, still full of life, looks at him imploringly. Without delay, he takes a thermos of tea from his sack and gets him to drink a few mouthfuls. The first drops to warm his bones. Simple gestures, few words. The helicopter is ready for the evacuation, there is no time to lose. Iglesis Alain takes Jamie in his arms and clips him on to the cable which is hanging fifty metres below the helicopter. In seconds Jamie is snatched from the Droites, from the Calvary which he has lived with his companion. Life will continue, life must continue.

We are in the Alouette III a few dozen metres away when the Lama lifts its precious load and begins the descent to the Grands-Montets. We see behind us a private helicopter turning above the Droites and quickly realise that it is a TV crew intent on having exclusive pictures of the rescue. We tell them to get out of the way. The Lama continues down to the Grands-Montets ski area. It is a beautiful day and there are many skiers out on the pistes who aren't thinking about what the helicopter passing over their heads may be carrying. The contrast is poignant.

With Philippe Pouts and Jerome Morrachioli, we receive Jamie Andrew at the intermediate helipad at the Grands-Montets, which has rapidly been prepared by a piste machine. With our poor English, we say a few words of comfort to him. While putting him in the stretcher, we touch his legs, hard as wood up to the knee, frozen. The hands also are concrete. We exchange looks of horror. Daniel's Alouette III comes to pick him up in order to take him to the hospital with Jerome, the doctor: he will live, it is written in the annals of fate. The Lama has already left to get the other Jamie.

In a sky of deep blue we soon see the Lama coming back with a body hanging below it, his arms crossed, crucified in his youth for his love of the mountains. We receive him in silence, and once more the Alouette returns to take him to the hospital. At the helipad, when Julio is brought back by the Lama, we feel a profound relief. The rescue is over. When he is put down by the Lama on the helipad, tears roll down Julio's cheeks, his eyes misted.

The rescue was a particularly intense experience, but it is nothing in comparison to all the emotion undergone by the families, to the life that goes on. Jamie Fisher leaves parents devastated by the death of their son, while Jamie Andrew is going to have to learn to live without his legs and hands, to rebuild his life in another way and to find the strength to overcome this terrible handicap. His alpinist's wings have been clipped, but he will be able to show us with his courage that one can travel one's road without these precious assets.

The rescue operation is over, the press are at the helipad at Les Bois, desperate for information and details. The deadlines for the afternoon papers are in a few minutes and we have to relate the conduct of the rescue as succinctly as possible, feed them what they want so that finally we can regain some peace. After a few interviews the mob is satisfied and disperses from the helipad in various directions. We are at last by ourselves, some sort out equipment, others talk about the rescue, life resumes its course and other rescues await us.

However, this exemplary operation did not come to fruition by chance, it woke in me the need to understand, the need to explain this extraordinary profession. I look into history to find the deep meaning of our action. I need to go over the origins of this mountain rescue mission in order better to understand it today. Some people have drawn the parallel between the rescue of the two Jamies on the Droites with other stories in the past, thus showing the continuity of our effort. We are only here thanks to the work, commitment, courage and sometimes the sacrifice of our predecessors, those who opened the road to a professional rescue service. This is a heritage which we owe it to ourselves to pass on to our successors.

Jamie Andrew

For Jamie Fisher, tragically, the rescue came only hours too late. For me it arrived at the very last moment, snatching me from the jaws of death. When Julio reached the brèche, forced hot tea between my lips and helped me into the rescue harness, I revived sufficiently to be aware of what was happening. I could see that the helicopter was unable to hover over the brèche and wondered for a moment how I was to be attached to the winch line. Seconds later the aircraft made a pass straight overhead, trailing the winch line beneath it. Julio deftly caught the hook as it swung past, and in one action clipped it into my harness. A moment later, before I had time to prepare myself for what was about to happen, I was jerked bodily into space and was spinning high in the air, the pristine white glacier far below. The last thing I saw as I was borne swiftly away was Julio in his blue uniform crouching over the slumped form of Jamie – my best friend, dead.

Many considered the operation on Les Droites to have been a failure. One of the climbers was dead, the other as good as dead, losing his hands and feet, a fate unthinkable to a mountaineer. But the rescue was far from being a failure. To the PGHM I owe my life and that is the most precious thing that any of us have, far more important than hands and feet, which I have learned to live without. And I know that if Jamie Fisher had survived and I hadn't, he would have grasped the second chance with just the same enthusiasm. So with every day that passes I am thankful for the success of my rescue from Les Droites.

The Venomous One

Hamish MacInnes, Reup Brooks, Noel Williams, Steve Hayward

Ben Nevis is the highest mountain in the British Isles, though only a mere 1,344 metres above that finger of the Atlantic, Loch Linnhe. However, if you consider the weather pattern at this latitude and its exposure to storms, then it can become a formidable opponent, especially for the ill-prepared.

This is a tale of a father and son pursuing their passion for the hills and observing the rules, who were caught up in events beyond their control which will haunt them for the rest of their lives. It illustrates the determination of individuals to get out of a situation under their own steam, until they were overwhelmed by obstacles in their way. It is also a tribute to rescuers who put the evacuation of both the living and dead above their personal safety.

There are few mountains in Scotland which have the same fatal attraction as Ben Nevis; possibly because it is the highest mountain in Britain. Everything, probably including the proverbial kitchen sink (certainly a piano), has been dragged to the whale-back summit in the name of charity. Platform heels and the ubiquitous carrier bag in lieu of a rucksack are often the artificial aids of the intrepid peak-bagger. Various forms of transport have been used to convey the adventurous to the top, one of the earliest being a motorcycle, but probably the best known vehicular ascent was that by Henry Alexander in a Model T Ford in 1911. He repeated the feat in 1928, driving the car from Edinburgh for the ascent!

The whale analogy for Ben Nevis is not that far out, especially in winter when the Ben, viewed from the south, resembles

Captain Ahab's big white adversary. The Ben is not a friendly mountain and the interpretation of the name may come from a Gaelic compound word, Beinn-neamh-bhatais. The *neamh* refers to cloud or heaven and *bhatais*, the top of the head, a name describing a peak with its head in the clouds, not unlike the Maori name for Mount Cook, Aorangi, the Cloud-Piercer. Certainly, on a stunning spring day on the summit, one could imagine being transported to even loftier heights. However, another interpretation of the name is "venomous" or "malicious", appropriate for a mountain buffeted by the full fury of Atlantic storms in whose track it lies.

The first recorded ascent was in 1771 by one James Robertson, a botanist who was collecting specimens for Edinburgh University Museum. The poet John Keats gained the summit in 1888 and, diverting into the realms of meteorology, there wrote a sonnet on the all familiar scene:

> Read me a lesson, Muse, and speak it loud
> Upon the top of Nevis, blind in mist!
> I look into the Chasms and a Shroud
> Vapourous doth hide them; just so much I wist
> Mankind doth know of hell: I look o'erhead,
> And there is a sullen mist; even so much
> Mankind can tell of heaven . . .

It is the north-east face of the Ben that attracts mountaineers and generations of them have trudged to the mighty cliffs through the boot-topping squelch of the Allt a' Mhuillinn glen for over a century. These great cliffs are the most impressive in Britain but it's in winter they come into their own. North-East Buttress and Tower Ridge are enormous flying buttresses which prop up the 1,000-foot high precipices of this lofty leviathan. There is also a host of smaller ridges and faces and a profusion of gullies in the wings. On its right flank is Carn Dearg which offers some of the best rock climbing in the country.

Getting to know the Ben is like a protracted relationship. Eventually you become intimate with its gullies and buttresses which are as complex as a computer motherboard. In winter it can offer pristine white cover, persuading you into thinking that no human has ever stepped on it before. These winter gullies and faces were the birthplace of modern ice climbing and devotees come from all over the world to pay homage with the ascent of its classic routes. But the quick-change weather ensures that for many a given climb on your personal tick-off list is more often than not re-scheduled for next time round. One has to be patient to winter climb on this great north-east face; a straightforward route, especially in winter, can transform chameleon-like with a passing snow cloud.

An early weather man, Clement Wragg, was a motive force behind the establishment of an observatory on the summit in 1883. Later there was even a summit hotel whose guest book prompted the now popular entry: "Missed the view, viewed the mist." Wragg's tenacity in daily walking and climbing the fourteen miles to the summit from Fort William, regardless of weather, earned him the title of Inclement Wragg.

Few people, unless they dabble in particle physics, know that the idea of the cloud chamber was first conceived by Charles Wilson who spent two weeks in September 1894 working as a student at the summit Observatory. Later he was awarded the Nobel Prize.

The Observatory was a relatively short-lived experiment which suffered several narrow escapes from the elements. In June 1895 a shocked occupant recorded: "a blinding flash of lightning illuminated the Observatory, followed instantly by a terrific crash. Bluish spurts of flame and a cloud of smoke burst from the telegraph instrument and the cook, who was sitting in the office at the time, was pitched on his back and rendered unconscious." The cook survived – though slightly overdone – but the telegraph apparatus was wrecked, "melted beyond recognition". During the operation of the Observatory the annual rainfall averaged 160.69 inches, with 1898 holding the record – twenty feet!

Chucking away litter isn't just a modern Scottish trait. They did it on Ben Nevis, using Gardyloo Gully as a skip. This elegant chute takes it name from an early Edinburgh custom of throwing the contents of chamber pots out of bedroom windows onto the street below with the accompanying call of *Gardez l'eau!* In its skip chute capacity Gardyloo Gully played a role in the final demise of Britain's highest building. Two tough gentlemen, who will remain anonymous, spent several months, including their Army demobilisation leave at the end of the Second World War, stripping the Observatory roof of its lead. This they neatly rolled up like high density Swiss rolls and launched them down the hard spring snow of the gully. Then after weeks of back-breaking work carrying them to Fort William under cover of darkness, they borrowed a truck and drove to the yard of a heavy metal dealer in Glasgow. The post-war boom had inflated the price of lead, but ironically on that precise day the bottom fell out of the lead market – they barely recouped their expenses. There must be a moral here.

The ascent of the great natural features of the Ben elicited the attention of the pioneers at the tail end of the nineteenth century. The brothers J.E. and B. Hopkinson succeeded in making the first ascent of the North-East Buttress in September 1882. Not to be outdone by the Hopkinsons, the indomitable Norman Collie, with Solly and Collier, two other redoubtable cragsmen, climbed Tower Ridge in the winter of 1894. Even today this snow and ice climb is considered a three star outing using modern gear.

In the year 1861 William Henry Burroughes of the renowned billiard table makers, Burroughes & Watts of London, together with a party of seven, arrived by steamer at Fort William to scale Ben Nevis. They had hired an experienced local guide, Duncan McMillan, for at this time there was no proper track up the mountain. The guide seemed to have little control over the gentry and the fitter ones pressed ahead, keen to get to the top before dark. Henry Burroughes was however feeling tired by the time they had reached the 4,000-foot contour, about a quarter of a mile short of the summit. This was at a fountain called Spring Nevis. He told Duncan that he would stay there until they returned.

Duncan instructed him the route to follow to the top, should he wish to continue, then dashed off to catch up with the wayward vanguard. After a breather, Henry did decide to follow, but the weather was closing in, and he stopped once more to await the return of his friends. An hour later he thought that they too must be lost and attempted a lone descent. Crawling and slithering down wet rock for over a thousand feet – now in zero visibility – he realised that he had lost the way altogether and was in what appeared to be a corrie and resolved to stop for the night. He had with him the equivalent of a modern bivvy bag, an oilskin cape and "squeezing between two immense blocks of granite on the side of the mountain, and close to one of the numerous streams of water winding down its stupendous sides," there he spent a miserable night. At dawn it appeared to be clearing and he started to ascend, intending, if possible, to find out exactly where he was and "in which direction he should steer his course". But the mist enveloped him again and he decided once more to descend – this time in a different direction.

What he did for the remainder of the day is a mystery, for it was late afternoon before he got below the base of the cloud. And the "sea" (Loch Linnhe) was revealed with Glen Nevis "illuminated" by the bright rays of the setting sun. It took him over an hour to cross a raging torrent and he was almost drowned in the process. Then he "descried a shepherd accompanied by his dog". The shepherd was looking for lost sheep, not a lost walker, nevertheless he took him down to his cottage and provided him with "refreshments", then drove him five miles to his hotel in Fort William in his rustic pony cart, an improvement on the sixteenth century when a bard described Glen Nevis as being inhabited by "thievish folk of evil habit".

Henry's friends were overjoyed, for they had feared for his safety and "all supposed he was lost beyond recovery". The summit party and the guide had not been lost and the group had assumed, when they reached the spring, that Henry must have decided to return to the Fort. They had called out his name as they descended, but there was no response. Reaching their hotel they were dismayed to learn that he had not showed up. "Being night it was impossible to prosecute a search until the next day, when, according to arrangement, eight guides were sent out at daybreak, not returning until night, and just before the safe arrival of the missing tourist, they being quite dispirited and sad, more especially the one who had been their guide on the ascent."

It was a happy conclusion to the often tragic adventures on the Ben and it is interesting to note that an experienced search party was dispatched so quickly. These Fort William guides formed what was probably the first *organised* rescue team of mountain guides in the British Isles.

There have of course been countless lost souls on those rugged slopes since then and many fatalities. Probably more have died on Ben Nevis than on the notorious Eiger and some of the tragedies have been heart-breaking, especially concerning the young.

On Christmas Eve 1956, when a great storm was brewing in the Atlantic, five poorly equipped Lancashire lads ascended South Castle Coire, a straightforward snow climb on Carn Dearg, that great rocky north-eastern outrider of Ben Nevis. At this time of year there are only about eight hours of daylight, if you're lucky. When they exited the gully onto the flat top they were assaulted by a hurricane-force wind whipping up spindrift like shotgun pellets. They dragged their way to some icy rocks and huddled, trying in vain to get shelter.

It was already getting dark and they could sporadically glimpse the lights of Fort William 4,000 feet below. By daylight four of them were dead. But one survivor managed to stumble down, having spent the night on the top, and reaching the town, staggered into the police station. The police on duty first thought that he was drunk, a Christmas reveller. He was there to report a tragedy! Four of his friends were still up there in a white hell of snow, wind and ice and, unbeknown to him, they were all dead.

A rescue team comprising five policemen set off to try to locate the party in the severe storm. They met two well-equipped climbers descending from the mountain and Sergeant Henderson, who was leading the party, asked if he could borrow an ice axe. One of the climbers eventually agreed, but requested a signature for it! They warned the police rescue party that conditions were appalling on the summit.

The police posse continued upwards but as conditions were getting progressively more stormy and icy Sergeant Henderson told his men to take shelter at some rocks and pushed on alone, crawling across the edge of the summit plateau with his borrowed ice axe driven in ahead of him to avoid being plucked off the mountain. Gusts of wind sounded like exploding shells, followed by an uncanny silence. Then it would start all over again. Though he didn't know it at the time, he had to give up about fifty metres from where three of the bodies were eventually found. The fourth body was located close to the edge of the cliffs two days later.

The bridle path (now the tourist path), which was constructed as access to the Observatory, also created a hazard. Here a dogleg on the trail, on the south side of the mountain, leads into the precipitous defile of Five Finger Gully. Close by, another great runnel known as Surgeon's Gully, also awaits the unwary. Surgeon's Gully is 1,500 feet long and, surprisingly, still awaits a complete ascent. The first ascent of the greater part of the gully, in twenty-one pitches, was made by two of my oldest climbing friends, Dr Derek Haworth and George Ritchie in August 1947. This climb didn't include the top section of the gully or the direct ascent of a couple of the major pitches as these were beyond the skill of even Derek Haworth. However, many of these pitches had in fact been climbed previously by Dr Donald Duff and Jimmy Ness, both members of the Lochaber Mountain Rescue and the gully is called after Dr Duff who was the surgeon at the Belford Hospital in Fort William for many years. Above a deer track, which cuts across the gully, is the final section, where the gully splits into three separate drainage channels like the triple heads of a mythical monster. The superstitious could be forgiven in thinking that these three abysses, and the adjoining Five Finger Gully, are specifically placed to await the unwary descending from the country's highest mountain, to transform a day of elation into one of tragedy.

There have been numerous accidents at this location. In 1993 a party was caught out here. I have been fascinated by this incident which befell a father and son. It is a strange case of cause and effect: the cause, a navigational problem, and the effect, a remarkable escape, literally from the bowels of the mountain, accompanied by a gruesome discovery. But it wasn't until a few weeks prior to writing this that I picked up the telephone and rang a number in rural England to obtain more information. This came from one of those involved, Herbert Henry Alfred Brooks, known as Reup. He takes up the story.

Reup Brooks

On returning from work the message was "Mountain Rescue wants to speak with you!" Even after nine years, the poignant reminder of that long day flashes back into my mind. Instantly the cold chill tingles up the spine and the events of the ordeal stirs my soul.

Let me start at the beginning in the sleepy English village of Rolleston on Dove where we live. We, that is my two sons, Stuart then fourteen and David twelve, and our friend Peter Collins and I, had planned to drive to Scotland to climb Ben Nevis.

It was the end of May 1993 when we piled into the car for the long journey north. I remember that there was a feeling of anticipation as there often is when embarking on a holiday venture. This one was to celebrate my fortieth birthday. We were lucky, the traffic wasn't that bad and as we sped up the M6 the usual banter ensued. At Carlisle we broke the journey and stayed at the Youth Hostel overnight and after a late snack, hit the sack.

Next day we were up early, bright eyed and bushy tailed, and were soon rolling once more. It was only when we were rising on the A82 above the nondescript village of Tyndrum that we felt we had reached the Highlands. We sped through the dark defile of Glencoe and about half an hour later entered Fort William. Here we got our first glimpse of our main objective, Ben Nevis. However we had decided to stay further up the Great Glen, some miles north-east of Fort William, at Loch Lochy Youth Hostel. This proved a wise choice as the Youth Hostel in Glen Nevis, situated at the foot of the Ben, is mobbed during the popular spring months.

There was a long-standing joke between Peter and myself concerning a popular BBC TV documentary programme which was currently running called *999* – a series of real life rescue stories. Peter thought that I had a secret yen to star in one of the episodes, but it was never clear if I was supposed to be cast as victim or rescuer. This speculation proved to be the source of some amusement.

I was up early next morning, cooked breakfast and made a substantial packed lunch. I asked Peter if he was ready for a good day on the hill. Big Ben was our objective.

"Of course, but are you?" he returned.

I muttered something about too much black pudding for breakfast and being not just spot on. We piled into the car once more. The morning was clear and, as we drove back to the outskirts of Fort William, somebody brought up jocularly the amount of petrol that the car was gobbling. We turned off on the Glen Nevis road and drove up the single-track road to arrive at the car park at the head of the glen. Here the Water Slab, which cascades down the south side of the Ben, sparkled like liquid tinsel in the morning light.

Our plan was to ascend Carn Mor Dearg, to the east and north of the Ben, connected to the summit by a rocky tightrope called the Carn Mor Dearg arête. From the summit of the Ben we would descend to the Youth Hostel in Glen Nevis by the tourist path.

We got out of the car and sorted out the gear. I had the extra large packed lunch in my rucksack. Peter and the other two were well aware of the fringe benefits of hill walking with me! We were well equipped, with all the essential mountaineering gear, map, compass, first aid etc. It was great to be heading up the trail through the dramatic Nevis Gorge, then skirted the pristine white Steall waterfall and on across the flats, a sheep-studded meadow, even as a shinty pitch. In minutes, we were at Steall ruins – an old croft house. One of us remarked, I can't remember who, how the scenery was so fresh, green and beautiful. Then we followed the course of the Allt Coire Guibhsachan. I was feeling better now, the black pudding had made peace with my stomach. On the path, where I took over the lead, we met two people. I greeted them with, "Safe travel, folks." With hindsight it would perhaps have been more appropriate for one of the descending party to have said this to us!

The day was dry when we left the car park but above 1,000 feet it was misty. We had read the weather forecast in Fort William the previous day, and it was reasonable. Of course we had experienced such misty conditions before in the Lake District. However, this was the first time we had ventured into Scotland.

Eventually we reached the summit of Carn Mor Dearg. Normally this is a stunning viewpoint for the Ben cliffs, but we were unlucky with the cloud cover and took the easy descent to the arête which connects with the loftier Ben.

We passed four other walkers on the way. It was calm, but the poor visibility was a nuisance, being down to about twenty metres. I stopped and shouted, "Look what I've found, Peter, a 5p coin!" This seemed to amuse everyone. "Good old Reup, searching for small change even at this altitude."

At 2.00 pm we all shook hands on the summit and took some photographs. We noted that the temperature had dropped and that there was a great deal of snow around. Visibility was deteriorating. We remarked at the number of people on the summit, it certainly seemed a popular place and it was at this point that I handed the map and compass to Peter who took a bearing.

We aimed, as mentioned, to return to Glen Nevis by the tourist path, but within minutes of leaving the summit, David, my youngest son, complained of the cold and wanted to put on his Gore-Tex jacket. I stopped within sight of him and said, "Put the jacket on, quickly now." He did so, but in the time it took him to do this, the other two were out of sight. "Don't worry, son," I said, "we'll soon catch them up . . . Mum won't want to loose the Family Allowance!" The other two, not realising that we had stopped, continued on down.

We angled down rapidly along the track in the mist, feeling sure that we would soon make contact with Stuart and Peter. But this didn't happen. With no map or compass we were not sure of our position. We descended a faint path, then a scree slope, followed by a grass track, unaware that we were heading for Carn Dearg South West. At this point, the saying "up the creek without a paddle" came to mind, but in reality we were on a mountain with no map or compass. Annoyance, then anger ran through my brain, having had the map and compass for the ascent. But we didn't panic! I stopped, staring at the outline of a footprint and became more aware of our predicament. We continued down at a great rate. It was as if we had an obsession to get to the floor of Glen Nevis, to get down out of this cloud and orientate ourselves. We knew that we were lost and kept heading to our right, hoping to hit the tourist path.

I asked Dave if he was OK. He was, and showed no fear. To him this was just another Follow-my-Dad situation. Going down ever increasing gradients we entered a gully, hoping to follow the watercourse into the valley.

Now we could hear motor vehicles, which I assumed were in Glen Nevis, but I was also aware that we were in a dangerous situation. We scrambled and slid down this steep rocky watercourse and came across a dead deer. Despite our perilous predicament I was excited by this find and went to great effort to try and remove the antlers as souvenirs. No chance! I had to come to terms with the something for nothing syndrome. It was off limits today. I thought it would have been a different scenario if I had my Swiss knife.

Below was a more serious drop of some ninety to a hundred feet. It was nearly vertical. I didn't relish this with a large rucksack on my back! I uttered an expletive, but Dave calmly stated that such comments would solve nothing. How wise are the young . . .!

We proceeded, I slipped and commenced a horrendous slide for about sixty feet, thinking my bum's on fire as I bounced down the face, ending with a splash in a rock pool. The air was now blue with more than one expletive! Miraculously, my only injury was to my ego. I was really lucky, I could have broken my neck.

Dave, who later matured into a capable rock climber, picked his way down, making difficult waterfall descending look cool. He now went ahead of me. Here the walls of the gully rose to an intimidating height. Turning a corner in the gully bed Dave remarked, "The mountain rescue have been here with a dummy." But it was no dummy! It was a decomposing body! I retorted, "Don't be so ****** stupid. It's a woman with fish net tights and a cardigan." It's amazing what you come out with when the adrenalin's pumping and the stress level has topped the scale.

David, even after all those years, still has a vivid picture of events. "The smell was indescribable, we both didn't eat anything for three days, and my dad even lost some weight! It was disturbing enough to see the decomposing body, but the fact there was little clothing, no bag or shoes was the worrying thing, especially in such a harsh environment."

Reup

What next I wondered. What next? Life can throw up some weird situations, but I had a fixation with "what next?" Numbed, both mentally and physically, we climbed down and round the cleft and the gully opened up. Moving cautiously, we peered anxiously over a brink, the water was leaping between our boots into space. What we saw was a hundred-foot waterfall directly below. Even in our mental state we knew that there was no chance of descending this other than by falling, and there was no way back, or escape up the vertical gully walls. "Let's just shout for help!" I muttered.

After more than six hours in one spot you've plenty of time to reflect on life. It's only when you experience the consequences of your leisure activity first hand that it comes home to you – the hazards and tribulations that go hand in hand with pleasure. We continued to shout from our misty perch.

At times the visibility improved and we could see Glen Nevis below. Later, in the early evening, we spotted mountain rescue vehicles arriving in the valley bottom. Eventually, at 9 pm, we were located by a member of the Lochaber Mountain Rescue Team. Once the full team arrived one of them was lowered by rope to join us.

For the next part of this scenario, let's go back a few hours. Two female hikers were walking in Glen Nevis, enjoying a fine day, even though it was a bit cloudy on the Ben. It was Monday, 31 May 1993. Above the muted noise of the River Nevis, which was taking a leisurely meander down the glen, and the occasional passing car on the single-track road, they thought they heard a cry – a cry for help. Checking this out they realised that it was indeed a distress call from the long steep slope above leading to the shoulder of the Ben. They could see from where they were, the two savage gashes of the notorious gullies rising in great steps as if they were the private stairways of the guardian of the mountain. Shortly afterwards one of the women reported the calls to Fort William police station and the duty sergeant sent a constable in a patrol car to investigate.

Jim Ness, who has already appeared in this tale, is a climber and an ex-member of the Lochaber Mountain Rescue Team, the busiest mountain rescue unit in Scotland. That day he had driven up Glen Nevis with his wife to go for a walk. On their way home they came across the police patrol car and Jim, realising that something was afoot on the mountain, stopped and had a word with the PC.

Though none of them could hear any call for help from where they were, Jim knew that shouts from the depths of either of the gullies could be very directional, probably due to the deep walls, and said that he would go up the glen a short way to try and find a better spot. He was acutely aware of the problems of anyone straying into these two gullies. When he had gone about a couple of hundred yards up the side of the river, he heard the help calls himself, and was sure that they were coming from Surgeon's Gully, so he retraced his tracks towards the car to confirm this. Sure enough, he had only gone a short way when they ceased, even though he had continued to shout. He then decided to ford the river to make absolutely sure. Once on the lower slopes of the mountain he was convinced where they came from and that they weren't the bleating of sheep which can often be mistaken for calls for help.

On the way back he met Terry Confield, the Deputy Team Leader, fording the river, and put him in the picture. Donald Watt, the Team Leader, had been called to the police station with Terry a short time before.

Where in Surgeon's Gully was now the problem. Terry started up the west bank, shouting as he ascended. Shortly he heard the calls again – "Help, help" – and traversed closer to the edge. Though he couldn't see the party, he could hear them below.

Already more of the team were making their way up the face and he shouted down to tell them the calls were coming from one of the bigger pitches. Some other team members were taken by a SAR Sea King helicopter to a point higher up the flank of the gully. Noel Williams, who took a lead role in the next phase of the rescue, takes up the story.

Noel Williams

From the floor of Glen Nevis we could hear frantic cries for help, and it was obvious that someone was in real trouble high above us. The cries were echoing around the glen, and at first we weren't certain which part of the hillside they were coming from. So after wading across the River Nevis near the old graveyard, we split up and separate parties headed for Five Finger, Antler and Surgeon's Gullies. However as we gained height we confirmed that the cries were definitely coming from Surgeon's Gully itself. So we all then converged on a recognised scrambling route up the left side of Surgeon's known as Surgeon's Rib. The cries were being sustained at a very loud volume and this spurred us all on. We raced uphill as fast as possible. Surgeon's Gully is an impressive gash on the west flank of Ben Nevis. A few years previously I'd tried to make a winter ascent of it. Although we had approached by walking across a frozen River Nevis, we had been disappointed to find a lot of water still flowing deep inside the gully itself. It really is a different world in there. After struggling up several long pitches, we had been stopped by a big waterfall. We only managed to escape from the gully with great difficulty by clawing our way up horribly loose rock and heather on the left wall.

We now had the problem of entering the gully in the right place to rescue whoever was in trouble. We realised that the shouts were coming from above a big waterfall pitch. It was very difficult to look into the gully, but we eventually managed to reach a point above where the shouts were coming from and shouted down that help was on its way. Everyone was gasping for breath and we were sweating profusely. It soon became evident that there was no way we could get into it without a rope. One of the team was still struggling up the hillside with one of our long pre-stretched ropes in a big rucksack. Whilst we waited for this to arrive, we looked around for a belay to anchor the rope to. The ground consisted mainly of steep heather and loose granite blocks, but by an extraordinary stroke of good fortune there was a small outcrop of sound rock just where we needed it on the hillside a short distance above. We were able to place a big tape around a bomb-proof rock spike and also fix a large metal nut in a crack. Meanwhile the shouts from below seemed ever more urgent.

When the rope arrived I tied onto the end and, with several team members taking the strain, I was lowered over the side. I was soon dropping down a vertical wall, and spied two figures some distance below me. When I hit the deck I was delighted to find that both man and boy were uninjured, although the adult, not surprisingly, was getting hoarse from shouting. It was obvious that they were extremely relieved to see me. Both walls of the gully were sheer at this point and there was no way that they could have got out themselves. It turned out that they had come down the gully from the summit. Looking up from where I was this seemed a mind-boggling achievement. I then heard that on their descent they had come across a dead reindeer. I didn't like to point out that this must in fact have been a red deer. The nearest reindeer I knew of were sixty miles away in the Cairngorms. The father was in an extremely excited state. He said that he had fallen down a big pitch but had landed in a pool unscathed. Somehow his young son had followed suit. He then astonished me even further by telling me that they had come upon a decomposing body in a pool a short distance back along the gully from where we were. The rescue team had no knowledge of a climber being missing on the mountain, so this was a real surprise.

Time was pressing however, and the first priority was to get the two of them out. I quickly improvised a sit harness for the young lad, and radioed the team above to haul the two of us up. They did this with gusto. I managed to hold the youngster away from the rock wall as we shot up, but I caught my arm on a sharp flake and ripped the sleeve of my jacket in the process. It was already dusk, so as soon as Dave was unclipped from the rope he was escorted by one of the team to a more open position where he was uplifted by a rescue helicopter.

I related the story of the dead reindeer and the dead climber to the lads holding the rope. Kevin, ever quick with a quip, remarked, "Oops! There goes Father Christmas." Amid laughter I was lowered back into the gully and retrieved the father. (On the way up this pitch Reup recalled that he had missed that day's episode of *Coronation Street*.)

By the time the two of us had been hauled back up and all the gear packed away, it had become too dark for the helicopter to fly. So we all had to pick our way back down to the floor of the glen by torch light. We were very pleased to have rescued two folk uninjured, but still puzzled by the corpse that had quite understandably given the pair of them the heebie-jeebies.

Reup was eventually reunited with his two sons and Peter at Fort William Police Station He sums up the ordeal.

Reup

We returned to the base of the gully the following day. Typically, the weather was brilliant and we could pick out the line of our descent. It was traumatic for us all. We asked ourselves why did this happen to us? Could it have been avoided? How much longer would the body have remained there had David and I not been funnelled down that frightening gash? Even now, I still think of that eventful day and have the occasional flashback when something triggers my memory.

Although we had considerable experience of walking in all seasons in the English Lake District and Wales, we realised that we still had a lesson to learn when we went to Ben Nevis. Our trip nearly ended in tragedy, all because we became separated and didn't each have a whistle, map and compass. After the experience of discovering the body, and the involvement of a full scale rescue, we both suffered delayed shock. My son required many months of counselling to overcome those traumatic experiences. We still ask questions: should we have returned to the summit of Ben Nevis, once we became separated, and joined another party to descend the mountain?

We left Scotland hardly able to believe that we had nearly died in Surgeon's Gully.

The corpse wasn't, as Reup and party had thought, brought down the next day. There was a problem in getting a helicopter. There is a ruling with RAF SAR helicopters, that they are used to save life, and not necessarily for the recovery of dead bodies.

The rescue team at that time used to frequent the Nevis Bar, a watering hole in Fort William strategically placed as the first pub when descending from the Ben. The conversation of those team members who went there after the successful rescue that night inevitably turned to the missing body. It was an unusual incident to say the least, for none of them had seen the body in a pool, despite Noel having been down to the top of the long pitch where the father and son had been found.

In the history of Scottish mountain rescue this surely stands out as one of the strangest incidents. No one had been reported missing. How long had the body been there? Who was it? Lord Lucan (a peer who had mysteriously disappeared)? This fanciful thought had run through Reup's scrambled mind when he saw it. It is not an uncommon occurrence in the Scottish Highlands for someone to vanish, and it may be years before the body is found. At any given time there can be several individuals who have just disappeared, seemingly into thin air, under avalanches, into deep heather or, in this case, down a deep gully.

It was arranged that the following morning a small party would return to the gully, by helicopter if possible, and try to locate the body. These were Willie Anderson, Brian McDermott and a member of the CID. It's usual for police to be involved in an investigation of a fatal accident, even in the most inaccessible places. However, early next morning the clag (an affectionate term for Scotch mist) was still clinging to the flanks of the Ben like candy floss and, as a SAR helicopter wasn't available that day, the trio set off on foot.

The three rescuers ascended the west flank of the gully and traversed into it via the deer track, which cuts across Surgeon's at the only possible place – clever deer! Here Brian and Willie first checked above, at the base of the three top branches, but there was no sign of a body there. It must be lower they reasoned, and started to descend. With them they had three long abseil ropes. The solitary representative of the law was instructed to remain where he was at the deer bypass as the terrain below was steep and dangerous for all but experienced mountaineers.

Below, the other two came across the bones of a stag, complete with handsome antlers and they wondered if the Brooks, in their stressed state, had imagined these as human remains: but this seemed impossible. Reup and David had been adamant about seeing a body in a pool. Willie and Brian continued down until a longer pitch necessitated an abseil. Brian, belayed by Willie on a safety rope, went down a full rope's length, but he could see no sign of a body. He then climbed back up the pitch. This was probably the waterfall down which Reup had fallen and David had climbed.

They called Terry Confield on the radio for confirmation as to the body's location – if indeed there really was a body in the gully.

Terry, who was acting as base in Glen Nevis, came back on the walkie-talkie, saying that there definitely was a body there, and it was about a hundred metres below the deer track, but he would double check this with the police station just in case anything further had come to light. By this time Brian and Willie felt that they had done as much as possible that day and went back up to collect their personal policeman. He greeted them like long lost brothers. "You're a pair of mad bastards . . ." All three descended to Glen Nevis.

It was apparent now that it was going to take a concerted effort by a bigger party to find and recover the body. But there was no doubt, it had been double and treble checked, there was a dead body up there! But whose was it? Was it a man or a woman? And why had no one been reported missing on the Ben?

At 10.00 am on Thursday, 3 June 1993, five members of the Lochaber Mountain Rescue Team were airlifted to the gully by a SAR Sea King helicopter from 202 Squadron RAF Lossiemouth. The pilot was Steve Hayward. They all knew that the chopper was the best and quickest means of locating the man in the pool and of getting him out.

Surgeon's Gully boasts of the most dramatic gully architecture in Britain, with its depth, massive pitches, cascading waterfalls and ability to make you seem insignificant, like a fly in a high-angled canyon. It didn't look any more benign looking down on it from the Sea King, where the rotors appeared too wide for the gully. This was a problem for Steve; he describes his side of the job.

Steve Hayward

The 3 June had started as a routine day on shift at D Flt 202
Sqn, RAF Lossiemouth. I was the duty captain for the day and
if nothing else happened I was going to fly a regular standar-
disation sortie with our Squadron instructor, Harry Watt. We
had all heard about the rescue of the father and son from
Surgeon's Gully a few days previously and the report of the
body in tights and a cardigan that was still supposedly lying in a
pool below one of the waterfalls. You see and hear some odd
things in Search and Rescue but this one still sticks in my mind
many years later. Just after shift handover we were requested to
go down to Ben Nevis to lift members of the Lochaber team into
Surgeon's Gully to allow them to search for and recover the
body in the pool.

We flew a recce of the southern side of the mountain to try
and discern where exactly we would need to put the team, but
from the air, without detailed on-the-ground knowledge, it was
difficult trying to pick out the spot. We landed at West End car
park in Fort William to pick up the team and get a brief from the
police about any special requirements for the task. Fortunately
the weather was kind with light southerly winds and good
visibility. The team directed us to the area of Surgeon's Gully
they needed to access; it didn't look especially promising; a
deep, narrow gash, running back into the side of the mountain.
The top of the gully looked slightly wider but it rapidly became
vertically sided.

This was likely to present a couple of challenges. We needed
to make a closer assessment. Having brought the aircraft into a
free air hover by the mouth of the gully, we examined the
problem. The Sea King has a seventy-five-metre winch cable
and we were going to need quite a lot of it if we could get into
the gully. It was unlikely that we would be able to hold the
winchman against the side, allowing him to treat the trip down
as an abseil. So the winchman was probably going to get spun in
the aircrafts downwash. That downwash was also likely to be
the cause of other problems. A hovering helicopter pushes
down a column of air as it sits in the hover, usually this
dissipates outwards below the aircraft. In a tight steep-sided

gully this 50 mph breeze would be concentrated, having no space to escape into, and could dislodge anything loose, potentially hazarding anyone below the aircraft. Furthermore, the little downwash that could escape could finish going up, round the sides of the rotor, and being reingested by the rotor. This aerodynamic phenomena is known as recirculation, and it can dramatically increase the power required to maintain the hover, sometimes beyond the available power.

However, after spending a short time assessing the situation, we decided that it was worth seeing if we could safely manoeuvre into a position to deploy the team. In order to give ourselves, and everyone else on the aircraft, an escape option if things did not go as planned we needed to reverse into the gully. The winchman, Tony, and winch operator, Clive, were both very experienced, so with one of them kneeling by the large open door and the other peering out of the bubble window on the opposite side we began to back slowly into the gully. During a manoeuvre like this the pilot is flying the aircraft following as exactly as he can the guidance from his rear crew, as he can see nothing of the area he is manoeuvring into. A very particular form of words is used (a misunderstanding in such circumstances is not desirable!) to ensure that the aircraft is manoeuvred in exactly the right direction, in three axis, at the required speed to put it over a particular point and keep it there. Everyone must trust everyone else implicitly, this is very much a team game.

Having carefully manoeuvred the aircraft to the required point, we were positioned well back in the confines of the gully. The clearance from the tips of the blades to the rock face on either side always looks to be less than it actually is – I would not have wished to be much closer. All I had to do now was stay put while Clive and Tony organised the deployment of the rescue team. We had decided to put Clive down on the ground and he was soon lowered on the winch cable, 180 feet later his feet touched the ground in the floor of the gully.

The winchman went down first, close to the lip of the waterfall on which Reup and David had stood three days before. Five members of the team then repeated this descent, Terry Confield, Ian Sutherland, Brian McDermott, Willie Anderson and

Ed Grindley. The gully almost proved to be a death trap for the rescuers, on account of the downwash from the huge machine in this narrowing defile. The stream was whipped up and soaked the party. Worse, stones were falling, dislodged from the gully walls. Terry wondered, when he was being lowered, what was hitting his face – it was maggots!

Steve

From a flying point of view, we did our best to keep it nice and accurate; concentrating on being relaxed is allegedly the secret of a good hover. Brian and Ian Sutherland landed about twenty feet up from the edge of the big pitch and, as there were so many rocks crashing down, Willie, who was the next lowered, was pulled by Brian beneath a small overhang on the gully wall where there was a degree of protection. They then climbed the rocks above and peered over a lip at eye-level with a pool. Floating a few feet away was the body of a dead man and a plague of beetles. Brian and Ian pulled him to the edge, while the others took the stretcher, which had also been lowered, up closer to the pool.

It was now a matter of getting everybody to hell out of there, including the corpse, which they installed in a yellow bivvy bag. Willie and Brian where the first to be winched up together on two strops – again the winch cable was almost at full extent. Rocks rained down just as they were spiralling upwards. Then there was blur and a tremendous crash, heard above the roar of the turbines, a large rock flake shattered on the gully bed between Ian Sutherland and the stretcher with its new customer aboard. It was a close call! Amazingly, everyone got winched out without injury, thanks to the skill of the pilot and crew and, as the last man swung aboard, the Sea King nosed its way out into the vast air space of Glen Nevis.

One of the team said later, "What that chopper did represented the best rescue flying I've ever been involved with – and that's going back thirty years."

Chief Inspector John MacFadzean, who is also a keen hill man was called on a team radio. "Line up the drinks, John. We have the body."

There is a footnote to this last phase of the Surgeon's Gully affair. The helicopter landed at Corpach, a village near Fort William whose name appropriately translates as The Place of the Dead. As they got out of the Sea King, Willie Anderson jokingly remarked to John MacFadzean that the police would probably manage to identify the body by the next millennium. The Chief Inspector retorted that he would bet him a pint of beer he would know all about the deceased before teatime.

True to his word he did just that, but not without a few setbacks. At the mortuary the man's name was discovered in the remains of his wallet, found in the back pocket of his trousers. When the name John O'Brien, with a Putney address, was fed into the Missing Person's Index on the Police National Computer nineteen missing O'Briens came up! But not a John. As the Chief Inspector later pointed out, "You would have expected this number of missing individuals with a common name like Smith or Brown, but not an O'Brien." He went back on the computer for clarification and was asked for a Personal Description File. Supplying this and contacting the closest police station to the Putney address, and checking other evidence found on the body, a railway ticket and a bank withdrawal slip, the investigation leapt forward. He quickly had the Fort William banks checked and found that a John Michael Joseph O'Brien had withdrawn cash from the Royal Bank of Scotland, possibly on the very day he died on Ben Nevis. These clues had survived being submerged in water for three months. It transpired that his relatives were not too concerned at not hearing from John, for he tended to keep himself to himself and would often go on protracted walkabouts.

That evening John MacFadzean enjoyed a well earned pint at the Nevis Bank.

Steve – a postscript

The Sea King crew, when it landed at Corpach, had only two hours of their twenty-four-hour shift left; they were then re-tasked to a helicopter crash south of Aberdeen . . . but that's another story.

We Recover the
Bodies of our Comrades

Ludwig Gramminger

The Eiger North Face, the Nordwand, will for ever stand as a milestone for those formative years of mountaineering, the 1930s, but it has also served as a gravestone for the unlucky who died on its flanks. The popular press had their first taste of mountaineering tragedy some fifty years before when Edward Whymper's party crashed to their deaths on the Matterhorn. Though Whymper himself survived, he was obsessed with the stigma of this tragedy for the remainder of his days.

Most of the climbing fraternity as well as the public condemned those Eiger North Face climbers who, they said, risked their lives and the lives of the rescuers who went to help them when they got into trouble. Yet those tigers of yesteryear were sensible young men who were only exercising an urge basic to all of us, to try something new to conquer the frigid vertical heights by the most direct route to the summit. They were mostly of German or Austrian origin, possibly because the use of pitons and slings as climbing aids first evolved in the Eastern Alps and, without their assistance, such ambitious goals as the Eigerwand were then out of the question. Those who condemned this new breed of climber were themselves too timid to contemplate tackling such routes.

One can expostulate on the pros and cons of big wall climbing, but the courage of those who attempted those north faces as well as the courage of their rescuers is beyond question. For decades the Eiger drama has been re-enacted on page and screen, yet it will always demonstrate an extraordinary facet of human nature, this deep-rooted desire to attempt a problem, knowing full well the odds are against one.

Austria and Germany have always been in the forefront of mountain rescue development, especially in the pioneering days of big cliff rescue, where steel cables were first used in place of conventional ropes. The German Bergwacht, the Mountain Guard, were then the stars of rescues where the stage was some great alpine north face. Ludwig Gramminger was the leader of this determined band involved in what will remain probably the greatest sequence of mountain rescue operations of all time, in days when the helicopter wasn't the bird of mercy it is today. I have made many landings by winch wire on the Eiger North Face and I can vouch for the skill and the daring of the pilots on those operations. But their exposure to danger is brief, compared with the hours and even days spent by rescue teams in the past on the icy ramparts of this hostile mountain.

During the war most of Ludwig Gramminger's companions were away in the forces when in 1942 he got a call to go to the Eiskarlspitze in the Karwendal of the Austrian Tirol. A climber had fallen and was subsequently killed. It meant abseiling down a 350-metre face with the corpse. Perhaps the best introduction to Ludwig is to listen to his own description of how, when almost down the wall, his colleague, who had gone first to prepare the anchors for the ropes, had failed to complete the final belay on one of the steepest sections:

For the last abseil, I asked myself, had Stadler only put in one peg? I could only see one, but this was inconceivable. Was it an oversight as we were nearing the foot of the cliff? But there was no excuse for a single piton. It's dangerous enough roping off a solitary peg at the best of times, but frightening when carrying the additional weight of the body of a large man. Perhaps, I thought, the eight pitches which Max Stadler had already organised from the top had taken too much out of him? Anyhow, I secured myself to the peg using a sling, but didn't take off my abseil rope. When Michel, the other member of our rescue trio, arrived alongside using his own abseil rope, he could hardly get a footing as the wall was so steep. He too clipped onto the peg. As well as staying on my abseil rope I had taken the precaution of knotting it so that it couldn't creep through the karabiner brake I was using. Michel now came off his abseil rope, for he had to help me to change over to another rope for the final descent. To our horror we saw that his extra weight was making the peg bend and as if in slow motion it came out of the crack. I grabbed him and in so doing took some of his weight. In desperation he linked himself to me with a karabiner so that we were all hanging, two climbers and a corpse, on my abseil rope. After recovering from the initial shock we had to do some slick thinking. It was a good thing that I hadn't trusted that peg and also that I was attached to it by a sling, otherwise we would have lost the rope that Michel had transfered to it. We yelled down to Stadler to tie some pegs and a hammer to the end of this and in a short space of time we had sound anchors in place. We then lowered the dead man to the bottom of the face and quickly followed, glad ourselves to be down alive.

To climbers that's the sort of stuff that nightmares are made from, but it is only a small incident in the long rescue career of Ludwig Gramminger. The following adventures have been narrated before in various forms, but seldom by the rescuers themselves.

In 1936 the Eiger North Face was the last main unclimbed face in the Western Alps. German climbers had been much to the fore in the other great ascents; the Matterhorn North Face was climbed by the brothers Schmid in 1931 and the Grandes Jorasses in 1935 by Rudi Peters and Martin Meir. That same year Wiggerl Steinauer and Hans Ellner scaled the North Face of the Aletschhorn. All these climbers came from Munich.

Climbing was just beginning to get public attention and the Eiger North Face represented to many a vertical arena of drama and tragedy to which the accidents of 1933–6 were the curtain raisers. For this was the time of the first attempts on that notorious wall and the press were to have many a bonanza reporting and misreporting the assaults on the 1,800-metre high face.

It was again a Munich party that first set their hopes on this great North Face. Max Sedlmayr and Karl Mehringer were both members of the High Level Group of the German and Austrian Alpine Club. They left Bavaria in August, travelling by car to Grindelwald and took up residence in a hayshed at Alpiglen. Alpiglen snuggles in meadows at the bottom of the Eigerwand on the Kleine Scheidegg railway. Here they spent some time carefully studying the possible lines on the face. It was no easier then than now to keep your objective secret if the Eiger North Face featured in your itinerary and news leaked out that they were to attempt a direct route up the westerly section of the wall – straight to the summit.

They set off at 3.00 am on Wednesday, 21 August and after three days of hard rock climbing they reached the Second Icefield. Due to heavy stone fall here they had to bivouac early.

It was on that Friday night that the whole Eiger region was subjected to a savage storm. The face, which forms a northern bastion of the Alps, is a buffer to all the foul weather from that quarter; it attracts storms as a magnet attracts pins.

On the Saturday the telescopes of Kleine Scheidegg and Alpiglen were trained on the face looking for signs of the two men, but nothing further could be seen. They were known to be excellent climbers and were well equipped, so it was generally thought that they would have survived the blizzard. Unfortunately, dense cloud rolled in and blanketed the whole face and a heavy snowfall commenced. It got increasingly colder (–8°C at Kleine Scheidegg) and the danger of avalanche on the face was considerable. On the Sunday around midday a portion of the wall was visible for a short while and then the two climbers were spotted higher up, presumably continuing the climb. But very soon the cloud closed in again and for the next few days not much more was seen.

Now with the continuing bad weather, the position of the two was critical and in Grindelwald preparations for a possible rescue were being made. In Munich our rescue group, the Bergwacht, received the following report at 9.30 am: "The weather conditions on the Eiger North Face are extremely bad. Today, Wednesday, 28 August it has snowed lightly on the upper slopes; in the valley it was raining. The snow is lying about fifty centimetres deep on the upper section of the face." A Swiss military plane had to give up a search on the following day because of poor visibility. There was nothing to be seen or heard, no signs at all. The face was under the constant observation of the Grindelwald rescue post, but the prevailing conditions precluded any mercy mission for the time being. Further reports arrived. In Munich our group was preparing to go to the aid of the missing climbers who would by now obviously be in a very serious condition. As soon as the conditions allowed, nothing would stop us doing everything we could to rescue our friends. We left Munich that same day at 9.30 pm in the Bergwacht Mercedes Kompressorwagen, driving through the night for Grindelwald. We had the best of equipment and rations and we departed in streaming rain convinced that we would bring help to our colleagues. There were four of us – Rudi Peters, Franz Hausstätter, Heine Sedlmayer and myself.

We arrived at Grindelwald around 9.30 am and our first call was at the rescue post which was also the guides' bureau, where we were given the run-down on developments to date. From this moment we were supported in every possible way. Herr Moser, President of the Grindelwald section of the Swiss Alpine Club and the manager of the Hotel Oberland, took care of our equipment and vehicle. Herr Direktor Grob from the travel office gave us lots of photographic material of the Eigerwand to study. Herr Direktor Luchtu gave us complimentary tickets for the Jungfrau railway. From photographs the guide, Fritz Steuri, and others showed us the line of the Sedlmayr-Mehringer climb and we weighed up the possibilities for rescue and recovery. In a short period of time we acquired a lot of facts. Later we took the train to Alpiglen where the missing men had made their headquarters. The bulk of their equipment – bivouac clothes, the second petrol cooker, spare sleeping bags, etc – was still in their hayshed. On Tuesday the 20th, we were told, they had established a food dump on the summit, and, according to reports, set off on the climb on the Wednesday at 3.00 am. From observations made from the West Flank when taking up the food dump, they had formed the impression that they could climb the face in three days and had therefore taken less equipment and emergency food with them. From the hotel owner at Alpiglen we learned more about their proposed climb. One thing that was absolutely clear was that everyone who had seen them climbing was very impressed with their ability. The news of the first attempt on the Eigerwand had spread like wildfire. Two other Munich climbers, Haber and Prosel, who were holidaying in the vicinity, had already begun searching the day before, but due to the snow and stone falls they had had to give up.

We reviewed the overall situation and came to the conclusion that there was still some hope for Sedlmayr and Mehringer, if they had found a sheltered bivouac site. Swiss airmen had already flown across the face three times, for an hour on each occasion, but without success. Now it was very cloudy, though we hoped that the following day we should be able to search the wall ourselves with the telescope. We dumped our gear at the start of the climb for, in the event of a rescue bid, we should start from the same spot. Should the weather permit (which we doubted in view of the constant avalanches) we proposed setting out the next day. For the time being we stationed ourselves in a barn and, as agreed, sent reports on the rescue situation back to Grindelwald, from where Munich was informed. Friday, 30 August was a beautiful clear day. We travelled to the Eiger-gletscher station on the Jungfraubahn and there split into two groups. Haber and Prosel climbed the West Flank of the Eiger to get a view of the face from there. The rest of us went up the railway tunnel to just below the Eiger window. Here there are a few galleries giving access on to the wall. They were originally used for dumping rubble during the construction of the tunnel. We attempted to get on to the face by the gallery window closest to the route. It transpired that the conditions were as bad as they could be, but we still wanted to make an attempt. Peters went out on to the face belayed on a double rope. Because of the heavy snowfalls of the previous few days, it was quite wintry and during this time avalanches, some of them formidable, thundered down, often releasing great clouds of powder snow. Obviously, any search work would be very difficult in these conditions; the danger was so great that after a few hours we had to give up the idea of getting any further out on to the face. The rock was covered with an ice layer 10-cm thick; no sooner had we cut steps than they were immediately filled with cascading powder snow. So, back to the gallery window.

The Swiss flyers were not idle this day either; they took photographs, hoping that something would be revealed when they were blown up. From this visual material and various observations we concluded that a spine of rock on the Second Icefield would probably have seemed a logical line to the two mountaineers. So they had possibly left their bivouac equipment and rucksacks beneath it and attempted to climb it in reconnaissance. But they must soon have realised that it wasn't feasible and therefore descended to their rucksacks – this clambering up and down had been observed by a gamekeeper. They then bivouacked in a niche they had already found and probably due to the cold and the snow storm went to sleep never to awake. It seemed to all of us that something like this must have happened. To reach the Death Bivouac, as it was later called, in good weather would be possible only with great difficulty and risk. We would need to consider carefully whether it was feasible and indeed justifiable to undertake such a venture to recover two corpses. We decided to wait until the next morning. Two more Munich climbers arrived to strengthen our team, Hans Teufel and Albert Herbst.

The next day, Saturday, the six of us went up to the start of the face. From very early in the morning avalanches of stones and snow were hurtling down, as if trucks were continuously dumping their loads off the top. They were sweeping the wall like torrents. The marginal crevasses going round under the face were filled with avalanched snow. Despite the poor visibility, we decided to proceed to climb to the Eiger window in three parties. That was a wearisome business, traversing upwards, for one minute we were in an avalanche runnel that was so hard in places we needed crampons, then it was ploughing through fresh deep powder snow. At 14.00 hours the sun came out and all hell let loose. Avalanches like a great barrage opened up unpredictably all over the wall. It meant we had to take cover from these under overhangs and in holes as quickly as possible and wait until 19.00 hours when the sun had crept off the summit rocks. The face soon became quieter and in a short time everything was frozen, covered in ice. We were certain that the missing men could not be lying on the lower section of the Eigerwand, the middle of which is smooth and steep. In the event of a fall nothing would come to rest here. Tired and depressed we retreated to Alpiglen. There we discussed our efforts so far and resolved to go up the West Flank right to the summit the next day and from there descend the wall.

On Sunday, 1 September, we went to the Eigergletscher station again equipped with high-power binoculars and a tripod. The West Flank was certainly the easiest route to the Eiger summit at 3,975 metres, despite the fact that the conditions demanded good climbing know-how, and as we had to scramble up every ridge and eminence that gave us a clear view, great care was necessary. It was all in vain; we didn't see any sign of our friends. We reached the summit around midday and by descending the ridge a short way to the north-east, we had a good view of the North Face. To climb down this wall, however, was impossible at that time because several cornices overhung the ridge; there was besides two metres of snow lying on the summit and we could not find the food dump left by the two missing men. A descent would have required at least three bivouacs and indeed whether it would still be possible during the remainder of that year was the big question. Powder snow avalanches continually leapt down the face. So again we had to return to our base having achieved nothing.

On Monday another attempt was made to get on to the face from the Eiger window, but again it had to be called of as the weather conditions had hardly improved at all since Friday. With heavy hearts we now resolved to abandon the attempt because of the advanced time of year and the deep-winter-type conditions. It seemed impossible to us that the two could still be alive. We had tried everything humanly possible, but the unanimous view of the company was that not only would any further attempt put our own lives at risk, it would be irresponsible and foolhardy. The mountain was stronger than human skill or will. But we resolved that the following year we would come again and bring down our dead comrades and return home with them.

Back in Grindelwald everyone was most sympathetic over the fate of the two lost men. We took our leave and made arrangements with the Swiss guides that, should there be an unexpectedly fine autumn and the face become free of snow, we would return. We had experienced the fullest co-operation from all quarters, including the Swiss authorities.

The journey back to Munich was a bad one; it rained very heavily and we were still very preoccupied with the trauma of the search. At Berne the sun suddenly appeared and our spirits rose. We were starving but had little money and we wondered how we should overcome this problem. Then Rudi Peters had a bright idea. He knew a well-known writer who lived near Berne whom he wanted to visit. With luck, he said, we should get plenty of food there. He was right! A great spread was provided and we sat around the table and ate our fill. Nor did the hospitality end there; the writer's wife made us masses of sandwiches for our journey. But we had barely gone twenty kilometres when we came to a big orchard. We all agreed that this would make a delectable interlude as the apples were asking to be picked. Naturally, both sandwiches and apples disappeared in this impromptu picnic – climbers are renowned for their prodigious appetites. The journey back was a pleasant one after the rigours we had been through and our Kompressorwagen went like a dream; we were able once more to smile on life and enjoy the wonderful scenery and the fact that we were alive.

After a few weeks we heard from Grindelwald that pilot Oberst Udet with the mountain guide, Fritz Steuri, had made a flight across the Eiger face and had sighted one of the missing men at the Death Bivouac. He was sitting huddled up, face on hands, and the snow reached to above his knees. It was assumed that his companion was probably still in his bivvy sack buried under the snow. This flight proved that due to the heavy snow it would be totally impossible to recover them till the following year. For the victims' parents it was some small comfort to know at least where they were.

In the spring 1936 we were in touch with Grindelwald again. We received regular reports on weather and the snow conditions on the face. On 5 July I went with the then leader of the German Bergwacht, R. Siebenwurst, to Grindelwald to arrange accommodation for our rescue team and to discuss the situation with the local guides. These men knew their mountain better than anyone and could give the best advice. We also intended to take a look at the face from the West Flank to see if a plan I had hatched would prove possible to put into practice.

On the West Flank at about 3,500 metres there is a gap in the ridge into which a chimney from the North Face leads. This chimney is some 150 metres long and links up with the band of rock that crosses the face (the upper limit of the Third Icefield). I now thought that we could abseil down this chimney by means of a 6-mm wire rope from a winch established on the ridge. Traversing the band would then not be so desperate as there were good belay possibilities at the junction of the ice and rock.

But most of all the retreat and recovery of men and equipment could be guaranteed more quickly and safely. We wanted to get everything ready on the spot.

When we got to the Eigergletscher station we learned of an accident a couple of days earlier on the Schneehorn to two of our last year search helpers. Hans Teufel was dead, and Bertl Herbst injured in Lauterbrunnen hospital. After a successful ascent on the extremely difficult North Face of the Schneehorn, an ice peg had pulled out on the descent. Teufel fell and died instantly from a broken neck. Herbst only sustained a few grazes and bruises. He had to pass the night beside his friend on the ice and it was only the next day that his cries for help were heard by the Eigergletscher station. We enquired at the hospital after Herbst and were told by the doctor that we could take him back to Munich with us in a couple of days' time. All sorts of rumours were abroad; some said the pair had been in training for the Eiger Nordwand, others that the two had been sent out to see what the conditions were like with a view to recovering last year's victims.

After we completed the reconnaissance from the West Flank we descended and near Scheidegg met the first two recruits for an Eiger attempt that year, two Austrians, Edi Rainer and Willi Angerer. We visited them in their tent at the foot of the face. Both were splendid young men and made a good impression as climbers. The day we left Grindelwald they made their first recce of the wall. As for us, we drove round to Lauterbrunnen and collected Bertl Herbst. He was very depressed and could barely reconcile himself to the death of his friend. It was tough that the mountain had again demanded a victim, and very painful for him to return home without his climbing companion.

Once back in Munich we learned via the communications network we had organised that Rainer and Angerer had got company. Toni Kurz, a guide, and Anderl Hinterstoisser, a climber from Berchtesgaden, had set up their tent close by, having come from the Dolomites where they had climbed some of the hardest routes, including the North Face of the Cima Grande. They were apparently very fit and experienced. There was no rivalry between them; in true mountaineering spirit they made a joint reconnaissance climb and discussed their plans and proposals together. On the 17th the weather was somewhat better and on the 18th the two parties were able to make a start on the face. They had dumped food and equipment up to 3,000 metres.

The major difficulties began from the bivouac site below the Rote Fluh. Angerer and Rainer had already had an abortive attempt on this section. An overhang was passed on the right and the easier terrain reached by an extremely difficult overhanging crack, about the level of the First Icefield. Now, however, steep smooth slabs blocked the way to the Icefield. However Hinterstoisser overcame these difficulties with panache. He traversed using a rope in a pendulum movement. They now reached the first bivouac site which had taken last year's contenders two days. They had reached in one day the same level as Sedlmayr and Mehringer's third bivouac. It was obvious to all who watched that the two parties were moving well and working as a unit. On the Sunday morning the four climbers were seen to leave their bivouac. Shortly afterwards a veil of cloud encircled the mountain and nothing could be seen, but above the clouds the top third of the mountain was showing throughout that Sunday. The reappearance of the climbers was awaited with much anxiety. But nothing happened. Neither party was visible beyond the spot where Mehringer and Sedlmayr were seen for the last time the previous year, before the storm enshrouded the mountain.

Shortly before 8.00 am on the Monday the climbers were seen again, continuing their attempt, albeit very slowly. But something was amiss. Towards midday, shortly before the face was again covered by mist, all four were back in their Sunday bivouac. There was much speculation amongst the various observers manning the telescopes. Had they given up? Were the difficulties insuperable? Or had something happened to one of them that prevented their continuing? Several people noticed that one of the climbers didn't seem to move so well as the others. It was thought that perhaps one of the many stone falls that had been seen had injured him. Again cloud and shreds of mist veiled the mountain and hid the 3,600-metre bivouac site of the two parties from view. Anxious hours passed; everyone hoped for the best. Another night came and went and by morning the weather had again taken a turn for the worse;

there was nothing to be seen. Then suddenly for a brief moment the mists parted and the face was clear. There was a mad scramble for the telescopes. The men were seen on the Second Icefield above the Rote Fluh. They were therefore retreating. It was easy now to see that one was injured, for two of them were continually helping him. The descent with the injured man was a very time-consuming business. At 8.30 pm they reached the bivouac site that Sedlmayr and Mehringer had used for their second night.

On the morning of the 21 July it was pouring with rain and above there was fresh snow on the face. It would be hard to describe what it is like to climb in such conditions after a frigid bivouac. Their rope must have been as stiff as a wire hawser (we were still using hemp rope at that time) and the rocks encased in a sheath of ice. Again clouds rolled in forming thick curtains; stone falls tumbled down and over the rock overhangs torrents of water and snow avalanches poured in continuous destruction. The traverse to them must have seemed impossible and so they resolved to abseil down the overhangs on the face below. They deliberated a long time over this abseil because the vertical and overhanging section below required several pegs and they only had a few. As the first one descended, a railway worker came out of the gallery window and called up the face to see if everything was all right. They called back, "All's well." It may have been the encouragement of finding themselves once more within shouting distance of other people. The linesman marked their position using a shovel as a pointer and went back to his work.

When he returned two hours later, he could hear cries of help from the face. He ran to the Eigerfenster station and telephoned the Jungfrau railway office for immediate assistance. There were three Wengen guides at the Eigergletscher station, sheltering from the storm. They were Christian Rubi, his brother Adolf, and Hans Schlunegger. A special train was ordered to take them to the gallery window, as the guides assembled their rescue gear – despite the ruling which had gone out that no life was to be put in jeopardy on the Eigerwand.

As the three climbed out of the gallery window, they were immediately assaulted by the violent storm raging on the face. It took all their strength to make a traverse of around 200 metres, running the gauntlet of continual stone bombardment and avalanches, until they were within shouting distance of the climber. His calls for help were getting increasingly more urgent. They heard, "Throw down a rope from above, no more pegs . . ." It was the cry of only one man. The guides shouted to him that it was impossible to get above him that day, he would have to wait until tomorrow. In agitation he shouted back "No, no, no!" It was terrible to hear; then he shouted something else about "Dead", but his words were carried away by the storm. The storm was so strong by then that the guides only just had time to withdraw to the gallery window before complete darkness set in. Between the crash of avalanches the man outside could be heard yelling for help like a wild animal. The icy face hurled back the inhuman, demented cries. It pierced everyone to the quick. Could he withstand the night?

Next day as soon as it began to get light the Swiss guides went once more through the gallery window and out on to the hostile face. The cries for help still came down from the wall. What must he have endured during this long night – yet he still lived! He grew quiet when he heard that they would now attempt to rescue him. They reached to within forty-five metres of the difficult section where Toni Kurz was hanging beneath an overhang in a single rope sling.

"Are the others still alive?" one of the guides shouted.

"No, they died yesterday. I am quite alone. One is frozen above me, one fell yesterday and the other hangs below me on the rope, he too is frozen – dead."

"Can you free yourself from the corpses? Try it and save as much rope as possible." Kurz climbed down twelve metres to his dead friend and with his ice axe cut the rope. Then again he climbed up to the other body and there, too, cut through the rope. The section of rope thus gained was frozen solid, but with incredible perseverance he began to separate it, untwisting the strands, with only one hand. (The guides had noticed that he only used one hand when he was abseiling, the other was frozen.) Only an experienced climber can appreciate what an achievement that was. When he had unravelled the frozen strands, he joined them so that he had a piece fifty metres long. He weighted it with a stone and lowered it to the guides. Hours had passed. One can but marvel at his will to live, his stamina! This man Kurz would have climbed the North Wall if the weather hadn't put a stop to it. Now the guides fastened a forty-metre rope, pistons, karabiners and hammer to the line and watched as it was raised by Kurz. (A second rope should have been sent up to the trapped climber.) Kurz hammered in the pegs and then the guides waited to see if he would pull the rope in any further. For a while he did; powder avalanches were meanwhile falling all around, but at last the rope stopped and Toni Kurz appeared over the overhang. He had therefore secured the rope above and was abseiling on it single. Slowly he came closer but the guides noticed the nearer he came, the more his strength ebbed. He was using a sit-sling for abseiling and the rope ran through a karabiner. There was no other method he could employ using only one hand. By holding the rope taut from below the guides gave him some assistance. But now he was coming to the knot where the ropes were joined. What would he do now? It would be impossible for him to get the bulky knot through the karabiner which was four metres above the guides. He realised this. Up till then his energy and his tenacious hold on life had been remarkable, now defeat threatened. Encouraging words were no longer of any help. The guides could see that suddenly it was all over. He tipped forward and didn't move any more. His face was red and frozen, his hands swollen and from his crampons hung long icicles. When it had appeared that rescue was almost achieved, his flame of life had been extinguished. Numbed and dazed, the guides took their difficult route back, immersed in the memory of the skill and courage of the young climber who still hung from the rope.

What happened on that Tuesday? What the misfortune was which cost the lives of those four young hopeful climbers we shall never know for certain. We have the sketchy details that Toni Kurz told the guides; climbers can only surmise the rest. The last one knows for certain of the party is that after the railway worker's call they decided to abseil down the eighty-metre overhang. This was because a retreat over the traverse was not possible. Hinterstoisser must have been injured by stone fall or avalanche and fallen either attempting this traverse or preparing a stance for the abseil. He took the rope and pegs for the abseil with him when he fell. Angerer, too, came off, either in the same stone fall or attempting to help his fallen comrade, but he remained hanging on the rope to which Kurz also was secured, held by a peg. Rainer was above them, at the beginning of the traverse, and must have frozen to death when, after Angerer's fall, he was yanked up like a puppet and left hanging jammed against the piton. Kurz was the only one not pulled off when all this happened, perhaps he was well belayed. The Swiss guides did all they could, we can corroborate that. There was nothing more that I could have done myself, taking into account the conditions at the time and the rescue methods in existence then. I was to learn a lot from these experiences and they helped us to develop new rescue techniques.

The police had raised the alarm and summoned our Bergwacht as soon as cries for help were heard on the Eigerwand and we had in fact arrived at the gallery window and were preparing to climb out, as the Swiss guides returned from their attempted rescue. Deeply shocked, they told us the story. We couldn't believe it. We could only inadequately thank them for their effort in trying to assist our friends, despite the terrible weather. It now remained for us to recover our dead.

The next morning we arrived at the gallery exit early. We took the same route as the guides had done the previous day. Again there was masses of new snow, and we had therefore to be very cautious. We fixed up a hand-rail, as we wished to take Kurz's body down to the gallery window. It was terrible seeing Toni hanging free on the rope some four metres out from the face and about three metres above our stance. We considered how we might get the body off the rope and down to us without it falling off into space. From its long exposure, Toni's rope was encased in ice making it as thick in diameter as a beer mug. We were amazed that the rope could withstand this weight of ice (it was forty-five metres long) as well as the weight of the body. There was therefore no way of getting up to the body by prusiking up the rope. We had with us a four-metre long pole and with a sling attached to the end of it we tried to get hold of a foot, arm or head and thereby belay him before he fell off into the depths when we cut the rope. We tried for three hours without success; when one of us got tired, another would take over, but it was all in vain. We were secured on a double rope; even so it was extremely difficult to move freely on our stance.

We therefore decided to cut the rope without belaying the body and duly fixed a knife on to our pole for this purpose. He fell, as we had predicted, on to the smooth slabs a few metres below us. The ice broke off him and, separated from the rope, he shot down over the rock and snow runnels until he disappeared from our view. We would not be able to reach him until the following day in any case, but we wanted next to attempt to recover Rainer who was still hanging frozen above the great overhang. We crossed under the overhang a little further to the right and were then able to see him.

We knew the whole business was being watched through the telescopes at Kleine Scheidegg. On that lonely stance we discussed all possible aspects of recovering Rainer's body, but had to retrace our steps to the gallery entrance as we were under constant threat from falling stones. We knew it would not be feasible to effect the recovery in these conditions. Added to which, the dead man was completely frozen into the ice; once it thawed perhaps he would fall down unaided. So, wait a bit, we thought. There were now three bodies at the foot of the face; they would need to be recovered from Alpiglen.

In the evening we sat with the Swiss guides and Fritz von Almen, the owner of Scheidegg Hotel. It could be seen with all of them, in word or gesture, these tragic events had left their mark. Fritz von Almen told us a bit more about the route, with the aid of his big telescope, which was invaluable. Early on Friday we climbed up to the lower section of the North Face. This consisted of a whole series of steep snowfields with rocky buttresses in between and avalanche-scoured gullies. Everything had to be searched. But our diligence was rewarded – we found one of the fallen men, whom we later established to be Angerer, hanging in a steep gully. We wrapped him in a casualty bag and carried him down. The rest of the men not required for the transport continued searching. They found various bits of camera equipment and a watch. This was in the main gully into which everything from above is channelled. It was therefore where Toni Kurz must have shot down when we cut him free. Checking the fall-line, we saw a huge marginal crevasse at the bottom which in places was completely filled with newly avalanched snow. The parts of the crevasse that were still open were under constant bombardment from falling stones. So we had to abandon this to await better weather conditions before we could search it.

We did, however, find a second body that day. It turned out to be Sedlmayr from the previous year's attempt. So the mystery was solved; the two men must have been swept from their bivouac site by avalanches and carried down. But of his companion we found nothing.

Several days' searching went by and it was decided we could have another attempt at bringing down Rainer who was still frozen up in the crack. Our party was six strong; we climbed out of the gallery on to the face with enough rope to cross the Hinterstoisser Traverse at the end of which Rainer was suspended. We had to do the climb the same way as the climbers had done it. Steep sections of the face with broken rock led to the so-called Difficult Crack, which is very overhanging. The stone fall danger in this part of the face is considerable, for the stones come down in free flight from 400–500 metres above, over the Rote Fluh.

When we were standing on the band from which the Hinterstoisser Traverse drops down leftwards, we saw Rainer very clearly forty metres below. The ice had completely cleared. It took a while before we had four men up there and were all ready for the abseil – suddenly there was a strange noise and we couldn't believe our eyes – Rainer and the ice beneath him fell into the depths.

Shattered by this sight, we took a while to recover our senses. Actually we were relieved because who knows whether the recovery would have been completed safely? We now abseiled, and were very pleased to get back to the safety of the gallery window without incident, except for the loss of some ropes. We left them in place because they had been exposed to stone fall, so would be no more use for rescues, and they were used by later parties retreating from the Traverse.

During the following days we were again at the foot of the face and recovered Rainer from one of the marginal crevasses. We were unable to find Toni Kurz. There was still too much avalanche debris in the crevasses. We decided to postpone that search for a later date. In fact the conditions were such that his body wasn't recovered until the following year.

In a sense we left Grindelwald without success – we were not able to help our friends, but at least we were able to recover their bodies from the face and that was some comfort to their relatives. But what was as important was that none of our team suffered any mishap. We had been lucky, considering the conditions. In my mind it was as if our good intentions were rewarded with good luck.

When we got back home we kept ourselves prepared and equipped to rescue other climbers from the Eiger. For we knew that this face would feature more and more in the sights of good climbers; we were proved right.

The Eigerwand, 1957–62

Hamish MacInnes and Brian Nally

The first British ascent of the North Face of the Eiger was a prize plum in our mountaineering orchard. I was well aware of this and during the spring of 1957 I contacted Chris Bonington who was then serving in a tank regiment in Germany to see if he was interested in attempting the climb. We were old friends and though I was aware that he hadn't climbed in the Alps before, I said in my letter to him, "Where better could you get such a fitting introduction to these Alps?" He wasn't totally convinced, but his spirit of adventure outweighed his common sense and we met in Grindelwald in July, 1957. Meantime, he had done a bit of Eiger research and was somewhat perturbed when he discovered that the wall then had only twelve ascents and had claimed fourteen lives. Anyhow, I managed to allay his fears, saying the climb was in the bag and, clutching a postcard with the route marked on it – our only guide – we set off. He didn't have much equipment and I gave him the plastic cover off my motorcycle to serve as a bivouac sack.

Our first acquaintance with the Eigerwand was of a passing nature, for after setting up a bivouac on the lower wall, threatening cloud caused us to scurry like squirrels for the valley and spend the remainder of our climbing holiday on the Aiguilles of Chamonix.

A short time after that abortive pioneering attempt, where we barely tickled the soles of the Eiger, a rescue swung into operation on the North Face which was a further instalment on this wide screen where Death invariably plays a principal part. It is a production where a "hit" is a collision with a falling stone. The rescue of Claudio Corti from the Exit Cracks of the Spider confirmed Ludwig Gramminger's faith in the use of steel cables for big wall rescues.

Ludwig's Bergwacht joined forces with Erich Friedli, a Swiss rescue team leader who shared a similar outlook to rescue work and techniques to Gramminger. Erich had assembled a formidable band of internationally known climbers on the summit when the Bergwacht arrived and the winch equipment was set in position for the very long operation down the face. Alfred Hellepart was lowered 320 metres on a thin steel wire to the trapped climbers. He reached Corti and discovered that Corti's companion, Stefano Longhi, was also alive 100 metres away. Hellepart succeeded in getting Corti up on his back, hauled from the top by the winch wire. But when Lionel Terray took over Hellepart's role and went down for Longhi, the radio failed and the attempt had to be abandoned. Longhi died, as did the other two men that had joined forces with them on the climb, two young Wurttemberg climbers, Gunther Nothdufft and Franz Mayer. After Longhi got injured, they had pressed on for help, leaving their vital bivouac sack with Corti who had exhausted himself trying to help his companion. After completing the climb, the two German climbers had died on the descent on the West Face of the mountain. Their bodies were not found until four years later.

I have avoided writing, or rather using a full account of this rescue as it has been well documented elsewhere, often with more than its fair share of hypothetical speculation on the actions and motives of the participants. The last words should perhaps be from Alfred Hellepart, for this quiet-spoken member of the Bergwacht was surely the hero of the operation. After a hellish night out on the descent with Corti, where a bivouac tent was torn to shreds by the wind, they continued down the following morning.

Alfred later wrote:

Our small group of German friends stumbled down that last rock buttress to where the others were already waiting. Amongst those there were some who were more interested in making capital out of the whole business than in helping. We didn't want to have anything to do with these people. Up above we had become aware of something quite different, sacred to us, no one could rob us of these memories. We could understand each other without lengthy dialogue. This was apparent as we pressed hands and looked each other in the eye as we bade goodbye. May it always be so in the mountains.

Though I returned to the Eiger hopeful of the first British ascent, it was not to be. Like so many before me, heavy snow and bad weather made any attempt out of the question. However, Chris persevered and on one occasion with Don Whillans rescued Brian Nally from the Second Icefield. Nally's story as narrated in an interview for the BBC documentary, "The Climb Up To Hell", is one of the most moving in the annals of mountaineering. Brian had teamed up with a student, Barry Brewster, a highly proficient rock climber, though he didn't have a great deal of snow and ice experience. The previous year Brian had made the first British ascent of the Matterhorn North Face with a Scotsman, Tom Carruthers. Tom was later killed on the Eiger. I knew Tom well, he used to sleep under a bridge close to my house when climbing in Glencoe. There was so little room under this bridge that its occupants had to crawl about. He and his friends who frequented this doss were known as the "Bendie-Bendie Boys". Brian Nally was a painter and like Barry Brewster came from southern England. Brian describes the climb:

We approached the Hinterstoisser; it's not a very difficult move, but it's got quite a strange psychological effect. The Hinterstoisser is the Rubicon of this mountain. In theory, if you leave a rope on it to traverse, you can come back across, but in actual fact only a handful of men have crossed it and come back. No British party had been across. It was a setback and it happened to be my turn to lead. I was a little wary about it. I looked at the weather, almost hoping for it to be bad enough for an excuse to turn back. But it was clear. I looked down at Barry and he simply said "Best of luck, Brian," and that was it. That was the decision made and, once it was, everything settled into place. We went across, through this torrential waterfall, up a chimney and into the Swallow's Nest. We reached there just before nightfall and everything so far was going to plan. We were happy that night because the decision had been made, everything now was just to get to the summit. It didn't freeze that night, but we didn't worry too much about that.

After that bivouac they continued up on to the Second Icefield the next day.

We got to the Second Icefield; we knew it was a long one, but the distance was enormous from where we were to the first rocks. It was late now and the Second Icefield was water, ice and slush. It was in very bad condition. We resolved to plough straight across rather than go for the rim. We decided to cut steps, firstly because the condition of the icefield wasn't good and, secondly, in case we had to retreat. So we ploughed across and the stones started coming down; we'd been through stone fall many times before, but we hadn't seen anything like this. The icefield was raked in every quarter and then suddenly all Hell would break loose. We turned in to face the ice and tried to dodge the big ones and hope the little ones wouldn't catch us, though we got hit several times. But we just pressed on and on. The icefield is incredible, it's endless . . . We were glad that the Second Icefield was over.

Barry said, "There's a pitch of Grade Five up above." (This is one grade below the highest standard.) Now I belayed to a ring peg and watched him as he set off up his pitch, the start of the Flatiron. Higher up Barry put in two other pitons then he went out of sight . . .

Everything went quiet for a bit. The rope stopped, then paid out again. Suddenly, from high above I heard him yell "Stones!" Instinctively, I dodged and kept close to the rock and at the same time I heard my name sharp and clear and I looked up and Barry was falling backwards through the air. He went hurtling past me, the two top pitons pulled out. He crashed on to the ice about a hundred feet below. For a moment I just stood there staring at the ring piton, not believing that it could have held and then I looked down at him. He was upside down on the ice. He wasn't moving. I stayed there for a minute and then I put a piton in and tied the rope to it and unroped, climbed up to the ring piton and hit it back in. Then I climbed down to Barry; he was very badly injured and unconscious. From the position of his body I came to the conclusion that his back was broken.

I formed a harness in the rope, took all the weight off his chest and hung him in the sling. Normally, it would have been quite a comfortable position. The stones were still coming so I started to hack out a platform and this took a long time. It had to be long and wide enough for his full length. I was grateful that he was unconscious, hadn't got any pain. When this platform was completed, I pulled him back into it, secured him and put him in the sleeping bag. Then I took my crash helmet off and put it on him and . . . and then tried to form a barrier between him and the upward slope. It was late in the afternoon by then and everything looked . . . everything was lost. It wasn't a question of just one of us being injured. This was the Eiger and it was both of us, you see. Once or twice I went up to the rock where I'd left some gear, brought it back and settled down for the night. I sort of placed myself between him and the upward slope and just waited for the morning. Stones were relentless. We were immediately in a path of one of the shutes that has a direct line to the summit where all the stones funnel down. We couldn't have moved to the right or to the left. We just had to stay where we were.

During the night I had to make the decision whether at first light I should leave Barry and try and go for my friends to help, or stay. It was obvious Barry was very badly injured; the point was, I couldn't bear for him to regain consciousness and me not to be there. It was a most terrible decision to have to make, and I spent the whole night trying to make it, but even at first light I hadn't made that decision. Because I wouldn't admit that he wasn't going to pull through and, though he'd been unconscious, he had moved once or twice, but he hadn't really woken. At first light I tried . . . tried to really make this decision and he appeared to stir a little, moved an arm and he seemed to regain consciousness a bit, so I went back again up the slope and got a stove, thinking that I'd make a drink or some soup or something if he could take it. I started to make this and he seemed to come to a bit. He opened his eyes and seemed to know where he was and who I was and said, "I'm sorry, Brian," and he died.

Everything went dark; it really was the end of – everything.

First reaction was to go for the summit at any cost, because that's what we'd come to do; I couldn't bear the thought of going down. But time passed, I rationalised and came to the proper decision. So I secured him once more with ice pitons and cut the rope above him and took the rope, meaning to try for the descent. I went up again to the belay but came down once more to Barry and just stayed there for a little while. I couldn't bear to take any of the pieces of equipment that were so vital to me now. I couldn't bear to take the crash helmet or the ice screws and pitons. So I left everything just where it was . . .

I knew this was the last time I was leaving him and I started to go back up the slope; the stones had kept up all night, but they seemed to increase now. The whole field was raked from every quarter again. Suddenly, I felt this was bigger than usual; I started moving a bit faster and I was about twenty feet away from the rock when tons of rubble and ice came down; I was directly in the path of the rock avalanche. I raced for the rock and just got there, but turned round to see that this avalanche whisked Barry's body away and took it over the edge of the ice into the blackness. This was the cruellest thing that could have happened.

Chris Bonington and Don Whillans were not aware that Barry and Brian were ahead of them, having set out twenty-four hours previously. When Chris and Don reached the foot of the Second Icefield, they realised that the weather was worsening and decided to retreat. They were just about to descend when two figures appeared from below. They were Swiss guides and they told them about the accident above and asked for their help. Chris and Don volunteered this without a moment's hesitation and set off across the vast expanse of the Second Icefield. They were continually subjected to stone fall and after a particularly bad one they looked across towards the Flatiron which was the direction it had come from and to their horror saw the tiny figure of a man being swept off into space. This was Barry Brewster. The guides promptly returned to the gallery window while Chris and Don pressed on towards Brian Nally who was visible as a mere speck of red at the top of the icefield.

Despite a storm, they got Brian down safely, a remarkable feat considering that Chris had lost his ice axe on the way up. The guides recovered Brewster's body from the bottom of the face. Later Brian Nally was presented with a bill of several hundred pounds for the rescue operation which he couldn't pay. This included a special train and the services of fourteen guides, which seems a bit ironical. It is also a sad reflection on journalism that for some unknown reason the train which was to take the soaked and exhausted climbers back to Kleine Scheidegg remained for almost an hour in the tunnel whilst reporters prised the whole story from Brian, who was still severely shocked.

Chris was to return to the Eiger later in that same year, 1962, and this time he was successful. Ian Clough was his companion, but even then death was at their heels, for behind them Tom Carruthers and an Austrian, Egon Moderegger, whom they had passed, had fallen to their deaths from the Second Icefield.

Now with helicopters capable of winching people off the most inaccessible parts of the face, the Eiger has lost much of its sting, but its place has been taken by other great walls in the Himalayas or the Karakoram; there will always be an Eiger.

Two on the Dru

Hamish MacInnes

Because it is so overcrowded and offers so many testing climbs, the Mont Blanc massif is one of the world's blackest spots as far as mountain accidents are concerned. In both winter and summer climbers flock to the Chamonix area. It is a testing ground for higher regions, such as the Andes and Himalayas, as well as a mountain playground in its own right.

There are many dramatic and horrific tales to tell from this wonderful region, but let me start with two which both took place on the Petit Dru, a slender mountain of great beauty and one of which I have vivid personal memories, as my first narrative will explain.

My own tangle with the Petit Dru was in 1958. My climbing companion was Chris Bonington. We had first met up in 1953 in Scotland where we had launched assaults on hitherto unclimbed gullies and faces and later in 1957 had made a short-lived attempt on the Eiger North Face, a route then unclimbed by a British party.

Our quixotic sortie on the flanks of the Eiger had only served to whet my appetite for Alpine firsts, but had had the opposite effect on Chris. He wanted to get an established route or two under his belt, not waste his time chasing dazzling possibilities and great last problems. So when we took up residence in a tumbledown goat herder's hut at Montenvers the following season there was a constant running argument between us, me holding out objectives like the Shroud on the Grandes Jorasses, Chris muttering about suicide routes and Highland idiots. As the weather was desperate, with heavy early-season snow, much of the great debate was academic anyway. So we sat there reasonably amicably tucking into army compo rations left over from Chris's last tour of duty with his tank crew in Germany. My contribution to the catering was for some reason twenty-five pounds of figs and a gallon of molasses, an unfortunate choice for the general atmosphere of the hut and one necessitating frequent nocturnal dashes to the shrubbery.

We eventually settled on a compromise. When the weather lifted I agreed to go on a training climb before we ventured on more serious objectives. We made the ascent profitable by de-pegging the route, that is to say, extracting all but the essential pitons, thereby making it a more enjoyable ascent for those who were to follow and bringing our ironmongery reserves up to scratch. Such is the logic of the impecunious.

Now, with a known climb under our waist loops, it was my turn, and I suggested a new line to Chris on the Pointe de Lépiney.

"Just the thing for you, Chris, bugger-all snow and lovely warm smooth granite."

"I'll believe it when I see it," he muttered.

Our stepping stone for this enterprise was the Aiguilles de l'Envers hut, perched crazily on the south side of the Charmoz like a fairy castle, though perhaps squarer in profile. It still boasted a beautiful princess in the form of the custodian's daughter, the only person in residence. No doubt dutifully remembering the "Auld Alliance" of France and Scotland she took me under her wing, much to Chris's chagrin.

Our new route lived up to Chris's worst fears. Our attempt turned out to be a fiasco. We soon discovered that the reason it hadn't been climbed was because it bristled with overhangs. On one of these, after we had a frigid bivouac, Chris fell. He didn't injure himself, and consequently went back at it again with the determination of a Jack Russell terrier. He got up, only to find other overhangs sprouting above, even more menacing than the one just vanquished. After a meeting of the partnership we decided to retreat with what dignity we could muster, and I had the bright idea of descending a couloir which seemed to be the shortest distance between two points – our present position and the glacier a thousand feet below.

In an hour we were in the innards of a horrendous chimney with water beating on our heads. I had gone down first and was hanging from a peg which I had inserted with difficulty. When Chris joined me to share the only mini-foothold, we found that the abseil rope had jammed. Showing great fortitude Chris went up the rope using the painstaking technique of prusiking, a special sliding knot which locks when weight is put on it.

The final sting in the tail of this Aiguille route was a rimaye at least ten feet wide. That's a gap between snowfield and rock face. When I abseiled down, Chris was ensconced on a mantel-shelf-sized ledge above this intimidating slot like an eaglet contemplating its first flight. As the rope was long enough, I continued past him, kicking out from the last nose of rock on an overhang, and just managed to reach the snow on the far lip of the gap. It was a hairy business.

Bedraggled, we slunk down, pride hurt and bodies aching with this abortive encounter. The two young knights who peacocked about the Aiguilles de l'Envers hut on the way up now stole furtively past the door in case the shapely *gardienne* should spot us. Finally, to make bad worse we lost our way among the crevasses of the Mer de Glace in the dark, and what normally takes half an hour took us three.

We had now been joined in our hut by two young Austrians, after whom our abode would eventually be known as the Chalet Austria. Walter Philip was twenty-one, tall and dark with panther-like movements; Richard Blach, three years younger, was quiet and slightly built. Despite their youth they had done some impressive climbs in the Eastern Alps. Chris and I immediately struck up a friendship with them and we pooled our gastronomic resources. The diet of the two Austrians was almost as monotonous as ours. They had arrived with rucksacks bristling with salami and very little else. As they feared for the lifespan of their protein cylinders, I suggested they use the Mer de Glace as a refrigerator. With due solemnity they lowered the salami into the depths of a crevasse, not before I had made an exchange for some figs and molasses, and the nocturnal atmosphere deteriorated accordingly.

At last the sun struggled out and Chris and I reached an honourable solution as to our major objective. I proposed what was still regarded as probably the most serious rock climb in the Alps at the time, the Bonatti Pillar of the Petit Dru. First climbed by Walter Bonatti, who had done it in a breathtaking solo lasting five days in 1953, the South-West Pillar had been climbed four times since, but none of the parties had been British. I knew it would tempt Chris.

"The Pillar's right up your alley," I encouraged. "Rock most of the way and good rock at that."

It was agreed and Walter and Richard would make it a foursome. The previous year Walter had made a fast ascent of the West Face of the Petit Dru, a 3,000-foot sweep of smooth featureless granite which borders on the Pillar, and so he knew the way down, always a reassuring factor should the weather take a turn for the worse.

We were, however, at a loss where to obtain a description of the Bonatti Pillar and descended to Chamonix to recruit Donald Snell, a local sport-shop owner, to obtain this for us. We succeeded. After steak and chips at the Bar Nationale we hiked back up the cog railway to Montenvers and our shack.

This (1958) was before the days of routine helicopter monitoring, where parties are often checked each evening from the air to see if they are all right. An accident on such a climb as the Bonatti Pillar was too awful for us to contemplate, but we made a simple arrangement with the stationmaster at Montenvers next day as we left with laden sacks. We would give him a torch signal to record our progress on the climb. "Every night at nine o'clock, André."

There was a great feeling of relief in leaving the penned-in area of Montenvers where hundreds of multi-coloured tourists gaze at the mountains and cluster round the large pay-and-look telescopes.

We crossed the dirty slug of the Mer de Glace and climbed the steep moraine on the far bank – a hazardous business as it was then a cliff of scree. The normal bivouac for the start of both the West Face and the Bonatti route is the Rognon du Dru, a pleasantly located rock "dwelling" comprising an overhang which, if the wind is from the right quarter, and it doesn't rain or snow, offers one-star comfort for uncomplaining alpinists.

Just before dusk we saw two figures approaching with large rucksacks. As they came closer we could see that one was almost as broad as he was tall. Like me he wore a flat cap. We immediately recognised him as Don Whillans, one of the foremost climbers of his generation and probably the greatest

British alpinist ever. It was Don who had made the first British ascent of the West Face with Joe Brown. His companion now was Paul Ross, one of the English Lake District's star climbers. They had long French loaves fingering from their packs.

"How do," Don spoke. It was a gruff but neutral-sounding greeting, neither friendly nor aggressive. He gave his home-rolled fag a drag and studied us with his small beady eyes, obviously weighing us up.

"Hello, Don," Chris responded. "Heading for the Bonatti?"

"That's right, Chris." Don looked steadily at me. "I hear that you have a description of the Bonatti, Hamish." It sounded as if I had just filched some classified documents. "I was in at Snell's," he added, explaining how he had gleaned this intelligence.

"Not much of a description, Don," I returned. "You know Bonatti is as tight with his route descriptions as a Yorkshireman with brass!"

"Aye. Well, we'll be seeing you." Don gave another draw on his cigarette. "It looks as if this doss is fully booked so we'll mosey up higher to see if we can find somewhere to bivvy."

We set the alarm for 2.00 am and settled down for what sleep we could get. But that early reveille, shared by bakers and alpinists, proved to be cloudy, so we turned over and Chris soon announced with snores that he was at peace with the world.

By 5.30 am the weather looked better and I gave him a shake.

"Wake up, fella, time to move." The Austrians were already up and Walter was champing at the bit.

"Could be a good day, Walter," I greeted, "even though we'll be keeping office hours."

"Ja, Hammish, we will have much fun."

I was later to reflect on this observation.

As we entered the jaws of the couloir we could see two small figures above. Don and Paul were already roped up, but when we reached the rimaye between the lower snowfield and the rocky start to the couloir, Walter suggested that we should climb unroped to save time. We agreed, which proved to be a somewhat foolhardy decision. For, preparing to make the long stride from the snow to gain the rock, Walter fell when the lip of unstable snow which he was standing on collapsed. He instinctively threw himself backwards thereby avoiding a rapid and chilly descent into the hole. Undeterred, he jumped across and raced up the rock on the other side as if he was in four-wheel drive. There was a lot of grit and stones on the smooth granite which made it very treacherous.

In a short time we had caught up with Don and Paul and it was the classic hare and tortoise fable. Don was leading and Walter clambered past him as if he was in the fast lane, with a brief "Good Morning".

When Walter was just above the stoic Mancunian, he slipped and fell on top of Don, who only with considerable effort arrested Walter's fall. It was a close thing and I thought Don was most restrained. The MacInnes, Bonington, Philip, Blach combine belatedly decided to rope up!

So we emerged at the wall of the Flammes de Pierre which effectively blocks off the top of the couloir. I had been pushed into the lead for the previous few hours on the false assumption that I could cut endless steps in the hard ice. The top of the couloir was steep snow and ice and as there was only one pair of crampons in our party, steps were essential.

From the cold dark depths of the couloir, we could see the Pillar above wrapped in a golden brown with sunshine. We were elated, just as druids must have felt when addressing the dawn.

In a slot in the rock at the very base of the Pillar, we found a walking stick, as if it had been placed in a hallstand. We never did find out who left it there. Here was the sun, its warm rays probing our bodies and rejuvenating us. But there was work to do, 2,000 feet of it, some of the most intimidating rock climbing in the Alps. Don now came into his own and for me it was the start of a long association from which my respect for him as a master alpinist grew.

"Aye, well," he drawled, "I think you, Walter, and your mate Richard should go in front and Paul and I can follow behind and give you a spell if you get tired."

"Zat is all right by us," Walter responded eagerly.

"Fine. Paul and I can do the sack-hauling up the pitches and Hamish and you, Chris, can take up the rear de-pegging."

"Suits me, Don, I've got the 'Message'." I brandished my large piton hammer made in a Clydeside shipyard.

In minutes the Austrians had vanished like inspired chamois. The climbing was a kaleidoscope of overhangs, cracks, dièdres, slabs and walls, all at crazy angles. None was easy and we realised that this was climbing of a high order. It had taken us five hours to get up the couloir, which was normal, but now on warm rock we were keen to make fast time. We soon concertinaed, however. It was becoming harder and Walter had trouble getting over a large overhang. He did this using an étrier, a short rope ladder, which he clipped into the pegs and wedges in a crack. Don, who was watching this exhibition of gravity defiance, told Paul that he'd start sack-hauling here and he tackled the pitch with deliberation. He climbed it by holding on to the pegs but instead of continuing up the line which the Austrians had taken, which is the normal route, he climbed directly up a groove, a new variation which was desperately hard. When he was above, Don hauled up all our rucksacks and Paul joined him at his stance. When it was Chris's turn to lead this pitch, he had a struggle, but he didn't ask for a top rope, which he could easily have had from Paul. Chris admitted to me later that it was one of the hardest pitches he had ever led. I agreed that it was desperate and I had the security of a top rope when it was my turn, thankful as I thrutched upwards that I hadn't had to lead it.

Above, the climb became very exposed and the void below our climbing boots seemed to have a magnetic quality as if trying to pull us into the depths of the couloir. I could see Don above. He had let Paul lead and somehow both ropes had got threaded through the karabiners with the result that Paul couldn't now haul the rucksacks. Don had two of these on his shoulders and was climbing an overhanging pitch free, with his fingers hooked through the loops of the wedges. We heard him yell for the rope to be taken in, for there was slack, probably caused by friction through the runners. A peg he was holding on to with two fingers of his left hand was slowly coming out, but with a burst of energy he grabbed a small wooden wedge above and succeeded in fighting his way to the stance. He said later that this pitch had caused him more exertion than the rest of the climb put together.

A couple of hundred feet above, there was a pendulum move across the wall from a flake. Actually, it was a tension traverse where we swung across a vertical smooth wall holding on to a short rope secured to a piton above; an exhilarating experience when there's 2,000 feet of fresh air beneath boots that don't have anything to stand on.

After a short steep chimney we found ourselves on a luxurious ledge and as it was now late in the afternoon we decided to call it a day. Walter and Richard had gone up some eighty feet to a further small platform, which they informed us was quite adequate for their humble needs.

We consulted our abbreviated bible, Bonatti's description, and discovered that we had made good progress. It was obviously the wise decision to take advantage of this horizontal haven in such blank verticality. Directly above, the rock rose in one mighty sweep as high as the Empire State Building.

One of the fascinating aspects Himalayan and Alpine climbing have in common with hitting your head against a wall is that it's wonderful when you stop. Not that you hate the process of actually climbing, but when you settle down for the night in some airy bivvy, you have time to reflect and collect yourself, and, if it's a good evening, soak in the view. At such times one almost feels like a bird – like Tennyson's eagle, clasping the crags, lord of all you survey. It was such a night on our bivvy ledge on the South-West Pillar. The lights of Chamonix twinkled like a fairground, and across the valley above tourist-deserted Montenvers, the Grépon and Charmoz stood to attention in the twilight. My thoughts took me back to when I was a young lad traversing those peaks solo.

Actually, I was following the famous French guide, Lionel Terray, who allowed me to tag along behind him and his current client. In this way I gained alpine experience and he kept a fatherly eye on me.

That particular excursion, however, had a drastic ending. We had reached the top of the Charmoz and I was following them down in a series of abseils, when the sling I was abseiling from snapped. It had held for both of them. I fell about forty feet, fortunately stopping on a small ledge. Lionel, who was a few hundred feet lower, saw me fall and was with me in ten minutes.

I had injured both feet and my knees had jack-knifed into my eye sockets with the impact, so that I couldn't see. Lionel was obviously going to require help to get me down and after ascertaining that I could descend on a rope, decided to get me below the main difficulties and then go for help. He couldn't abandon his client though, who was looking anxious, no doubt concerned at being left on his own.

With Lionel telling me where hand and footholds were, I moved down stiffly and painfully. I could face in all right, but couldn't put weight on my heels. I could just see through a red film; but we both realised that I would have to be carried back to Montenvers. I couldn't walk on level ground. Lionel spotted the guide Raymond Lambert on the Grépon and shouted to him to come and assist. In some twenty minutes Raymond and an aspirant guide joined us. In such distinguished company I had made steady progress back down to Montenvers.

My ruminations were cut short by the need to make our 9.00 pm signal to our friendly stationmaster. In a few minutes answering flashes winked up at us. It was comforting to know that down there, across the Mer de Glace, someone cared and took the trouble to keep in touch.

Don and Paul also had their stove roaring and the aroma of soup and compo wafted luxuriously around the Pillar. It was so peaceful. I can still recall thinking that when there was a hideous cacophony of falling rocks; they were below, piling into the couloir, sending up showers of sparks. They took ages to sweep down the rock and ice of this bowling alley and presently the appetising smell of soup was replaced by the pungent smell of brimstone, a smell to me associated with death and destruction.

"Just as well that bloody lot didn't roll this morning," Don remarked drily, "there wouldn't have been much of us left."

All was quiet again, even more so after that shattering interlude. Then a high-pitched whine, like a ricochet from a sniper's bullet, cut through the silence. It had that confident, predestined note, which we all felt meant it was destined for us. I was the prime target. The rock bit into my scalp like a blow from a stone axe, catapulting me forward under its impact so that I was left hanging from my belay. Momentarily I was stunned. Instinctively my hands went to my head and I could feel warm blood oozing between my fingers. I can't remember a great deal of what happened next, but I gather that Chris, who had a wound dressing in his rucksack, pressed it over the gash to stem the bleeding and tied it under my chin.

Seating arrangements were changed and we all huddled back

against the wall of the Pillar, out of range of any other stray missiles. I was poised above Chris in a shallow groove and several times during the night I slumped unconscious on top of him. It was cold and I for one was in no state to think of tomorrow, but the others did. There was no question of retreat, the couloir was just too dangerous and it would have been difficult to abseil down the Pillar in any case, due to the traverses we made on the ascent.

In the morning we unfolded like newly exhumed zombies, our joints cold and stiff.

Chris asked, "How are you feeling, Hamish?"

"Not a bundle of fun, Chris, but I'll get by." I must have looked a mess, for Richard, who was above, sharing a perch with Walter, turned pale when he first looked down.

We had a brew and Chris suggested that Don should rope up with me as he was the strongest member of the party.

"I'll take out the pegs with Paul, Don."

"Aye, all right," Don looked thoughtful. "That may be the best policy. You think you'll make it, Mac?"

"I'll have a go," I said, trying to muster confidence. "Not many alternatives, are there?"

The Austrians had already started and the ring of pegs being driven home echoed from the rock. Walter was fighting his way up a line of grooves which scored the otherwise smooth face of the Pillar. It was climbing of a high order and Walter demonstrated his talent for pegging by inserting each new peg at the absolute limit of his reach, and he was tall. Sometimes it was possible to get finger jams and if it hadn't been for my nocturnal mishap I could even have enjoyed it. As it was, from time to time I could feel the Dru and my surroundings slipping away from me as I lapsed into wonderful unconsciousness where, for a minute or so, all was peaceful. Don played me like a sluggish fish, not giving me an inch of slack and exerting a persistent and welcome tension, and on the hardest sections literally hauling me up.

I looked up to where Walter and Richard were spreadeagled on the smooth red wall. For the last half-hour Walter had been requesting more and more pegs.

"That's the bloody lot," Don yelled up as he tied on the last six pitons which Chris had extracted below – a strenuous and frustrating task.

"You watch my rope, Hamish, if you can, and I'll take a mosey round the corner to the right, there must be a bloody easier way than up there."

In a couple of minutes he came into view again, a small broad figure with his large rucksack making him look like a hunchback gorilla.

"It's this way," he jerked a thumb, a wide grin on his face, "up the biggest overhang in the three kingdoms."

When I went round to join him I saw this was no exaggeration. A great roof hung over the face up which ran a crack punctuated with wooden wedges in various degrees of decay. My heart seemed to stop, for I realised that I just didn't have the reserves to climb it.

Walter was recalled, de-pegging the long pitch as he abseiled. He had put a tremendous amount of work into attempting that terrifying red wall, all to no avail.

I secured myself to a small chockstone in a daze and craned my neck backwards to where Don was now swinging from the wedges. It seemed as easy for him as climbing stairs. I had to give up watching after a time, for it hurt my head. Presently the others joined me on my small ledge.

"What's it like above?" Chris shouted up.

"A bit steep, send up some more pegs."

"It's getting late," Chris yelled back. "It's almost seven o'clock and it'll soon be dark."

I could see Don looking at his watch.

"I'll come down," he returned. "We can bivvy on the ledges where we spent most of the afternoon."

He pulled the two ropes up through the pegs and lowered them, where they hung out beyond us in space. When he abseiled he had to swing in and Walter fielded him and pulled him on to our ledge.

We climbed down to the wider ledges, feeling despondent that we had made so little progress that day. Don had virtually pulled me up every pitch and I was feeling a burden to the party. But it was a matter of carrying on and not giving up, and I only hoped I would feel stronger in the morning. Chris signalled to the stationmaster, just the usual signal – we were continuing.

It was a night which didn't seem to end.

I huddled in a crack above the others with a peg belay behind me because I didn't want to descend any more than I had to, and Paul sent up my dinner, two bangers, on the rope. Anyhow, I suppose in some ways I fared better on my perch than Chris. He shared Don's bivvy bag and as Don was a chain smoker and Chris a non-smoker, one puffed and the other coughed all night. We hadn't had anything to drink since the previous morning and our throats felt swollen and sore. The cold was insidious, seeking out every chink and gap in our bivvy sacks and, as we were hidden from the morning sun, it took ages to sort out the frozen ropes and to thaw our boots. Breakfast was an oatmeal block which looked and tasted like plastic wood.

Don suggested to Walter that he should lead.

"I'm going to have to help Hamish up this." He pointed a gloved finger in the direction of the roof. "It's a bit strenuous."

I watched Walter climb. He seemed to have tremendous drive and literally threw himself at a climbing problem; usually he got up – but not always. He later told me of his attempt on the North Face of the Cima de Laveredo, when he fell from the second pitch and plunged the total length of the rope, a fall of 300 feet. At the full extension of the nylon he just touched the scree at the base of the climb and escaped with minor injuries. I felt envious as I watched him snap off icicles to suck as he climbed the overhang.

It seemed to take me ages to get up that pitch. Don couldn't give much assistance and from time to time I passed out. It was strange coming to again to find myself swinging from a rope threaded through pegs and wedges – a reversal of the normal nightmare situation, here reality was the nightmare. Chris coming up just behind was a comfort, he described me as "hanging like a corpse from a gibbet".

Above the roof was another, but not so overhanging. I was part way up, thanks to Don's persistent tension on the rope, when the sun hit me. It was now the time of day when more sensible people were sitting down to lunch and there was considerable power in those life-giving rays. Before I reached Don's ledge the heat was beginning to get to me and Chris, who was still wearing his duvet jacket, found it almost unbearable. It seemed amazing in so short a span of time to suffer such extremes of temperature.

Paul was behind Chris de-pegging the overhangs. I sat recuperating while Don made a brew using ice he had found in a crack, his dixie piled up with this frozen aggregate, for it had a high gravel content. I heard a call from below and peered over the edge. It was Chris. He had reached a peg on a hard blank pitch and was feeling shattered with the combination of cold, heat and dehydration. He asked for a top rope. In a couple of minutes he had tied on to this and joined us on the ledge, his eyes lighting up when he saw the brew – even if it was only a gritty mouthful each.

It was a strange situation. There was now standing room only, as the ledge was the area of a kitchen chair and with three of us on it everything had to be done by numbers. Walter and Richard were still ahead, and from what Don told us they were having trouble route finding.

Five minutes later we heard a cry from above. It was Walter. He had found the right line and was almost at the Shoulder, he said. The top of the Bonatti Pillar was close at hand, hallelujah!

I remember finding the last pitch of the climb desperately strenuous. With each new rope length my energy had ebbed. I felt completely done in, with a dull diesel-like throb in my head, realising that I couldn't go much further. Don kept saying that each pitch was the last – the very last and definitely the last. At least he kept me moving. Lines from "Hassan" ran through my mind – "Always a little further: it may be Beyond that last blue mountain barred with snow."

Not that the ultimate pitch was particularly hard. I simply seemed to have used up all my steam.

During the day we hadn't noticed that the weather was getting progressively worse. Now leaden clouds were seeping in from the south and the wind had a razor's edge to it. It didn't need a prophet to tell us that we were in for bad weather.

The snow started to fall steadily and heavily and soon everything was blotted out. I remember seeing the Grandes Jorasses being swallowed in a white froth of cloud. We bivouacked on the broken rocks close to the summit. Don knew the route over the top of the mountain, but he felt that this would be too dangerous in the present weather. Walter, on the other hand, had gone down directly from where we were when he completed the West Face route the previous year, and felt that he could find the way. But not today, or rather that evening, for it was essential to get into our bivouac sacks to avoid being frozen. In ten minutes we were tied to our pegs, tethered like cowed dogs.

It was an even worse bivvy than the previous night: bitterly cold, and the fine driven snow seemed to find every cranny and tear in our bags so that we were first soaked, then frozen as if set in casting resin. Our only food was one packet of soup divided by six. There was not a great deal to be cheerful about; no joy in having climbed the route, only a numbed realisation that we had got up, but what was now much more important was to get down, and fast, for we knew that we couldn't survive long in such conditions.

We witnessed dawn through storm clouds. It was still snowing and everything was plastered: a world of white and metallic-looking ice. The ropes were again frozen solid and our plastic bivvy bags, now the worse for wear, cracked like celluloid when we tried to fold them.

Walter led the descent of the West Face, abseiling into a white nothingness on slippery ropes. The wind was so strong now that we could barely communicate. We had gone down about four rope lengths when Don, who had an acute instinct for danger, called a halt.

"Walter," he shouted, "I think you're wrong. This is too dicey for the descent route." Indeed it was becoming desperately steep.

The Austrians, snow-covered figures on a minuscule ledge, were another rope length down.

"I think you are correct, Don. We will try further to the right."

But they had trouble joining us again, and when they came alongside I could see that Richard was in a bad way, suffering from exhaustion and exposure. Don and Chris had already set off on the proper descent line.

Now, for some strange reason I was feeling stronger, possibly because I was descending, which required less effort, and I was probably more used to these abominable conditions with my Scottish background of blizzard and flood than our Austrian friends.

I tried to help Richard as best I could, while Paul and Walter were preparing the abseil belays. Walter had fallen when coming up from the low point of his descent and appeared in a nervous state. Now he launched himself on the next abseil. I could see, as if in slow motion, what was about to happen but my brain wasn't working fast enough to prevent it. He had looped a sling round a sharp spike of rock so that there was no slack, and his abseil rope was threaded through this so that when he put his weight on the doubled rope the tight sling was under great strain. It snapped when he was a few feet down, but luckily Richard, who had him on a top rope, prevented a very nasty accident.

I heard a call from Don below. "The Flammes de Pierre, Chris. We're on the right route now."

I breathed a sigh of relief. With my revival I could now grasp the seriousness of our situation, but in fact the worst was behind us. Both Walter and Richard, who had got into such a physical and mental state, possibly through lack of food, now responded like a pair of huskies that had scented home base.

Abseil followed abseil, and with the lower altitude the wind dropped and we came out of the snow clouds. It was still miserable, but we could see the broad couloir below and shortly afterwards the hut.

We decided not to stay at the Charpoua hut that night, but carried on in the gathering dusk to Montenvers where we ate and ate until we finally staggered off to our sleeping bags at the Chalet Austria. Above, a great storm raged in the Aiguilles, but we didn't give a damn.

It was the end of my holiday for I had to return to Britain nursing a fractured skull; an injury which with its legacy of headaches and blackouts was to remind me of our Dru epic and for ever make me grateful to Don, without whose help I may have remained on a lonely ledge on the Bonatti.

I had been fortunate to be with some of Europe's leading alpinists who knew exactly what had to be done when I cracked my skull on the Bonatti Pillar. We rescued ourselves. At that time perhaps you might say we had little option to do anything else.

The case was different in 1966 when the evacuation of two young Germans from the West Face of the Dru precipitated one of the greatest rescue operations of its kind in the world, and hit the newspaper headlines with the impact of an international crisis.

The first ascent of the West Face of the Dru in 1952 had opened a new chapter in alpine climbing history, though there had been considerable controversy over the ethics of the first ascent. After ascending two-thirds of the wall, Guido Magnone, Lucien Berardini, Adrien Dagory and Marcel Lainé had to give up due to threatening weather and lack of water. When they returned to continue their assault, instead of going back up by their own ascent line, they took the North Face route to the point where their high point was within a hundred feet. This was frightening territory: blank, featureless rock falling sheer for some 2,000 feet above the base of the couloir. The only possible way to cross this smooth wall was by drilling the rock and inserting expansion bolts. The bolts are still there today, and have provided a providential escape route for climbers trapped on the West Face in bad weather.

Hermann Schriddel and Heinz Ramisch lacked both the experience and the ability to take advantage of this escape route when they joined forces with more enthusiasm than good sense to attempt the West Face in 1966. It was hardly the sort of climb on which to discover the limits of a new climbing partner, and they compounded their folly by failing to realise that the upper part of the mountain was sheathed in ice, something that was obvious even from Chamonix.

Hermann Schriddel, thirty-two, was a motor mechanic from Hanover. He was fit and experienced, though the West Face was by far the most serious climb he had ever contemplated. Heinz Ramisch was a twenty-three-year-old student from Karlsruhe who had recently completed the South Face of the Aiguille du Midi, the peak overlooking Chamonix up which the famous Mont Blanc cable car runs. The fact that this climb had taken him about eleven hours when it is often done in three should have acted as a deterrent to him, for in 1966 the West Face of the Dru was a very serious undertaking.

They bivouacked, as others before them, under the rock at the Rognon de Dru, had an early start and crossed the bergschrund in the couloir at 1.00 am. Their progress was slow and they must have had some trouble in climbing the slabs and terraces which form the initial part of the climb. Here the rock is loose and great care must be exercised.

Fortunately the weather was fine. Conditions, at least low on the face, were good, but when they decided to bivvy for the night they had only reached 10,700 feet (3,260 metres). Next day the weather still held but they were now involved with a different league of difficulty. Hermann had a thirty-foot fall, but didn't injure himself. The weather was beginning to break, with a build-up of cloud to the south. Once again they decided to bivouac, for the day was well advanced. They had only ascended 350 feet and were now at the bottom of the 295-foot dièdre, one of the great features of the climb. It started to snow.

It was a cold night and their bivouac gear left much to be desired, a duvet jacket each, a simple two-man bivvy bag and waterproof anoraks. The next day the gods smiled on them but perhaps it was a somewhat ironical smile, for had the weather continued bad they would probably have decided to retreat and they could have done so without too much difficulty, but with blue skies they decided to press on. From where they were they couldn't see the top of the face, which was plastered in ice.

Hermann had his second fall when a piton came out, but Heinz held him, burning and cutting his hands in the process. It took them all day to get to the top of the dièdre. They were both shattered and one wishes they had considered the escape route across the face on the expansion bolts to the North Face. The first bolt was only a few feet above them. However, they decided to bivvy on a minute ledge, which they knew from their route description was out of sight round a bulge. To get to this they had to do a tension traverse across a blank and vertical wall. A fixed rope hangs here and once down and across the slab, there is no way back except by climbing the rope, which is very strenuous and extremely exposed. Once over, they had really crossed their Rubicon.

With the closing of the day – 16 August – the cloud clamped in and their third bivouac on the wall was not a pleasant one, for their duvet jackets were now soaked, and they couldn't lie down on the ledge as it was minute.

In a dawn of hanging cloud, they made a right traverse on very exposed rock which took them to the base of a 100-foot crack, wide and very difficult. From this pitch there is a sheer fall for over 2,000 feet to the couloir and it is very intimidating. Hermann encountered ice at the top of this section.

At last the penny dropped and the two Germans realised that they were in serious trouble. Once up the next pitch, a crack which snakes up through the overhangs, they had verified what they already knew. The climb above was impossible for them. Fighting one's way up ice-plastered vertical rock requires skill of a high order. That skill they didn't have. With their tails metaphorically between their legs they retreated to the tiny ledge on the wrong side of the tension traverse. They were exhausted.

Their friends back in Chamonix, who had been monitoring their progress through gaps in the cloud, were a little concerned when Hermann and Heinz retreated from the overhangs and came to a prolonged halt on that tiny platform, and as soon as they got a prearranged signal from the climbers that they needed help they informed the rescue service. Hermann and Heinz settled into their eyrie, little knowing that they were going to be there for seven days. To make matters worse Heinz had developed a sore throat and couldn't swallow, while Hermann was in pain with bruised ribs, a legacy of his falls.

With threatening weather, it was decided that a helicopter reconnaissance should be made, for it was assumed that one of them at least must be injured as they hadn't moved. Though the chopper managed to hover quite close to the pair it was impossible for the crew to ascertain if the climbers were hurt.

Next day, Thursday 18 August, Colonel André Gonnet, Commanding Officer of the Ecole Militaire de Haute Montagne (EMHM), deployed a team of forty alpine troops and guides who reached the Charpoua hut by midday. He had decided to implement the rescue from above using wire rope to get to the two Germans, a distance of 1,000 feet from the top position, 500 feet down the North Face and 500 feet down the West Face, a formidable undertaking. There were others who did not agree with this strategy and they, too, would soon be swinging into action independently. In the meantime, the troops kept advancing up the South Face route, the *voie normale*, to reach their objective, the Quartz Ledge, which is a couple of rope lengths short of the summit. Here there is a hole through the peak running north and south. Others had stopped en route at prearranged spots, so that a human link could be maintained up this route to expedite the movement of equipment, but there was a great deal of snow above 11,000 feet and this hampered their progress. A further hazard to the alpine troops was electrical discharges, and several of them suffered burns.

It is normal for the media to swing into action in the wake of a big rescue operation. This case was no exception, and as the West Face of the Dru was one of the most formidable climbs in the Alps, the rescue was obviously going to provide good copy for several days. *Paris Match*, never regarded as sluggish when there is a tragedy in the offing, gave a wide spread to a photograph of the rescue helicopter hovering close to the two Germans huddled on the tiny ledge on that unique expanse of verticality.

Two climbers, one American and one French, were independently worried about the plight of Hermann and Heinz and both decided to do something about it. René Desmaison is a French guide with a long history of first ascents, who accurately describes himself as a maverick. Certainly his next adventure, rescuing Hermann and Heinz, was going to add to the controversy connected with him and lead to him being banned from the Company of Chamonix Guides.

On that Thursday afternoon, Gary Hemming was sipping coffee in a Courmayeur café, just across the Italian border from Chamonix, when he picked up a copy of *Dauphiné Libéré* and read an account of the plight of the two Germans. He knew the West Face well. In fact, with fellow American Royal Robbins, he had made the first ascent of the American Direct, a line right up the face from the Dru Glacier which avoids going into the deadly couloir. It was an impressive climb. Gary turned to his German companion, Lothar Mauch, and asked if he wanted to come with him to try to rescue Hermann and Heinz by climbing the West Face from the bottom. Lothar was more than willing, so without even finishing their coffee, they set off for Chamonix.

I think perhaps I should say a few words about Gary, who was a bit of a cult figure at the time. Gareth Hemming was born in Pasadena, California in 1933 and, after finding life at San Diego State College boring, he hot-footed it to France, where he began studying philosophy, that subject which can camouflage other motives and interests so effectively.

Like many American climbers of that generation, he lived on a shoestring budget, a mere five dollars a week which his mother sent him, and acquired comprehensive bivouac training, as he slept under the Seine bridges for several winters and generally bummed around. His summer retreat was usually Chamonix where he was easily recognised by his thick long blond hair and six-foot six-inch height. In fact there is an account of a journalist asking him how tall he was and Gary telling him that way back he was only six foot four inches, but during internment by the Japanese in the Pacific war he was stretched as a punishment. After the reporter had dutifully taken note Gary said to him, "No, I'm kidding, I was actually this height at birth".

He had remarkable looks and a serene expression, yet beneath it I don't think he had found the elusive Nirvana he was looking for. I met him several times and one couldn't help being impressed by the man, both as an individual and as a climber. With his thick red pullover and the coloured patches on his trousers he reminded me of an impecunious knight errant.

In Chamonix, Gary called to see Colonel Gonnet and volunteered his services. He had met the colonel before, but in somewhat strained circumstances. Gary had been nominated to attend a special training course for talented climbers at the prestigious Ecole Nationale, but the long-haired American was refused admission unless he got a haircut and removed his beard; Gary did neither, so he didn't get on the course. However, the colonel wasn't one to bear grudges. He supplied the tall American with a walkie-talkie and other equipment and wished him "bonne chance".

After enquiring at a climbing shop as to which top-ranking alpinists were in town, Gary tracked them down and enlisted their help. There was a German called Gehrad, two leading French climbers, François Guillot and Gilles Bodin, and lastly, a friend of mine, Mick Burke. Mick had been on the West Face before, but was forced back from the ninety-metre dièdre, one of the crux pitches, in nasty weather and with an injured companion. They had abseiled right down Gary's route, the American Direct, a feat which Hermann and Heinz could have done had they been prudent enough. Mick was always willing to help a climber in need and I was later to respect him for this on an attempt to find a colleague who had been buried under séracs in the Everest Icefall.

While the military operation was being consolidated on the Quartz Ledge, high above in atrocious conditions, Gary's party set off up the couloir at 10.00 am on 19 August. It was about 2.00 pm when they traversed left over a section known as the grey slabs. The weather was deteriorating and they prepared to bivouac on rock ledges there. Over a thousand feet above, Hermann and Heinz resigned themselves to another freezing night. Yet despite their prolonged incarceration, on their prison with one wall, they never lost hope and knew that they would be rescued.

Meanwhile, René Desmaison had also taken things into his own hands and landed by helicopter with his friend Vincent Mercie on the Dru Glacier. He had earlier volunteered his services to the Guides Bureau but had been told that the bureau hadn't been consulted or asked to help, so they rather huffily hadn't called out any of the guides.

Though conditions were desperate on the summit, it wasn't exactly a picnic for those at the bottom of the face either. Cloud had a tenacious grip on the Dru and it was raining at the bottom of the couloir. Stones and rocks came whistling past, intent on destruction. Undeterred by these missiles, René and Vincent climbed quickly, using a 160-foot-long climbing rope. Higher up, the couloir narrows in a bottleneck and stone fall was so concentrated here that they realised they would never get through unscathed, so reluctantly decided to bivvy for the night. Rain turned to snow then back to rain again and a soggy mist made the gully an eerie place, but the ledge which they had found was reasonably missile-free even though it lacked creature comforts. At least they felt that in the cold of dawn the narrows of the gully would be safer with the rock debris above frozen in place, until the temperature rose.

That day, Gary's party had seen the chopper coming in and later spied the two figures making their way up the couloir. Everybody on the mountain had had a miserable night, possibly those lower down suffering the worst.

On 20 August the weather hadn't improved. Visibility wasn't even the length of the climbing ropes. René and Vincent ran the gauntlet of the couloir narrows and they could see Gary's party, only a hundred feet above them on the ledges where they had lodged for the night. To speed their progress over verglased rock, Gehrad, one of the Germans, dropped René a rope. With the addition of the two Frenchmen, the rescue party was now up to eight. It was 9.00 am, and Gary had perhaps optimistically said that they could reach the two trapped Germans in a day. That might have been possible on dry rock, but conditions were abysmal and not going to improve. René thought they were moving too slowly so they agreed to have the fastest climbers out front: Gary and François Guillot, followed by René and Vincent. The others were to follow, carrying the bulk of the equipment, and caching some of it on the ledges.

So while René and Vincent got a brew going, Gary and François set off. But Gary went off route. Though he had done the much harder American Direct to the left, he hadn't in fact done the lower part of the West Face route and a couple of pitches up René and Vincent caught them up. Gary's error was soon corrected and he carried on, leading towards the Fissure Vignes, one of the hard sections of the climb.

About this time, 12.00 noon, down in Chamonix another decision was taken. The Ecole Nationale and the Guides Bureau agreed to send a group of top guides and instructors up the North Face of the Dru to try to reach Hermann and Heinz from that side. Now the Germans were being approached by every possible way. The media were having a banquet of drama and they made the most of it with national television coverage and international press saturation. As always in such situations, there are individuals willing to crawl out of the woodwork to pass supercilious judgment, and René fell victim to a great deal of this by his act in pre-empting what in fact his organisation, the Guides Bureau, did later.

The North Face party had one of the most dangerous approaches, for they were in direct line of fire from above, where ledges were being excavated in the snow and belays installed. All debris from these operations came right down their route.

The group climbing the West Face weren't now subjected to objective danger – the huge overhangs above ensured that, but it was still unpleasant and difficult climbing, with icy water running down their sleeves. Even so Gary was laid back and expounded his philosophy of life to an exasperated François.

Higher up on a pitch called the Forty Metre Wall, René had a twenty-foot fall when a peg came out, but he was unhurt. The rock on this section is so steep that he fell clear, but it must have been disturbing to peel with such a dramatic backdrop and only air below, for 1,800 feet.

It was dusk by the time Gary had ascended the Jammed Block pitch. This derives its name from a huge chockstone jammed into a very steep chimney. The boulder effectively blocks the chimney and has to be climbed by a thirty-foot overhang. Needless to say the scalp of this huge rock holds snow, as the sun doesn't reach it. But as temperature rises during the day some does melt and with a night frost, ice forms, sometimes in quantity. That evening it was meltwater which was cascading down, directly on top of the climbers so that they were soaked to the skin. They settled down for the next bivouac there – another uncomfortable night. It was 11.00 pm. They shouted up to the two Germans, who they knew were now quite close, but there was no reply.

That day the weather had been so severe on the summit that virtually nothing was done. The helicopter which was scheduled to transport the winch to the Quartz Ledge party couldn't fly.

The Hemming/Desmaison party still had 300 feet to go to reach the Germans, but this involved some very hard climbing. Above was the ninety-metre dièdre. It was now 21 August and Gary started up at 6.00 am with François. The cloud had cleared and they hoped their luck was going to change. Alas, this wasn't to be. René and Vincent delayed their departure from the Jammed Block to organise equipment ready to assist the Germans back across the pendulum pitch. Meantime, down below, Mick Burke and the others were busy hauling up ropes and equipment for the abseil down the face.

By the time René and Vincent had climbed the dièdre, Gary was moving across the pendulum pitch. He was now very close to Hermann and Heinz. He shouted to them, "I'm coming." They replied but their call was unintelligible. In a few minutes Gary had reached their ledge, followed quickly by François. It was midday.

Hermann offered Gary a nut. For six days they had been on a starvation ration. Gary dryly mentioned to Desmaison when he arrived that had the Germans been French they would have gobbled all their nuts on the first day.

One is tempted to compare this rescue to spiders converging on a pair of flies. Just at this moment the two separate ropes from the North Face gained a ledge not more than a hundred feet away and slightly higher. Yves Pollet-Villard was in charge of this group and he had direct radio contact with Chamonix. Now developed a discourse on how to dispose of the prey. Yves, as representing the establishment and the official rescue party, was all for taking the two uninjured Germans down the North Face. René pointed out that this route was too strenuous for the weak and shattered climbers, and Gary, who had been the first to reach the Germans, was given the casting vote. He advocated abseiling down the West Face. In the meantime, high above, Wolfgang Egle, a young German friend of Hermann and Heinz, somehow got snarled up in his rope while abseiling and was strangled.

The Germans were given dry warm clothing and after they had been fitted with safety harnesses the long descent began. Gary and François set off and did two 130-foot abseils down to the Jammed Block. Vincent then abseiled one rope length and waited at a stance. René sent down Hermann, abseiling with a safety rope on. It was an incredibly exposed situation, but he managed it. Vincent untied him once he had reached his minute ledge and prepared him for the next stage down to the base of the dièdre. Meanwhile René was busy sending Heinz down.

Below they met up with the rest of Gary's party and all decided to bivouac as it was 4.00 pm. There were now ten of them occupying the bivvy ledge. For a cushion they had snow, which melted underneath them. They were all saturated and shivering. But they were soon to forget that particular misery as an electrical storm of unusual violence lit the Aiguille in a blaze of light, racking them all with violent body-arching shocks. They were desperate to escape from this charged and sulphurous hell, but there was nowhere to go. They were effectively chained to the rock by their karabiners. To unclip would have been instant suicide. The fact that there were bunches of metal pitons about didn't help matters. Gilles Bodin, who was sitting on a pile of these pegs, as a "damp course" in his personal pool of water, had a series of shocks through sensitive regions. René

Desmaison was the worst affected: his face was swollen, and he had trouble breathing. Hermann and Heinz, who were beneath an overhang, had a reasonable night. It is interesting to note how these two young men withstood the strain of their prolonged stay on the face. The fact that they had always been confident that they would be rescued must have played a part in their ultimate survival. There is nothing worse than giving up hope of rescue. It seems that if you give up hope, hope gives up you. Another danger for the rescued is the tendency to relinquish the struggle once the rescuers arrive, when in many cases the casualty still has to display determination to win through and get off the mountain.

At 5.00 am they were up to a fresh snow cover and at 6.00 am they were off. Over the walkie-talkie they heard that the weather was to improve. Mick and Gary started abseiling first. It was their intention to establish a continuous line of rope for almost a thousand feet. While the Germans were being safeguarded on their abseils, the ropes above were retrieved and passed down to Mick and Gary. Hermann and Heinz now made up for their slow ascent for they were expedited down that intimidating face at high speed to a heroes' welcome.

Gary was the man of the hour and the press latched on to him as if he were the principal character in the crucifixion. The two Germans were taken to hospital, but there was little wrong with them. Their friend, Wolfgang Egle, still hung from his rope at the top of the mountain and would be taken down to rest as soon as the weather improved.

The inevitable rescue post mortem got under way in the press. It had been one of the biggest operations of its kind, with many alpine troops, guides and climbers risking their lives to help. In fact Hermann and Heinz could possibly have been reached and evacuated by any of the routes employed and the way they had been taken down had proved entirely viable.

Gary continued his nomadic life in the high Alps, but now he was recognised everywhere he went. In 1966 he earned some money clearing the roofs of tall buildings in Chamonix after winter snow, and when spring came round he set off for Alaska, still outwardly his normal carefree self, taking the handout of life as it came. He returned to the United States and on 6 August 1969, just over three years after the Dru rescue, he was found shot dead in the Grand Teton National Park in Wyoming. It was accepted that he had committed suicide. Why he returned to the stately Tetons to die no one will ever know.

Mick Burke and I went on two later expeditions to Everest's South-West Face. On the second of these, in 1975, Mick disappeared when close to the summit. It is very possible he had reached it first.

Shibboleth

Andrew Fraser

I suppose if you take any given area of the earth's crust, it will have its tale to tell. What secret does a square yard of battlefield hold or the floor of a prison cell? To mountaineers and rescuers certain climbs and peaks present obvious hazards and can be poignant with memories. The Eiger North Face, for example, is notorious for stone fall and storms, the Everest Icefall for tottering séracs and abysmal crevasses, and Mount Washington for high winds. Each rescue team has its local accident black spots into which team members would never dream of venturing in bad conditions of their own accord. A call-out removes the option.

Buachaille Etive Mor in Glencoe is a peak which seems to stand as self-appointed guardian over the Moor of Rannoch. By international standards it is not a big mountain; but like many smaller peaks it reaps its macabre harvest as assiduously as its big brothers: probably more climbers have been killed on this conical lump of porphyry than on the Eiger itself.

Great Gully of the Buachaille is a steep-sided wound which appears to have been gouged out by an almighty bulldozer and left unhealed for those wishing to inspect the innards of the mountain. In summer it spews forth rocks at irregular intervals and in the winter, avalanches. From its sombre depths we rescue unfortunate climbers every year. In summer the gully does not present a rock climb as such, though it possibly has a soggy attraction for athletic botanists. (Winter is another matter entirely.) But in summer the walls on either side of the gully present sport of a vertical and intimidating nature, especially the great sweep of rock on the left, known for obvious reasons as Slime Wall. To its right, with the symmetrical uniformity of a dank tenement close but superbly executed, is the slit of Raven's Gully. To the right again, separated by a buttress, is Great Gully. Raven's Gully and Slime Wall both present a challenge to mountaineers. The uncompromising steepness of Slime Wall provides a playground for those to whom movement on rock is an art form. In winter Raven's Gully presents high-angled overhanging sport to climbers who dare enter between its claustrophobic walls.

In winter too Great Gully is the climbing M1 of the Buachaille and appears to induce motorway madness in climbers attracted to it when it is obviously poised with unconsolidated snow and hopelessly out of condition.

This tale takes place in 1958, before the formation of the Glencoe Mountain Rescue Team, the venue Slime Wall, the route Shibboleth. The climbers were Andrew Fraser (now a retired microbiologist) and Robin Smith. I knew Robin well. He was possibly the most promising climber of his generation, a man of apparently unlimited strength, with an analytical mind. In a few years he had created a new dimension in mountaineering, raising the standard in both winter and summer. Sadly, he was to fall to his death four years later on a descent in the Pamirs with Wilfrid Noyce. One slipped (an eye-witness is not sure which one) and pulled the other off. Though the first person to fall managed to stop he couldn't then hold his companion on the rope and so both plunged to their deaths. I remember Robin awakening on my floor in Glencoe where he used to doss from time to time, covered in feathers which had moulted overnight from his ancient sleeping bag. The down clung to his hairy cardigan, a legacy from his grandmother, and there it remained until the west-coast winds plucked it off and he again took on a human aspect rather than a cross between an eider duck chick and an orang-outang. As Andrew Fraser, author of the following account recalls, Robin is the hero of Slime Wall.

My account of the climb is taken from the *Edinburgh University Mountaineering Club Journal* of 1959. It is a period piece, written with student enthusiasm, but it may recapture something of the flavour of climbing with Robin Smith in those days when he was establishing himself as one of the finest climbers of the time.

A few paragraphs will help to set the scene. Robin was a student at the University of Edinburgh, but his philosophy course left him plenty of time for climbing, the dominant obsession of his life. During these years the EUMC gave him a good supply of enthusiastic seconds; I had an easy term, a tent and the occasional use of a vehicle and was quickly drawn into the summer's schemes. The forthcoming new edition of the Scottish Mountaineering Club *Glencoe Rock-Climbing Guide* was a great incentive to polish off the best remaining lines on the Buachaille before the editor's deadline, and most weekends found us in the cluster of scruffy little tents at Gunpowder Green at the base of the mountain. The rival camp usually arrived in Graham Tiso's old Ford Popular – Big Ellie, Dougal Haston, Ronnie Marshall and the legendary Old Man Marshall himself, one of Scotland's great climbers.

Jimmy Marshall dominated our activities, subtly stirring up the competitive spirit amongst the young tigers, pitting Robin against the Currie Boys (where Dougal Haston came from), and hard men against soft students; Edinburgh youth against Creagh Dhu classics. Rivalry bred gamesmanship. Plans were kept secret. Robin would mutter vaguely about strolling up to have a look at one of the golden oldie routes, if he felt up to it; Dougal and Ellie would talk of maybe getting into training on a V. Diff or two; Jimmy would apparently prepare to sleep quietly in the sun at the camp site. But each nursed his own schemes. Despite a leisurely start, the casual walk up the hill would turn into a race for the cliffs, with Big Ellie's ribald roars chasing us up Great Gully, and always the possibility that Jimmy Marshall would materialise by magic at the foot of the great new line before we reached it, even though we had left him still in his sleeping bag at the camp. Insults and taunts flew between the cliffs. Standards rose. The Buachaille was cleaned up, and the focus could move further down Glencoe for next season.

Robin's writing was as influential as his climbing, and his articles for the *Edinburgh University Mountaineering Club Journal* have become classics. His own tale of Shibboleth would have been very different. When I wrote this account of our climb we spent many hours in the little café in Forrest Road, Edinburgh, where so many of our plans were concocted, going over the details with my crutches propped against the wall.

This is the story of Shibboleth – the true story behind the sensational headlines in the *Daily Record* of Monday 16 June 1958. "SEVEN INCHES FROM DEATH" shouted the inch-high block letters; "Hurt Youth Saved on Mountain" ran the subheading . . .

But, to begin at the beginning. The principal characters in the tale are a certain Robin Smith and a cliff on the Buachaille Etive Mor, promisingly known as Slime Wall. Early in the summer Robin set his mind on forcing a Great New Route straight up the virgin verticality of this fearsome face, but up till June the weather kept him grounded. He passed his time thinking up a worthy name for his adversary, eventually, for reasons known only to himself and certain of the Gileadites, to fix on Shibboleth. He pondered long on the choice and was often to be seen in some small café of the town with a visionary gleam in his eye, muttering the word to himself, weighing it up, savouring its quality, testing its quantities, passing slowly from initial soft sibilant syllable to linger long on limpid labial and liquid "l", endowing the word in a rapture of phonetic sensuality with almost oracular portent.

When at last summer arrived and the slime had drawn sulkily back into streaky patches, Robin decided to renew the attack. He lacked only a sufficiently docile second to hold the other end of his rope, so, with glowing tales of a Great Natural Line, he lured me off to Glencoe. When he had tied me securely to the first belay and I had time to study the projected route, all I could make out of his Great Natural Line was a series of highly unnatural cracks and corners extending tenuously up the 500 feet of sheer rock above me, linked, or rather separated, by sections of steep smooth slab. This is one of those spots which drive home the meaning of "vertical, if not overhanging" – a phrase much used on the ascent.

This is not the place for a detailed technical description, but a vague sketch may prove of use. The climb is 550 feet long and consists of six pitches, each of which is of very severe grading [then the highest standard]. The first pitch is shared with a climb called Guerdon Grooves and merely serves as mild preparatory exercise. Pitch 2 is the hardest and never falls below VS over all its 90 feet, while pitches 3 and 4 are nearly as hard. The last two pitches are more straightforward again and are even separated by a platform big enough to stand on without using the hands, though the exposure discourages this somewhat. At the hard bits a harsh croak emanates from Raven's Gully, while at the desperate bits I had the distinct impression of vultures hovering behind me, though this may have been merely imagination.

We spent two weekends on the climb. The first day we climbed the lower three pitches. Robin spent a considerable time clinging to the face below the crux, trying vainly to stem the oozing slime with a towel borrowed from an unwitting friend some months before. He abandoned this eventually in favour of simple levitation, and we made fine progress till he was turned back by approaching dusk and the severity of the resistance on pitch 4. We escaped from the face by following the magnificent flake of Revelation, the climb that runs up beside this pitch, but further to the left.

Next day we returned by the start of Revelation to our turning point of the day before. Robin contemplated the fourth pitch anew. The sun was shining all around, accentuating the perpetual damp depressing gloom of Slime Wall. Shibboleth was exerting all her subtle insidious powers of dissuasion. No doubt malnutrition and camp life had left their mark on us too. Anyway, the more we contemplated the situation, the more obvious it became that the ideal way led up the flake pitch of Revelation to the left. From its top one could resume the original line with ease. Robin swore it would be more aesthetic to include such a unique pitch in such a fine climb, while I argued that it was in fact the more direct line. And so, up the flake we swarmed, revelling in its beauty and exposure, leaning out carefree on huge undercut holds over a sheer drop into Great Gully some 300 feet below. At the end of the day we emerged on to the hillside above, with the rest of our climb safely behind us.

It was then that a chill breeze of doubt first struck us, and faint echoes of mocking laughter wafted up out of Raven's Gully. Shibboleth obviously considered that by the inviolate middle pitch she retained her virtue. We could feel her exulting in her subtle triumph. Reluctantly, we climbed down by a fearful loose chimney on Cuneiform Buttress opposite to review the situation. There was no doubt about the direct line.

And so we returned next weekend, vowing to prove for once and for all who was master. An alpine start from base camp saw us at the foot of the climb by midday. The second pitch provided some entertainment when it came to my turn to follow Robin's graceful lead. At the crux he had fixed a piton. This was the only one used in the whole climb apart from belays and was essential for security, the nearest runner being thirty feet below and the next hold being fifteen feet above, up a smooth over-hanging corner. Since the piton filled the vital handhold before the crux, I at least was very glad to use it quite unscrupulously. But being second, I had to remove it as I passed. The only position in which I could hold on with one hand and hammer with the other was so low as to be prohibitively exhausting. So I had to pull up to the piton and lean fully out from it with my left hand and hammer with my right while Robin took my weight on the rope from above. There was only a trace of a hold for my left foot while my right just pushed flat against the gently over-hanging wall stretching massively on my right down to the last belay.

I hammered till I was exhausted; the peg wiggled freely, but was firmly pinched about its middle. At last I got permission from Robin to leave it behind. Just before con-tinuing up I gave it a couple of desultory blows as a final gesture – and found myself floating gracefully away out from the climb and in again to the impossible wall on my right, clutching the recalcitrant peg in my hand. Great gusts of drain-like laughter echoed down to me. All I could do was push off gently again and hope to arrive back where I had come from. Somehow I managed to wedge a fingertip in the empty piton crack and hold myself into the cliff, but once there the situation called for urgent action.

I was exhausted. I could not rest from the piton now. I could not climb on, deprived of the piton. I could not face the thought of being lowered right down and starting again – without the piton. The only solution was an inelegant but quick and effective technique specially devised for following Robin on such occasions. It involves liberal use of rope handholds, a jerky and positive "tight-rope" policy and unscrupulous use of such minimal rugosities as may appear on the actual rock. Any lack of co-ordination tends to leave the second upside down dangling helplessly at the end of the rope, but happily we had perfected the trick on other occasions and all went well.

It is, however, a fairly energetic procedure. When I reached the belay I was utterly shattered and had to cling weakly to the rock for several minutes before I could find sufficient strength to weave myself into the network of loops that constituted the belay, and could let myself relax and recover.

After this all went well for a while. The virgin fourth pitch was assaulted and duly succumbed to Robin's persuasive tactics. It proved a very worthy pitch and we emerged from it with triumphant feelings – Shibboleth had at last fallen, nothing could take that away from us now. There only remained two pitches. We had agreed beforehand that I should lead the next pitch as a reward for my patience over the many hours we had spent on the climb.

It was the easiest pitch we should encounter, or rather, the least difficult, and I had followed up it quite competently the week before. Robin was belayed to a piton in a reasonable stance, and as I set off he was chortling Shibboleth in a happy way to himself and working out suitably laconic descriptions for the guide book. But Shibboleth is a lady of strong character and she could not take this defeat lightly. She had to be avenged for her fall, and nothing short of human sacrifice could satisfy her outraged pride!

I climbed fifteen feet up and to the right, to the foot of a shallow overhanging corner. This was fifteen feet high and the crux of the pitch, followed by easier rock to the large platform and a fine stance. I remembered that Robin's runner had fallen off as he climbed this corner so I cast around for a better one. Classic rock spikes are not one of Slime Wall's notable features, but at last I managed to chip out a crack with the hammer so that a single strand of baby nylon would just lie in it. Hoping it was adequate, I clipped one of the ropes into the karabiner and attacked the corner. It was typical of Slime Wall. The main face sloped gently outwards over me, while the shallow right-hand wall remained obligingly vertical. There were a few sideways holds in the crack inside the right-angled corner, and one or two little ledges on the walls but nothing much bigger than fingertip holds.

I was nearly at the top when I realised that my hands were

feeling the strain of seven and a half hours' struggling on this cold, damp, steep, sunless wall. My fingers began to feel soft and weak, and showed an alarming tendency to straighten out when I put my full weight on them. But I just had to put my full weight on them, for I was in a sort of layback position, my feet pressing in rather than down, since there wasn't enough to press down on, and my body leaning down and out on my arms, since the slope of the wall pushed it that way. My right hand had its fingers curled backhand against a vertical groove on the side wall, while my left hand was pulling sideways against the corner crack and taking most of my weight.

The next move was obvious. There was no choice. I had to lean fully out on my right hand and throw my left hand up on to a ledge above me. This ledge was quite large and flat; it sloped outwards, had a rounded edge and no trace of a grip for the fingers on the inside. I could not lean out on this hold, I could only push down on it as I overtook it. Thus my right hand would have to take my full weight as I moved my foot up to a small ledge at knee level, and gently straightened my leg – leaning right out on my hand. Then my left hand could get a push hold on the ledge while I threw my right up on to large holds and could climb out of the corner to safety.

The more I thought about it, the less likely it seemed that my fingers could hold out. Yet the longer I waited the more tired they became. I couldn't possibly rest them in this position and it was even more strenuous to retreat. To have shouted to Robin would have meant psychological defeat – my fingers would have loosened at once. I knew he was watching me in any case – he had even stopped singing his usual appalling skiffle. I just had to try that move.

I summoned up my last reserves of energy and leaned right out. I put my hand up on the ledge and moved my foot up. But I felt my hand weakening as I tried to straighten my leg and swing up gently, and then my fingers turned to putty. I seemed to be watching impersonally as I saw them straighten out and leave the rock. I started to fall. Classically my whole life should have flashed before me but my mind remained a rather peaceful blank; it was almost a feeling of relief – I had done my best and it was out of my hands now.

The next thing I knew was a hefty jerk at my waist which

doubled me up, and I found myself dangling at the end of the rope some thirty feet down, at a level with Robin but over to the right. I contemplated cursing roundly but decided it was a little melodramatic. The runner which I had spent so long making had stayed put. The rope had not broken. Robin had held me. His piton hadn't come out. Everything seemed to have gone off classically until I became aware of a burning heat in my right leg. A quick glance down led to an instant diagnosis of broken; my foot was swinging about quite regardless of what I did with my leg. It must have hit the ledge where the runner was, for it was so steep elsewhere that I had fallen quite free of the rock and wasn't even bruised or scratched otherwise.

But the fates had kindly provided a nice ledge a couple of feet below. Robin lowered me to it. It was about a foot wide and eighteen inches long, and was quite unique on the face – there was nothing comparable in sight. I managed to sit sideways on it dangling my leg over the edge. Robin passed over his end of the rope and I tied it to my waistline so that I was really suspended on to the ledge from the runner and couldn't fall off if I fainted. I had the rock behind me and to my right and the two ends of the rope like braces in front of me. I was as comfortable as I could hope to be, though a little cramped, and all I had to do was to prevent my foot swinging about.

We shouted for help, but our cries were swallowed up in the echoes of Great Gully. So Robin tied the end of his rope to the piton and traversed off more or less unprotected over some sixty feet of far from easy rock at a considerable exposure. From my ledge one could have spat, if one were that kind of person, straight to the bottom of Great Gully, 300 feet below.

I looked at my watch – 7.30. Then I set about examining my leg. Both bones were obviously broken clean through about halfway up the shin; I could feel the ends grinding together on the slightest provocation. As long as I kept perfectly still it only felt hot, but any movement was distinctly painful. All the rules told me I should develop shock, but my pulse obstinately refused to rise over the 100 level. Then I wondered how I was going to be got off; there was 300 feet sheer below me and 200 feet above. As I couldn't solve that one I tried not to think of the immediate future. How long did a leg take to heal? Six weeks, I seemed to remember. I hate to think what I should have felt if I had known it would take six months! Then my foot began to feel numb and cold, so I loosened the lace of my boot very gently.

It seemed quite soon, though it was actually two hours later, when I heard Robin's voice from the edge of the cliff again. The rescue party was on its way. He climbed over to me and kept me cheerful till the experts arrived to mastermind the operation from the far side of Great Gully. Apparently people had never fallen off in such an interesting place before, or at least they hadn't survived to be rescued. Splints were lowered and we fixed them fairly efficiently. The stretcher was manhandled up Great Gully beneath us with much gentle cursing. The air was ringing with Glasgow and Edinburgh voices and the hillside seemed to be alive with climbers.

Ropes were lowered to us from above, knotted to reach down the 200 feet. I tied myself into a cradle arrangement, leaving my legs dangling. Then Robin tied another rope on to me – I don't think he trusted my knots – and tied himself on to a third. I tied my feet together to give me some control of my right foot. Two more ropes were brought over from the side of the cliff, where there was a largish platform on North Buttress, and we tied on to them too. Then we let the top ropes take our weight, while we were pulled over and up to the platform. Robin was half-pulled and half-climbed across the face, protecting me and controlling the ropes, while I rested on his arms and fended off with my hands. It was quite a feat getting five long stretchy ropes to work in perfect co-ordination.

Five hours after my fall I was off the cliff and safely on the platform. I could lie down at last and stretch myself again. A unique hot drink consisting mainly of chocolate had been brewed on the hillside, thanks to Graham Tiso who worked for Cadbury's. Then I was carefully inserted into a Thomas splint, wrapped in a sleeping bag and blankets and strapped securely into the stretcher. Familiar and unfamiliar faces floated into my sight and away again – I didn't gather who half the people were, but they seemed to be from a good mixture of Scottish climbing clubs.

Now the real work started. Happily I had chosen a fine clear midsummer's night, but even so the North Buttress is no place to take a stretcher down at midnight. So the route lay upwards.

The technique was magnificent: five ropes were tied to the head of the stretcher and teams of seemingly inexhaustible climbers simply pulled me up the buttress. A Glasgow man was in the straps at the foot of the stretcher and he was pulled up too. He just had to walk up the face steadying the stretcher in a sort of inverted abseil. On the less steep bits indefatigable relays of climbers manhandled me up the hillside, half sliding me on the ski runners. It was a strange sensation to be relaxed and comfortable, vertically ascending the Buachaille at midnight, with the whole of the Moor of Rannoch, the Kingshouse, the camp site and the Etive laid out flat at my feet in the mid-summer dusk.

I was hauled up the hill for some time, then over long scree traverses under grey cliffs, the rescuers slithering and scrabbling round the mountain until we could make our way down Lagangarbh Gully and over the moor to the road. I didn't quite keep track of the whole journey, nor could I contribute much to the general flow of conversation of the party; the stretcher was so comfortable and so smoothly carried that I felt more inclined to go to sleep.

The rescue party was magnificent. A better, more experienced group of climbers it would be hard to assemble in Scotland; most of the best-known characters in active Scottish climbing were there. They had been dragged from their tents or the Kingshouse back on to the hill for an exhausting all-night expedition, many without their suppers, but the tone of the party was amazing. I would never have imagined that a rescue could be so cheerful; everyone seemed to regard it as the most entertaining expedition of the season. There was a lot of good-natured inter-city banter and abuse; I gathered that one Glasgow fellow seemed to think that Edinburgh had been trespassing on *his* wall, and that my fall was the just and awful retribution of the gods. Another had the distinct impression that this was a god-sent exclusive scoop for his newspaper and promised me headlines next day. We all joined in with suggestions that would really impress the great British public, but I have to confess the actual result was even more sensational.

We reached the roadside as dawn was breaking and everyone lay around exhausted, wondering whether to eat or to sleep first. Eventually they divided the day fairly evenly between the two;

happily the weather wasn't of the sort to tempt them on to the hill again. A Bedford van took me to Fort William. When we met the ambulance after a mile or two the owner of the van just persuaded it to go home again empty and very kindly took me all the way. And so, just twelve hours after I had fallen in the most inaccessible spot on the Buachaille, I reached the Belford Hospital and the friendly capable hands of Dr Duff and his charming staff.

Sixty Years on Beinn Achaladair

Hamish MacInnes

These stories of Beinn Achaladair span a period of sixty years, and they are linked by some curious coincidences of people and places.

The mountain seems insignificant enough, a well-rounded heap of grass, scree and rock in summer. In winter it is popular with hillwalkers, but not something to take a rope to, though its seemingly innocuous slopes are often subject to icing.

Beinn Achaladair is one of several mountains which stand to the east of Loch Tulla, the large natural water receptacle on the southern fringe of the Moor of Rannoch. The West Highland railway line skirts the bottom of the face, giving it the appearance from across the valley of some great force trying to undercut the mountain. Further up this line a group of bowler-hatted railway engineers once nearly succumbed to a blizzard when prospecting the rail route to Fort William. It goes without saying that the area should not be treated casually by walkers, bowler-hatted or otherwise; winter storms can be sudden and severe.

For the purpose of relating these case histories, we start in 1983 and go back in time.

On 12 November of that year I went to an exhibition of paintings by the artist William Cadenhead in Edinburgh. In the gallery I was approached by a tall man who announced himself as one of four climbers the Glencoe Rescue Team had rescued a few years previously from Beinn an Dothaidh, one of Beinn Achaladair's close neighbours. I remembered the incident well and was glad to see that he, for one, seemed none the worse for his encounter with the mountain or our team.

The reason for my journey to Edinburgh on that cold 12

November was twofold. In addition to artistic exposure, I was also there to visit and photograph that august Victorian structure, the Royal Bank of Scotland in Exchange Square. This strange assignment stemmed from three Amazonian expeditions in search of Inca gold, tenuous clues about which had led me from the arrow grass of the Llanganatis of Ecuador to this edifice of prosperity. Certain documents suggested that part of the Incan hoard had found its way by a devious route to the coffers of this most Royal Bank.

Having taken my photograph, visited the art gallery and bidden farewell to Bill Cadenhead and the rescuee, I drove back to Glencoe, passing a bleak cloud-covered Beinn Achaladair en route, and as I sped along the A82, between Loch Tulla and Beinn Achaladair, my thoughts took me back over the rescues on the mountain.

I had just arrived home when Willie Elliot opened the door. As the Glencoe Ranger, Willie looks after the property of the National Trust for Scotland, an area embracing most of the glen. He and his brother Walter have been rescuing people off the local mountains since they were boys, though they are not climbers in the rope and ice-axe mould.

"Aye, Hamish. There's a call-out near Beinn Achaladair. I got a call from Jimmy Bannerman. He was contacted by the Oban Police."

Jimmy Bannerman was our local policeman.

"Well, I suppose it's back across the Rannoch Moor, Willie. What's the score?"

"I've got a map reference, it seems as if a chap's fallen to the north of Achaladair on Meall Buidhe, but I don't have any more gen."

"OK, Willie, call out the boys and we'll meet at Achallader farm. Can you arrange for both the truck and the Land Rover to be taken over?"

Up until 1975, Beinn Achaladair was within the Glencoe Mountain Rescue Team's jurisdiction under the Argyll County Police, but after regionalisation, it came under the umbrella of Strathclyde, a large area administered from Glasgow. As assistance from Glencoe hadn't been requested immediately, by the time we got to Achallader farm, the Strathclyde Police Mountain Rescue Team had arrived from the Divisional Headquarters in Dumbarton, over sixty miles distant, together with police from Oban.

It was dark by now and visibility was very poor due to cloud cover above 2,000 feet. We set off, armed with the map reference. There were about ten Glencoe Team members and Willie set up base in our truck close to the farm buildings. Achallader farm had been run by the Smith family for two generations. Both father and son were involved in these stories.

A problem that dull typical November Saturday was that the telephones in the area were out of order. Consequently the survivor of the accident, a Dr Manson, had to drive sixteen miles to Crianlarich to raise the alarm. Apparently he and his companion, John Burke, were hillwalking when, close to the summit of Meall Buidhe, Burke's bootlace came undone. Dr Manson strolled slowly on, assuming his friend would catch him up. On looking back, however, the doctor saw to his horror that his companion had strayed to the edge of the north-west face and fallen over. Dr Manson tried to see where his colleague had landed but the ground was steep and festooned with rock faces. He descended, cutting round the bottom of the face with difficulty. Finding no sign of his friend, he decided the best course of action was to get help. He immediately set off for Achallader farm, where he discovered that the telephones were out of order.

This, together with the map reference, was all the information we could muster.

We did a sweep search up the open corrie leading to the map reference; the police on the left flank, the north side, and the Glencoe Team on the valley floor and to the right, the south side. The group I was with eventually joined a police party as the valley narrowed and we stopped all together for a breather. Discussing the problem with some of them, I mentioned that the name of the man who fell was John Burke, that he worked in banking and was a regular visitor to Glencoe.

"John Burke? John Burke?" A policeman was searching his memory for something. "Surely the signature John Burke is on the Royal Bank of Scotland notes?"

Those who had wallets quickly took these out and looked through our paper money. Sure enough several of us had notes with Burke's signature on them.

As we moved into the head of the corrie, visibility became worse and our headlamp beams diffused in the dense cloud. After several hours' search there was still no sign of the missing man and we had a further discussion. The police team decided to call it a day, return to base and recommence the search at first light. They planned to stay at Bridge of Orchy Hotel for the night. I told them we would pack it in after we had completed a quick once-over at the bottom of the topmost cliffs. Most of our team are climbers so this was easier for us to do as the ground was steep and treacherous. A short time later, Peter Weir reported over his radio that he had just come across a formidable landslide, no doubt a result of torrential rains which had washed the Highlands over the previous weeks.

I and a few others followed a weakness in the cliffs to the west of this, which leads up steeply in a grassy ramp interspersed with rocky outcrops. But here the cloud was so thick we could barely see ten feet. Meanwhile, the rest of the team in the corrie below were getting the itchy feet associated with a lost cause, so I too decided to call things off for the night. Searching in such conditions was really farcical.

The call-out for the next day was at first light, which during November in Scotland doesn't mean an early start. Alan Thomson, Richard Grieve and I were the first to arrive at Achallader. In the gloom we could see the lights of an RAF Wessex helicopter landing at the farm. It had flown from Glenmore Lodge in the Cairngorms where there was a weekend rescue exercise.

The winchman came over as I pulled up. He had to shout above the helicopter's still-running engines. "We've found the man. He's dead and in a difficult place. Can a couple of you come up and give us a hand?"

We found John Burke at the bottom of the face we had been on a few hours previously. He had plunged across the ramp we had climbed and smashed into the top of the landslide. Difficult enough to spot in daylight, he would have been almost impossible to see at night as he lay at the bottom of the rock face in a field of boulders. Apparently the helicopter flew directly to the map reference en route to Achallader farm and had spotted the dead man immediately. A fine bit of mountain rescue search work.

Once Alan and I were winched down on steep scree below where Burke lay, we quickly climbed up and brought him to a point where the pilot managed to lower the winch wire. The rotors were literally a few feet from the cliff, but thank goodness it was a still day. Otherwise, as the pilot said later, he wouldn't have been in there at all.

That was the end of that particular incident, and unfortunately, the end of a remarkable man. John Burke was highly respected in financial circles throughout the country. The mountains and the freedom of the hills were to him a release from the pressures of big business. In solitude he could lose the responsibilities of his office. In so doing, he lost his life.

After his body was taken away in the ambulance, John Grieve, Richard's brother, recalled another local story about John Burke. A couple of years back he had been staying at the Onich Hotel while on a climbing holiday in the Glencoe region. At the end of his stay he asked the receptionist for his bill, and wrote a cheque for the amount. When she asked for his bank card, he had to confess that he had left it at home. She insisted that she couldn't accept a cheque without the card. John Burke then took a ten-pound note from his wallet and, handing it to the girl, asked if she would kindly compare his signature on the cheque with that on the note.

It never ceases to surprise me how coincidence, as well as fate, seems so much part and parcel of rescue work. Earlier that year, above Crianlarich, where Dr Manson went to raise the alarm for his fallen friend, two climbers had fallen and been killed. One of these, Alan Jessiman, was the Chairman of the Bank of Scotland, another eminent Scottish bank.

Now we must go back to an unlucky 13 January in 1977. Four climbers from the Grampian Club of Dundee set off to climb a gully on Beinn an Dothaidh, a close neighbour of Ben Achaladair. The northerly aspect of this peak is known locally to Gaelic-speakers as the "clenched fist" from its tight formation of gullies and buttresses.

When they failed to return I got a call from the Oban Police. It was bleak weather with soft snow above 1,500 feet and an icy south-easterly wind. There is little daylight in these high latitudes during January, and dusk had fallen when we left

Achallader farm. It was the sort of evening we would have preferred to be sitting by our respective fires.

The RAF Leuchars Mountain Rescue team had already searched in vain. Now it was our turn. We split into three groups, each taking a different area, but all three parties initially heading up the Allt Coire Achaladair to gain our respective search blocks to the south of Beinn Achaladair.

Ian McCrae, a local gamekeeper who knows every nook and cranny in these mountains, was with us. We spread out with our headlamps on as we ascended from the valley floor forming a wide sweeping, overlapping line of light. Further up, it was even colder and windier. The blast cultivated spindrift, making it appear as if we were walking on a shallow white foaming sea. After four hours we had to call it a night and return to search at first light.

At Achallader farm the following morning we found that the police had mustered reinforcements, with teams drawn from various parts of the Strathclyde Region as well as rescue dogs. The RAF Leuchars team were also back.

A helicopter which had been promised for first light got diverted en route for a serious accident in the hills above Crianlarich, but it was hoped that it would come later in the day. Some of the police top brass had arrived and I suggested they request a Naval Sea King helicopter. These are based at Prestwick where they are normally used for anti-submarine patrol work in the North Atlantic.

"We'll be needing white sticks in that crap above, how's a bloody chopper going to fly?" commented one of the lads as we struggled back up towards the cliffs of Beinn an Dothaidh.

But fly it did, in horizontal driving snow and nil visibility.

We spread out in line to sweep up the corrie, really a sloping shoulder with a depression in it, treading up left towards the summit. Ian Nicholson and Ed Grindley went off to the left to check the principal gully climb on the face and the plan was, by the time they had done this, we would hopefully have swung round to meet them on the summit. But they found the climbing too dangerous, due to the high avalanche risk.

Our hunch of this corrie the previous evening paid off. We heard a call, which sounded unreal – but it was a call for help. It came from the gully and through a window in the cloud we saw a figure emerge from the snow at the last pitch. Then another, then a third.

It was obvious that our best course of action was to tackle the problem from above, and after making radio contact with base, Ian McCrae as the fastest man on the hill this side of Tyndrum, volunteered to bring up the 500-foot rescue rope.

By the time we got things organised on the top and had ascertained (by shouting) that the trapped climbers below were uninjured, Ian McCrae was spotted with the long rope toiling through snow-choked boulders.

We had learned by now from the climbers that the leader had fallen 150 feet, but fortunately the rope snagged. This possibly saved them all from plunging to the valley below. The leader, though uninjured, didn't relish the thought of retackling the final pitch of the gully, which was at a high angle, and capped with a formidable cornice. As descent was also dangerous, he had wisely chosen to stay with his less experienced companions. They found a suitable bivouac spot behind a snowed-up chockstone infinitely more snug than our windswept nocturnal venue.

When the rope arrived I grabbed an end and, inching over to the cornice, cut a V in the snow. I then chucked some coils down, shouting to those below for one of them to tie on. After about five long cold minutes we heard a faint cry which we interpreted as "OK". The team didn't need any prompting; all were wanting to get to hell out of this wind-blasted place as it was bitterly cold. They started to pull in line, each grasping the non-stretch Terylene rope in ice-coated mitts like a snowman tug of war team.

I stayed close to the edge, monitoring the lift, and gave my radio to one of the younger team members to relay the operation to base. He hadn't used a radio in such a public way before and was obviously nervous with so many "high hed yins" at base.

The haul rope bit into the snow edge as effectively as a cheese cutter. My shouts of "Hold it! Hold it, for God's sake!" were snatched by the wind. Also the lads were finding it more expedient to run backwards with the rope, rather than pull it in from a static position; their crampons afforded excellent traction. After a few seconds I could barely see the closest snowman hauler through the swirling snow.

But where I had failed by command, compression and friction on the rope in the root of the cornice succeeded in slowing up the rising man. Now the rope strained to a halt. I could see melt water from the ice exuding from it. It was obviously in considerable tension.

Suddenly, just in front of my crampons, the snow surface exploded and a balaclava'd head shot out of the hole as if fired from a cannon on the floor of the corrie. The first man had been rescued!

He was none the worse for his adventure, and like a patient who'd had an aching tooth extracted, seemed glad it was all over.

The subsequent hauls, though perhaps not so dramatic, were certainly faster as there was no cornice left to hamper the team's efforts. The last man, who was also the lightest, materialised on the plateau at speed, appropriately wearing snow goggles.

While this was going on I had forgotten all about the young team member who was relaying our progress to base. It wasn't until years later that I discovered that his commentary had caused great consternation in the upper echelons of the Strath-clyde Police Department. Every few minutes or so, they had received a sombre message.

"First fatality now up."

"Second fatality now up." And so on, until four had been effectively dealt with. Only then did he realise his mistake, hurriedly adding, "I mean climber, not fatality."

Right on cue, we heard from base that a Sea King was approaching, and asking if it could be of assistance.

"Yes please," I replied. "The climbers we pulled up may be suffering from hypothermia. We'll take them to the west of the summit to see if visibility's better. I'll call you in fifteen minutes, over."

Some of the RAF Leuchars team had joined us by now and they could contact the chopper on their frequency.

We helped the four stiff men across the plateau, hoping for a window which would allow the Sea King to approach.

At the westerly side it was clearer, and we could see down the slope for about fifty yards or so, through a very small opening in the cloud. Below, the edge of Loch Tulla materialised. We could also discern the large brown and black camouflaged helicopter, outlined above the water. I hurriedly took a bearing on it and asked one of the RAF lads to relay the back bearing of this to the pilot so that he could approach. Just as this was done, the cloud socked in again, but we could hear the machine approach, though too far to our left. It wasn't until later I realised that when I snatched the bearing I had been standing alongside Alan Thomson, a keen photographer, and his exposure meter must have affected the compass. Fortunately the Sea King is equipped with radar and it nosed its way along the ridge. Then the cloud cleared sufficiently for the pilot to spot us. It was a bold piece of flying.

At that time we didn't have much experience with large helicopters and the downwash took us by surprise, blowing several of us over. Luckily, the plateau was wide and there was no danger. The four frigid climbers were bundled aboard and, as there was plenty of room, several of us joined them. In minutes we were back at base.

It was a good rescue, no one was hurt, and I for one wouldn't have missed the sight of the first climber's head breaking through that cornice for anything.

Next we go back just over a decade to a crisp January night in 1966. In those days we couldn't rely on much being done for us by the paraffin budgie, as helicopters were known to the rescue teams. It made for a tremendous team spirit however when everything on a call-out was down to us.

I had just finished dinner after seven hard hours on the hill, and decided to pick up an Agatha Christie novel, *The Labours of Hercules*. The title seemed most appropriate, for that day I had hauled four climbing-course members up a new route in Glencoe's Lost Valley.

In Glencoe, we get two distinct types of conditions for accidents. The first is heavy snow cover with bad weather conditions, when people either get caught in storms or are avalanched, or both. The avalanche is probably the most dangerous rescue situation we face. The other accident condition involves hard frozen snow and exposed boulders, the one promoting rapid acceleration, the other ensuring a sudden and dangerous stop. These were the conditions that starry night with just a flurry of snow, teased by a fresh westerly wind, but above 1,500 feet it was as hard as roughcast.

The telephone shattered my armchair detecting. I knew before I picked up the receiver that it most probably meant trouble.

It was an operator on the line.

"Meester MacInnes" – she had a lilting West Highland accent – "will you accept a reverse charge call from Bridge of Orchy? I think it's an emergency."

"Yes," I sighed with resignation. It could just be some friend who had run out of petrol.

"Is that Hamish MacInnes?" I didn't recognise the voice.

"Yes, what can I do for you?"

"There have been two accidents on Beinn Achaladair. One to my friend, Kenneth Dunn, who's fallen and is still up on the west face. Another chap, I don't know his name, is injured in the corrie to the south."

"Are they badly hurt?"

"I don't know, I ran down for help. The third member of my party stayed with Kenneth."

This was a common enough situation for us. Often the survivor of a mountain mishap rushes down for help before first establishing the seriousness of the victim's injuries or even if help is required. Neither do they stop to work out exactly where their companion is lying. This, especially at night, can be time-consuming for rescuers.

"We'll be over as quickly as we can," I told him. "Stay at the farm and I'll get more information from you when we arrive."

In those days our call-out procedure wasn't so sophisticated as it is now. I phoned the Clachaig Inn, where the owner, Rory MacDonald, was a team member, as were John Gray and Alec Morrison, two of his employees. On dozens of rescues, customers had been abandoned to serve themselves as Rory and his staff took off on their roles as good Samaritans.

This time, it was John Gray who answered the phone. I told him what I knew and asked him to contact the Elliot brothers while I let the police know.

Making fast time across the long straights of the Moor of Rannoch, as the road was clear of snow, we turned off to bounce up the dirt road leading to Achallader farm. The stocky figure of Duncan Smith, the farmer, was framed in the open door of the farmhouse. As we got out of the car, I could see beyond through the snow flurries the stark outline of the Fortress of Achallader. It was within these now crumbling walls that in 1691 the first Earl of Breadalbane conferred with the Highland chiefs on the pacification of the clans, then in arms for King James. Before the Massacre of Glencoe, a Campbell party spent a night here. Luckily, there were no Campbells in our rescue party that night, because even today, Campbells are still frowned on in this area. That's a long time to hold a grudge, as the Massacre of Glencoe occurred in 1692.

I left the car headlights on as we unloaded our rescue gear. A few minutes later I was speaking to Duncan Smith and Graeme, the climber who had telephoned, when we saw a blood-covered figure staggering through the farmyard gate, a macabre sight, like something out of a horror movie. This was the victim of the other accident, who had got himself down. Despite his gory appearance he had no serious injuries, only multiple lacerations and bruising.

Vehicles started to pour into the yard. John Gray and Alec Morrison arrived, followed by Hugh McColl, a Glencoe farmer and a special constable. Just behind, Denis Barclay, Will Thomson and John Hardie emerged from their vehicles and our local police sergeant, Douglas McCorquodale, drove up in his Land Rover with a full complement. Out jumped Constable George Cormack, Rory MacDonald of the Clachaig Inn, the two Elliot brothers and Ian Clough, my partner on the winter climbing courses. The rest of the police team were on their way from Oban.

Duncan Smith who knew the hill like the back of his hand, had been piecing together the climber Graeme's description of his fallen friend's position.

"He'll be just about the same place where that man died way back in 1925," Duncan informed me confidently. "You won't remember that, but my father found the body. It's across on the middle of the face, on the long scree slopes." He pointed a finger into the dusk to the right of the castle ruin. "The snow line's quite high just now, so you shouldn't have too much trouble getting there."

"Thanks, Duncan. Have you got the searchlight, Willie?"

"Aye, and it's fully charged."

"Good, we'll probably need it."

Duncan Smith went on helpfully, "There are long streaks of scree where the chap'll be lying, Hamish. You should be able to make your way up those between the snow without crampons."

"I hope we don't need any gear." It was Alec Morrison who spoke. "I've bugger-all with me. I didn't think that there would be any snow over here." Some time before Alec had been a member of the RAF Rescue Team at Leuchars and came to live in Glencoe when he finished his service.

We did a rising traverse from above the railway line and were soon on to large sheets of ice. As Duncan Smith had mentioned, there were scree ribbons fingering down through the ice sheets and edging the shallow gullies. We took to one of these, but after fifty minutes' hard going, realised we were too high. We were going to have to traverse.

Alec Morrison wasn't the only member of the team without crampons who had thought that the rescue was going to be a piece of cake. They were soon in trouble. Those of us who had crampons put them on. With Will Thomson, who helped on our courses, I started to cut steps, Ian Clough taking up the rear, in case anyone got into difficulties.

I heard Willie Elliot's voice somewhere along that crocodile of light.

"This searchlight's a hell of a weight, would anybody like to take a turn?"

"Well, if you're feeling past it, Willie, I'll have a go." It was Alec Morrison.

Later, Willie told me that instead of getting a lighter burden he found that Alec's rucksack was almost double the weight of the searchlight. Rory MacDonald was carrying the folding stretcher and for once was not sporting the kilt, his normal attire for pub and rescue.

I now realised how high we had climbed, as the face here was riven with narrow icy runnels which proved difficult to cross. The steps which Will and I were cutting had to be well formed for, had someone fallen, it would be akin to descending the Cresta Run without a bob, with the added hazard of a multitude of lethal boulders below. Not a pleasant thought.

John Gray, who regained his balance after a stumble, dropped a large hand torch, which bounded down the face. We gazed at it in silence like astronomers observing a new comet.

"That's one way to snuff it," Denis Barclay observed dryly. Thereafter we progressed even more carefully.

Alec Morrison put the searchlight on. Previously we had been conserving the battery and now the vivid white beam picked out the injured man, Kenneth Dunn, with his companion Bill Jack, on an island of rock. Kenneth had his rucksack propped up in front of him. I shouted, "We'll be with you soon." But it took us about twenty minutes. Kenneth was desperately cold, having been lying out for hours.

With the help of the searchlight we found that he had back and hip injuries and extensive bruising. He was in considerable pain. Carefully lifting him on to the stretcher which Walter Elliot had carried over the last part of the traverse, we secured him inside the casualty bag. Bill Jack told us that Kenneth had fallen at 2,400 feet and, after shooting down ice, had smashed into a boulder sixty feet down, which, though stopping him, had caused the damage.

We tied a couple of 200-foot ropes to the stretcher and started down. These were well V'd out to give maximum control and also to prevent stones or lumps of ice hitting stretcher and patient. It was only when we had descended a hundred feet or so that I realised how lucky Kenneth Dunn was, for had he not met his boulder on that rocky island he would have continued several hundred feet and would surely have perished on the rocks.

I was getting worried about these rocks – and the ice.

"What do you think, Ian? It's a bit dodgy for those without crampons."

The lads were kicking their heels into the icy surface with very little effect.

"They'd better go down one of the scree strips," Ian Clough replied, shining his headlamp to the right.

"I think so too," I responded and I shouted instructions accordingly.

The powerful beam of Alec's searchlight picked out the steep verglas-coated rocks. Though not inviting, at least one couldn't fall far in the event of a slip. About eight of the team made their way to this frozen gangway. Those of us with crampons took up the stretcher "reins" and continued down.

We had been going for some ten minutes when I heard a

shout and the searchlight beam spun across the dark curtain above before hurtling down the slope, with Alec Morrison still attached. Alec was the only one remaining with the stretcher party who hadn't crampons. As he was operating the searchlight he didn't want to abandon us and leave us short handed. It was a strange sight to see Alec, followed six feet behind (the length of the flex) by the lamp. The battery was still in the rucksack on his back. He did several cartwheels, eventually coming to a halt 300 feet below, when he hit frozen scree resembling a carrot grater.

In our concern for a fellow rescuer we almost forgot Kenneth and his stretcher, which was also eager to be off. I had to yell to the team to hold it or we'd also lose our patient.

Three of us quickly cramponed down to where Alec lay. We were relieved to find that he wasn't badly hurt, mainly abrasions, but he had injured his back. While we attended his wounds, the stretcher was lowered down to us.

Below I saw a host of lights.

"That must be the Oban Police team," I said to Ian Clough. I spoke to them on the radio, asking if they had another stretcher. They had, and as it was being carried by Ian McCrae, the gamekeeper and special constable who lives just a mile or so from Achallader farm, I knew it would be with us pretty quick.

Though initially Alec insisted on painfully hobbling down, he soon succumbed to the indignity of being carried when Ian and the stretcher arrived. We brought both men down to the farm. The lower slopes of the mountain, which we had avoided coming up on our rising traverse, proved to be like an angled skating rink, sheathed in wide expanses of ice, and made slicker by a thaw which had by now set in. Both casualties were taken by ambulance to the local doctor at Dalmally and then to Oban hospital.

I have always found it a point of interest when thinking of this rescue that Kenneth Dunn was found very close to the location of the 1925 accident. That early rescue occurred at a time when there were no official rescue facilities in the Scottish Highlands, and psychic assistance was volunteered in the form of "magic writing", which may or may not have given clues to where the missing climber lay.

I have been interested in the mystery of the Beinn Achaladair letters for over twenty years. Every time I go on a rescue in that area my thoughts take me back and I am forced to believe that there are some happenings on earth which, at the present time, have no logical explanation. I knew several of the people who took part in the search and have spoken with them at length about this strange affair.

To begin, we go back in time to 1925. It was a cold Sunday morning on 22 March. The time, 5.30 am when Douglas Ewen, Archibald MacLay Thomson and Alexander Lawson Henderson left Inveroran Inn, an old droving stance, to walk to Beinn Achaladair.

The high tops were still in winter condition and there was a crisp clear frost but none of the party had knowledge of snow and ice climbing. Thirty-year-old Alex Henderson was the most experienced of the group, having made some ascents on the continent.

In 1925 the A82 highway across the Moor of Rannoch, which links Fort William and the West with Glasgow, had still to be built. They took the old road as far as Loch Tulla, then followed the loch edge and crossed the Water of Tulla at a ford opposite Achallader farm.

The north-west face of the mountain rose above them as they crossed the railway line. It was 7.30 am.

To a mountaineer this aspect of Beinn Achaladair presents no great difficulty, being an almost uniformly angled slope to its summit. The three men chose to ascend a wide snow gully in the centre of the face.

They had been warned that conditions on the mountain could be icy and even lower down on the slopes they had to kick steps. From below, the long treadmill of this slope is foreshortened.

It was 9.30 am before they stopped for breakfast at 2,000 feet. Already they were finding the going difficult and, with little thought of the possible consequences, they took an hour over their meal. Alex Henderson, who felt cold, kept stomping about and impatiently got off ten minutes ahead of his companions.

As Douglas and Archie climbed they could see Alex ahead, but at about 11.15 am he slanted leftwards and they lost sight of him behind some ice-coated rocks. But by now they had other problems to occupy their minds. They were experiencing difficulty with hard snow and higher up they found themselves on iced rock. They were so gripped by their predicament that they resolved not to descend by this route.

It was 1.25 pm when they emerged on the summit of the mountain. No sign of Alex. At first they were puzzled, then alarmed, and for two hours searched the final slopes, even using a hand siren in the hope of attracting his attention. Archibald Thomson also lowered himself on their climbing rope over a cornice to a ridge below. This was the continuation of Alex's line of ascent. There was no sign, nothing – just a vast angled whiteness interspersed with ice-coated rock.

The two men were baffled by the disappearance of their friend and decided to head for the col between Achaladair and the adjoining peak, Meall Buidhe. They had difficulty climbing to this and had to resort to step cutting on the icy slope. But nowhere could they find any tracks suggesting their friend had come this way. They returned to Achaladair summit at 6.00 pm and after ten minutes' deliberation decided to descend to Achallader farm to raise the alarm.

By the time they got down to the north-east corrie it was dusk, but they made a hurried search at the foot of the steep slopes and satisfied themselves that the only marks on the snow had been caused by falling rocks. There were no prints in the floor of the valley, but in the failing light they were not sure if the broken slopes at the head of the big central gully contained tracks or not.

At 7.07 pm the light failed and they abandoned the search and continued to Achallader farm.

It was 8.40 pm by the time they got down to this place of refuge, and they were fed by Duncan Smith, the father of my late friend, and his wife. The two tired men were asked to spend the night, but they felt that there was a possibility that Alex had somehow crossed over the summit and had perhaps descended to the east towards Tyndrum.

They left Achallader at 10.35 pm and walked the ten miles to the Tyndrum Hotel. It was now 3.45 am on the Monday morning. There was no sign of Alex. Both men were shattered, having traversed forty-four miles in just over twenty-two hours, some of that up and down the steep slopes of Beinn Achaladair.

Robert Stewart was the hotel owner at the time and he organised a search party which set off by mid-morning. In those days the arrangement for rescues was to recruit shepherds, gillies and casual climbers locally, and alert the Scottish Mountaineering Club, who would sally forth with all expediency from Glasgow or Edinburgh or indeed from both cities.

Robert Stewart had sent the club a telegram that morning but it was Wednesday evening before it was found in the Scottish Mountaineering Clubrooms in Glasgow. It had been accepted on the Monday by the charwoman who hadn't thought it was necessary to inform the club secretary! That evening the club's topic was a paper on the installation of a mountain indicator on the summit of Lochnager. The account of this operation by the Cairngorm Club was read by the Honorary President, J. A. Parker. The situation was reminiscent of Drake's game of bowls with the Spanish Armada looming over the horizon. The audience knew of the urgent plea for help at the start of the meeting and as soon as the paper was concluded the president put the matter to the members. It was resolved that a party should set out for Tyndrum immediately. With this rescue party was Alexander Harrison, a future Honorary President. Despite the telegram which went astray, several Scottish Mountaineering Club members in the area were already helping the search. These were J. H. Bell, A. J. Rusk and E. C. Thomson, names renowned in Scottish mountaineering circles. Frank Smythe, the well-known mountaineer and writer who had been climbing with Dr Bell, had to return south and couldn't take part.

Throughout the Thursday a fifteen-mile radius round the mountain was combed, but without success. The weather had deteriorated with driving rain below and snow above. While police, gillies and other volunteers scoured the lower slopes, the SMC members concentrated their efforts on the more precipitous parts of the mountain, where they thought it more likely that Henderson had come to grief. They concluded that he could have reached the summit at least half an hour ahead of his two companions. It was just possible that they had missed his prints, or that he had kept to harder snow, where his tracks had not stood out, especially in the fading light. With this in mind they felt that the missing man could be anywhere in a wide area, even in Glen Lyon.

On the Monday, eight days after Henderson's disappearance,

a set of old prints had been found lower down by some of the local searchers, but these had run out in treacherous ground where the rescuers themselves were exposed to considerable danger.

That day, when the rescuers were on the hill, a strange letter arrived in the post at the hotel. It was addressed to Mr Garret. The hotelier, Robert Stewart, decided it must be meant for a Mr Garrick, who was an experienced Glasgow-based mountaineer in charge of one of the search groups. The letter ran thus:

Dear Sir,

This is going to be a difficult letter to write, and beyond making use of the information it may give, I would ask you to be so good as to keep it to yourself as far as possible. A friend and myself have, within the last three months, received startling proof of the accuracy of the information regarding unknown people, which we have received from a supernatural agency. I cannot go into details of these now – it would serve no purpose . . .

Yesterday (Tuesday, 24th) it occurred to us that we might be able to get useful information as to the whereabouts of the lost Mr Henderson and at 12.00 noon we approached the usual source of our information, and requested that a "scout" be sent out to get any information possible. In the evening about 6.30 pm we asked for news and the undernoted is verbatim:

The answer is slow in coming, but our messenger now reports that it is raining, and one, I think his name is Cameron, is heading towards the col, where the man is lying. The snow is deep here perhaps twenty feet and it may be that Cameron is not sure of his feet and we cannot influence him sufficiently; it may be I say three, some six weeks ere he be found. Jim says he is warm yet . . .

Some time later: Where may he be found? Can no directions be given?

Such information as I have is scant, but news is that he is warm, and we are not led to think that he is asleep.

What do you say of Death?

There is no Death.

Where is he?

He has not yet passed, but his needs are worldly. It is a col. Ask one, I think his name is Cameron, where he was at 4 o'clock today. They are still searching, and we are trying to help!

Now we do not know a single member of the search party, but should there amongst them be one of the name of Cameron, that would be one point correct, indicating an intelligence of some kind behind our information. I would say that in all probability the whole information as to location of the spot for which you are searching is correct, and that the information should not be treated lightly. Neither my friend or myself are spiritualists, but interested in investigating phenomena we do not pretend to understand. In view of the nature of the information we feel conscience-bound to pass it on – it can do no harm and may be useful.

The only signature was "Anxious to Help".

Though most of the club members were sceptical about the weird letter, there indeed was a Mr Cameron in the search party and he had been on the col at 4.00 pm on the 24th. Also, it had been raining (a not uncommon phenomenon in this part of the world). It is understandable, however, that the letter wasn't treated very seriously by those hard-bitten mountaineers.

The search continued and a large-scale operation was planned for the weekend as the weather seemed to be improving. Some thirty quarry workers were taking part, travelling from nearby Ballachulish slate quarries by bus. John Kennedy was one of these. Gillies, police and shepherds all turned out in force; the shepherds with their dogs hoped that the collies could locate Henderson if he should be buried under the snow. Some thirty years later I was also to use my dog to find a buried avalanche victim only a short distance away in Glencoe, but was soon to realise that dogs have to be specifically trained for this work, especially for locating bodies. As a direct result, I later started the Search and Rescue Dog Association.

The climbers in the 1925 operation felt that there was little hope of finding Henderson until a thaw, for on the 25th eighteen inches of snow fell, which they rightly concluded must have effectively covered the body, unless he was lying on a windswept slope.

The weekend search was to no avail, although many pinned hope on the dogs. By now considerable public interest had been aroused and on Sunday 29 March an aeroplane from Renfrew airport circled low over the mountain, where over seventy men could be seen sweeping the slopes and corries, but they saw no sign of Henderson. In fact it later transpired that several of the search party had passed close to the fallen climber, but hadn't spotted him due to the snow cover.

Meanwhile, Anxious to Help had become a diligent correspondent. Another undated letter arrived for "Mr Garret", offering the following information from the supernatural:

> *My news is but little, for the "scout" is not yet returned. You ask me many questions, and these I will attempt to answer. The loch mentioned is not so much a loch as a widening in the Water of Tulla, and some miles form the Loch Tulla at Achallader House, and the ruins of the old castle of the same name. This is Ford.*

We did not know of a place named Ford's whereabouts, and had asked for particulars.

> *From here, if they follow the valley, some say corrie, to its source, and at altitude 3,060 feet, they will get as near as I can tell you at present. Today many have passed fairly near, but only a few are out, and there is no sign of a thaw.*

We asked for a sketch of the place, but were informed that the "scout" was with the searcher, one McLaren. You will know if such a person was out, and accept it, if so, as further proof of a direct intelligence.

Still Anxious to Help

Captain McLaren was a well-known climber and actively engaged in the search operation, and curiously it was he who opened this second letter addressed to Mr Garret. Hard upon it, another letter arrived, dated 2 April, and addressed this time to Mr Stewart, the hotelkeeper, at Tyndrum:

Further to my letter of Yesterday addressed to "Mr Garret", the following, together with the rough sketch, is sent from our source of information and for what they may be worth. Neither any friend or myself is acquainted with the locality, and do not know from which side of the paper the sketch is to be read; but to those on the spot it should be evident if the sketch corresponds to the definite places named on it – we got two separate sketches drawn and they seem to be similar. They are reputed to have been drawn for us by the "scout" sent to the spot, and the following is his information asked by us for further directions:

Leave Loch Tulla and go along the road until you come to Ford, which lies between the castle and the big house, and go up the corrie. You go east and climb up the corrie on your right hand.

Asked if nothing could be done, we were told that the only hope was a thaw – for recovery of the body.

My friend and myself would give our names but in view of the publicity the accident has occasioned we prefer not to do so. My friend knows you personally, Mr Stewart, and I am therefore addressing this to you as likely to be able to make use of the information should it be worth anything.

Anxious to Help

The "spiritual" sketch showed Loch Tulla, Achallader farm and the castle, but the ford is marked in the wrong spot.

The next letter was dated 3 April.

Further to my letter of yesterday the following information, since received, is sent for what it is worth.

There is little to report; we have found a definite aid to the climbers. It is in the shape of a tin box and many . . . (interrupted)

Has our letter to Garret been received and opened?

Yes, it has been opened by one of the name Mak Lairen, but to the box, some say tin, well, this they will find not one hundred yards from the spot.

But we cannot say will any of the climbers associate the box, some say tin, with the man you mention.

Can the tin be seen?

The tin is quite visible, though snow is falling.
Where exactly is it?
It is near the corrie Achallader, and if they are quick they will find it. A strange message reaches me, and this I will repeat on verification.

Later.

The message is small account; it says the box is empty save for a small bit of linen – the contents of the box is linen and is stiff with batter.

Asked for further directions.

The stream of the corrie is starting at Ford. Yes, you follow the corrie, or some say coire, and it goes to the bogland at altitude already mentioned – 3,060 feet.

Yes, it is a burn, though the word is new to me.

I regret my gernadion [messenger] is no longer here, but from the report delivered the news was on climbing the corrie, or I believe korrie, I noticed a box I think he called it, and in it a cloot (I think it is a cloot with a k sound) of linen. This, I am afraid, is the extent of the message, which I will repeat in one particular. The word of the gernadion is in Scots and represents box-mullie.

What is a mullie?

The error is mine – I am sorry my Scots is poor, but it is new to me. The gernadion spoke of the box or a tin as a mull-lie, a diminutive of mull – that is a little mull.

This is all for the present, but he will return with more news and I fear more Hieland jawbreakers.

Later.

There is little more to report, but this may interest you. Tomorrow no search will take place and all trace of the mullie – I use advisedly the word of the messenger – will, I fear, be lost. This, though, I say. To climb the corrie is easy – it is commonly used by – help me with this – ghillies – pronounced ghilly, a species of gamekeeper, from (locally known as) the Big House, I believe Achallader House, near Ford. This route adhered to will prove the great help. The snow still falls increasingly, and I fear that many clues already known to the helpers will be obliterated. One thing remains that it is at about altitudes about 3,060 feet that the find will be made when they do, weeks likely from now.

This is sent with the hope it might be useful – in any case no harm could be done by trying to verify it – one route is as good as another when looking for something where no clue already exists.

Anxious to Help

The next letter addressed to Mr Stewart was dated 6 April 1925.

Dear Sir,

I am sorry we have much to give you since my last, but it may be of interest – especially to the "speculators"!

Saturday, 3.00 pm

I say they have your letters, and whilst laughing in their faces I should say it is not in their hearts – they say what is this, who is this? Yet do they say they know something of the affair. Today, but not yesterday, a large force is working and two men are going in the true line of search.

Who are they?

That I fear me is all I can say until the return of the gernadion.

[Captain McLaren and a fellow rescuer were, at the time indicated, heading in the right direction.]

Saturday, 9.00 pm

The gernadion is not yet with us. I regret to say the box, or as we have said, the mullie, has not been seen, nor can I wonder. My last advice is take the corrie at Achallader House, which is to say ford, and at altitude given, and to the north you should encounter your object. There is a dark stone ridge – I forget the technical name – at or near the spot.

Is the ridge covered with snow?

Well, it is as though the snow had covered up the middle part without covering the top or the bottom. It is visible.

This last in answer to a question I forget what.

To the searchers I say, walk warily for it is deep.

Is there a precipice?

Yes it is a precipice – I could think only of cliff, and that was not the word. I think Mak Lairen said Heugh or Kleugh.

Has he been near the spot?

Yes, and Captain McLaren several times. [This was verified by McLaren.]

11.00 pm

The gernadion has returned. Here is the report. Much talk at Inveroran, and much talk at Tyndrum. They are speculating as to who the comrades are, (ourselves I suppose). They say they too have a definite clue. But I do not believe them as they were too far north. Tomorrow if weather permits, a still greater search will be made. Two of the company believe your good faith – one is called Walker. That concludes my report.

Will the information about the ridge be any good as a further report?

No, I cannot say it will help any more than what I have already written.

Have they got the rough map I sent?

Yes, and they say it is the copy of a map.

Can they make anything of it?

Yes, it is quite intelligible to them. Ford is well known to them.

On the back of the map there was reverse drawing. It almost looked as if it had been drawn on carbon paper. Considerable confusion was caused in attempting to interpret this on the wrong side, for the rescuers at first thought it to be an independent map.

Monday, 4.00 pm

My sole news is that owing to bad weather the large company did not materialise and no search of the high ground was possible. The letters (Ours I suppose) have much comment and some heed is now being paid. Stewart says, "I know no one in Peterhead."

We might only remark that the sketch we sent was not a copy of a map if such a criticism has actually been made. It was sent in good faith by us as we got it and for what it was worth. The only ford we knew was at the far end of Loch

Awe, and we could not connect Achallader with that direction – hence the questions and answers regarding it. We have failed to see any news in the *Herald* since Friday of the search, and all our information we have got from the unusual source originally indicated. We may say that a copy of the *Oban Times* came into our hands on Saturday (of the previous week), and we got a number of particulars of which we had been unaware – such as that the missing man had parted from his friends apparently after a considerable climb had been made. This would indicate that those on the spot must be aware of the original route taken at the start of the climb – this we were not aware of.

Still Anxious to Help

The search was rewarded by success on Sunday 13 April. A considerable thaw had now taken place exactly three weeks after Henderson went missing. Duncan Smith found the body lying face down in a small depression almost exactly where it had been indicated on the "spiritual" map, and at the altitude given – 3,060 feet. Alexander Henderson was lying most probably in the position in which he had come to rest, with both arms in front of his face as if to protect it. The toes of his boots were still pressed into the snow as if they had been arresting his fall, but he most likely came to rest on this easier ground through colliding with a frozen rock, which was supporting him between his legs. He had no broken bones, but there was a large gash on his forehead, two of his upper teeth were missing also his lower front teeth. Later his ice axe was found 150 feet higher and this seems to indicate that he fell from the steeper rocks above, made highly treacherous with ice. Henderson's body was carried down to Achallader farm, then to Bridge of Orchy church before he was buried in his home town of Cupar.

Though Duncan Smith denied that he obtained any help from the sketch map and the letters, indeed maintained that the information misled him, the fact remains that he did find Henderson at the exact point indicated on the "spiritual" map.

Regarding the other "clues", the box or tin or "mullie" was never found, though in Henderson's rucksack, which he was still wearing, a broken vacuum flask protruded through the canvas. Some said this could have been the object mentioned by the gernadion, others thought it could have been a tin with a linen-backed map inside. A cloot is an old Scots word for a pudding cloth. And as for the mullie, that's a diminutive of mull, which, as well as a promontary, can also mean a snuffbox.

There was considerable interest as to the source of these strange letters and a reporter from the *Dundee Advertiser* succeeded in tracking down the writer if not the source. The trail led to one Mr Norman MacDiarmid at Buchan Ness Lodge at Boddam in Aberdeenshire which at one time had been a shooting box for the Earls of Aberdeen. He was thirty-eight years old, born in the West of Scotland, educated in Glasgow, and a man of private means. He contributed articles on natural history to magazines. Though Norman MacDiarmid would admit to no part of the letter writing, a statement was obtained from a close friend of his. The account of his friend, who wished to remain anonymous, is as follows:

> Altogether there were six of us gathered together in my house – a friend, my wife, my daughter, myself and two others. The medium and writer of the messages was my friend, who has previously had most startling messages sent in this way. He simply sits down with a paper on his knee and a pencil in hand, which commences to write backwards. The written matter has the appearance of what might appear on blotting paper after it had been used to dry the ink of a communication, and has to be read by means of a mirror.
>
> On this evening my friends and the others were sitting in the room chatting and joking, and while we were thus engaged his hand began to write. Previously, when in his own home, he had got a sketch drawn by this method, but up to then he had not been able to interpret its significance. The words came through slowly, and gradually the story unfolded itself. We immediately saw that we were getting information with regard to the Argyllshire mystery. The message indicated that we would be guided by a "mullie" or tin, in which would be a linen "clout", and that although snow was still falling at the moment, the tin would still be visible.

Interspersed through the message came most irrelevant matter, some of it silly stuff, but this we had just to sift out. I can vouch for the fact that the whole thing was genuine. I was a bit sceptical up to that time, but I am now convinced, although spiritualism has absolutely nothing to do with it. The whole thing came through without any inquiry being made about the Argyllshire affair, and when we were discussing other matters.

There was nothing of the nature of a seance about the meeting, which was purely a social affair in my own sitting-room. As a matter of fact, I was pottering about with my wireless set at the time.

It was apparent that Norman MacDiarmid had a gift before this incident. He and some of his friends had held seances for entertainment. On such occasions he would suddenly commence to write backwards at great speed. One such seance had uncanny accuracy. MacDiarmid's hand had drawn two cars, one large, one small. The small car had the word "Me" beside it and underneath the name and address of someone in Musselburgh. Next day they were all shocked to read that a youth of that name and address had been killed in a road accident in Musselburgh about the time Norman had drawn his sketch.

I'm sceptical about spiritual assistance in searching for missing persons, and know of several instances where it was tried unsuccessfully. However, the Beinn Achaladair incident does make one think twice about ESP and it appears that the information volunteered had a degree of accuracy. At the time it must be said that members of the Scottish Mountaineering Club were suspicious of the letters, and George Sang wrote an article debunking them in the *Scottish Mountaineering Club Journal*; but even he had grudgingly to admit that Henderson's body was found where it was shown on the sketch and at the precise altitude.

Perhaps we should allow Sir Arthur Conan Doyle, who had an abiding interest in spiritualism, to have the last words on the matter:

I would say a word as to the Achallader case, which is an extremely instructive one. It is perfectly clear that some one or something brought information to Mr Norman MacDiarmid as to the position of the missing man. That is certain and undeniable. Even names of the search party were given. Now, who was it who brought that information? There are two possibilities. It may have been an unconscious extension of Mr MacDiarmid's own personality. This is an explanation which should never be lost sight of. We are spirits here and now, though grievously held down by matter. What a spirit can do we can do if we get loose. I am just as sure that the explanation of many Mediumistic phenomena lies in this direction as I am that there is a large residue which could only come from external intelligent beings.

Let us, however, exhaust this possibility. It means that the medium's spirit went forth exploring and brought back information. But we have the evidence that the medium was perfectly normal at the time. We should have expected trance had his soul really left the body untenanted. Then, again, this strange messenger did not know Scotch. He had to ask for information from the medium. Is this consistent with the idea that he was actually part of the medium? Finally, he used some strange words which Mr MacDiarmid (who courteously answered my enquiries at the time) could not explain. I think that these words cast some light upon who this helpful spiritual being may have been.

The first word was "gernadion", used evidently in the sense of a messenger, an inferior messenger, apparently, who was sent out by some superior control. Upon Mr MacDiarmid asking what language "gernadion" was, the answer was "Eschadoc". Now Eschadoc in Greek signifies "beyond the limits of humanity" and gernadion is connected with a Greek root which gives the idea of one who is bearing something. The latter may be obscure, but the former is perfectly clear. It was while discussing the incident with Mr H. A. Vachell, the famous novelist, that this discovery was suggested by him. It would seem then, that the main control is a Greek – probably an ancient

Greek who retains some memory of his old Speech. It would certainly be interesting to know what knowledge Mr MacDiarmid has of Greek, but undoubtedly in his normal state he was not aware of the derivation of these words.

This fact disposes also of the possibility that the messenger was actually the spirit of the lost traveller. The only supposition which covers the case seems to me to be that Mr MacDiarmid's control or guardian spirit is a Greek, that he interested himself in the case of the traveller, that he had messengers at his beck, that he sent them forth, and that he then conveyed the result to the brain and the hand of the medium. If there is any better explanation which does not ignore the facts I should be glad to hear of it.

The Matterhorn and the Bergschrund

Ludwig Gramminger

*It was in the wake of the last war that I first made acquaintance
with the Zmutt Ridge of the Matterhorn. As a kilted, inexperienced fledgeling, I was taken under the wings of two established
canons of the mountains, George Ritchie and Derek Haworth, the
first a solicitor, the second a doctor. With the objective of the
Matterhorn's Zmutt Ridge determinedly implanted in our minds
we made our way to the Schönbühl hut; our guidebook a postcard
bought in Zermatt. My financial state was reflected in my lack of
equipment; I didn't even have crampons.*

*The normal way to climb the Zmutt Ridge is from the Hörnli hut
at the start of the ordinary route up the Matterhorn. We set out
about 2.00 am when the saner Swiss dream of sheep in green
pastures. In so doing, with only the light of a flickering candle
lantern, we lost our way and inadvertently ventured into the jaws
of the notorious Penhall Couloir which spewed rocks as soon as the
sun touched the summit.*

*We endured the adventure, as did fortunately, Ludwig Gram-
minger and his companions several years later, for in 1956 in this
same high angled corridor Ludwig was faced with the appalling
prospect of getting his three injured companions back to safety, one
of them gravely hurt. He describes the ordeal and, typical of the
man, passes lightly over the momentous labour in rescuing his
friends. It was an exacting test of his ability as a rescuer and of
his proficiency as a mountaineer.*

In the summer of 1956 two climbers from Saxony, Vogel and
Zireis, got into difficulties on the Zmutt Ridge of the Matterhorn. They had come to Zermatt by motorbike with the

intention of training on the Matterhorn for an attempt later on the Eigerwand. They set up their tent at the foot of the mountain on the banks of the Visp. The two, both from Saxony, climbed to the Hörnli hut, spent the night there, and then set off to climb the Zmutt Ridge and descend by the Hörnli Ridge. They left their sleeping bags in the Hörnli hut. After eight days the empty tent on the Visp bank drew attention. Police enquiries indicated that the two had not returned from their Matterhorn climb. The weather was very bad at the time this was discovered, but as soon as it improved, a guided party and two guideless Viennese climbers started up the Zmutt Ridge. After the Zmutt Pinnacles at the point where one traverses into the Carrel Gallery (Carrel's Corridor), one of the Viennese spotted a climber in front, above and to one side, wearing a red ski cap. At first he thought it must be the guide of the second party but quickly realised that this was silly for they were behind. He waited for the guide to catch up and pointed out his discovery. The guide was puzzled and traversed across the face to discover a frozen climber in a bivouac. The man had frozen to death in a sitting position, secured to a peg. The guide took a few photographs, then cut the body free and dropped it down the West Face. This upset Herr Caplan, one of the climbers in his party, and he protested strongly against the guide's action.

In Zermatt later the incident was discussed; it was a delicate matter for the father of one of the missing men, Herr Vogel, had already offered a reward for the finding of his son's body. It was perhaps fortunate that from the photographs one couldn't tell if it was Vogel's body which had been found or his companion, Zireis. After these events the weather became very bad, the guide announced that he had made a search for the body, but had found nothing.

Some time later Herr Vogel came to the offices of the Bergwacht in Munich and asked for their help to locate his son's body. He said that he had no further confidence in the Zermatt guides. I had to tell him that after the recent bad weather and heavy snowfalls high up, there was very little prospect of finding the missing men that year. "Even the best Swiss guides would have small chance of doing so," I added.

Understandably, Herr Vogel continued to press for a search,

so I relented and promised to organise one right away. For my companion I chose my old friend, the guide Anderl Heckmair who was then nearly fifty, and as the weather had just turned for the better, we decided to leave immediately for the Valais. It was 1st October, 1956. At the last moment Herr Vogel brought along two men to accompany us, two friends of the missing Saxons, Lothar Brandler and Klaus Buschmann. We weren't enamoured of the idea but, as there was room in the car, we agreed.

In Zermatt we first spoke to the police, then with the guides, to discover if anything else had been found in the meantime. Nothing had, so all four of us went up to the Schönbühlhütte on the west side of the mountain, accompanied by a Swiss lady. At the hut we met Ludwig Steinauer and he promised to keep the Schönbühlhütte open, as it had already closed for the season. We had brought up with us a half-Akya stretcher with transport wheel. The weather was fine but very cold, which was good for our task.

Early next morning we set off from the hut and crossed the Zmutt Glacier to the foot of the Matterhorn's West Face. The Swiss lady remained in the hut. In about two and a half hours we reached the bergschrund. This was some two to four metres wide, with a fifteen-metre high vertical ice flank to climb on either side. There were also two snow bridges which proved very difficult. The lower slopes and the avalanche cone under the face yielded no trace of the victims and we came to the conclusion that in all probability the dead were buried under the masses of new snow. We roped up to search the area above the bergschrund to the start of the rock face, and to take a look into the couloir coming down from the Zmutt Ridge.

Anderl told Klaus and Lothar that they, too, should rope up and try to cross the bergschrund and the ice slope. Klaus, who tried first, didn't manage it, but Lothar then had a go and succeeded in reaching the upper edge of the dangerously steep, smooth ice cliff above and got a good stance. The vertical distance was about fifteen metres. Now Anderl and I made a serious error. We didn't go as a two-man rope, but attached ourselves with karabiners from our chest harnesses to the rope from Lothar, belayed above. We all reached the upper stance and let Lothar go on right away. Above, the conditions were good and without thinking too much about it, we were able to climb together on the rope using our twelve-point crampons and axe points. The going was excellent on the hard firn. It was at an angle of about 50°. It was a mistake, but we didn't give a moment's thought to the fact that one of us could make a false move; we only had eyes for the icefield around and above us which we were scouring.

We had already put a few rope's lengths behind us; but moving together without resting was too strenuous for me and I was puffing and panting.

I called to Anderl who was second on the rope above, "I'm going to untie from the rope and traverse over to the left to the Zmutt Ridge and get on to the rocks. Perhaps I can find a good stance there. From there," I added, "I can search the upper section of the face with the glasses."

"Right," he shouted back. I unclipped from the main rope and moved up to the left, where I had to cross a small hard gully down which stones hurtled in the afternoon when the sun was on the West Face.

I was scarcely a metre above this gully when I heard a noise above. I looked up and couldn't believe my eyes. A man was shooting head-first towards me. It was Lothar Brandler, who had been leading. It all happened so quickly and the reason I didn't get torn off with him was because I had already crossed the gully and was out of his direct descent line. Anderl's attempt to arrest the fall with his ice axe failed as Lothar was already falling too fast and the firn snow was very hard with ice beneath. I saw the whole thing clearly as if in slow motion. Anderl now swept past me, plucked from the face. I shouted to him, I forget what now, and then saw Klaus, the last man on the rope, receive a terrible jerk; he was projected off backwards, as if by catapult, down the mountain without being able to do a thing about it. Helpless, I could only watch, numbed, unable to intervene. It was dreadful to see one, then the other, whipped off into space, to see arms, legs, axes, rope, tangled, flailing, whirling down the gully, and then to watch them disappear over the edge of the vertical cliff. It was a fifteen-metre drop – had they fallen into the open bergschrund? Far below, I was able to make out the avalanche cone again and I waited anxiously to see if they would reappear there where it ran out, but no. I now feared that they had fallen into the schrund. I shouted and listened alternately. Nothing.

Thoughts jumbled in my head; I had to force myself to consider carefully what to do – I can hear myself now, how I counselled myself out loud: "Wiggerl, you must think very carefully what is to be done!" It was as if I was rooted to the snow, standing there on the steep slope to one side of the hard gully, with four of the twelve crampon points in the firn and clutching my axe. I felt very alone; I dared not make a wrong move – those below needed me. It would have been dreadful had I fallen too . . .

Two of the others had lost their axes in the fall. They were still sticking in the ice of the gully. Ice axes can be very useful items on a rescue operation, for splinting and transporting the injured. I must retrieve them, I thought. Carefully, step by step, I climbed downwards, then across and I had them. I could move well enough with two, but with three – what'll I do with the third one, I asked myself? I was tempted to stuff it across in my chest harness, but that could be dangerous if I should fall too, so I hung it by its wrist loop to one arm. With extreme care and yet not slowly I reached the top edge of the bergschrund and the fifteen-metre ice wall. At last I could see what had happened and was somewhat encouraged. Two of them lay close together on the steep slope below the schrund, the rope ran up from them and into the crevasse. So one of them had fallen into this and the other two swept right over it and were now held by the rope. It should therefore be possible to get the one in the crevasse out. I shouted and then shouted again, and at last received a response, from the man in the crevasse. I asked him whether he was injured, but he only said he would see if he could climb up the rope. I called down that I would soon be there to give him a hand. The two others were lying motionless and I feared the worst.

But first I had to direct all my concentration on the difficult descent of the ice wall with the three ice axes as a handicap. Immediately below the open bergschrund yawned blackly, too deep to see the bottom. I moved with circumspection, careful in case something should break off, or in case I should fall, yet at the same time angling diagonally down so that I shouldn't fall into the crevasse if I did slip. I have forgotten how I managed to get down this tricky little wall without assistance. I certainly had luck on my side – with a last strong leap I reached the other side of the crevasse and stood beside the rucksacks that we had left there. In the meantime, the man in the crevasse had climbed up the rope and was now out, and I greeted him. It was Lothar Brandler.

When I saw his face I was shocked but without letting it show – it was badly lacerated and covered with blood, and then I saw that his hands and arms were in the same state. He talked in strange, disjointed fragments and I realised he was suffering from shock. His behaviour confirmed it – he didn't look at me and even wanted to throw the two rucksacks down the steep slope of some 250 metres. I had difficulty getting him down to the others. I carried the rucksacks myself and as I descended I could see that Anderl Heckmair was lying crumpled, unconscious and bleeding very badly from a gaping wound in the back of the head. Klaus Buschmann lay on his back, groaning loudly. He was having difficulty in breathing. I examined him and saw that he was not in fact badly injured. This eased my mind somewhat, but Anderl was quite still.

I told the two Saxons to clench their teeth firmly and only do what I told them, at the same time belaying them both to their ice axes. Then I encouraged them to help me get Anderl settled more comfortably. As a first measure I bandaged his nasty head wound, and as I was doing it, he awoke for a brief moment and though semi-conscious, complained of pain in his right shoulder and arm. I had a closer inspection and saw he had dislocated his shoulder. He passed out again. His unconsciousness was now to my advantage and his; with some exertion I managed to get his shoulder back into place. He awoke immediately after this operation and right away recognised the Dent d'Hérens North Face which was the first thing he saw. He named it but didn't connect it with his situation. He didn't remember the accident or why he was there. I was touched that he recognised me right away and immediately said, "If Wiggerl's here, then everything will be all right."

Like Klaus he was having great difficulty with his breathing. I realised this could only mean broken ribs. After this preliminary first aid, it was now important to get them out of the danger zone, off the steep slope. Above, the sun was creeping across the West Face and we could expect stone falls soon. The gully above was like a cannon barrel aimed directly at us, only awaiting the final triggering of the sun. Therefore we had to get out of the firing line as fast as possible, but how?

I gave the two young men precise instructions once again, securing them, one close in front of me, the other behind. They were like zombies, almost immobile, not with it, and I had to shout at them sharply to urge them on. There was no alternative; the urgent thing was to get Anderl down.

Only when we had safely reached the bottom of the slope and traversed round a bit to get out of the danger zone, did I take notice of the other injuries of all three. Luckily, I had plenty of dressing material. As far as Lothar was concerned, after taking care of abrasions to both arms, the worst was over; Klaus also had severe abrasions as well as bad bruising to his back and his difficulty breathing. Later it was confirmed he had a broken rib. Anderl was in the worst state. Fortunately, the dislocation was now reduced and I strapped his arm to his chest. But I was particularly worried that he couldn't hold up his head; it kept dropping on to his chest or falling to one side. I considered what this might mean. Then from a pair of nylon overtrousers I made a kind of cravat, a collar, wide, thick, strong and yet soft. There was an immediate improvement. Further investigation suggested that the difficulty in his breathing must be connected with other serious injuries. I was aware that he must have several broken ribs. I had a big over-anorak with me and used this as a strong support bandage-wise over his chest. This was extremely painful for him but I felt it would be the best thing in the long run. But what could I do about the many contusions Anderl had suffered? He was unable to move on his own and was in great pain if he tried to do so. It was impossible for him to stand on his own; I had to support him continually. First I tried to lay him on his back, but that presented further problems; I realised then that the lumbar vertebrae must be damaged. I tried all possible ways of getting him into a carrying position so that we could move him without causing him undue pain. The best seemed to be if he leant sideways on to me, clinging to the straps of my rucksack with his one good hand, his left one. I secured the rucksack firmly to my back, then put my right arm round his waist and grasped his belt. By this means I succeeded in easing things for him so that he could take tiny steps, albeit with great pain. There was no other choice, this was the only way we could, with luck, hope to get back to the hut in daylight. Perhaps, given time, he might have got along better by himself. But he could only put one foot ten centimetres in front of the other, not a centimetre more.

We were all still wearing crampons. So we painfully progressed. Later when the snow surface became soft, I took off Anderl's crampons. Every twenty or fifty metres I had to call a halt. The one way Anderl could rest was for me to go behind him, a little higher so that he could lean against my chest and sit on my knee. I very quickly lost all feeling in my feet in this torturous "resting" position. For me these stops were the worst of all. But how could we have made this difficult journey otherwise? I had thought of all sorts of possibilities: such as attach him to the rucksack and carry him, but he would have suffered unbearable agony like that. No, this was the best, I concluded.

There was the additional problem of the two young men. I had to safeguard them across crevasses and supervise their every movement. Whenever it was time for a rest, the one in front would simply drop to the ground and the other would similarly crumple behind me and I could do nothing but look on. Anderl and I had difficulty instructing them in the simplest basic mountaineering rules; things like climbing down a glacier with crampons. I had to shout loudly, it was the only way I could get through to them. I knew that we still had in front of us a steep pitch of blank ice and that there the greatest difficulties awaited. Once at this impasse, I had to safeguard them step by step downwards, and then follow with the immobile Anderl. At every crevasse I had to traverse until it was a mere crack; only there was it possible to cross. Anderl still took the tiniest of steps. We had already been going five hours and finally had the glacier behind us. But now came rock and moraine that was almost more difficult than the ice. The good thing about this section was that finally I didn't have to worry about the two young men. There was no longer any danger, no crevasses, no fear of slipping; it was just wearisome. We could see the Schönbühlhütte and from time to time tried calling. But there was no-one to be seen.

After another hour, we heard shouts and saw climbers descending the moraine, which we had to reach to gain the hut. We were overjoyed and I was enormously relieved to see them. It would have been quite impossible for me to have overcome the sixty-metre high moraine wall without the help of a rope and a belay from above. Now a climber with a rope came down towards us, which enabled this last obstacle to be overcome.

Above, on the edge of the moraine, was the track to the hut and once there I would be faced with a difficult decision. With the help of the climbers I could be in the hut with Anderl in half an hour, but ought we not get all the injured down to Zermatt right away? Even with assistance from the climbers from the hut we couldn't get the three injured men down to the valley in less than four hours. It had already taken seven from the scene of the accident to the hut path. Moreover, we were all shattered. I tried to talk to Anderl, asked him how he felt. He was of the opinion that if he could rest and be taken care of in half an hour at the hut that would be best. I agreed that to get him into a good comfortable position was top priority. Also he, like the rest of us, needed rest.

We carried Anderl up to the hut in a rope seat, as quickly as possible, but I could see that his condition had deteriorated. That night I stayed up very late working out the method for transporting Anderl down to Zermatt. The Swiss lady, too, had her hands full after our arrival, taking care of Anderl who was completely helpless. The pain of his bruises got steadily worse and began to swell badly. There was also the problem of Lothar and Klaus. Klaus's contusions were giving him a lot of trouble now. He was covered in blue patches with terrible black swellings. I thought by morning he would surely be unable to use his limbs.

I got up very early and got our half-Akya assembled ready to carry Anderl. It was padded with our sleeping bags so that he would be more comfortable, with his legs secured to a bridge splint. Lothar and Klaus seemed to be completely incapable of movement. I explained to them that only exercise would ease their condition and allow them to move again. Once more I had to use strong words to get that message across. Two of the Swiss climbers helped me with the difficult business of evacuating Anderl to Zermatt and things went better for the two young

Saxons once they got going. Anderl was reasonably comfortable on the journey and I was now thankful that I had let him rest in the hut overnight. It had been the right decision.

Arriving in Zermatt, we went straight to the doctor in the hospital. This was purely to have a look and see what was broken. Our resolve to get Anderl back home right away, come what may, was unchanged. He was given a firm, wide strapping over the whole chest. Luckily, the hole in his head turned out to be only a cut, probably caused by his ice axe. His shoulder was back in place and was in order, but it was established that he had a fracture in his cervical vertebrae.

Our car was in St Niklaus and when we fetched Anderl from hospital the next morning, the doctor expressed doubts about the wisdom of the long journey. But we made up a bed padded with sleeping bags by pushing the front passenger seat right back without its back rest. Lying with his legs bent, he travelled without pain over the Furka and Oberalp Passes, then through the upper Rhine Valley. After crossing the border at Oberstdorf, we took Anderl to hospital. A thorough examination revealed that he had also a fracture to a lumbar vertebra together with a fracture of the right clavicle. Six ribs were broken. Since the ribs forced Anderl to lie perfectly still, no plaster cast was necessary for the vertebrae.

Anderl, the first conqueror of the Eiger Nordwand, passed his fiftieth birthday in the hospital. We were both thankful it was all over; after all, we realised, it could have been a lot worse. I have often speculated on what would have happened if I hadn't untied from the rope above the bergschrund. All four of us would then have lain injured on the glacier and help, if it had come at all, would certainly have been too late. Above all, the fact that Lothar Brandler, who was still very young at the time, took the lessons of the accident very much to heart was gratifying. Later he gained extensive experience in ice techniques and, already being a fine rock climber, developed into an outstanding mountaineer.

Plucked from the Pillar

Emmanuel Schmutz

Emmanuel Schmutz has taken part in many evacuations in the Chamonix Alps and, typically of a climber and guide who has to deal with high drama as a daily routine, this tale stands as a memorial to understatement. It is difficult to imagine a more impressive location to enact a rescue. It was completed competently by true professionals.

Nearly fifty per cent of all mountain rescues in France take place in the Mont Blanc massif. The number of incidents increased from about twenty-four a year in 1959 to an average of over three hundred in the 1980s, a frightening escalation in twenty years. In the five-year period up to 1985, 245 climbers have been killed in the Mont Blanc area and over a thousand badly injured. Two-thirds of the accidents occur in July and August when there can be more than two thousand climbers a day on the mountains.

Mountain rescue for the Mont Blanc massif at Chamonix is now based on a specialised unit, the PGHM (Peleton de Gendarmerie de Haute Montagne), about forty strong, most of them guides or aspirant guides. Before, it was the province of the guides of the Chamonix Company, but by 1958 the number of accidents in this overcrowded part of the Alps made people realise it was essential to create an organisation whose sole purpose was mountain rescue. The need for a force like the PGHM was driven home by the tragic accident on Mont Blanc at the end of December 1956. It was obvious on this rescue that the set-up was totally inadequate.

Various other interests were later incorporated within the

structure of the PGHM, the army (EMHM: Ecole Militaire de Haute Montagne), the Ecole Nationale de Ski et d'Alpinisme (ENSA) and the Company of Guides, which provides a back-up to the PGHM.

At present [1987] two Alouette III helicopters which can carry seven people are available. These two machines are owned by the Gendarmerie and the Civil Security and stay in the Chamonix valley during the peak summer period. Their off-mountain duties include the evacuation of road accident casualties and general hospital ambulance duties.

The present policy is to use these helicopters for ninety per cent of mountain rescue situations, which is now possible due to their more powerful turbines and sophisticated winches, able to control a fifty-metre cable.

On a busy day there can be ten rescues; without helicopters it would be impossible, as most of the evacuations are difficult and dangerous, both to patient and rescuer.

In ideal conditions, using the Alouettes, an injured person can be delivered to the Chamonix hospital in as little as ten minutes after the accident. In the past, it would have taken one or even several days, involving dozens of rescuers.

Previously, the guides coming back home exhausted from a rescue had sometimes to set out again the next day. Now, as in other parts of the world, the helicopters have taken much of the drudgery out of the job.

The detail of some tragic rescue is often vividly retained in the rescuer's memory, though the media reports may make little of the tragedy. A major effort on the part of a skilled rescue team may be only a few lines amongst the news items: "The mountain strikes again: Two deaths in the Goûter Couloir . . ." leaving readers indifferent to the suffering of those concerned. For bad news is good news as far as selling papers is concerned.

That's why I've chosen to tell a happy story: a tale of two young people, not really aware of the dangers in the mountains, but fortunately everything turned out well in the end. It could so easily have been a tragedy.

On Saturday 19 June 1976, Paul Vincendon and Didier Hendry set off to climb the South-West Pillar of the Dru. Though it wasn't what they expected, they profited in experience and went forward to maturity. It was the kind of character-building adventure which is said to be so beneficial when you are in your late teens.

Paul and Didier bivouacked in the open at the Rognon de Dru, ready for an early start in the morning. The Rognon de Dru is a wonderful place; one feels overwhelmed by the sheer scale of the West Face above. In daylight, if you're lucky, you can spot climbers like coloured dots, seven or eight hundred metres higher, perhaps at grips with the difficulties of the American Direct, the West Face or the Bonatti Pillar. At night it is certainly one of the most beautiful "bedrooms" an alpinist can imagine. This cathedral of the Mont Blanc massif has attracted millions of people, both climbers and tourists, thanks to the cog railway from Chamonix to Montenvers, the station across the Mer de Glace. From there, with the aid of telescopes, they can fight, slip, sweat, or Walter Mitty-like, believe they are the heroes of an unfair struggle with the smooth and vertical rock of this giant above them.

In the morning our two young men prepared to tackle the first difficulties. Before leaving the valley they had sensibly given their schedule to the OHM (Office de la Haute Montagne), as well as an intended return date from the climb. The OHM was the brainchild of the late Gerard Devoursoux. It supplies information on snow conditions and weather, and also informs the PGHM if a party is overdue.

Though the night was mild, the snow grated under the boys' crampons, indicating that it was freezing. At 5.00 am they crossed the rimaye with the aid of an étrier. They were making fast time. The Dru Couloir, which angles steeply up the bottom of the West Face, is a death trap down which rockfalls thunder unpredictably. Many climbers have been killed and injured here. The Couloir is effectively blocked off at the top end by the wall at the Flammes de Pierre. Here is the start of the Bonatti Pillar, probably the most majestic sweep of rock in the Alps.

It was now 10.00 am. Crampons and ice axes were returned to the rucksacks, for the next few thousand feet would be rock climbing. Paul and Didier were relieved to be out of the Valley of Death. But their shoulders already ached with their large rucksacks, even the minimum is too heavy. Both boys had been training hard for this expedition; first at the climbing school, then on their own, wearing climbing boots on exacting rock routes rather than the specialised lightweight ones favoured by climbers for hard rock problems on lower crags. On such serious climbs as the Bonatti Pillar the axiom is let's not get too ethical: if there is a peg in a crack you use it. There's no one about to point an accusing finger. Time and storms are the adversary.

If the telescope addicts were in position below they would be thinking in headlines. "Cheating Death by the Skin of Their Teeth", watching them thrutching up a Grade IV athletic! They probably wouldn't know that the IV of the Mont Blanc massif is often harder than a Grade V in the Vercors or Calanques.

In the Mont Blanc massif guide, the route doesn't seem frightening when you read the description "V, A1, A2" and so on. There never seems to be exceptional difficulty. However, the truth can quickly be felt in the arms, especially with the dead weight of the rucksack hanging from your shoulders.

The two men agreed to lead alternate pitches. But after the second one, Didier, the weaker of the two, let Paul go first. It was soon clear to Paul that the climb was too serious for his companion who was making heavy weather of the difficulties and seemed to take ages.

Time was slipping by, but they didn't even eat, and in the afternoon, the weather became overcast, more like August than June. A violent hailstorm swept over them with devastating suddenness, followed by torrential rain. They were forced to bivouac where they were, soaked and frozen.

Making the best of a bad job they settled down for the night on a minuscule ledge. Later the clouds cleared, giving way to a cold which seemed to settle into their bone marrow. There was no hot food to eat, they had left their stove behind to save weight. Even so, they were still in high spirits; such is the temperament of mountaineers.

The stars glimmered that night, glimmered with cold. If only the sky could be overcast, Paul thought, it would be a bit warmer at least. Getting going in the morning was hard; they had had a sleepless night. And on this South-West Pillar the sun does not get round to thawing out frozen cracks and numbed muscles before the end of the morning. But the sky was now azure blue and the young men had no desire to retreat. They felt optimistic, despite the desperate night. So they pressed on, Paul still out front: he had already completed some major climbs in other parts of the Alps and was confident he could lead his friend to the summit.

Each year younger and younger climbers tackle fashionable routes, especially rock climbs such as the American Direct on the West Face of the Dru, or the Dru Couloir. Their record times are evidence of this youth revolution: North Face of the Droites, three hours; West Face of the Dru (solo), three hours ten minutes; Grand Pilier d'Angle, three hours; each year faster and faster: now the Matterhorn North Wall, the Eigerwand *and* the Grandes Jorasses in a day! Paul hadn't yet graduated to this elite band.

Immediately after leaving the bivouac Paul had to tackle a testing pitch, made worse by the cold. The crack was graded IV athletic but it was hard. Didier, when it was his turn, climbed up the rope, assisted by Paul.

An artificial pitch left them in a cold sweat. The wooden wedges inserted by earlier climbers looked as if they had been manufactured from offcuts left over from the Ark.

Paul felt sure that they must be the first party to do the route that year. It was necessary to check every piton, every wedge. In 1976 aluminium wedges or chocks weren't widely used by French climbers and they tended to use pitons whose regular insertion and removal from the cracks left permanent scars.

After climbing for some hours, the two men found themselves at the bottom of the Red Wall. All the pegs were dubious and some positively insecure, and already half a day had vanished. They swallowed some nuts for lunch.

Further up is the Austrians' Crack and Paul started a new pitch which should take him to the bottom of this fissure which goes through a small dihedral at Grade V, then up a slab. But a peg at arm's length looked unsafe. To avoid it, he decided to move right to a small overhang, then up an easy crack.

There was a good wooden wedge in this overhang. Without thinking, Paul asked for some slack rope and clipped on to it with a karabiner. He realised as he continued that he did not have enough security, retreated to the wooden wedge and then clipped to a peg just below. He then attached his étrier to it and stood up – but not for long! Suddenly he was falling, rock was passing in front of his eyes; he struck a protruding piece of it and felt a stabbing pain in both thigh and ankle. After thirty feet he stopped abruptly and swung gently to and fro, horrified to see that a strand of the rope was cut just above him by the sharp edge of the rock.

Didier, apparently more shocked than Paul, desperately pulled him in to the stance. Paul had a struggle because of his aching right ankle, also his harness was cutting into his thigh and he thought he might have broken his leg.

There was nothing more they could do that day, it was 2.00 pm and Paul was stiffening up. He saw a small ledge below and they succeeded in getting to this tiny sanctuary poised high above the Couloir which they had climbed, what felt to them, so long ago. Gratefully they sat down. A short time later, in the middle of the afternoon, another storm blew up. They curled up against each other to keep warm, there was nothing else they could do. Lightning flickered round the Dru in a heavenly electrical display. Repeated shocks racked their bodies. Being soaked to the skin didn't help matters either. Later the skies cleared and a biting frost enveloped the mountains. It was going to be another frigid night.

Around 7.30 pm they heard the throb of a helicopter coming close. Having told the OHM that they expected to be down that evening, they thought it must be coming to see if they were in difficulties. But the helicopter didn't arrive. It was on another mission.

They decided to stay where they were the following day in order to rest and in case the pilot had seen them but couldn't get close enough and would try again next day.

This night between Monday and Tuesday was as cold as the previous ones. Their food had almost run out. When dawn broke, they saw the day was fine, but the sun, as ever, took time to reach them with its warmth. They could not face another day on that lonely ledge. There was still no sign of rescue, so they decided to try to get off on their own by taking the Weber route, a traverse which would allow them to escape across to the top of the Flammes de Pierre and then on to the normal route for the Petit Dru. Paul was unsure how his injuries would fare in this ambitious last-ditch bid to get back down to the Charpoua Refuge. A further short violent storm punctuated the end of the day, in which both climbers suffered more electric shocks and were again saturated. At 7.30 pm they heard a helicopter once more. This time it came closer and closer and hovered in front of them. Now they knew that they hadn't been forgotten. They made the conventional signals of distress, raising both arms in a V, meaning Yes, we need help.

Because it was so late, the PGHM decided to postpone the rescue operation till the following day, Wednesday.

That evening a team of eight of the most experienced rescuers was selected, and a quantity of equipment prepared to get the two climbers off the Weber route to the Flammes de Pierre. An essential item of equipment, the Pomagalski winch, was put in a rucksack. Being both heavy and difficult to carry, it was usually the responsibility of the latest recruit.

Very early on Wednesday 23 June the rescuers were warned by the Met Office that they would have a storm during the afternoon. But when? They could only hope they would beat it back before it broke. At first light, around 5.00 am, the rescue team were winched from the helicopter on to a small shelf on the edge of the Flammes de Pierre, some 250 metres above and to the side of the ledge where the two climbers were.

The problem for the rescue team was not in the vertical distance but in the horizontal one between them and the climbers. It is easy to rope down or to use a cable from a point directly above an injured party. But when traverses are involved, the problems escalate. They didn't know much about Paul and Didier, or if one or even both were injured. If it were a serious injury, evacuation was going to be highly technical.

As soon as they landed, the rescuers started to fix ropes across the difficult face above the climbers. Their rucksacks were heavy and made this manoeuvre hazardous. Eventually they found a steeply angled ledge, almost directly above the boys. They were now about a hundred metres above. It was essential to find cracks from which to secure the winch to pitons. Here, however, the rock was very compact and they had to make the best of a bad lot of belays; it seemed impossible to get a good piton in. Finally around 10.00 am (five hours after having been landed from the helicopter) they got the winch in place.

Even with the dodgy belays there was a volunteer ready to go down on the thin cable. It was Alan, one of the guides, who went down with a walkie-talkie. The lowering operation is fairly simple, just a matter of braking with the winch, which doesn't require much effort. After about eighty metres Alan had to make a tricky pendulum to get round a rock edge. He made it and arrived at the two climbers, who hailed him as if he were the Messiah.

Time was slipping away and they decided to winch up the three men together. Even though the winch can lift over a ton, the effort required from the rescuers was going to be considerable on the cramped and dangerous stance.

They knew that it would take the six of them nearly two hours to get the three men to their ledge. Later they were to realise that it would have been better to do it in two operations instead of one. That would involve two men at a time because you needed to keep a rescuer on the cable to prevent it penduluming. Eventually, after much sweating, they got the three men up to that uncomfortable ledge at half-past twelve.

The rescuers didn't mutter about the incompetence of the two climbers. There was only the satisfaction of having completed a difficult and dangerous job successfully.

From their lofty perch they could now see that the sky, which they had forgotten to look at, was getting darker. Another storm was almost upon them. Within a few minutes all hell broke loose, the same ingredients as the two men had experienced before. Lightning, rain and snow. They had to tie on to prevent themselves being plucked off the face.

Everybody was soaked to the skin. The sodden ropes froze into steel hawsers and the rescuers realised what Paul and Didier had been through in the earlier storms. They were lucky to have survived.

The problem now was how to get down. Just then it was out of the question to make a move. To untie from the safety ropes would have been suicidal. But if the helicopter didn't return they would have to start considering the long and laborious way down the frozen rock, towards the glacier and the Charpoua Refuge. Just when they had decided on this drastic course of action, which would mean leaving their heavy gear to be picked up later, they heard the comforting beat of the Alouette through the cloud. What a relief!

Over the radio the rescuers were told that both helicopters

were hoping to pick them up. It was to be a personal challenge for the rescue pilots. The machines inched their way towards that exposed rocky outpost. The first helicopter hovered overhead. Didier and Paul were winched aboard. In minutes, they were borne from that harsh environment to the Chamonix hospital. The second helicopter managed to get a skid on to the granite edge of the rock and eventually all the team were taken off. Paul fortunately had only sustained severe bruising and was shortly to be climbing again.

That night, the rescuers met in a restaurant to celebrate the success of the operation. They felt it was a call-out of considerable technical difficulty which doesn't happen too often these days, and what was even more important it had a happy ending.

An Airborne Avalanche
Detective work in the Tatras

Miloš Vrba

An avalanche to the layman is often simply regarded as a mass of snow shooting down a mountain, just like a load of sand or gravel being tipped off a truck. The word avalanche is an all embracing one conveying everything from rock falls to soggy messes of slithering mud and earth which can be a serious problem in some countries in the spring thaw. Then there are the thoroughbreds of ice, powder snow, wet-snow and an assortment of slab avalanches, or indeed combinations of all these.

Avalanches are just one of many dangers sprung on the unwary by mountains. They can descend with devastating force, but they are not all in a hurry. A small wet avalanche can tumble down a slope as if it had all the time in the world, but its more flighty brother, the airborne powder avalanche can scour a face in a blast of destruction, reaching speeds of over 200 mph. It can rip reinforced concrete to pieces, leaving only a skeleton of steel and reduce villages and even towns to their foundations.

Up till the early 1960s very little notice was taken of avalanches in Britain. It is true that climbers were injured and killed by them on occasions, but they were considered to be an act of God. Later, however, once the ice climbing revolution got under way in the mid 1960s, the number of mountaineers on the hills rose dramatically in winter; and so inevitably more were caught in avalanches.

One of the earliest recorded avalanches in Scotland is shrouded in folklore and legend, but the bare facts are interesting enough. A certain Captain MacPherson was known as the "Black Officer"; he was a despised recruiting officer, with whom many felt they had a score to settle. At one time he was reputed to have given a ball at Ballachroan and sent invitations to all the young bloods of the district. Though it wasn't a fancy dress ball, the wily captain had laid out a selection of smart red coats for the young men to try on, which they did with alacrity and laughter. Once resplendent in the uniforms they had signed their destiny. The captain's soldiers descended and pressed them into the service of the King. But in the end it was the Almighty who took vengeance and so the people of the district considered his death a fitting judgment.

On the 11 January, 1800 by the new calendar, but Old Yule according to the reckoning of the time, MacPherson and four other Highlanders went to Gaik, a remote bothy in the Cairngorms, to stalk. There were no witnesses to the catastrophe, other than perhaps a golden eagle or a red deer, when the avalanche thundered over that lonely lodge. The five men were buried and killed.

It was probably a wet-snow avalanche and it took the lodge apart as if it were made from old orange boxes. When a search party went up to look for the overdue hunters they were flabbergasted at the devastation, but they didn't have any tools with them to dig down to where the lodge had been, so they returned to Speyside and came back the next day with reinforcements, picks and shovels. They recovered four bodies including that of the Black Officer. The last man had been carried some way by the avalanche and was found much later in the year when the snow melted. The tremendous grinding force of the avalanche had twisted the hunters' guns which were found in the debris of the building. The accident created a lot of speculation at the time, for the Black Officer was said to to have been a buddy of Auld Nick as well as having other nefarious associations. A predecessor of McGonagall wrote:

. . . Gashed, torn by the demon, the merciless foe,
  In Gaick lie their corpses deeply swathed in the snow.

It is said that to be involved in an avalanche is to have one foot in the grave. When I began to take an academic interest in snow structure and avalanches in the early 1960s, I had already fallen foul of three, so I had more than a passing interest in them and, presumably, I already had a foot in three graves. Abiding by the axiom "better late than never", I read all I could on the subject. Some may wryly point out that as I've been engulfed in three more avalanches subsequently, these studies haven't done me much good! But most of these personal encounters and rapid descents were either in the Himalayas when caught out in bad weather, or on actual rescues on ground where, like a sensible angel, I would normally have feared to tread.

I resolved, however, to do something constructive about avalanche search in Scotland after looking for a buried climber, Professor Lata, who had been swept down in a small avalanche from the Aonach Eagach Ridge in Glencoe. It was really an apology for an avalanche – a narrow ribbon of snow which had slid down like a stair-runner for a thousand feet. But it was wet snow with virtually no air content. Burial in such liquid porridge, should there be no air trapped between the snow boulders, is fatal. The Professor's companion got free and fortunately survived. I had my dog with me when we started searching for the buried climber, but in those days we had no dogs trained for avalanche search and when she started to dig enthusiastically at the edge of the debris, which I thought was an unlikely place, I called her away. Next day we found the Professor's body where the dog had been digging.

In 1965 the Scottish branch of the British Red Cross sponsored my visit to the Swiss Avalanche Dog Course based near Davos. When I returned I started the Search and Rescue Dog Association and we held the first training course in Glencoe that winter. Though the dogs were to be primarily used for avalanche search, we incorporated in their training summer search technique, for locating people lost on hill and moorland. We had made a start.

I wasn't the only person with an interest in snow structure. Eric Langmuir, then the Principal of Glenmore Lodge, a government training centre in the Cairngorms, was engrossed in the subject and later became a leading authority on avalanches in Britain.

Eric made countless climbers and skiers aware of avalanche danger and also of the fascination of snow in all its varied forms. He invited Miloš Vrba, a Czech, to visit Scotland and lecture on the subject. At that time Miloš was an avalanche expert with the Czech Government and a member of the Horska Sluzba, their national mountain rescue service.

I first met Miloš when he came to Glencoe to talk to our rescue team and next day he gave us a demonstration on the hills. He surprised us, after he had taken a snow profile, by saying that he considered the snow unstable and dangerous. We were even more

*surprised next day when we found that he had been right. The snow
had avalanched overnight.*

*Miloš is a stocky man with precise speech and a perpetual
twinkle in his eye. We became good friends and later Eric and I
visited him in Czechoslovakia. Our whistle-stop tour with the
Horska Sluzba included a short stay in the Low Tatra; country
not unlike the Cairngorms with rolling hills which seem to invite
you to walk them. It winter they are snow-covered and give a
feeling of infinite space; in the forests on the lower slopes silence
prevails, only broken by the soughing of the pines. The sort of area
where one could imagine Good King Wenceslas with foot-weary
page hirpling through oxter-deep powder.*

*But the sequence of events which Miloš now relates are not
tranquil. It all started on a day in 1956 when hell broke loose in a
thunder like peal.*

The forester walked up and down in the roomy chamber of his
old wooden lodge, hands in pockets, gloomy, nervous. Nobody
remembered such a relentless snowstorm as this at the beginning of March. Yet there was no sign of any change. On the
contrary, it had been getting from bad to worse. It was nearly
dark in the room. The snowdrifts more than half covered the
small windows and the cloudy daylight hardly got in. The cribs
were empty and the deer were hungry. But it was quite impossible to think of going out with food for the poor animals.
The best friend of the middle-aged bearded man did not share
his master's troubles. The dog slept quietly in a corner.

If he could at least have a game of cards with the loggers
above. In normal conditions twenty minutes' walk would take
him to their hut and he could have a good time in a warm smoky
room with those hard woodsmen, some shuffling, cutting,
dealing; others telling stories into the night. Now, only a fool
would try to go there.

Living in such a lonely place was not a simple matter. One
must be constantly busy. Inactivity in solitude makes people
nervous and quarrelsome. No doubt the loggers above did
quarrel, especially at cards, but at least they had a choice.
Among twenty people you can always find a new partner either
for companionship or for a quarrel. However, to live only with a
quarrelsome female under one roof, that's martyrdom, the

forester reflected. No pipe allowed, each microscopic bit of rubbish discussed. Now such a clattering of pots and pans in the kitchen; it gets on one's nerves.

The loggers could at least swear at each other, man to man, and give vent to their furies. Twenty lumberjacks have a rich verbal reserve! But there were not twenty today – only nineteen. Jim left yesterday. Did he make it, the forester wondered? Probably, he reached town all right. It must have been difficult, though. If one could but telephone. However, as usual, the wires were broken under heavy icing and snow. The underground telephone cable will probably never be laid. No-one worries about such a forgotten forest lodge in the mountains and who would spend money for twelve kilometres of telephone cable? Certainly not the telephone company.

Time was dragging terribly. It was only half past nine in the morning.

There was a deep-throated rumble and the dog suddenly jumped up. It was always afraid of thunderstorms. It was true, though, that long low roar was really strange and there was no lightning. A thunderstorm on the 8th March? It was not usual, he thought, but here, in the Low Tatra of Czechoslovakia, it was not exceptional. We sometimes even have them at Christmas and New Year, so it's not so surprising, he assured himself.

The dog showed no inclination to go on sleeping. On the contrary, he grew restless and was obviously frightened. He followed his master step by step as the forester paced the low room, for he too felt uneasy. Finally, he sat down. So did the dog; close to the chair, staring at his master's face.

"Did you hear the thunder?" the grey head of the forester's wife appeared in the half opened door.

"Yes." The terse answer indicated that her husband did not feel like talking.

Nevertheless, the woman continued, "It's said to be a bad harvest when thunderstorms come so early."

Another deep thundering roar; this time stronger. The old wooden house trembled on its foundations. Still, no lightning, though that thunder must have been very close.

The dog howled and hid under the bed.

Darkness fell and a great wind broke tree-tops, some of which fell on to the roof. There was a crash of glass in the loft. Even the forester was taken aback. In order to camouflage his concern he reached for the pipe which was normally strictly forbidden in the room because it produced an awful smell, but now his wife did not take any notice. She only crossed herself and prayed.

"May be it's the Last Day," she said quietly, resigned to what may come.

"Perhaps Old Nick will take you off to hell," the forester replied jokingly in an attempt to boost their morale. He wanted to keep his wife in the room. Fear brings people together and they were both frightened. The dog slunk out from beneath the bed to under his master's legs.

The forester finally filled his pipe and lit a match. His hand shook. Neither of them could think of anything to say – it seemed as if time had stopped. They were not able to share their anxiety and to express their emotions. They both, however, instinctively felt that something must have happened, something quite terrible.

Their uncertainty was shattered by a heavy blow on the lodge door. The dog ran to it barking like mad, followed by the forester and his wife. When he opened it, a cloud of whirling snow burst into the passage and a man fell over the doorstep. They drew him in and quickly closed the door.

It was John, one of the loggers from the hut above. He was covered in blood and dressed only in a torn night-shirt. His bare legs were partially wrapped up in material obviously torn off the shirt. He was now unconscious, having passed out as soon as he fell through the doorway, and had multiple bleeding surface wounds but, at first sight, nothing more serious. They laid him gently on the bed.

He soon came round and opened his eyes.

"Tell me, Johnny, what has happened?" the forester asked quietly, but urgently.

"Explosion . . . There was this great blast . . ." John said with difficulty and closed his eyes again.

"Take care of him," the forester ordered his wife, "I'm going up there with the dog!"

The walk in deep powder snow and through muscle-aching drifts reaching a height of two metres was exhausting for both man and dog. The forester had the advantage as he wore snowshoes, while the dog's paws sank deeply into the powder and his master was obliged to help and even carry the poor animal over deep sections.

The snowstorm permitted only limited visibility – a mere couple of steps and the forester quickly lost any idea of distance and time. It seemed to be an endless white hell. He felt tired and was obliged to have a rest and leant against a tree. Immediately he was alarmed for he realised that it was one of the last trees and beyond nothing but a white emptiness. Where is the forest, he asked himself? Where are the old high spruces? He must have lost the way, he thought. But that was out of the question. He knew the way as well in darkness as in daylight, summer or winter. The forest had simply disappeared!

He stepped forward like a sleepwalker, having forgotten about his dog. The beast followed, wallowing through the snow masses. Fighting on through the whirling whiteness the forester reached a drift that looked like a swelling wave. Up until now he had sunk deeply into the white cover despite his snow-shoes, now the walking was surprisingly easy. He felt a hard base lightly covered with powder snow. He scraped away that thin surface layer and saw an ice-hard brownish snow beneath, full of stones, earth, twigs and needles. Incredible! What had happened, he wondered? Everything around had changed and now this strange snow! An explosion? What sort of explosion?

The dog sniffed, barked briefly and ran uphill, quickly disappearing in the whirling snow. The forester followed the dog's prints and soon he heard the sharp bark that he knew was a sign of some important discovery. Indeed, when he saw the dog it was digging and sniffing the snow.

When the forester came nearer he shuddered. The dog had uncovered two human bodies buried in the surface snowlayer. He quickly removed the snow from their heads and recognised two of the loggers. They were alive. He shook them and thumped their backs hard. This crude treatment seemed to have the desired effect for they opened their eyes, and stared dully but did not respond to the forester's questions. The dog did not mind their miserable condition. He jumped, barked, wagged his short tail with joy and licked the cheeks of his good friends.

The forester praised the dog and was about to tell it to sit when the animal disappeared. It had got a fresh scent. The warning barks changed to friendly ones and in a couple of minutes it returned out of the white snow-screen, jumping cheerfully in front of two men – evidently people it knew. The forester saw it was two young lumberjacks from another forest camp close by.

It was chance that they had left their mountain hut in a neighbouring forest, for they had run out of food. Taking shelter from the storm on the way back they, too, had been frightened by the "thunder". They had been heading back to their hut when the forester's dog scented them. Just as well it did, for its master would not have been able to evacuate the two men who were buried and they would surely have died if left.

"Hello, Charlie!" the older of the two men addressed the forester, "what the blazes has happened here? It doesn't make sense. We called at your lodge. Your wife's crossing herself and talking about Doomsday, John's lying on the bed bleeding and blabbering something about an explosion and these two blokes here looking as if they have just fallen from the moon. What the hell is going on?"

"As I see it, lads, a big avalanche must have come down. I've never known anything like it. I can't even imagine how it could be possible in this deep forest and so far from the mountains. But, no doubt, it was an avalanche. And I'm afraid that all the others from the hut must have been buried. You had better get these two to the lodge quickly, in case they are seriously injured."

"Right," said one of the woodsmen. "We'll take care of these two."

"Good. Then I'll have a quick look round with the dog," returned Charlie, "to see if there is anyone else to be found. Afterwards I'll go down to the village to ring for help. Our phone's out of order, as usual."

Though the dog worked well, it didn't find anything else. Finally it went out of the avalanche cone and sniffed at the base of one of the remaining trees. The forester assumed that the dog had lost interest, so decided to discontinue the search and go down to phone. However, just then the dog barked, calling him.

"What's the matter, you old fool?" he spoke to the dog good-naturedly. "You're outside the avalanche path here." But nevertheless he unwillingly went over to it, and quickly changed his opinion of his canine friend. The dog was no fool, for under a thin powder layer there were dark red spots of blood in the snow. Not only blood but also traces, shapes, strange impressions: not from bare feet, nor boots, nor snow-shoes. Simply shapeless hollows leading away from the tree, but surely made by a human being not by an animal.

The dog went on sniffing at the tree. However, he did not lift up his hind leg, as he would have done had another animal left its visiting card, but stood up on his back legs, his fore paws against the tree trunk and continued sniffing. The forester was puzzled because he saw above only broken branches, as on the other remaining trees. However, with careful examination he found hanging from the tree trunk a long drop of freezing congealing blood, almost black in appearance. Looking up again he saw a weird sight: a piece of John's night-shirt on a broken branch, high above the snow level.

What on earth had made John climb the tree? he asked himself. He had presumably fallen down from that branch, hurt himself and afterwards crawled downhill, leaving those strange hollow indentations with his knees which he had protected with torn pieces of his night-shirt.

There were too many unknown factors about this whole tragedy; he must get help urgently. Before noon the forester rushed into the village headman's house and described the situation, whilst still getting his breath.

"Charlie, I cannot believe that it was an avalanche," the headman said. "Couldn't it, after all, have been an explosion as John said? Tell me, have you ever seen or heard from your father or grandfather of an avalanche in the neighbourhood of your lodge? Don't forget that great barrier of forest separating you from the avalanche slopes higher up! I'm almost sure . . ."

"You're quite right, Tom," Charlie interrupted, "but time is running out. Whether it was an avalanche or an explosion is all the same now. Sixteen people are very likely still buried and another three lie in my lodge, perhaps critically injured. Do something! Telephone for help!"

"But, I've no idea what to do. Who've I got to call?"

"Everyone! Mountain rescue service, police, army, hospital, fire brigades. Simply everyone. The more the better! We need a lot of people, shovels, picks, saws, axes, food, bulldozers and I don't know what else. They will know. But, for heaven's sake, make those phone calls, Tom! Every minute is vital."

"Yes, I understand, Charlie. But I think you had better do it yourself!"

That day, in the early afternoon, I received a cable: AVA-LANCHE ACCIDENT LOW TATRA SOUTH. NINETEEN PEOPLE BURIED. AVALANCHE EXPERT NEEDED. COME PROMPTLY BY AIR-TAXI. CAR WAITING AIRPORT BANSKA BYSTRICA. The cable was signed by Joe, Rescue Chief of the Low Tatra South district. Joe was my good friend.

Great! In a trice everything turned upside down. The accident happened 400 kilometers as the crow flies from Prague where I was up to my ears with work. Instead of concentrating all my thoughts on the main problem of what to take with me, I began to speculate where the avalanche accident might have happened. I was a little confused because I knew very little of those southerly slopes of the seventy kilometre-long mountain chain. The majority of that hillside was inaccessible then, far from roads and railway, without hotels, lodges marked routes, downhill runs, chairlifts or ski-tows. Really, virgin mountain country with the only exception being the southern part of Chopok.

Deliberating on these things I lost a lot of precious time. But in spite of this I landed at Banska Bystrica airport by five pm and immediately went on by mountain rescue service car. The young man who met me couldn't tell me much because he himself knew little. He was, however, a skilled driver who, in spite of the twisting narrow roads, snowdrifts and ice, covered the fifty kilometers to the village Dolna Lehota within the hour.

It was from this village that the SOS call had been sent several hours previously, a small Slovakian mountain village in the old style, with low wooden cottages, a quiet idyllic place. But when I arrived this was no longer the case. Military vehicles, soldiers, lighting and telephone cables were everywhere with the unhappy villagers looking on in amazement.

I didn't have much time to take all this in but was impressed how much had already been done. I sensed that there was a good feeling of fellowship amongst the rescuers, a voluntary unit, a blend of intellect will and technical expertise whose common aim was to save human lives. Aware of these high ideals, I entered the village headman's house.

It now served as the headquarters of the commanding officer. The high-ranking army officer did not let anyone forget that he was appointed as lord of the avalanche and that everybody must comply with his orders without hesitation.

"You're late!" he greeted me with those tense words and a firm hand-shake. "Will you have a drink?"

"Thanks."

"Let's start immediately," he continued, "you are said to be an avalanche expert. Let's hope so." He looked at me steadily. "As you have probably seen, the army has undertaken the rescue operation, as we have the necessary equipment and men. But you must help us because we have no experience with avalanches. My second in command is avalanche commander above in the search area and he's been told to carry out your orders. The position is this," he cleared his throat, "there are about two hundred people above. Tomorrow, if necessary, there will be three or four hundred. You are fully responsible for their safety. Do you understand? You must safeguard them against further avalanche danger!"

"No, sir, I do not agree to your conditions!"

My reply took the officer unawares – he wasn't used to being talked to like this. His mouth closed with a click of teeth – I continued before he recovered.

"After eight days of snowfall there is a general avalanche hazard. That's all I can tell you. If you have taken on the overall responsibility for this rescue you must also reckon with the risk. I can only assure you that I'll assess the snow situation on the avalanche slopes above as soon as it is possible. Now it is getting dark and I can't do it until first light. I must tell you, too, that I've never been in this region before. I don't know it and won't tell you any fairy tales!"

"All right," he said slowly, "your points sound sensible. I'll ring up the avalanche commander. You go up there in about half an hour. I'll give you a tracked vehicle and a driver at your permanent disposal. Here is a large scale map of the area and I won't try to influence your decision tonight. It's your decision whether you will let the rescue go on, or stop it till tomorrow. I have ordered a helicopter for the early morning to observe the situation from the air. You will want to use this, I presume."

"For heaven's sake, no helicopter, no airplane, no noisy machinery at all!"

"Why the hell not?"

"The noise and the air turbulence of low flying aircraft could release additional snow masses and cause avalanches that might threaten your soldiers and the others as well."

"Yes, I see," he mused, rubbing his chin. I think he was beginning to appreciate that there was more to an avalanche than a pile of snow.

We went up as far as the forest lodge. The narrow road had been cleared and made wide enough for vehicles moving in one direction only. The traffic was controlled by the police.

Beyond this, I had to walk. It was not far, some 400 or 500 metres as far as I could judge in the dark. The trail was hard packed and wide, having been trampled by hundreds of feet. Somewhere in the dark to the right a diesel engine throbbed and the battery of lights ahead indicated my final destination.

In the harsh glare of searchlights I felt myself lost amongst a mass of busy people, mostly soldiers. However, Joe walked out from the dark, having seen me. Instead of friendly words of greeting he shone a powerful light on six mangled corpses lying on the dirty snow.

I was shocked. It was such a horrid spectacle that I was obliged to transform it in my imagination and thought of it as a Shakespearean tragedy in a theatre. A velvet-black background contrasting with the sharply illuminated foreground, the lights being focussed upon the terrible scene. A brilliant arrangement of light and shadow, indeed; Shakespeare himself wouldn't have prescribed such a cruelty. The only woman among those six corpses was scalped. Her long black hair laid out beside her bloody bald head.

". . . hardly 900 metres above sea level . . . no avalanche as yet . . ." I caught only fragments of Joe's speech; he must have been speaking for some time. I was full of horror and couldn't concentrate. I was simply not there.

". . . we wanted to probe but it was quite impossible . . . ice-hard snow . . . probes bent and broke . . . what do you say to this system of lengthwise and transverse corridors?"

"What? Sorry, Joe, I didn't get that."

"Parallel corridors or channels! Two metres apart. It was my idea to dig them and to probe horizontally from within. The snow is hard on the surface only, whereas one or two metres down it's possible to probe. When I saw so much manpower and tools it occurred to me to make use of them. It seems the only possible way to search the avalanche tip. There are also lots of tree trunks in the debris that must be cut. Do you think this is a sensible method of searching?" he asked me anxiously.

"Sure. Good work, Joe. I doubt whether such an idea would have occurred to me. Really first class. But tell me, why did you start just in this area? Was it intuition or lucky chance?"

"Neither. We started to dig in the same place where the forester's dog discovered two living men and where the forester himself found traces of one man who wasn't buried, but fell down . . ."

"Yes, I know. I've heard the story already," I told him. "Nine victims found in such a small area! Incredible."

"Yes, that's right. These six were discovered at a depth of about two metres. The dog couldn't scent them. It isn't a trained avalanche dog, of course."

"Your corridors are pretty deep. About five metres, aren't they?"

"Some even seven metres!" he returned.

"Joe, I think there are too many people concentrated in one area. Isn't it possible to enlarge the search area?"

"You had better tell it to the commander. He's just coming. I'll introduce you."

The avalanche commander was a young officer of lower rank. At first sight he appeared self-confident and energetic. I realised he expected something different where I was concerned. He surely thought I'd be some sort of superman, with an inscrutable expression, who would confidently point in an instant to where the missing ten persons were to be found. Instead, I presented the figure of quite an ordinary human being called an avalanche expert. Fortunately, he was immediately called to the phone in the signals tent, so that our first impressions were brief and we didn't exchange a word.

Later, when he returned, he came with an inconspicuous man.

"This is the forester," Joe made the introductions.

I immediately found the forester sympathetic; he was a man of the outdoors.

"Would you mind, Mr . . ., I am sorry, I didn't catch your name?"

"Call me Charlie like the others used to." He nodded towards the avalanche debris.

"Well, Charlie," I began, "could you tell me the story of the avalanche from the very beginning? You seem to be the only reliable witness and I must know all that's happened."

He described the events as he knew them, slowly but briefly. Suddenly I had a feeling of being observed by somebody. I was, but it was the dog who'd fixed his bright amber gaze upon me. When our eyes met I smiled and the dog wagged his short tail – our friendship was sealed.

Charlie noticed this and said, "This is my dog, Brok. I'm sure he's the only hero of this terrible day, though he's not aware of it."

"Tell me, Charlie, can you locate the lumberjacks' hut?"

"No, I can't. Everything has changed, and I'm puzzled. Maybe tomorrow in daylight. However, I still haven't finished the avalanche story," he continued. "I don't understand why John climbed that tree over there, you can see it silhouetted in the dark. What do you make of it?"

"Have you tried talking with him since he came round?"

"No, they took them all off to the hospital."

"I'm puzzled as well, Charlie. I don't understand it either."

Joe, Charlie and I sat down on a broken tree trunk near a fire made by the soldiers. The fire slowly sank down into a snow hollow. Brok, making the most of the pleasant heat, was cuddled upon a sack and soon fast asleep.

The young officer came back. He had probably received further orders from the C.O., for he immediately asked me for instructions.

"I understand," I answered, "you are in command of about 200 soldiers and policemen."

"Correct," the officer agreed, "most of them are working on the avalanche, the rest on the road, the generator and communications. There are also the cooks, lorry and bulldozer drivers. Then there is the medical staff. There are another sixteen mountain rescue personnel. However, they are under the command of the rescue chief here." He nodded towards Joe.

"Have you really sixteen people available, Joe? I've seen about half that number. Where are they all?"

"I'll tell you later," Joe said mysteriously.

I thought Joe's reply odd, but didn't pursue it just then.

"Tell me," I addressed the officer again, "when did you discover those six victims?"

"About three hours ago. They were found practically all at once, certainly within fifteen or twenty minutes."

"And since then, what else did you find?"

"Nothing. Oh, yes, there was a pocket watch belonging to one of the dead men."

"I see." I deliberated, then continued, "I think little more will be discovered in that area. A lot of people are wasting their energy and they cannot work properly as they are too concentrated. Let's arrange the search more effectively. Unless you have any objections, sir, I would recommend you to allow only fifty people to work here to enlarge the corridors, and another hundred should start the same operation at the end of the avalanche cone and work uphill."

"Are you sure that the missing ten men may be there?"

"No, I am not. But this is normal procedure for avalanche search if no other facts are known, and at the present I don't know any other facts. Unless someone can give you further information that could change my instructions? No? Well, I haven't, for example, any idea of where the hut was. I cannot, therefore, but recommend that you start digging at the end of the avalanche tip."

"All right, sir, I'll do it according to your instructions," the officer agreed, "but I have another twelve soldiers at my disposal. Am I to let them work here or send them down to the end of the avalanche tip?"

"No, I've an idea how best to employ those twelve men. I have seen that the rescuers piss any old place on the avalanche. Tomorrow morning an avalanche dog from High Tatra will arrive and such distractions will interfere with its work. Have these twelve men build latrines somewhere in the wood. Nobody should be allowed to pollute the avalanche further. You must give these orders immediately."

The officer's face was a picture of disenchantment. Such a mundane matter, piss houses indeed!

Up till then Charlie had been silent and meditatively smoking his pipe, but when the officer and Joe left he turned to me.

"I think you are right that nobody else will be found in this hollow. I was well acquainted with all the people from the hut. Those discovered in this small area, including John and the two men found by Brok before noon, came from one village and lived together in one room."

"And what about the dead woman?" I asked.

"She was their cook. Loggers from another village lived together in the second room. There was always rivalry between those two groups. The women caused most of the quarrels. You can well imagine the situation: eighteen virile men and two wives. The corridor between the two rooms often formed a boundary that couldn't be crossed."

"Wait a minute, Charlie! Eighteen men and two women. Unless I'm mistaken, that's twenty people and not nineteen! I was told that there were nineteen people in the hut, not twenty!"

"That's right," Charlie answered slowly, "one of them, called Jim, left for town yesterday as he has to stand trial today. He sells pigs on the black market and is charged with tax evasion. That swindle has saved his life."

"Did he live in the same room as the others discovered here?" I pointed to the holes in the avalanche.

"Yes, he did and, as I said, all in that room have been found. Now we must concentrate the search for the ten missing people from the other room."

It was midnight. The snow had stopped falling some time before; the wind had dropped, but now fog slowly crept in. Anonymous figures moved in it like blurred shadows on a screen.

Charlie with Brok had left half an hour ago and I sat on the broken tree trunk alone, thinking. They were not pleasant thoughts. I was helpless and could do nothing but wait. There was too little known about the circumstances of the tragedy and the known fragments of the jig-saw didn't help me to find a reasonable solution.

A phantom-like figure coming out of the damp fog turned out

to be the long absent Joe. He was accompanied by a pleasant smell of warm food for there was a soldier with him with a dixy of hot goulash soup. I suddenly felt awfully hungry because I had not eaten since morning.

As I tucked in, I asked Joe, "How many men did you say you have?"

"Sixteen, and tomorrow morning there will be another fifty coming from other districts."

"I've been wondering about your sixteen merry men. Where are they all?"

"Well, ten of them are working with the soldiers. They are probing the snow between the corridors and six are high up the valley above us monitoring any snow movements."

"Have they a radio transmitter?"

"No, we haven't any, but I gave them two flare pistols and instructed them to go up along the verge of the remaining forest as far as the mouth of side valley which is about 800 metres above."

"Yes, I know where it is. I've studied the map I got from the C.O. What's the precise function of those men?"

"They are to listen carefully. Should they hear a roar of a further avalanche they are to fire a warning flare. That's the agreed signal for the soldiers. They would then immediately run away from the avalanche tip into the forest."

"A sound idea, Joe! I only hope you don't believe that this precaution will be of any use?"

"I don't, really. It's only a safety gesture. A matter of psychology. I have been simply obliged to do it. I'm sure you understand."

"Sure, Joe. But now let's talk in earnest. Do you know this region? If so, tell me whether we are threatened by any further avalanche release. It's your subjective opinion I want to hear, not any theoretical precepts."

"That's a difficult question, Miloš. To tell you the truth, I don't know the area well enough. I've never been here during the winter season before. This region's not of interest to skiers or climbers. But I was here once in late summer, about three years ago. To the best of my recollection, the upper forest margin is two or three kilometres uphill. Above that there are grassy and steep slopes of about 30° inclination, reaching as high as 1,900 metres. Perfect avalanche runways. A lot of avalanches must hurtle down those slopes every winter but nobody worries about such a huge deserted area, inhabited only by real bears or by bears like Charlie here." He smiled good naturedly towards the other end of the tree trunk where the forester and Brok had returned and were about to sit down. Charlie had brought a bundle of branches and a bag of pine cones. I looked back at Joe.

"Go on! As yet you haven't answered the most important question: whether there is additional avalanche hazard or not."

"I don't know. Maybe yes, maybe no. What do I know of the snow masses up there? In two seconds a new avalanche could bury all of us and I don't want to talk about it any more. But tell me why are you so firmly convinced that the avalanche must have come from above? It might be a local snow release. Don't forget the great distance from the avalanche slopes! Between our present position and those slopes there are curved, narrow and afforested valleys. Also, the valleys themselves are not that steep. I worked out their inclination is only between 5° and 15°. No more. In my opinion too little for an avalanche to travel such a great distance, to overcome such obstacles and to reach down to here."

"I don't agree with you, Joe. An avalanche of enormous mass, energy and speed can do it. I've no doubt that the avalanche came from above. Look at the map, Joe! The margin of the forest runs pretty zig-zag. What does that mean? That's a result of previous avalanches, though none of them travelled as far as this one. Such avalanches may occur four or five times within a millennium; probably beyond human memory, especially in such a remote region. Though I haven't yet seen the situation above, I'm pretty sure about it. But I'm anxious on another point. The valley above is interconnected with another. The avalanche came down through one of those valleys and the valley through which it came is no longer dangerous because it has avalanched – all that snow is down now and cannot produce any additional avalanche. I'm worried about the other valley where perhaps no avalanche has been released as yet. Or, it might have been a double avalanche that came down through both valleys at the same time and merged into one stream of enormous energy just above the loggers' hut. That would be the most favourable condition for us."

"I cannot tell you anything further about that problem until daylight, Miloš. Then I'll send patrols to investigate."

Until daylight! I was told the same by Charlie when I asked him to locate the hut. Daylight was a question of another six hours. These thoughts ran through my mind. The trapped people might be alive and in need of help. Every lost minute may mean life or death, not only to those buried somewhere in the snow mass, but to all of us. Even now I didn't have any idea what was above. Could I take this appalling risk? Hadn't I better tell the commander the truth and ask him to stop the operation until daylight? I didn't.

I was frustrated and angry about my inability to do anything further. The commander returned just then. My face must have reflected my thoughts. I forgot even to thank him for the soup. He gave me a slip of paper.

"Something from headquarters. Not important for me but you will perhaps find it interesting," and he went off again.

It was a record of a telephone call with the hospital where the three who had been rescued were being cared for. All were suffering from severe shock. The two found by the dog still could not speak. They had internal injuries. John had only superficial wounds. The most interesting part of the message was his version of what had happened for he had recovered sufficiently to give a statement.

Before the catastrophe he was asleep and was awakened by a deep thundering. He was going to look through the window to see what was the matter but just as he reached the window a tremendous explosion tore the hut asunder and he was catapulted into the air. After what he thought was about twenty metres' flight he landed on the top of a spruce and fell down through the branches. His only thought was to protect his legs with pieces torn off his night shirt. Somehow, he reached the forest lodge. He couldn't remember anything more.

I got up and went to Charlie at the other end of the log. He had been busy working on something in the snow using twigs and pine cones. He also used a shovel from time to time.

"Look, Charlie, your problem is solved. John didn't climb the tree. He landed on top of it after a twenty metres long airflight."

"What?" He stared to me incredulously, his pipe in his hand.

"Here, you'd better read it yourself." I handed him the slip of paper. He read it slowly, probably several times. Meanwhile I observed his work. When I finally understood what he had done I was delighted. It was a relief model of the valley before the catastrophe. The valley was slightly curved. The steep hillsides were completely afforested, trees simulated by cones pressed into the dirty snow. The stream flowing through the valley was marked by means of twigs and thicker sticks were used for three-dimensional models of the two buildings, the forest lodge and the loggers' hut. This last model attracted my particular attention. It was situated on the same side of the valley as the forest lodge, on a plateau above the stream. The natural shape of the plateau had possibly influenced the location of the building for it was at an angle to it, so that one end of the hut bridged the stream on the side closest to the mountain. It seemed that Charlie had not yet finished this part of his task, because behind the hut he had heaped a high steep pile of snow without any cones on it.

"Haven't you finished yet, Charlie?" I pointed at this heap of snow.

"Yes, that's done," he answered absent-mindedly. "The rest of the hut was hidden behind a rock. That's the best I can do for a rock." He started to fill his pipe, his thoughts now obviously elsewhere. For me he had just uttered the most important fact, though he hadn't realised it. Until now all the known facts had fitted together but, unfortunately, did not give me a clear picture of events as a whole.

"That won't do. It's out of the question!" Charlie said finally in disappointed tones, brooding still on the message from the hospital.

"Why, what's wrong, Charlie?" I asked briskly. "With the help of your model you'll be able to locate the hut in a few minutes, using John's landing tree as a starting point."

It was a stupid oversimplification of mine, and I made an awful fool of myself by such a rash conclusion. Charlie stared evenly at me.

"It doesn't make sense," he said flatly. "The hut was situated two or three hundred metres uphill from here and from John's landing tree, as you call it. Besides, it was on the opposite side of the valley. Look here," he pointed to the inner curve of the valley model, "that's approximately our present position. A pretty long distance to the hut, isn't it? John must have landed on another tree, if at all. Not here. But then why is a piece of his bloody shirt still hanging on that tree, over there?" He pointed with his pipe.

"Why didn't you tell me sooner that the hut was situated so far off? It was my first question!"

"You asked me the exact position. An approximate one you can find on your map."

"No, I can't. The map is older than the hut, so it's not marked."

The forester turned his back upon me, kicked furiously at the snow model and sat down on the broken trunk. I felt deflated, but didn't say anything further and walked away into the dark and the fog.

Later, much later, when I went over that critical bit of information again, I realised my unforgivable mistake in accepting John's initial information. A man who is projected from a disintegrating hut by an unknown force cannot reliably determine how far he has been hurled. Information from eye-witnesses of any catastrophe is often wrong, being as it is influenced by fear, shock and a common human failing to exaggerate – though in John's case exaggeration was to prove to be the last thing we should all be accusing him of.

But for the present, was I perhaps being too meticulous – wanting too many details? Success, I thought, is for those who don't ask but give orders. Yes, I really had been about to call my driver, go down to the village and tell the commanding officer that the avalanche was beyond my experience and knowledge and that I was going home.

It was, however, lucky that I was also annoyed, having felt an injustice. A voice within me whispered, calling me a coward who wanted to leave the battlefield before the fight was decided. I was annoyed by my own shortcomings, but also those of others. No, I'd stay, not just because of the buried people, though they were probably dead, I'd stay because I'd demonstrate that I could get to the bottom of all this chaos and find the avalanche victims. But it would be a different Miloš Vrba who'd take over. Now there wouldn't be any more. "Can you . . .

would you be so kind . . ." Now it would be straight from the
shoulder, "You must!"

Meanwhile, I went over to the end of the avalanche tip where
the corridor digging and probing was in full swing. The officer
and Joe immediately joined me.

"No traces yet," the commander reported reproachfully.
"I'm sure this search area is quite useless."

"Carry on!" I retorted, ignoring his poignant remarks.

"At first light over 400 people will arrive," the commander
continued stiffly. "Are they to dig here or somewhere else?"

"Ensure that they have the necessary tools, and are instructed
about the emergency. At daylight you and the forester will go
with me, Joe, uphill to study the situation. Later I'll give my
instructions on procedure."

"Yes, sir!"

Joe was evidently surprised by my changed attitude and using
our friendship as a lever he tried to humour me by making a
joke, but I didn't react and told him, "At the first sign of dawn,
Joe, you will send two patrols up to investigate the avalanche
situation in both valleys. They will take two-way radios to
inform me of the immediate situation."

"We haven't any radios, you know that," Joe objected.

"The soldiers have and they will lend them to you."

"That's quite impossible," the commander protested. "No
civil person may use the army's frequencies. You must ask the
commanding officer for special dispensation."

"You will do that," I replied. "One of your operators will
explain to the mountain rescue team how to operate the equipment. We shall start at six o'clock sharp. One of your radio
operators will also come with us."

I left then. Both I knew were angry, but so was I. It was cold
during those long hours before dawn. I preferred, therefore, to
walk about within the circle of light cast by the searchlights and
fire. The rough snow surface littered with broken trees and
branches made the walking difficult. For something to do I
decided to investigate the opposite side of the valley.

The valley was about thirty to forty metres wide, really
slightly bow-shaped, the area where the search was being
conducted forming the outer curve. On that outer margin,
about 200–300 metres uphill was where the hut had been.

But how, I asked myself, is it possible that until now all the victims located were at the inner curve of the valley, and how is it possible that the trees on that outer curve are hardly damaged, whereas here the majority of them are smashed? That was at variance with principal physical laws and with my experience as well. After all, everything flowing, streaming, running and rolling is pushed outside on a curve, not inside.

I couldn't understand these anomalies, though I spent a long time investigating each particular spruce with the beam of my torch. My self-confidence sank again; the whole affair seemed a mystery.

A gloomy, foggy and watery dawn arrived. We started uphill, climbing the avalanche path. Charlie with Brok took the lead, followed by Joe and me and finally the commander with a radio operator carrying a transceiver. We went up slowly for it was rough going, though the slope wasn't steep. The shapes of the trees disappeared in the fog, and the valley grew wider. We didn't talk, not only because of the difficult terrain, but also due to the strained terms we were all now on. It seemed an endless and exhausting trip. Finally, Charlie stopped, looked round in the fog and turned to the left. We followed him. In front of us a rock rose out of the fog.

"Here it is," Charlie said.

"Are you able to mark out an approximate ground plan of the hut?" My voice sounded hoarse and breathless.

"I'll try, though the snow must be about seven or eight metres deep here."

He began to measure the distances step by step. Joe helped him, having brought up an armful of branches to mark out the walls.

Meanwhile, it got brighter and the fog lifted. I saw with interest the smashed trees on the steep hollow hillside above the rock and to the left of it. The piled-up timber made a crazy sight, as if a giant had smashed trees with his hands and tossed some with their tops uppermost above the rock, while at the head of the slope tree-tops were pointing down.

Suddenly, the radio operator raised his hand, drawing our attention to a signal coming in. The rescue patrols had reached the point where the valleys joined and reported that the avalanche ran down through the left valley only. The right-hand valley had been blocked by a ten metre high ice wall. They asked for further instructions.

"Bad news," I said, "tell them to go on separately to investigate the snow situation above."

"And you, sir," I said to the commander, "give orders that the support party which is due must not go into the avalanche tip. They will wait in the hillside wood for orders!"

"I cannot keep all those people waiting," the officer protested, "I was ordered by headquarters . . . Watch out, avalanche!"

We all quickly looked up, automatically pressing ourselves to the rock. Only the dog kept quiet because his animal instinct did not register danger. There wasn't any. The supposed avalanche was only a high wall of white snow which appeared out of the dissipating fog about thirty metres from us. In fact, it was the second step of the existing avalanche which had stopped not far from the hut. Probably it originated from the snow transported in the avalanche cloud which settled in that area after losing the majority of its energy, and thus formed an immense mass of white snow, contrasting sharply with the dirty avalanche tip coming out from the bottom of the terrible whiteness. The frontal wall was about ten metres high. Maybe even more.

"Joe, have you ropes and ice axes?"

"Yes, of course."

"Well, send four or five of your men to investigate the stability and hardness of that mass of snow. Very carefully!"

Charlie had almost completed his work. Both rooms and the corridor were already marked and he was just indicating doors and windows with sticks. I was busy observing the hillside opposite. The fog had gone so that I could clearly see every detail on that slope, though it was 200–300 metres from our position. An extensive bow-shaped area of smashed trees piled up in the same curious shape as on the slopes above us. All the broken trees on that distant slope had their tops lying towards us, however, and here I realised they tended towards the inner avalanche curve where John and the others were discovered. The full significance of this came to me. Take it easy, no hastiness, the inner voice whispered, and I smiled to myself. I was sure of everything now. It had all dropped into place.

"Charlie, tell me – No, I'll tell you. John and the other victims who have been found lived in this room," I pointed at his hut plan, "in the room which was over the brook facing the mountain."

"Do you read my mind or did someone tell you?" Charlie returned, looking surprised.

"No, I worked it out myself. I even know where . . ."

In that moment we were interrupted by another report from one of the rescue patrols. The men climbing up the right-hand valley had discovered a tip of a big avalanche that had stopped about 300 metres before the bottom. They thought that avalanche may have been released at approximately the same time as the other one, as there was only a thin layer of powder snow covering the debris.

"That was your first 'thunder', Charlie! Now, everything is clear, gentlemen. Let's get started."

"I don't understand," Charlie murmured, perplexed.

"Neither do I," Joe added. "What were you about to tell us, Miloš?"

"Simply," I said, "that I think I know exactly where the ten missing persons are to be found. Just here," I pointed. "Or, say, within a distance of fifty metres downhill. Not more."

"Sir, will you be so kind as to express your theories more clearly?" The commander's tone was petulant. "I must do something with the men waiting in the wood. There are almost 500 of them now."

"Clearly? Yes, and briefly! It was an airborne avalanche that came down in two waves from different directions and of different energy. The first one was a pressure wave of immense power. That wave ricochetted within the valley like a billiard ball. I understood what happened for the first time after having seen the patterns made by the smashed trees. The pressure wave destroyed the front part of the hut. John and the others living there were blasted and hurtled a distance of 250 metres in the curve of the valley. Not twenty metres, Charlie! John really landed on that tree, he didn't climb it. He fell down, out of reach of the additionally flowing snow. The others were not so lucky and landed in the avalanche stream where they were buried.

The avalanching snow, mixed with wood and stones, rolled down in the second wave. Those slower flowing masses of lower energy destroyed the back part of the hut hidden behind the rock here. The missing people living there must have been buried either in the base of the hut or dragged down along the outer curve of the valley, not too far off."

"Your orders, sir!" The officer asked impatiently, unimpressed with my dialogue.

"All your people with tools will come here, immediately," I said. This space where the hut was situated and an additional strip, say twenty by a hundred metres downhill, must be turned upside down as soon as possible. The organisation is your business."

"Yes, sir." He dashed off.

"Joe, I want to know urgently the result of investigation of that wall of white snow."

"Right, I'll see to it."

Charlie came over and said, "Last night. I was mad. I'm sorry."

"Charlie, I share the same sentiments – about myself. I talked like an idiot. Let's both forget it."

The commander proved to be an excellent organiser who knew how to direct a large number of people in those difficult conditions and how to allocate particular tasks to the right personnel.

Joe brought a report on the white snow wall and I was a little alarmed. The mass was rough and hard enough, though not so icehard as the dirty avalanche tip. This was good. But they had also found long narrow deep cracks in the snow.

"Longitudinal or transverse?" I asked.

"Longitudinal ones, and in the lower part only," Joe explained.

"If the cracks were transverse, I should be afraid of a glacier-like creep downwards. However, I don't understand the longitudinal cracks, I cannot explain those."

"Neither can I," Joe added.

"Tell them to keep a close eye on them."

Meanwhile, the soldiers dug a deep pit and had now uncovered the damaged floor of the hut. We decided to try the avalanche dog. But the animal refused to go down into the deep pit and the handler had trouble getting the dog to work. Finally, the dog got a scent at the back right-hand corner. Within a few minutes two victims were found. Two dead men were pressed against the timbers of the back wall, both still holding a hand of cards. There were no visible injuries. The doctor judged that they very likely died immediately after burial because no traces of ice were found in their mouths and nostrils.

Further victims were discovered soon afterwards, outside the former hut. The ninth corpse lay thirty metres downhill. Altogether eight men and one woman were found by eleven o'clock. The tenth man was missing.

"Charlie, what's the matter? Nine people again. Where can the tenth be? Haven't you any idea? Did he go into town with Jim?"

"That's out of the question."

"What about the out-house?"

"Dug out already. Destroyed, but the door was found in the frame and was closed from outside."

After a short noon break, Joe proposed to enlarge the area searched by making another corridor. I agreed, then remembered the snow mass above us and asked about the cracks. No change, was the report and I forgot about that problem for the time being, unfortunately.

I was occupied with another idea. I decided to make contact with the hospital, and question the lumberjacks to see if they had any idea of the whereabouts of the missing man. Charlie had told me his name. The reply was prompt: a few minutes before the catastrophe he took a bucket and went down to the brook for water.

"Charlie, do you know their path to the stream and the place where they got water?"

"Exactly."

The last phase began. The path to the stream ended only a few metres in front of the white snow wall. A wide corridor was quickly dug. A lot of people were at my disposal and they worked in relays. The pit at the foot of the white wall was soon twelve metres deep. But when both the corridor and the pit were complete, nothing was found. Not even the bucket. The soldiers standing on the bottom of the hollow reported that the brook was completely dry.

"Did you say dry?" Charlie wondered. "The brook was swift and never iced up even in severe winters."

A shiver went down my spine. There was something odd here! I was not surprised that the last victim wasn't found but I was by the absence of the stream.

"Look . . . look, there!" Joe cried, "the wall's giving way!" He immediately fired a warning flare.

The emergency worked perfectly. Everyone took his shovel, saw, axe or pick and ran up the hillside into the wood. In two or three minutes an immense snow block slowly broke out, rolled over and a fountain of water shot up from the white wall as if under the power of Moses' rod. Then the dirty stream cascaded downhill. Within minutes the search corridors and the avalanche tip were flooded.

A water avalanche! Something nobody had expected. Not snow but water threatened several hundred people. Thousands of tons of snow had formed a natural dam that collapsed due to the digging of the pit and corridor at the foot of the white snow wall which was actually a dam.

I stared helplessly at the streaming water and felt suddenly exhausted. Yet one of the last memories of that terrible avalanche rescue I'll never forget. An officer came from somewhere and though soaked and muddy he reported, "Sir, nobody is missing, nobody has been hurt. Some tools, several covers, one tent and one telephone have been swept away."

"Thank you very much," I managed to mumble.

It all happened many years ago, on 8 March, 1956. And the reference book facts when finally pieced together read like this: At 9.40 am two bulky powder avalanches released in a remote region of the Low Tatra mountains. One of those avalanches contained 1,590,000m of snow, weighing 380,000 tons and travelled a distance of 3,500 metres from the rupture zone. This great mass ran down into a narrow, curved and afforested valley. The immense avalanche, reaching a speed of about 250 kph was pressed into the valley neck. In that critical section the mass exploded in the air and turned into an avalanche cloud. The pressure wave and the avalanching snow buried nineteen people. Sixteen of them did not survive. Twenty-five hectares of an old forest were smashed. It took eighteen months to clear the smashed timber and the same time for the avalanche snow to melt. The last victim was found by the forester's dog six weeks after the accident, having been buried under an overhanging bank of the stream.

A Cauldron of Wind

Markus Burkard

I first met helicopter pilots Markus Burkard and Günther Amann in September 1973 when Dougal Haston and I were landed by winch wire at the Eiger's Death Bivouac. That lower, Dougal's first, must have been quite an initiation. Being in the rescue business, I had done many previous lowers, often in bad conditions, so it wasn't quite so alarming for me, but to be whisked up from that awesome face on a slender steel wire, out over the verdant pastures of Alpiglen, gives one pause for reflection with 7,000 feet of space beneath your crampons! It was Günther who was piloting on that occasion and it wasn't until the following year that I flew with Markus. Whereas Günther is inclined to be introspective and quiet, Markus is more carefree, though no less careful than his colleague. These two pilots have saved many climbers and skiers in difficulties in the Swiss Alps.

The insurance service provided by the Swiss Mountain Rescue Flight provides an excellent service. Its pilots, like their compatriots doing the same job in Chamonix, have proved beyond doubt that mountain rescue with helicopters is by far the most efficient means of taking the injured off mountains.

Helicopter winch rescue originated in Britain where it was developed for Air-Sea Rescue. It was first used in the Alps in 1961 on the East Face of the Watzmann, a peak near Berchtesgaden. The aircraft used was an old Sikorsky. Though many different types of helicopters are in use for rescue work today, the French Alouette has been the most popular workhorse and its souped up small brother, the Lama, is one of the few helicopters which can lift its own weight; it also holds the world altitude record of almost 41,000 feet. Now there are many new high powered kids on the block, such as the BK117, and some of these also give good high-altitude performance.

The Eiger North Face didn't succumb easily to this helicopter revolution. Here, too, as with other firsts, psychological barriers had to be broken and it wasn't until 1970 that Günther, as a rescue exercise, lowered Rudolf Kaufmann, a Grindelwald guide, on to various parts of the face, the Spider, the Flatiron and the Ramp. This was an amazing breakthrough, but prior to this the helicopters had played a combined operations role. For instance, a rescue team was flown to the summit ridge in the winter of 1970 with winching equipment and an injured Japanese climber was taken up from the Exit Cracks. Fixed belays were established at the top of the mountain, at the finish of the Ramp and the North Pillar, which meant that in the event of a rescue taking place in weather too severe for a helicopter to operate, normal winching procedure, as pioneered by Ludwig Gramminger and Erich Friedli, could be swung into action with the minimum of delay.

During the summer of 1970 that astute master of the telescope, the late Fritz von Almen saw from his base at Kleine Scheidegg that one of two Italian climbers had fallen, close to where the unfortunate Corti had bivouacked many years before. He informed the authorities and at dawn next day a rescue party was flown to the summit ridge and a guide lowered by winch wire to the scene of the accident. Angelo Ursella, a climber from Udine, had fallen thirty metres and unluckily some coils of his rope had caught round his neck. He was immediately strangled. His friend, de Infanti, was whipped off his belay, but being uninjured, managed to climb back up to his stance. The guide got de Infanti to the summit shortly after midday. Ursella's body was recovered later.

In September of that same year, the first exclusive helicopter rescue was done on the face. Günther Amann was the pilot. The circumstances leading up to this rescue, which fortunately ended happily, were rather bizarre. Two German climbers, Martin Biock and Peter Siegert, started up the original route. They were both strong climbers. Siegert, for example, was one of the first to try the Eiger Direct in winter and was also a member of the party that made the first winter ascent of the Matterhorn North Face. However, the Eiger didn't seem congenial, for at the Difficult Crack Biock dropped the rucksack he was hauling up a pitch and, though they recovered it some 200 metres below, Siegert's crampons *had been lost. One advantage of their close proximity to the 3.8 window was that it made commuting possible and Peter dashed down to the Stollenloch window, took a train to Grindelwald, where he bought a new pair of crampons and was back on the climb with Martin by midday.*

By now the sun was causing havoc and the usual stone trundles had started down the Hinterstoisser Traverse, so they decided to get to the Second Icefield via the Japanese Route, up the Rote Fluh. This is the intimidating overhanging red wall to the right of the Hinterstoisser. It was whilst bivouacking in hammocks from this huge overhang that night that they discovered their stove had been damaged in the fall and couldn't be used. For some reason best known to themselves, they decided to carry on next morning, but by the evening had only reached Death Bivouac. When they were at this fateful ledge the weather broke with a vengeance, typical of the Eiger, and the next two nights were spent at this isolated eyrie.

On the second night they signalled for help by torch and Kurt Schwendener, the rescue boss in Grindelwald, set the rescue machine in motion. The weather was still bad next day and in case Amann couldn't get in with the Lama, Schwendener also arranged for a group of guides to be ready at the Stollenloch. Despite intermittent cloud Amann got close enough to the bivouac to speak to the two Germans using the helicopter loud hailer, for he was not absolutely sure that they now wanted to be rescued. In the past many climbers had retreated from Death Bivouac and above, and it was assumed that these two were uninjured. Later, when the cloud cleared, Amann saw that they had abseiled two rope lengths to the side of the Flatiron and here they made definite signals that they wished to be picked up.

Rudolf Kaufmann, the guide, was lowered to the tiny stance (the size of a biscuit tin lid) and Biock was hoisted up and taken to Scheidegg. Fifteen minutes later both Siegert and Kaufmann were winched aboard in safety. In all, the rescue had taken less than an hour.

Between 1973 and 1977, I did many flights with Günther Amann and Markus Burkard connected with filming and TV. Most of the winch lowers were either on the North Face or on the West Flank. My last trip with Markus in 1971 was a hurried one. I had a meeting in Zürich about a possible live TV climb of the face and I had to check on one or two points, which meant a flight to a ledge high on the West Flank on a cold September morning. I had only four hours to complete this work. The well known Swiss climber and guide, Hans Muller, was with me and when Markus dropped us off on a snow-covered ledge, it felt both lonely and cold. The mountain was in the first grip of an early winter. The helicopter landed close to Kleine Scheidegg, keeping in radio contact with us for the return trip.

When our survey was completed we called Markus on the walkie-talkie and he picked us up. On the descent I asked him if he could fly close in to the Japanese Direct route to enable Hans to check on some ledges which we were wanting to see. Hans had done the route in both summer and winter. Markus nosed the Alouette into the wall like a dog scenting a lamppost, until we were below the great overhang above and to the right of the Rote Fluh. He then eased the helicopter beneath this so that the deafening roar of the rotors and the gas turbine bounced down on us from the rock roof. It was both exhilarating and frightening, yet he was in perfect control. His only apparent concern was before he took the machine beneath the rock when he asked Hans if the overhang was solid. Hans had assured him that it was. This is typical of the confidence which these pilots have in their crew, for both the winchman and the guide have to be experts also and equally cool in a crisis. Markus wasn't worried when he took us under that overhang and Günther wasn't scared when he dropped Dougal and me off at Death Bivvy and other places on the wall. When Markus in the following narrative talks of almost crashing the helicopter on a rescue, he must really have been out on a limb.

On Friday, 11 November, a group mostly of younger climbers from Belfort in France started from Rosenlaui in the Bernese Oberland for the Dossenhütte. The weather was fine, the sky cloudless, but the forecast was very bad. A depression had been threatening for days.

The group camped below the moraine, in the Gletscherhubel area and started the ascent on Saturday. As the day wore on, the expected bad weather front reached the Rosenlaui area. By evening it started to rain heavily, turning later to sleet and snow. Two days later, on the Monday evening, the Swiss Alpine Club rescue leader in Meiringen received a report from Belfort that several people were missing. Later when I was on duty I heard about these seven overdue climbers. The operations leader told me what he knew and I assumed that they were waiting in the Dossenhütte for better weather and a helicopter to pick them up. There are ten days' emergency provisions in the Dossenhütte and plenty of wood but, unfortunately, no telephone.

On Monday it snowed without stopping from 10.00 am onwards. For a while even the Brünig Pass was only passable with chains. Winter had started with a vengeance. Later on that Monday night an unusually severe storm raged over the Alps and on the Tuesday morning I heard on the news that the met. station on the Säntis had recorded a wind speed of 140 kph. During the night we were awoken several times by the noise of the storm. I had forgotten about the seven climbers, because the weather was so bad that a flight to the Dossenhütte was out of the question. A telephone call from operations headquarters shortly before 9.00 am changed the situation completely!

A twenty-two-year-old climber from Belfort had reached Rosenlaui absolutely exhausted and raised the alarm. He, with the six others, had left the Dossenhütte on Sunday morning, two days earlier, and had tried to descend to the valley. When they left, it had already been snowing all night, so they attempted the descent under the worst imaginable conditions. The normal route through the Dossenwand, threatened by avalanches, seemed too risky and there was no choice but to climb to the Dossensattel and reach the valley via the Rosenlaui Glacier.

Three of the climbers got as far as the first icefall at 2,500 metres. There they were left behind as they were unable to go further. A seventeen-year-old boy reached the shelter of the Dossen bivouac with a fourteen-year-old companion. The youth who later was to raise the alarm continued the descent accompanied by his girl friend. They failed to locate their tent at the Gletscherhubel campsite, an hour above Rosenlaui and were therefore forced to bivouac in the open. During the night the girl died from exhaustion and hypothermia. This was the sad news I was given.

Just then thick clouds made a flight impossible and so the rescue leader in Meiringen had to go about organising a rescue party from the Hasli. We promised help as soon as the weather improved. Rosenlaui was to be the meeting point. At Interlaken Urs Menet, the mechanic on duty with me, made the Alouette 319 ready for take-off. I obtained the latest weather reports. They promised some temporary improvements due to the strong winds. At 3,000 metres wind speeds of fifty knots and gusts up to sixty-five knots were reported. Above Interlaken there was a patch of blue sky. Shortly after 10.30 am Peter Winterberger reported that the Dossenhütte was clearly visible. We took off.

I had a sinking feeling – a glance at the peaks was sufficient. Everywhere the same picture presented itself; snow showers, wisps of cloud which rose, dissolved and reappeared, gusts of wind shaking the helicopter. Above Meiringen the valley was completely clear of clouds. We flew up to 2,000 metres and cast our first glance in the direction of Rosenlaui. Seen from the air, this glacier is one of the most beautiful of its kind, but today there was a storm above the ice. Everything seemed to be moving. The snow swept along the rocks, was hurled high in the air and formed eddies which jumped like dancers over the crevasses. A dim light lay over the scene. We flew into this cauldron and into the lee of the big Wellhorn. Terrible gusts of wind caught the Alouette. We were hurled upwards and the next moment we were hit from above, then once more pressed down into our seats. I required the full range of the controls in order to keep the machine in the air. I felt sick. During my thirteen years' helicopter experience I had seldom encountered such winds. This was hell. I flew a full circle 200 metres above ground. It was impossible to keep a look-out for people. I could reach the radio-controls only with difficulty, as this meant lifting my arm off my knee and this impaired my steering. There was nothing I could do – the force of the gale was overwhelming. I could not tell from which direction the wind was blowing – it seemed to be everywhere. On my right the snow swept over the rocks in the direction of our flight. On Urs' side was a counter-wind blowing across the glacier. I did not know what to do.

After circling for the second or third time, far away – 300–400 metres higher – we saw two figures, one of whom was waving. They were standing near an icefall where the huge crevasses begin. This meant flying higher, further into the cauldron. I simply had to overcome my feelings and control myself. For a moment the thought crossed my mind that the tremendous winds might snap a rotor-blade or ruin the tail rotor. I was terrified to crash out of control on to this cruel glacier. The upper end of the glacier was hidden by clouds consisting of snow and ice crystals. The cold hard snow swept in from a westerly direction and continued horizontally over the icefall.

Now we were above the two men. Only with difficulty could I keep the stick steady in my hand. It was being shaken by the strong bumps and the upwards and downwards currents. There was no question of flying on course. We thought that we would never get anywhere near our men. Still, I could not simply leave them, I imagined the long steep climb which the rescue party would have to face. I saw the threatening clouds on the Dossensattel on my right. The victims had been fighting for their lives for the last two days in this hell composed of wind and cold. Ice axes, half-buried rucksacks, ropes and scattered bits of clothing protruded from the snow. It was a horrifying picture. A landing was impossible as the angle of the glacier was too steep. At the utmost I could touch down with the nose-wheel and hover at the same time in order to try and get the victims on board. But first I had to get near enough. It just had to work! I was thinking of Sigi long ago on the Monte Rosa Glacier in the south-west wind and of that avalanche disaster behind the Testa. Here, however, was the Rosenlaui Glacier. I fought, I was frightened, I cursed, I was furious with myself and the profession I had chosen. Twenty times I asked Urs where the wind was blowing from; he probably thought I had gone crazy.

The first attempt ended twenty metres above the party; on the second we flew as fast as an express train over them, although I had chosen the same direction. During the following attempt, shortly before landing, we were caught in the down-current so badly that I had to open full throttle. The huge crevasses came towards us so fast that I believed we were going to crash. At the last moment I managed to pull away. The new turbine had to give its maximum power. I could not consult the confounded T_4 instrument any more. This was the moment when I wanted to give up. What was the use of smashing the Alouette and risking our lives? Urs did not say a word, but as a glider pilot he knew what we were up against. We headed towards safety, but after thirty seconds I had to turn back and try once more. Finally, we succeeded in touching the ground with the nose-wheel. Urs opened the sliding door and I shouted at him to keep an eye on the rotor. We were in a cloud of whirling snow. I had to correct the Alouette's position continually – it was like holding a bucking bronco. The silhouettes of the two men were my only landmark. Snow whirled through the cabin like dust. I was ready to take off at any moment before the rotor hit the snow.

Now the incredible happened. The two men did not stir. One of them was lying in the snow, secured to a red rope. Both held their heads hidden behind their elbows. The extra blast of the rotor-blades seemed to take their breath away. Urs made signs, I shouted which only served to soothe my nerves; the others could not possibly hear anything, but it helped me. Now one of them looked back – he understood that we could not land. My starboard main wheel was half a metre above ground and the Alouette was bumping. Several times the stick was at the end of its travel. I wanted to take these men on board, fly away, never to return.

Now one of them dragged the other over the snow to the helicopter. He was crawling like a worm over the ice. He must have been at the end of his tether. I wondered whether the two were tied together with the rope. If one of them was inside the helicopter and I had to take off suddenly, the other one would be left dangling on the rope, a potentially dangerous situation. However, it never came to that. When both men were at the level of the sliding door, outside my field of vision, I felt blinded. Everything around me was white, snow and ice.

I was left without any landmark at all. I had to take off, called to Urs to check that nobody hung on to the helicopter – and we were away. Like this we would never get anywhere and the only alternative was to fetch a guide to help us. If only all went well! I gave a radio message asking for someone to be ready and flew back to Rosenlaui. There we met Fritz Immer and Peter Winterberger, both guides used to flying. For reasons of balance I only wanted one of them. We shed all unnecessary material in order to be as light as possible. I did not even switch the engine off as I had to turn back at once to rescue the men before the weather made this impossible.

After starting I managed to warn Fritz Immer over the intercom to hold fast. The wind was as strong as before and snow eddies were whirling everywhere. The gusts from the Wellhorn shook us and I tried to meet them as well as I could. I was caught in an impossible situation where there was no way out; I simply had to carry on.

After several further attempts I managed to touch down on the ice with the nose-wheel, choosing a blue, half-buried rucksack as a beacon. Fritz Immer jumped on the glacier and now everything happened very swiftly. The younger man almost flew into the cabin, the older one, completely exhausted, was hauled in. Over the radio I could hear Urs' heavy breathing. Much strength was needed to carry the completely apathetic, almost paralysed man on board. I kept my eyes on the blue rucksack. Whether it was the wind or the moving men which caused my correcting manoeuvres, I did not know. I took off even before the door was shut properly, relieved to have rescued two. But during our descent I started to count: one raised the alarm, his companion is dead, two are on board – where are the remaining three?

On arrival I needed to stretch my legs and left the Alouette for the first time. My stop-watch recorded sixty-five flight minutes. During this time one flies from Interlaken to Zermatt, round the Matterhorn and back again. Normally our flight would have lasted twenty minutes, but now time was immaterial. I talked to the seventeen-year-old boy, who seemed to me in a reasonably good state. He kept on saying: "Nous sommes sauvés," (we have been rescued). He had spent two nights in the bivouac on the Dossen. This morning he had returned to the icefall and wanted to accompany the remaining three. However, only one was still alive – the forty-year-old man lying in the back of the helicopter. The woman had died during the first night. Marc, the seventeen-year-old companion, died the following day. Both lay buried under the snow.

A fourteen-year-old boy was still at the Dossen bivouac. Twenty times at least we flew over this small hut, but there was no sign of anyone. Once more we flew back, Fritz Immer jumped out of the hovering helicopter, ran the fifty metres to the hut and fetched the shivering boy. He dragged him by his belt over the snow. The boy's legs kept buckling under him. Into the cabin they went and we were off.

The three unfortunates on the glacier would have needed a further thirty minutes in order to reach the safety of the Dossen bivouac. They were not fully equipped and totally unprepared for a change in the weather. The boy was merely dressed in blue jeans and walking shoes.

We took the survivors to hospital. The forty-year-old man's temperature had fallen to 32°C. He was completely exhausted and his will to live at a low ebb, I do not think that he would have lived to see the arrival of the rescue party. Nobody can imagine what he must have gone through; to be helpless at the mercy of a storm for two days and nights; to have to watch one's wife dying and a cheerful seventeen-year-old collapsing, losing consciousness, never to wake again. It must have been terrible for him to wait and suffer up there, all alone. I am in no position to judge what they did wrong – nobody can do anything about that now.

Three people died. The guides found the two women later and when the wind had abated, we flew them back. The Rosenlaui glacier is Marc's grave. Officially, he is considered missing, but he is lying somewhere under the snow and has found his eternal rest in the mountains he loved. It is a sad story: in spite of having rescued several people and done our utmost, we cannot feel very happy.

On landing after a difficult flight, before we switch the radio off, it's customary to say thank you to each other over the intercom.

Avalanche on Beinn a'Bhuird

Hamish MacInnes

Scottish hills to the visiting tourist, perhaps blessed with fine weather, may seem serene and gently inviting. Indeed they often are in summer and even in winter when the weather gods smile on these northern latitudes, but in storms they can reveal their Jekyll and Hyde character and be as savage as a rabid dog.

This tale from the Cairngorms recounts one of the longest avalanche burials which anyone has survived in Britain.

Visitors to Royal Dee-side generally get the impression that the valley of the Dee is a tranquil place – as indeed it is – while the gently rolling Cairngorms look no more forbidding than a school of slumbering whales. However, three distinct features, weather, altitude and sheer size, can transform those leviathan-like peaks into deadly killers of the unprepared.

Much of the high ground is over 4,000 feet, but the height is deceptive because the mountains extend over a vast area; here one has much further to walk in order to reach a climbing area than in most other regions of Scotland. The weather is probably the most dangerous single factor. The Cairngorm tops form elevated plateaux whose height and open nature offer little obstruction to the high winds which, in winter especially, sweep in with alarming rapidity. These winds can soon sap a climber's strength and have a dangerous chilling effect.

The ferocity of Cairngorm storms has to be experienced to be believed. At the Ptarmigan Restaurant, on the forehead of Cairngorm, wind speeds of 150 mph have been recorded. It is not an exaggeration to say that severe weather in the Cairngorms rivals that found in any part of the world. In a blizzard it is an arctic no-man's-land.

Ben Macdhui (4,300 feet/1,300 metres) is the highest mountain in this range and, incidentally, the second highest in Britain. It is connected to Cairngorm by a broad plateau which nowhere falls below the 3,600-foot contour. The westerly slopes of Ben Macdhui fall steeply to the Lairig Ghru: this is a pass which connects Spey-side with Dee-side, and it lies between the portals of Braeriach and Cairn Toul on one side and Ben Macdhui on the other. It is twenty-seven miles from Aviemore to Braemar. No accommodation exists for twenty-two miles of this journey other than the odd bothy or barn. One such haven to the traveller, on the Braemar side, is Derry Lodge. For many years this isolated game-keeper's cottage was the home of Bob Scott who was head-keeper for Mar Estates. (Mar Lodge then a famous stalking and fishing centre near Braemar, is now owned by the National Trust for Scotland.)

Bob was a generous character, as free with his fund of tales as with his hospitality. He has been "father" to succeeding generations of young climbers from Aberdeen: such well-known mountaineers as Bill Brooker, Tom Patey and Jim McArtney started their climbing apprenticeship from his hay barn in the shadow of these hills. Bob took his role as guardian of the glen seriously. He felt that, living as he did in that remote yet popular area, he had a certain responsibility towards travellers. On a bad night he used to place a lighted candle in his window as a beacon for belated and lost walkers trudging through the Lairig Ghru down from those featureless tops.

His candle was lit as usual one wet, autumn night some years ago when, between 1.30 and 2.00 am, there came a knocking at his door. As he jumped out of bed, dressed only in his shirt, he realised that it was a terrible night of rain. It was bouncing like bullets from the roof of his cottage.

"Who's there?" he shouted above the cacophony of wind and water.

"We're lost," came a feeble reply.

"Are ye ladies or men?" asked Bob.

"Ladies."

"Weel, wait there a minute and I'll put on ma plus-fours," answered Bob, going back into his bedroom.

When he opened the door he saw that they were two girls; both appeared in a bad way, shivering, saturated and obviously wishing that they had never heard of the Cairngorms.

"I canna tak ye into the hoose," he said in his broad Dee-side accent. "It's full up. But we'll go oot tae the bothy and I'll soon get a fire going for ye."

In no time he had a big fire roaring in the bothy and went back to the house for food. After a few minutes he returned.

"A've brought ye half a loaf and a've brought ye a bit o' butter. A've got eggs and a've got cheese and a've got jam," he added, "Noo, ah don't think ye'll starve!"

One of the girls, who was as pale as plain flour, said, "We'll have to take our clothes off and there's no blind on the window." She pointed up to the solitary pane of glass which rattled in the driving rain.

"Och, ye don't need to bother with a thing like that here," he replied, laughing. "There's naebody aboot and a'm a married man, ye ken." Then he gave them two large great-coats which he said they could use to sleep in amongst the hay in the corner. From the doorway, he asked,

"What time do you want wakened at?"

"About seven would be fine," said one of them, shaking water from her flimsy cotton anorak.

"Goodnight then," said Bob as he left them.

In the morning when he went out to wake them up, they were sleeping, as he later recalled, "just like two corpses". He invited them in to breakfast and over the meal they told him what had happened. They had stayed the previous night at the Youth Hostel at Aviemore. When they asked the warden there whether it was possible for them to cycle through the Lairig Ghru he had told them – probably jokingly – "Sure, people do it every day." Since the girls came from Birmingham, they assumed that the route over the pass followed a rough road at least. However, as the going became progressively worse they were forced, much to their disgust, to carry the bicycles. Finally they decided to abandon them and continue on foot, intending to return to collect them the following day. But they were caught by darkness and became hopelessly lost. The rain had been growing steadily worse and eventually formed a seemingly unending downpour. At last, when they thought that they could go no further they saw the light in Bob Scott's window.

The next day, in better weather, they retraced their steps of the previous night and returned safely to Derry Lodge with their bicycles.

Not all the tales associated with Derry have such happy endings. Climbing conditions were poor on the 28 December, 1964. Earlier that month snow had covered the tops, crisp and deep but not necessarily even. This had consolidated and formed a good, hard base in the gullies and on the faces. However, about the 27th a fresh fall of snow occurred and the hills were then plastered. But, despite this, the temperature was unusually high for December. It didn't bode well for climbers. It didn't bode well for four men, carrying heavy rucksacks. They asked Bob if they could use his bothy for a few days. As usual, he told them that they could stay as long as they liked – provided they kept it clean and tidy.

"Whit dee ye hope to do, lads?" he asked.

Robert Burnett, the eldest of the party at twenty-eight, replied, "We hope to do some hill-walking, we've got a few days' holiday."

"Weel, watch the gullies just now," warned Bob, kicking at the snow under his tackety boots. "This stuff is very wet still."

Early next morning Bob was over collecting wood from the stick shed close to the bothy when the four lads emerged. The weather, though better, still had a damp, muggy feel about it; there had been no overnight frost.

"Morning, boys," he greeted them as they shouldered their rucksacks. He could see that they were well equipped. "heading off?"

"We'll just take a walk up Beinn a'Bhuird," answered Burnett.

"Ah well, take care then, as I telt ye," warned Bob. "I dinna like these conditions."

"Oh, we'll be all right," rejoined one of the others. "It's an easy climb."

They set off for the hill but one of them – he looked the youngest – came running back for something he had forgotten. Bob watched him as he hurriedly departed again to catch up with the others. He never imagined that, within four hours, the lad would be dead.

That day Bob and one of his gillies were traversing the lower slopes of Beinn a'Bhuird hind shooting. They saw no sign of the four lads, although they must have been descending from the summit while the keepers were on the southern slopes of the mountain. The climbers came off the South Top and were at this time in a gully which had a very big build-up of snow on the true right bank. One of the party, Alister Murray, was slightly to one side of the rest.

Few mountaineers, even today, take sufficient heed of possible avalanche danger. In 1964, though many climbers had been involved in avalanches, these didn't receive much publicity. People accepted them fatalistically – largely as an act of God – if they ever thought about them at all, just as they accepted unpredictable stone fall. I don't suppose it entered the boys' heads whilst they were walking over the snow cover, that the mass of snow in the gully was poised, only requiring the smallest vibration to trigger an avalanche. Avalanche it did. Starting with a fracture twenty feet wide, then extending across the slope as if severed by an invisible guillotine. It was a classical, wet-snow avalanche, starting initially from a fracture of wind slab.

Murray managed to keep clear of the main force of the avalanche but his companions were swept away. With considerable presence of mind he noted where he had last seen them and stumbled down the avalanche tip which extended several hundred yards down the gully. There was no sign of his companions but he shouted for them as he descended. The avalanche he judged to be about ten or eleven feet deep. He eventually gave up the search and did the only thing possible; he went down to find help at Mar Lodge. From there, at 5.50 pm, he telephoned Braemar Police Station.

In Braemar PC John Bruce answered the call. There was no organised rescue team in the area; in those days there were just a few locals who would go out in an emergency and evacuate a casualty, even though they themselves were inadequately equipped. Jim Fraser, a quiet-spoken Aberdonian, was then living in Braemar; a few years previously he had started a horn-carving business in the village. As he was a keen hill man, always willing to help, John Bruce went round to see him as soon as he had contacted headquarters. He also told John Duff, the other policeman in Braemar, who had recently arrived there. There was no police Land Rover in the district then, but a local farmer, Mr Pottinger, had one, so John Bruce contacted him to see if he could assist. This small party, with Gordon Fraser, a Mar Lodge game-keeper, PC Alexander Souter from Ballater and Jock Farquharson, who worked at Mar Lodge, climbed into the vehicle which spun up a rough track to just beyond a wood, close to the bottom of the gully. They considered themselves fortunate that the accident was so accessible; a most unusual occurrence on Cairngorm rescues. Gordon Fraser, the game-keeper, was the most familiar with the area so he acted as guide.

It wasn't a bad night, though there was no moon, but the stars gave enough light to allow them to see the outline of the peaks. There were, however, a few black areas in the night sky which indicated clouds and this didn't suggest any improvement in the weather. They found the bottom of the avalanche tip without much trouble. In those days even the official rescue teams which had already been established in the Highlands had only a vague notion of how to conduct a proper avalanche search. Nevertheless, the Braemar party worked their way up the avalanche tip, probing at random with some long, bamboo poles they had brought along, and about a hundred yards from the bottom of the avalanche they located the first man. They found him by pure chance in their random probing, buried three feet deep in avalanche debris. It was Alex McLeod who at twenty was the youngest member of the group. He was dead.

By the time they had dug him out of his icy tomb the light from their torches was reduced to a dull glow. They realised that they would have difficulty even getting back to the Land Rover, for the weather was deteriorating and it was really dark now. There was no hope of finding anyone else that night. There was no sign of the other two buried men in the area where Murray had thought they might be, nor was there any answer to the rescue party's frequent calls. The only thing they could do was to return at first light and conduct a more thorough search.

It was 3.00 am before they got back to the Land Rover. On the way they met Dr Irvin, the local doctor, and told him they had only found the one man. The doctor confirmed that McLeod was dead.

Next morning the Land Rover crawled once more to a point just beyond the wood. Ahead they could see the elephantine bulk of Beinn a'Bhuird encased in a dazzling mantle of snow. The scar of the avalanche was visible but looked small and insignificant on the massive south flank of the South Top. From this summit a broad, easy ridge eases down in a southerly direction, forming a blunt nose known as Bruach Mor; the avalanche gully is to the south-west of this and in summer holds a stream, the Alltan na Beinne, a tributary of the Quoich Water which in turn flows into the Dee between Mar Lodge and Braemar.

That morning they had gathered a few extra helpers, including at least one member of the Steele Combo Ecosse Band who were playing at Mar Lodge at the time. The noise of the Land Rover's engine broke the still of the lonely glen; when it was cut there was a momentary hush. Suddenly, a man shouted:

"I can hear someone calling!"

There was no doubt about it. From somewhere up in the direction of the avalanche tip there was a cry: "Help . . . Help . . ." It seemed so incredible that they could hardly believe their ears – they were absolutely positive that there had been no shouts the previous night for the wind had been too light then to drown such vigorous cries.

Grabbing their rescue equipment they proceeded up the slope as fast as possible. They passed the shallow and empty grave from which McLeod's body had been exhumed. The shouts were coming from the brink of a small, iced-up waterfall, somewhat higher up than Murray had indicated. Hastily, they went round the side of this and saw above them, in the debris, a hand sticking out of the snow and moving – it was whiter than the snow.

"All right, lad, we've found you. We'll soon have you out," shouted Jock Farquharson.

Though still breathless from the dash up the slope, they quickly dug round the buried man, careful not to injure him with the shovels. It proved to be a difficult task, since both his feet and the lower part of his body were encased in ice. When a wet-snow avalanche is subjected to pressure, as it often is in its rush through narrow parts of a gully, it rapidly freezes once it stops and pressure is released. This is what had occurred in

Robert Burnett's case. It had also become colder overnight and so any melt water which was about – probably the snow round his body melted by body heat – refroze and encased his exposed skin, for his shirt, pullover and anorak had been pulled up by the force of the avalanche. The ice adhered to his body as if it had been bonded with a powerful adhesive and when it was removed his flesh resembled a pin-cushion as a myriad of needlepoints oozed blood. Even using a pen-knife they had difficulty in removing the ice and large areas of skin simply peeled off. His hands were in a similar state for he had been frantically digging for hours; he was badly frostbitten.

It was then 12.30 pm. He had been buried for twenty-two hours – the longest avalanche burial survival recorded in Britain. The previous night, when the rescue team was searching, he must have been unconscious and this fact probably played a considerable part in saving his life, for someone unconscious uses less oxygen and isn't subjected to the same degree of shock as a fully conscious person. Burnett was put on a stretcher and taken down to the Land Rover; an ambulance picked him up at Mar Lodge and took him to Aberdeen hospital.

Meanwhile, the search continued for the one remaining man, Alex McKenzie. The rescue party again employed the bamboo poles to probe the avalanche tip. At 2.30 pm, as they were growing despondent at the prospect of failure, Jim Fraser finally located him; he was about three or four feet below the surface. He lay face down with the snow packed tightly about him. They knew before they dug him out that he was dead.

Later, when Burnett was interviewed in hospital in Aberdeen by Sergeant Massie of Bucksburn, he criticised the rescue team for abandoning the initial search despite the fact that their torches were dead. Even with later knowledge of avalanche search and rescue, I feel that the small volunteer party from Braemar made the only possible decision. Jim Fraser, later a member of the Search and Rescue Dog Association, thinks that if he had had an avalanche dog that night, Burnett would have been located with the minimum of delay, and he's probably right.

Burnett, I gather, took up pot-holing after his accident – the confines of a narrow pot-hole shouldn't hold any terror for him after his burial under the snows of Beinn a'Bhuird.

The Wellington and the Storm

Hamish MacInnes, Dick Brown, Stan Stewart

To the north of the Rannoch Moor and south of Loch Laggan, in the wilds of the windswept no-man's-land of Ben Alder lies Loch Ossian; a loch which takes its name from the most famous of Celtic bards. It is desolate country by any standards, especially in winter, where for months it can retreat under a blanket of snow. In olden times it was the hunting ground of Scottish kings, who had their base on an island on Loch Laggan, now, alas, submerged beneath industrial waters, for the loch is a hydro-electric reservoir today. Much of the lower ground round Loch Ossian is also submerged under a green sea of unimaginative coniferous uniformity: Forestry Commission planting.

Desolation, like beauty, is in the eye of the beholder. To a few discerning people the land round Ben Alder is a sanctuary in the bosom of Scotland. Only the thread of the West Highland line to the west intrudes on this haunt of the red deer, the golden eagle and the fox.

It was in December 1942 that a Wellington bomber number L7867 of B Flight, RAF Lossiemouth, took off on a cross-country day training flight. The weather was cold and blustery at Loch Laggan and on the peaks sleat hissed down. Visibility was bad. The pilot took the plane down through cloud to below 5,000 feet, thereby disobeying specific instructions. About 1500 hours it crashed into the summit of Geal Charn, 3,714 feet, just north of Ben Alder.

Duncan Robertson was then head-keeper of Corrour Lodge which snuggles amid trees at the north-eastern end of Loch

Ossian. That evening the kitchen door burst open and a man dressed in a flying suit staggered in. Quite coherently, he asked the startled housekeeper if he could take his harness off. He was Sgt. P. E. Underwood, RAF, the tail gunner of the Wellington. After establishing that his five fellow crew members were all killed, he had struggled down from the summit to the Lodge unaided.

Nine years later, again in the month of December, a survivor loomed out of one of the worst storms for many years, into the shelter of that snug kitchen, to announce that four men lay dead up towards the pass to Ben Alder.

The friends one makes in youth often have a lasting influence, especially climbing companions. There's an impetuous tendency to stick out your neck, mostly through lack of knowledge; nevertheless, upon this foundation experience is built, as well as mountaineering common sense. The obvious isn't always so apparent when you don't have anyone to show you the ropes! When I started climbing there were no climbing schools, either outward- or upward-bounding. The modern inmate of such establishments is crammed with instant knowledge and in such academic circles the snow hole is regarded with the sanctity of a church, and map and compass the bible and staff of the wayfarer.

When John Black, John Bradburn, Sid Tunion and I lifted our eyes to the hills it was with an abundance of enthusiasm and a distinct lack of equipment: an old hemp rope, clinker-nailed boots and, if we were lucky, a karabiner and sling between us. We had to make do with the minimum of gear, yet I feel that our shoestring education had a lot of compensations. It taught us to be self-sufficient and self-reliant, principles much lacking today. Now we have occasionally to go to the assistance of a party on a mountain that may only be "fatigued" and require an escort (often an ill-tempered one) back to the road.

Tragedy overtook those early climbing friends of mine one cold December in 1951. The events which befell this party and also included Sid's wife, Ann Tunion, had nothing to do with lack of equipment or lack of knowledge, for by then they were all experienced mountaineers with several years on the Scottish and Alpine peaks behind them. It was a type of accident which still happens today. The adversary is not mountain or avalanche, but the weather and that most insidious killer of the unwary, exposure.

I first met John Black, John Bradburn and Sid on the Cobbler, a small, savage, terrier-like peak which stands boldly above Arrochar at the head of Loch Long, some thirty miles from Glasgow. For generations it has been a kindergarten for budding rock tigers from the city. Its mica schist grudgingly offers the smallest wrinkles as a substitute for holds and when wet, which it often is, it makes the crags as slippery as oiled leather.

John Black was a lean-faced, serious man with deft movement who had the analytical mind of an engineer. John Bradburn was also in the engineering business, being a draughtsman: quiet spoken, always well dressed and giving the air of one contented with life. Sid was from tough stock. As a lad with his brother Sandy, he thought nothing of walking into the depths of the Cairngorms from Aberdeen where he was brought up. Aberdonians are hard men on the hills and Sid was no exception. All, including Sid's wife Ann, were honorary office bearers of the Glencoe Mountaineering Club, based in Glasgow. Though I was never a member, I used their bus at weekends and climbed with them. We taught ourselves the vagaries of the sport and rejoiced in the freedom of the hills. Another young climber who sometimes joined us was Jimmy Grieve. Those were carefree days and on a Saturday we used to rendezvous at Glasgow's St Enoch's Square and take the bus to Glencoe or some other far-flung highland destination. We even went to the Alps in the bus on one occasion.

But to return to the Glencoe Club party of New Year 1951. Hogmanay is a time for revelry in Scotland where the national drink is patronised with a fervour which must gratify the Exchequer. Climbers usually head for the hills at this festival; some to ensure their discomfort insist on camping on mountain tops, a peculiar diversion, you may say, when the summits are in the path of the North Atlantic hurricanes.

The Glencoe Club party decided to take in New Year 1951 at Ben Alder cottage in the Central Highlands. It is a snug abandoned bothy on the shore of Loch Ericht that seems to beckon the weary traveller, and it is reputedly haunted by the ghost of a hanged man. The area is wild, with no roads and even the trails owe an apology to the walker. It was close by that that sprightly Jacobite and alcoholic, Prince Charlie, took refuge in Cluny's cave, a rustic hideout by all accounts which, if it didn't operate on smokeless fuel, at least had a backdrop of grey Ben Alder cliff which would obscure any smoke signal to keen-eyed redcoats.

There are seldom good climbing conditions at the New Year, but being a perennial optimist I myself repaired to Glencoe that year with Charlie Vigano, a member of the renowned Creagh Dhu Mountaineering Club, in the hope of stealing a route before the Old Year escaped. Anyhow we agreed there was little climbing on Ben Alder and in those days I didn't go a bundle on either history or ghosts.

John Black, John Bradburn, Jimmy Grieve, Sid and Ann Tunion left Queen Street Station, Glasgow, on a Fort William train. Their intention was to get off at the remote halt of Corrour which comprised a brace of incongruous buildings and two lonely signals, set amidst god-forsaken country on the easterly frontier of Lochaber. On the train were other mountaineers with similar intentions, members of the Scottish Mountaineering Club who knew the Glencoe climbers. Dick Brown was one of the SMC party. With him were Dr Malcolm Slesser, Stanley Stewart, Gordon Waldie and several others. Dick Brown takes up the story:

> I think the first sign that things were going wrong that holiday was at Bridge of Orchy station when the train stopped. I went up the platform to see the driver, for I knew that the guard had been celebrating and you have to make arrangements for the train to stop at Corrour, it's not a regular halt. On the way along the platform I met another climber who told me that there was no point in going to see the driver, for both he and the fireman were in much the same state as the guard.
>
> The train jerked out of the desolate station of Orchy and skirted the Rannoch Moor. We did stop at Corrour, however, though as the train was long and the station short, the manoeuvre of stopping the guard's van at the platform was not successful. The Glencoe party, who had

their rucksacks with them in the carriage, got out smartly. But not so us, for our gear was in the guard's van beneath a mountain of other luggage. The guard came along and shouted, "You've got two minutes to get your stuff off." He then disappeared, but he was true to his word: the train pulled away before all our rucksacks and skis were unloaded. Stan Stewart and I were still on board and Stan, who incidentally is a solicitor, rushed into one of the compartments and pulled the communication cord. But the New Year breakdown in communications obviously extended to the communication cord. The train kept going. It was pulled again and the one-time merry guard came storming down the train, as black as an Atlantic depression, asking who was responsible.

I said to him as he barged in, "If you don't stop this train, I'll go right up to Fort William and make a complaint. I'm warning you!" The guard, realising that I meant what I said, released the vacuum brakes and stopped the train about a mile and a half beyond Corrour station.

By the time we got all our gear assembled on the snow beside the line, the day was well advanced and the weather nasty. Several old women peered through the steamed-up windows of the train with worried expressions, wondering where on earth we were going on such a night in such a place.

Malcolm Slesser, meanwhile, left behind with some of our equipment close to the station, had climbed the signal post to see if he could spy the wayward train. He couldn't, so he trudged up the line to try and make contact with Stan and myself.

Sid Tunion's Glencoe party had already got a lift in a lorry going to Corrour Lodge. It had waited some time for our group, but eventually had to leave without us. So we set off laden with skis and rucksacks to the Youth Hostel (which has no warden) at the south-westerly end of Loch Ossian, just off the dirt road to Corrour Lodge. There we spent the night.

Sid's party had a drum-up of beans and soup in the woods close to the Lodge and then, shouldering their packs, headed up the snow-covered track towards the pass leading to Ben Alder cottage. It was about 8.30 pm and though it was snowing a bit, there wasn't a great deal of wind. Anyhow, they knew that it was a fairly straightforward trek up over the pass then down to the cottage. They had heavy packs, with enough food for several days. They even had a pressure cooker.

They had been going about two hours, having covered some two and a half miles up the glen, when they found that the snow was too deep to continue. John Black, Sid and Ann Tunion decided to bivouac for the night, as they had plenty of equipment. They were at the junction of the Uisge Labhair and the Glas Choire streams at a place called the Tramp's Grave. John Bradburn and Jimmy Grieve carried on, but a short way beyond they, too, decided to bed down for the night.

At about six o'clock the next morning John Bradburn and Jimmy Grieve decided to push on towards the pass. The weather had worsened overnight and a strong south-westerly wind was blowing. Sid's party awoke about two hours later after an unpleasant night and decided, like their two friends, to continue. It was easier, they thought, to go with the wind in the direction of the pass than to fight it. They also knew that John and Jimmy would be worried if they didn't show up at Ben Alder cottage. But the weather was so desperate now that John Black, Sid and Ann couldn't roll up their sleeping bags. In any case the rucksack straps were frozen solid, like steel bands on a packing case. It was quite impossible to open their packs to stuff the frozen bags inside. They didn't have much to eat, despite the fact that they had ample supplies of instant food in the form of chocolate and shortbread. In such an environment, in cold, damp and the cutting blast of the wind, one doesn't have the inclination to linger over food in any form. The overriding desire is to get to hell out of the strength-sapping blast.

Meantime, back at the bottom end of Loch Ossian, the SMC party made their way after breakfast along the rough road to Corrour Lodge. Stan Stewart remembers that day well:

There was now a very strong south-westerly wind blowing where we were. The temperature was just around freezing or a little above. There were blatters of sleet and big wet flakes melted on landing and the gusts whipped up spray dervishes from Loch Ossian, so that the air was filled with cold moisture. Even with the wind at our backs we were soaked. I was wearing an old Home Guard great-coat, cut to jacket length, which I had proudly thought to be my personal armour plate, proof against anything. But its hidden qualities included a large capacity for absorbing moisture and by the time we reached the far end of Loch Ossian we were only too ready to sink our pride and beg the shelter of the estate bothy.

The keeper, Andrew Tait, after looking over the wretched soaking party, asked them where they were headed, and when they said Ben Alder cottage, he asked, "Are you from Gartnavel?" (a well-known mental institution near Glasgow). But like most Highlanders, the keeper's bark was worse than his bite and he took them to a snug bothy and ordered his men to cut a pile of firewood for them. The keeper's boss, Sir John Stirling Maxwell, the owner of the estate, was also a member of the Scottish Mountaineering Club.

A short way up the pass a life and death struggle was being enacted. It was about 9.15 am when Sid's party, fighting their way up the glen, met John Bradburn and Jimmy Grieve coming back. This was at Lochan Allt Glas Choire. John Bradburn told them about the bivouac they had and how at six o'clock they had pressed on with the gale whipping the fresh snow into a frenzy. But they had found that they just couldn't make it and had decided to come back. They all now turned into the wind and headed back towards Corrour Lodge.

At about ten o'clock Jimmy decided to abandon his rucksack. Today, such irrational behaviour is recognised as a sign of impending exposure. So far he hadn't appeared too bad, just a bit slower than the others. Presently it was John Bradburn's turn to act strangely; he threw his torch away, complaining that it was too heavy! When they reached the bivouac site which Sid's party had used the previous night the rest decided to abandon their rucksacks. Though the storm had been too bad for them to eat a meal, they did have some chocolate – probably about three ounces each – as well as some butterscotch. Ann, who had been sick earlier, had fortunately recovered.

John Bradburn and John Black broke trail, always a soul

destroying and energy absorbing task. Then Sid and Ann gave them a break. The wind was so strong now that they had to lean steeply into it and keep moving, otherwise they would have been blown backwards. Hailstones straffed them, projected by the worst storm for years in an area renowned for severe winter weather. Not long after this, only about half a mile beyond the bivouac site, Jimmy died. Half a mile further John Black and Sid collapsed. Vainly Ann tried to shelter them from the blast, but to no avail; they both died. John Bradburn was somewhere ahead. Ann left the boys about 1.30 pm and managed to reach the Lodge in under two hours.

At the bothy the SMC party had made the most of the relative comfort; the previous night both Malcom Slesser and Dick Brown had produced chanters and there was a light-hearted competition in the intricacies of piping, with the pibroch (classical pipe music) being discussed and played by the log fire. Outside the storm raged. It created havoc throughout Scotland, bringing down trees and causing widespread structural damage. A short time after 1.30 pm the SMC group heard the heavy tread of keeper Andrew Tait's boots outside the bothy. He opened the door and announced: "Look here, there's a woman in my house. She tells me there's four dead men in the glen. Can you come and give me a hand?"

With the keeper and two of his men, the climbers found the bodies of John Bradburn, John Black and Sid in the fading light. Jimmy's body was located the next day. During the night Andrew Tait had made up stretchers with saplings and jute sacks and with the help of the deer ponies the bodies were taken down to the Lodge.

It is easy to appear complacent over the passage of years and say such things don't happen to experienced mountaineers any more. Now we are aware of the dangers and the sudden onset of exposure. In 1951 exposure, if indeed anyone thought about it, was assumed to be a gradual process. Its symptoms are now well known to include faulty vision and irrational behaviour; manifest in this party as they abandoned their rucksacks and John Bradburn threw away his torch. Or was it? Certainly they must have been suffering from exposure, but leaving their packs might have just saved them by diverting their last straws of energy to locomotion rather than carrying a burden. One can hypothesise endlessly on the tragedy, but the fact is that they were reasonably well clad with windproof though not necessarily waterproof clothing, and of course damp soaks away vital body heat like a deadly wick, with a wind in excess of fifty mph and an actual air temperature of 32°F. The effective chilling temperature that day must have been in the region of –10°F.

John Black suffered from asthma, and I remember Sid on some occasions lagging behind when we were climbing. It was only later, after I knew him better, that I discovered he suffered from a pelvic war wound. He had served in the Royal Artillery. These may have been contributory factors.

The accident rocked the Scottish climbing fraternity to its roots. Here were four climbers, and I can personally vouch for their fitness, who were adequately equipped with plenty of food, who died on what is usually an easy mountain path. It just didn't seem possible, yet it happened.

Ann survived unscathed except for the terrible trauma of losing her husband and three friends. A short time later the Glencoe Club was disbanded.

Death in the Giant Mountains

Miloš Vrba

*Miloš Vrba, the Czech avalanche expert, relates another remark-
able tale from the mountains of his homeland.*

"Attention! Warning by the Mountain Rescue Services: Heavy
snow storm conditions in the mountains. Do not leave huts and
chalets situated above one thousand metres! Abandon ski tour
projects; evacuate downhill runs and ski slopes! All chair-lifts
have been stopped.

"I repeat: Warning by the Mountain Rescue Service . . ."

The weather is invariably atrocious in the Giant Mountains
over Christmas. Fine powder snow falls on Christmas Eve and
turns soggy on Christmas Day. Then fog sets in and the
thermometer doesn't creep to zero till New Year. It's an
unpleasant time of low air pressure, with people irritable,
quarrelsome and bored.

The weather was no exception in 1959 and it was what sparked
off a rescue operation that made a perfunctory few lines in the
local newspaper. But for me it was something more. I took part in
the rescue. What I experienced during the last two nights of 1959
and the first waking hours of 1960 forced me to ask myself the
reasons for what happened. I tried to understand the physical and
emotional motives of that poor boy. The official verdict was that
he was himself to blame because he had ignored the warning of
the Mountain Rescue Service and overestimated his physical
capabilities. This was true. However, I also learned some background facts which, while they did not change the cause of the
accident, at least enabled me to understand the behaviour of that
unfortunate young man called Jan.

The Meadow Chalet is reputedly the largest mountain hotel in Central Europe. At an altitude of 1,410 metres (4,626 feet) it is situated in the middle of an extensive plateau girdled by summits. However, with the exception of the highest peak in the Giant Mountains, Snezka (1,605 metres, 5,266 feet), the altitude between the foot and the top of the plateau fluctuates only between fifty and one hundred metres, so that the area is extremely exposed. Storms predominate throughout the year.

In spite of such climatic conditions, people have built houses here since time immemorial. In the first half of the seventeenth century, after the battle of White Mountain near Prague, the persecuted evangelical Protestants found a safe refuge here when leaving the country. The Polish frontier is a short way from the Meadow Chalet. The reason why people choose to build on that windy, foggy and inhospitable plateau is because of the excellent pasture and a constant source of spring water. One tributary of the river Elbe, the White Elbe, has its source in the neighbourhood of Meadow Chalet. It descends as a torrent through the long, sheer avalanche-prone White Elbe Valley. Not far from a spot called Spindler's Mill it joins the Black Elbe for the long journey to the North Sea.

On 30 December 1959 few people skied, though there were over 400 guests staying at the Meadow Chalet. In spite of dense fog, four young men left the chalet at 9.30 am. They were university students spending their Christmas vacation in the mountains. They were fed up, and with good reason. Up until now it had been a week of bad weather, the usual continuous fog and heavy snow. In two days they would be returning without having even seen the place. Only one had visited the Giant Mountains in winter before, the other three boys were beginners. As well as this, Jan, who was one of the group, was extremely clumsy and held back the others who had quickly acquired the basic principles of skiing. That day, after having haggled about what to do, they agreed to attempt a ski tour as far as Spindler's Mill, an ambitious plan for aspiring skiers. It's a hard trip in heavy snow and at the end there's a steep downhill section.

They made it, arriving about noon at Spindler's Mill saturated, after countless falls. What would they do now, they wondered? Soon they got cold. The only thing they could agree on was to go to the snack bar, though they hadn't much money. It seemed as if everybody in Spindler's Mill had the same idea, for it was lunchtime and the snack bar was hopelessly over-crowded. Jan felt self-conscious and uncomfortable, for he was a country boy and his skiing clothes were baggy and makeshift. He didn't feel he fitted in with the confident crowd in the snack bar and he was in a hurry to leave. Not so his three friends.

At about one o'clock Jan's patience ran out. He decided to return to the Meadow Chalet alone.

"Hold on, Jan, we're coming too." His friends paid their bills and left with him. They walked as far as the main road without a word. There a quarrel developed because Jan wanted to turn left and the three boys to the right, to the valley station of the chair-lift.

"Why to the chair-lift?" Jan asked petulantly.

"That's a stupid question! Upwards by the lift and, after-wards, we ski our same route back."

"No other possibility," put in the one who had been to the Giant Mountains before.

"I know another way to reach the Meadow Chalet," Jan retorted. "I found it on the map: the White Elbe Valley! It's longer, of course, no chairlift, no ski-tow. But I'm sure it won't be crowded. I can't bear those crowds on the plateau and all over your route."

"Don't be silly. Do you want to climb six hundred metres in this snow and fog?"

"Look, the fog's gone!" Jan pointed towards the mountain with his ski pole.

It was true, the fog had disappeared and the ridge above was clearly visible. But at the same time, the temperature must have dropped for the wind was now cold. Snow began to fall and envelop the mud and slush. Black clouds above the summits indicated more snow was coming.

"Don't be crazy, Jan! Come with us. Within three hours it'll be dark and you don't know the way. There's not much daylight just now."

"Three hours! That's plenty for me! I'll go alone if none of you are up to it. I bet I'll be there before you. You all ski like snails."

So Jan went off to the left. The others, after some head

shaking, turned right and shuffled towards the chairlift. A long queue had formed but they decided to wait, though it meant hanging about in the now heavier snowfall and cold wind.

Now, at last, Jan felt in a good mood. He whistled like a small boy, looking forward with pleasure to the coming battle with the elements. Here his old clothes didn't matter. Unfortunately, it is often the case that the feeling of elation and satisfaction is of shorter duration than that of depression and disillusion. Fully occupied by his dreams of solo adventure, he didn't notice a group of youths and girls from the university.

He saw them too late to take evasive action round the corner of the post office for they had already spotted him. One of them was Vera. His newly regained composure was shattered. Vera was one of the most popular girls in the student skiing parties that season in the Giant Mountains, and Jan had long nursed a secret and fruitless passion for her. Secret because he did not know how to approach such a goddess. Fruitless because now, as always, she was accompanied by the handsome guitar-playing Vaclav who effortlessly managed to be all the things that Jan was not.

To his surprise, however, Vera and Vaclav and their friends seemed perfectly happy to sweep Jan along with them to drink tea in their hut in the village of St Peter. Flattered and confused, Jan explained that he couldn't stop as he had to get back to the Meadow Chalet before dark.

"Then why are you going this way?"

"I want to explore new country in White Elbe Valley on the way."

"What? Going all that way alone? It's too far to solo," one of them warned. "If you want a tour through a lonely region, why not go the shorter and simpler way through the Long Valley?"

"Where's that?"

"On beyond St Peter. Then it leads direct to the Eagle Owl hut. You know where that is?"

"Oh, yes. We passed it this morning."

"Then come with us to have a cup of tea and, afterwards, ski up the Long Valley, and you may meet your friends at Eagle Owl hut at the top."

It was snug and friendly in the village. Brew followed brew and Vaclav tuned his guitar for another song when the Mountain Rescue Services Tannoy system resounded through the wooden walls with the advice about worsening snow conditions. *Do not leave huts and chalets above one thousand metres. Abandon ski tour projects.*

"Well, Jan, now you must stay here overnight!" Vera teased him.

"No! No, I'll not stay!"

She turned to the guitarist. "I'm sure you'll stay, Vaclav."

Vaclav smiled ironically and plucked a string.

Jan spoke up. "I'm not scared! On the contrary, I'm glad that a blizzard is brewing; it's to my taste. I'm leaving!"

"Don't be silly, Jan! It's getting dark. Go down to the inn, ring them and tell them you'll be up tomorrow."

Vaclav's impatient advice was the soundest he would get, but the last person Jan was going to listen to was Vaclav. Watching him and Vera together had fed his self-pity and frustration. Now here was a chance to show he was somebody, somebody who could snap his fingers at warnings, somebody with the guts to risk his life and fight the blizzard. As they all watched him in silence he just wished he had something more stylish to put on than his old threadbare anorak and his leather motorcycle helmet, and that his skis weren't made of ash with beak tips and with two long hazel ski poles.

Perhaps Vera knew that a word from her could have changed Jan's mind, but she was tired of him and thought he was behaving stupidly. However, on an impulse, as he opened the door on to the swirling snow, she grabbed a handful of biscuits and all the sugar lumps left in the food locker and pressed them on him.

"It's a long trip, Jan. You'll be hungry."

The Meadow Chalet seems to be a world unto itself especially in bad weather, and is almost independent of the outside world. It has its own well, its own power station driven by the water energy of the Elbe stream; it has its own laundry, bakery and various workshops in the cellar. Upstairs that December night 450 young people, mostly university students, made the two dining halls reverberate with their boisterous high spirits. However, three young men, sitting at a table with one vacant chair, would have caught the attention of an attentive observer.

They were evidently worried, speaking to each other in low, urgent voices.

"Look, it's gone too far. We must do something!"

"What, for example?"

"For a start, alert the mountain rescue!"

"Wonderful suggestion, but it's too expensive."

"Why expensive? Nothing's charged for rescuing."

"Not unless you've been bloody stupid."

"Well, that's his problem. He would go alone through that White Elbe Valley!"

"Take it easy! It's a long walk. Maybe he rested in some hut on the way . . ."

"Don't talk nonsense. There's no hut in the White Elbe Valley according to the map. He hasn't a torch and it's been dark since four o'clock. Now, it's half-past eight! Also, he doesn't know the way. Something must have happened. I'm worried, very worried and I'm going to tell the rescue service."

A siren started, a terrible sound, bringing back to many the sleepless and fearful nights of the war; a sound which tells that human life is threatened.

The engineer of the chairlift was the first one to leave his cottage on the hillside, and he ran down to the station to prepare the lift for the rescue teams.

At the other end of Spindler's Mill an attractive girl hurried out through the garden of her parents' house, buttoning her short fur coat as she ran to the telephone exchange. She had to be at her post as the exchange was operated manually.

The teacher put aside his red pen from correcting a pupil's essay, and reached for the blue ski-trousers and orange anorak of his Mountain Rescue Service uniform.

The waiter stopped gliding through the dining hall, put a tray of full beer glasses on a vacant table and disappeared in the direction of the staff quarters to get his gear.

The joiner shuffling cards in the bar put the pack down beside his glass, pocketed his winnings and left without saying a word to his companions.

The postman awoke from a heavy sleep. It took him a couple of minutes to realise what was wrong, then he sprang out of bed, dressed hurriedly, and grabbed his rescue rucksack from the corner of the bedroom.

The doctor and the druggist, who were playing billiards in the tearoom, looked at each other, silently put their cues in the rack and left the inn. The head waiter didn't say anything. They'd pay later. They had other things to think about right now.

I help my wife run a private hotel for employees of a Prague factory not far from Eagle Owl hut. So I am well placed for my special snow and avalanche research and for lending a hand with rescues when Otan, our local leader, gives me a call, as he did the night of 30 December 1959. One of the hotel staff, a lad called Honza, is also in the team. I slipped along to his room where he was snoring loudly. I hesitated to wake him as he had had a hectic day. However, he wouldn't forgive me if I didn't and I couldn't go out alone in such a storm.

"Honza, get up!" The snoring was uninterrupted.

"Get up! Quickly!"

". . . What's the matter?"

"Call-out. We've not much time."

"To hell with all those idiots! Just before New Year's Eve, just like last year, remember? Avalanche or broken leg?"

"Nothing like that. It's a missing man. Otan's just phoned. It's a young man who left the snack bar in Spindler's Mill about one o'clock for the Meadow Chalet. He didn't arrive."

"What time's it now?"

"Quarter past ten. We have to check the area both sides of the track from here to Eagle Owl Hut, then as far as Meadow Chalet. We rendezvous with the other groups at 1.00 am."

"Does Otan know where the man might have gone to?"

"Yes. White Elbe Valley. That's Otan's patch. He's taking most of the team there, but he's also sending small groups to check all possible routes from Spindler's Mill to Meadow Chalet."

Honza dressed and picked up his rucksack.

"Do we need any other gear?"

"Nothing special. I've a Very pistol and flares. You take the searchlight. Come on, Honza, get your finger out, it's half-past ten already."

As soon as Honza and I slammed the outer door and turned

the corner of our hotel, we caught the storm face on. Conversation was out of the question – the din was horrendous. But years of working together in the mountains meant we understood each other perfectly without speech.

The ridge was marked by three-metre-high wooden posts at ten-metre intervals. Some of these hardly protruded above the afternoon snow cover. We quartered each side of the marked route, concentrating on hollows scooped out by the wind around stunted hill-pines. Visibility was good here, for both fog and falling snow had dispersed. The snow had stopped about six o'clock, but the wind was ferocious and seemed to be getting worse.

From time to time we used the searchlight and I fired several white flares to illuminate larger areas and give an indication of our position to the missing man. We knew the hill region between us and Meadow Chalet intimately. I'm sure we would have detected any unusual object among the scattered pines.

After about an hour's thorough searching on our skis, we cut through corrugated hard-packed snowdrifts and reached Eagle Owl hut. At that time it was Eagle Owl hut in name only as it had burned down soon after the war and new premises had not yet been built. In place of the once luxurious hotel a shabby canteen and telephone had been installed at this point and simple meals were available, with a couple of emergency beds.

Eagle Owl hut is at one of the most important and dangerous crossways in the Giant Mountains. The popular ridge route connecting Spindler's Mill with the Meadow Chalet intersects here with the path from the ski villages of St Peter and Pec.

It wasn't until we dropped into the snow hollow where the hut is located that we caught a glimpse of a dim light behind frozen window panes. In our searchlight the ugly barracks of a canteen shone like a fairy cottage dipped in silver. We didn't want to stop and take off our skis; so we knocked on the roof with our ski poles. The canteen keeper came out.

"What's the news?" I asked.

"Nothing."

"Ring rescue control and tell them we are continuing."

"Right, boys. Good luck."

As far as this point the plateau is almost level, but beyond Eagle Owl hut it rises abruptly towards a saddle between two hills, a notorious funnel for the prevailing north-west winds to attain their greatest velocity.

That night it must have been in excess of 100 kph! as we couldn't breathe or even keep upright. We wrapped scarves over the lower part of our faces and pulled down our goggles. I headed to the edge of Broad Ridge above the Blue Valley. Honza followed using the searchlight from time to time. It was a difficult section.

The black sky suddenly lightened. There was a glare behind us. A rescue group going up the Long Valley must have set off a white illuminator.

A rescue team ascending the Blue Valley from the village of Pec replied with another flare. It was heartening to realise that we were not alone in this snow-filled wilderness. I replied by firing one against the wind to indicate that we were on Broad Ridge.

As our comet-like flare was falling, I saw something strange to the left, quite a way off. I touched Honza with my ski pole and pointed. He understood immediately and without a word we headed for the spot.

That quick decision to abandon the search on the Broad Ridge and investigate a strange object off our search area later caused me sleepless nights. At the moment of our diversion we were the first two rescuers anywhere near Jan, but we had no way of knowing this. Had we continued in our original direction of search we might have found him.

Our diversion was abortive: the strange object was a freight sledge from Meadow Chalet, full of frozen meat. It was almost buried in a snowdrift. The tractor driver hauling the sledge up from Pec was probably caught by the snowstorm in the afternoon and decided to abandon the freight, rating personal safety above punctual delivery.

Having investigated the sledge, we continued searching the area leading to the saddle. I forgot the section on Broad Ridge which we had missed by doing the diversionary search. We reached the saddle. This next section proved to be the worst. We had to lean against the wind like ski-jumpers, otherwise we could not have moved. The prevailing good visibility seemed strange. The light of the summit hut on Snezka looked like a star and we could see the dimly lit windows of Meadow Chalet.

Far below across the ridge we recognised Polish towns and villages. Though it had stopped snowing, when we stood still our skis and boots were completely covered by a dense layer of snow crystals drifting in the hurricane close above snow level. It looked like a flying carpet.

Three green flares appeared in the black sky. One o'clock. Time for the rendezvous at Meadow Chalet. We skied down the slope.

For the rest of the night we searched through the White and Devil Meadows. Though there were about fifty of us we didn't find anything.

On 31 December 1959 it was foggy, damp and cold. The wind of the previous night had abated in the early hours to be replaced by fog. By three o'clock in the afternoon it was getting dark and people were preparing to see in the new year. The self-service grocery at Spindler's Mill was chock-a-block with customers. Skiers forced off the slopes by the fog consoled themselves by stocking up with wine for the evening's festivities, while the wives of the rescue team wondered whether they'd be greeting 1960 on their own again that year, as their menfolk were still up in the mountains hunting for the missing skier.

One of the long-suffering wives was standing in the queue at the check-out behind a couple of students wrangling amicably over the rate of sugar consumption in their lodgings. The boy laughingly accused the girl of giving it all away to Jan yesterday, and she had rounded on him saying was she expected to let that ridiculously ill-equipped idiot set out into the blizzard without anything to chew on all the way up to Meadow Chalet.

The village woman could contain herself no longer and broke into their romantic bickering to find out if they knew whether their Jan was the same man that her husband and many others were out looking for. "They were out all last night and today in the White Elbe Valley."

There was a pause while the young couple, sobered now, digested her information.

"Why are they searching in White Elbe Valley?" Vaclav asked.

"That's where he told his friends he was going."

"No, he didn't go that way. He went into Long Valley."

On the information gleaned from this chance encounter Otan re-briefed the rescue team and we prepared for another new year on the hill.

We had only been skiing for a short time when we caught a glimpse of white flares in the foggy sky somewhere in the direction of Eagle Owl hut. As we approached we also saw green lights in the fog. This was a signal to meet up. We were annoyed as we had now to descend the steep zig-zag trail. There was quite a large group of rescuers already there. Otan was looking at something in the snow on the steep slope bordering the path. Footprints had been found, leading directly uphill, ignoring the winding path. All the rescue team now followed Otan. The prints were partly covered under a thin layer of fresh snow so that only faint indentations were visible. The covering of fresh snow indicated that they must have been made the day before, just before the snow stopped at about 6.00 pm. This would fit with the knowledge we now had that Jan had left the St Peter hut at 4.00 pm. An inexperienced skier without a torch could take at least two hours to reach Eagle Owl hut. The climb was long and tiresome. After we finally left the wood and reached the open plateau, the footprints disappeared, covered no doubt by the drift in yesterday's storm.

Otan had now to decide what to do. Where had Jan gone? Straight ahead? Left or right? Such crucial questions usually occur during the course of a rescue operation. Further development of the rescue depends on sound psychological reasoning and, sometimes, good or bad luck. Discussion is often impossible because of the severe conditions. The leader must decide on his own which direction the operation will take.

Otan later explained that he remembered the example of the Babes in the Wood. When they lost the way they looked for a light and went in its direction. Jan probably did the same. From the edge of the plateau he would only see the lights of Richter's Chalet because the Eagle Owl canteen, though closer, was hidden in a hollow.

"This way!" Otan pointed with his stick to the right. "Richter's Chalet. Do a sweep search, check absolutely everything!"

This was a sound decision. Within fifteen minutes we found one of Jan's hazel sticks in a direct line between the last footprints and Richter's Chalet. Jan couldn't be far away. To be without a ski pole is like being minus a leg.

Unfortunately, the stick was the last clue that night. Although we made various sweeps and cross-sweeps, checking every dwarf pine, we didn't find anything. As the night progressed we became depressed and quarrelled about nothing. I'm sure that none of us knew the exact number of line searches we did to Eagle Owl canteen, then down as far as Richter's Chalet, uphill again, downhill again, across, back. Nothing.

The fog turned red.

"Look, a red flare!"

A red flare was the agreed signal to halt the rescue operation. But why stop it? Who would give such an order? The flare was a long way off and Jan couldn't have gone as far as that.

"It's midnight!" One of our party looked at his wristwatch. "A New Year is just beginning!"

"I strictly forbade anyone to shoot flares to celebrate tonight." Otan was very angry.

"They're drunk, Otan," I said. "They don't know what they're up to."

We started to search again across an icy face. We were all silent. I imagined the others shared the same thoughts: millions of people were wishing each other a Happy New Year at that moment. We just got on with the job.

With dawn the fog seeped into the valleys. The dark blue, cloudless sky turned slowly lighter and the snow on the mountains glared like polished silver. Finally, the sun, that eternal wonder, rose and changed the angry dark mountains into an idyllic picture of tranquillity. We returned home depressed.

I took little notice of the toy-like figures emerging from the forest far down the Blue Valley. They were in a long line on the steep snow-covered slopes. It was a rescue team from Pec taking over. Just then I was indifferent to the situation: I had no interest, no sentiment, no emotion. I was spiritually low. I was exhausted.

Bohous, a skilled mountain guide and rescuer, was on the extreme left of that line in the bed of the Blue Stream. They had been detailed to go as far as the so-called Grave, a sheer gorge where the Blue Stream starts. During his long years of rescuing, Bohous had found several victims there. But there was nothing that day, other than fresh fox prints. Bohous was also a dedicated hunter and seeing the fresh spoor awakened primitive instincts. He forgot the search and followed the fox prints. The fox had gone straight uphill towards Broad Ridge. So did Bohous. But the rescue group continued through Blue Valley veering right so that the distance between them widened. Bohous did not even notice this, he was too absorbed. Out of breath and sweating, he felt a satisfaction in his choice of climbing wax. The skis did not slide back one millimetre.

Cresting the steep slope the fox skirted round a stand of slender pines. It was at that moment that Bohous had his first glimpse of the animal, but it got scent of him and immediately took off as fast as the deep powder allowed.

"Now it's given up its scent," Bohous thought, disappointed.

"But what's the reason for it coming up here? There's bugger all here. Food? Its an icy desert. I wonder – could it have caught the scent of . . .?"

Bohous felt the hair on the back of his neck stand up. He took out a cigarette. His hand trembled as he lit it because he felt he was being watched by somebody behind him. The feeling was so strong that he forced himself to turn his head. It was an involuntary action. He didn't want to turn, but was compelled to do so. He knew exactly what he would see.

His eyes locked on a pair of wide open light blue eyes. They stared at each other for a long time. Bohous's living ones full of fear, the dead ones full of horror.

Jan was sitting against a pine trunk. He had his leather helmet on and his face was sheathed in ice which reflected the cold New Year's Day sun. The rest of his body was covered by the snow.

Otan arrived at our hotel one afternoon in early January. It was an unexpected visit. Honza brought coffee and cigarettes and discreetly left the room immediately.

Together we drank coffee and smoked, we didn't talk. However, I felt something important would be said. After a long time Otan asked:

"Are you sick? Your wife told me that you're not right."

It was true that I didn't feel well, but it wasn't sickness. It was a mental state which had plagued me since New Year's Day when Bohous had found Jan on the Broad Ridge. I just couldn't find my previous peace of mind. The wide-open eyes of the dead man with that transfixed look of horror had made me blame myself for Jan's tragic end. I told Otan about it and he listened in silence.

"I led the search towards the Broad Ridge that first night. I shot a white flare and, seeing a strange object far to the left in front of us, I abandoned the Broad Ridge search. Jan must have seen us, he must have cried out when he saw us moving away. I am sure that he died from despair which was mirrored in his eyes even in death."

Otan looked steadily at me. "No, you're wrong, Miloš. The boy died between 7.00 and 8.00 pm that first day, due to exhaustion and shock. At least four hours before you reached that area. I received the result of the autopsy today."

"Are you sure, Otan?" I asked.

"Quite sure, I had guilt pangs like you. I made a mistake, too, during the search the second night. As soon as we lost his footprints near Eagle Owl hut, I was sure that he went towards Richter's Chalet, because he would have seen the lights. That was basically correct, and finding one of his hazel sticks convinced me. Do you know why we didn't find anything more that night? Because when you go down towards Richter's Chalet, the lights disappear again behind a snow bank. I went back in daylight and saw my mistake. After the boy lost the lights he must have turned left towards Broad Edge where he met his end. I'll have to get to know my mountain again, Miloš. I know nothing."

This was the longest speech I had ever heard Otan give and he had not finished.

"In the end it was that fox hound, Bohous, who found him, and none of us could have helped him. He was dead before we knew that he was missing."

In January 1975 Honza Messner perished tragically on the icy mountainside of Snezka attempting to rescue an injured tourist, and Otan Stetka died nine months later, of a heart attack.

Duel with An Teallach

Hamish MacInnes and Iain Ogilvie

Just occasionally one hears of an act of bravery which seems to go far beyond the bounds of rational action. It may be someone saved from drowning by a complete stranger or a child snatched from the teeth of a blazing inferno by a passing samaritan, but usually such acts of mercy are of short duration, at least those which involve a single rescuer, though both lifeboat crews and various teams of rescuers can be exposed to danger for long periods.

The striking thing about Iain Ogilvie's attempt to save his friends on an ice-bound mountain in western Scotland is that it was a protracted effort by one man. There was no other alternative, for to have left his friends and gone for help would have certainly sealed their fate. As it was they had a chance, however slim, if he stayed with them and moved them to a safer place on that hostile peak.

First let me describe the mountain in question, An Teallach, which means the Forge in Gaelic. Heading north towards Ullapool in north-west Scotland, one first catches a glimpse of the castellated peaks of An Teallach from the Dundonnell Forest beyond Garve. It's not a forest of trees, but a deer forest, squelchy bogs, bouncy heather and of course deer. The road to the doorstep of An Teallach forks left from the A835 to Ullapool. Skirting the Corrieshalloch Gorge, it weaves downhill on the Road of Destitution, a name inspired by starving natives of the area who built it during the potato famine of 1851 – payment was made in potatoes!

This road gives the best tourist's view of the mountain; few peaks in the British Isles can vie with its rugged profile, it looks as if it was carelessly built by a crazy architect. What one can't see from the Road of Destitution is Toll an Lochain, an inkwell-like lochan huddled beneath the great cliffs. Around it for threequarters of its circumference An Teallach bends like a cross-cut saw. The highest peak is Bidean a'Ghlas Thuill (3,483 feet/1,062 metres). Eight further summits curl round the lochan to the west and south, the southerly aspect terminating in An-Sail Liath, the Grey Heel.

On 17 April 1966, three friends travelled north from London and parked their car in a lay-by off the Destitution Road. They were Iain Ogilvie, fifty-three, a member of the Alpine and Scottish Mountaineering Clubs; Charles Handley, fifty-nine, known as Tommy, who was of the Alpine Club and Climbers' Club, Peter Francis at thirty was the youngest member, a good rock climber – but he didn't have the snow or ice experience of the other two.

Shouldering their packs they climbed to the col east of An Teallach and made a high camp. There was an unusually heavy covering of snow for the time of year – moreover, it was extremely hard; as hard as Iain Ogilvie, with his wide knowledge of Scottish conditions, had ever experienced in early spring.

It is not uncommon for parties traversing An Teallach to pitch camp to the east of the mountain as these three friends did, otherwise the traverse would be a long day. Furthermore, they welcomed the solitude of the Highland snows. The scenery alone pays dividends to those prepared to carry a tent into this hinterland. Few places can rival the sheer grandeur of the cirque of An Teallach, while to the north, the horizon is dotted by peak upon peak endowed with such magical names as Cuinneag, Bein Dearg and Cul Beag. Beyond Ullapool on the fringe of the North Atlantic are the Summer Isles, small idyllic jewel-like islands on a romantic sea-board.

The object of this particular expedition was to go over all the ten tops of the An Teallach range. The first peak of the day was Sail Liath. Ahead, the peaks clustered in a series of icy pinnacles with a great precipice of 1,500 feet falling to Toll an Lochain. On their right they passed the gaping mouth of Constabulary Couloir, first climbed by Dr Tom Patey and members of a police rescue team. Presently the three climbers arrived at the main obstacle on the traverse, the face of Corrag Bhuidhe Buttress, in summer a steep rock face, in winter often plastered in snow and ice.

It was lunchtime when Iain Ogilvie and his two companions reached the summit of Sgurr Fiona. During the morning they had enjoyed traversing the top of Sail Liath, the four pinnacles of Corrag Bhuidhe and Lord Berkeley's Seat, a draughty and exposed "armchair" which is a promontory on the ridge. From below this last point an easy snow slope led them to the top of Sgurr Fiona and they realised that the main difficulties were now behind them.

At this stage, Tommy and Peter decided to miss out a subsidiary summit to the west, Sgurr Creag an Eich. Iain, however, had finished his sandwiches before them and, as he was feeling fit, he decided to take in this top. He asked his friends if they would wait for him and this they agreed to do, Tommy adding, "But if we get cold, we'll move on slowly and if there's any difficulty – anywhere that needs a rope – we'll wait for you."

So Iain set off to bag his peak.

He had covered almost half the distance along the snowplastered ridge to Sgurr Creag an Eich before he looked back and saw that Tommy and Peter already had the rope on and were climbing down the ridge of Sgurr Fiona towards Bidean a'Ghlas Thuill. Since the understanding was that they would wait for him, should the rope be required, he concluded that they must have thought that the rope wasn't really necessary for someone of his own ability, but that Tommy had thought it prudent to have Peter safeguarded as he wasn't so experienced.

As Iain considered this possibility, he turned and looked back again. He could see them quite clearly, silhouetted against the bright northern sky, now drawing slightly nearer as they bypassed a rocky step on the ridge. He stopped to watch them. Neither was moving now and he wondered if they were debating the best line of descent, or were they going to wait there for him? He went on but soon turned round again; for no obvious reason he was feeling distinctly uneasy. To his horror he saw they were both falling, sliding down the steep, hard snow at a high speed, hopelessly out of control. They shot over one low cliff, then over another where the rope caught and they were left hanging on the snow face. There was no movement, no sound, just silence. Iain Ogilvie describes what happened:

I ran back to the col and put crampons on over my tricouni-nailed boots. I recalled as I ran that Peter Francis also had crampons and Tommy had nailed boots the same as mine. Once at the col I found that I was at their level, but to reach them involved a long but fairly straightforward traverse of a quarter of a mile over hard snow interspersed with scree patches. On a later visit in summer I found that there was a deer track along this line but, of course, with the snow cover there was no sign of it then. The snow was banked up against the upper cliff on which they hung and it was much steeper than it is in summer. Several jagged rocks protruded from the slope down which they had fallen and I saw, as I approached, that the rope was snagged on one of these, so that they were both hanging from it. The particular projection on which the rope caught was very small and obviously had only a hair-trigger grip. If, I told myself, I could get them onto safer ground, then the most sensible thing to do next would be to go for help.

There was another vertical drop below them, but about thirty feet away to one side there was a steep tongue of snow and ice leading through the difficult sections below. I couldn't see to the bottom of it, but I realised that this was the best chance – my only hope of getting them down. This was essential, as I couldn't leave them where they were to go for help; it would take hours and, though they both appeared to be unconscious, it was just possible that one of them would come round and any movement might have sent them crashing once more down the face.

All this took only seconds to run through my mind. I quickly cramponed over to where they were hanging and discovered that they both had severe head injuries. With some difficulty I secured their rope where it was already caught. They were tied together with a fifty-foot length of full-weight nylon climbing rope and I had a further 120 feet in my rucksack. I went down to Tommy and tied him on to an end of my rope; as there was no suitable anchor to which I could tie him, I drove my ice axe into the steep slope for a belay. I then cut the rope on which he was hanging so that his weight came on to the ice axe on my rope. I had secured the other rope at the rock spike so that it wouldn't run free with Peter on the end of it once it was cut.

I then swung Tommy across the hard snow in a pendulum motion to the top of the tongue of snow – my only hope. Once he was on the correct line of descent, I proceeded to lower him until he was out of sight over a bulge. When all the rope ran out there was still considerable tension on it, so I knew that he hadn't yet reached the bottom. I had no alternative but to descend the steep slope. Using my crampons, this stretched me to the limit of my capabilities, for I had no ice axe, as it was holding Tommy, and I dared not put any more weight on the rope because the belay wasn't all that secure. My two friends had lost their ice axes in the fall and the only thing I had in lieu of an axe was a piton hammer. I tried to drive it in above me as I kicked the points of my crampons into the snow. Suddenly, as I was inching down, I slipped and fell over a short rock step of about six feet, landing on my chest on the slope beneath. The snow was still iron hard here and, even as I tried to regain my breath, I knew that it was imperative to stop: otherwise I would be killed. Putting my full body weight on to the head of the piton hammer, so that the short spike bit into the snow, I slowed up and scraped to a halt. I was shaken, bruised, but otherwise uninjured. I had been carrying two rock pitons which I had intended to use to bring Peter down, but these were lost during my fall.

I worked my way over to where Tommy was hanging at the end of the rope and realised that I would have to secure him before I could go back up to release the rope and get my ice axe. I had with me an ice screw but the surrounding ice wasn't suitable for it, so I had to jam it into a crack in the rock nearby. I realised that it had only a fifty-fifty chance of holding, but things were getting desperate; risks had to be run.

I was now able to use the hanging rope as a handrail since Tommy's weight had been transferred from it to the piton, and I quickly reached my ice axe and descended again without further incident. This time I lowered him a complete rope's length, using the ice screw as a belay. When the rope was paid out its full length he had reached the foot of the Torridonian Sandstone rock bands and was at the top of another steep snow slope. I climbed down to him and started to cut out a ledge in the hard snow. All this, I later discovered, took a great deal of time, but eventually it was completed and I laid him out on this cold ledge and covered him with most of my clothing.

I then started back up the slope for Peter. As I removed the rope from the screw at Tommy's last belay on my way past, the screw actually fell out of the crack and bounced down the slope. I had been right – it wasn't secure! However, I told myself that this was no time to think of narrow escapes.

When I reached Peter I suspected that he was already dead but, having come all this way, I decided to try and lower him down. As I now had both ropes available I could secure him from much further up the slope. Also, I had my axe which made my own position safer, though unfortunately, I had to use the axe again as a belay for the second lower to Tommy's ledge, because the ice screw had vanished.

After a lot of hard but uneventful work, I brought him down to Tommy's level. I knew then that I would have to run the gauntlet once more and descend the treacherous slope without an ice axe. There was no alternative for once more the axe wasn't safe enough to risk our combined weight.

The last ten feet down to where Peter hung were at a steep angle. I slipped again. I might have saved myself with my hammer, I suppose, but I tripped on Peter's body and pitched headlong over it. In seconds I was travelling at an alarmingly high speed. As soon as I tried to dig the hammer pick in, it was snatched from my hands by the force of my fall. I shot down about 500 feet, hitting two rocks sticking out of the snow en route. Fortunately, I stopped before running on to the scree and boulders at the bottom. I was badly bruised and skinned and, as I found out later, I had slipped a disc in my neck.

By this time it was after 1.00 pm. There was no possibility of getting up again. Even if I had managed to reach them there was nothing more that I could do. The only course left open was to go down for assistance and return with help. I knew also that I must get down for my own survival, as there was no shelter and it promised to be a very cold night. All my warm clothes were covering Tommy. Even the prospect of going for help was a bleak one. I had five miles to travel and 2,000 feet to descend down the rough valley from Coire Mor an Teallach. It was 5.30

pm before I reached a crofthouse at Ardessie, from where I telephoned to Dr Tom Patey in Ullapool.

As soon as Tom had the message from Iain Ogilvie, he alerted the local police sergeant, Roddie Lovat, who in turn contacted his headquarters in Dingwall. Both Ross and Sutherland Police Rescue Team and the RAF Kinloss team were told of the accident.

Tom arrived in his Renault at the croft house at 6.30 pm. Meanwhile, Iain Ogilvie had not been idle: he had marked on his map the exact location of the accident.

Iain had not met Tom before. "My first impressions of Dr Tom were very true of the man. He took my map, listened patiently to me for about half a minute, and then said, 'If you got yourself all the way down from there on your own, the district nurse can deal with you. I must get up before it's too dark. Tell the rescue party to follow.'"

Tom Patey was born in the small township of Ellen in 1932. With the wild Cairngorms as his playground in his early years, he grew up with a high degree of physical fitness which, combined with his natural musical talents, made him the ideal companion for hard, long climbs, followed by nights of song. Tom was a song-writer and a singer who had a magical touch on his accordion. He was involved in quite a number of rescues in north-west Scotland and devoted a considerable amount of his precious spare time in helping to train the local police, for he shared my view that you can't teach people to rescue on mountains until they have learned to climb.

Tom set off dressed as usual in a pullover, an old pair of dark trousers, with an anorak tied about his middle, and a great coil of rope slung over his shoulder, grasping his old ice axe. He followed the trail of blood left by Iain Ogilvie. In an hour he had covered the distance – which gives some indication of his fitness – but he had trouble in locating the two men. They were both dead when he found them. It was 8.30 pm as he started to cut steps down the slope for another 500 feet in order to help the other rescuers.

He saw them coming up the valley below – a small band of figures in red anoraks: the Ross and Sutherland Police team, led by Donnie Smith. As darkness was now close at hand Tom decided that he had better start lowering the bodies, since the police party had only limited experience on snow and ice and he didn't want any further accidents. Combining the length of his rope with the 170 feet which Iain had left by the bodies, he succeeded in lowering the first corpse. The length of this lower was exactly 500 feet – the distance that Iain had fallen.

Tom quickly climbed down the face and joined the police as they were strapping Peter's body to the stretcher. The next day the RAF team recovered the other body.

Iain Ogilvie was awarded the MBE for his part in the attempted rescue of his friends, while Tom received the Queen's Commendation for Brave Conduct.

Not a Place for People

Pete Sinclair and Al Read

We were slumming in what must be the most despicable "hotel" in the length of the Andean chain: the place, the Ecuadorian town of Ambato. In the courtyard idle peons whittled wood with keen knives, whilst others played cards with our gaunt, wily de-poncho'ed landlord. The game was strategically conducted at the bottom of rickety stairs which led to the balcony from which our room sulked in shadow.

This cell, for it resembled a cell more than a room, had at one time, perhaps when Pizarro was a breadsnapper, boasted white walls. The remaining plaster bore witness to this. The only furniture was three wooden platforms serving as beds. On these lay Joe Brown, Yvon Chouinard and I. We swotted flies and absorbed the incessant cacophony of the market crowd; assailed by a proliferation of smells which is South America. The other "fixture" in the room was a large rat – it hadn't moved for ten minutes. It looked me over with a calculating eye from its sanctuary beneath Yvon's bed.

We had come to look for treasure and to find emptiness in the Upper Amazon. So far we had discovered flies and had been engulfed by numerous, gregarious, but essentially friendly Ecuadorians – but that is another story.

"You know you were asking about that rescue in the Tetons, Hamish." It was Yvon speaking. I looked up expectantly. He continued, "There's a guy, Pete Sinclair, who can possibly help you. I think he was involved. He's a professor of English now, I'll give you his address."

Well, Pete Sinclair did help. He knew about the rescue all right, he was on it. So was another American climber that I knew, Al

Read, who then lived in Kathmandu where he ran Mountain Travel, the trekking organisation.

Both Pete and Al had done a lot of climbing in the Tetons, the range on the Wyoming-Idaho border; compact mountains rising up to 6,000 feet from an alluvial carpet of river flats interspersed with aspen and cottonwood, a veritable rock candy upthrust, studded with pearly lakes. From both sides of the massif water drains to the great Snake River, which, true to its name wriggles 900 tortuous miles to the Pacific. Early trappers called the three main peaks the Grand, Middle and South Teton – Les Trois Tetons, the three breasts, which makes one speculate on the suggested angular profile of pioneering maidens!

Unlike those in the bum's song, these are real peaks, they can be hard, cold and unrelenting. There is snow and the wind does blow in these mountains.

The back room of the Jenny Lake ranger station served as a country store on stormy days or rest days. The cabin had a stove because in the winter it was used as a patrol cabin; there was also running water. It was a good place to make tea and to talk. Leigh Ortenburger spent quite a bit of his research time there when he was in the valley and since he was our historian, the back room became one of the two storytelling places in the valley. The climbers' campground was the other one. Once Yosemite climbers started coming to the Tetons to rest from the intensity of the Yosemite walls, the campground and ranger station became the communications hub of American climbing through most of the 'sixties.

Late in July, 1962, there was one storytelling session going on with Leigh Ortenburger and Dave Dornan in the group. Dave wanted me to work on No Escape Buttress with him. Mount Moran's south buttresses presented Teton climbers with a chance to do something that resembled Yosemite wall climbing. The easternmost of these buttresses, No Escape Buttress, was the last and most difficult of these problems. I was not in any way prepared for a climb of this difficulty but I had to try. Dornan wanted this climb. He was born in the valley, had been a climbing ranger with me and was now an Exum Guide. He had accepted the Yosemite challenge. That is, he did not expect to become as good as Chouinard or Robbins but he wanted to be good enough to carry on a conversation with them.

There were encouraging signs in the heavens as we rowed across Leigh Lake in a rotting plywood skiff, one rowing, one bailing. I had never seen clouds so massive or as black as those which were piling up on the Idaho side of the range. Such clouds in the morning indicated that this was not to be an ordinary storm; we were sure to be stormed off the climb. The prospect pleased me, we'd do a couple of pitches and then go home. That would give me time to psyche myself up for a serious attempt later. As it turned out, I was to be busy for a while.

In a different part of the range, another climber was discovering that he had backed himself into a commitment which was to prove very serious. Ellis Blade had led a group of nine Appalachian Mountain Club climbers up Teepe's Snowfield on the Grand Teton. The snowfield is steep though not extreme. But the snowfield had become Blade's personal Rubicon.

Dornan was near the top of the first lead when the storm hit us. He rappelled off and we ran for the lake. Crossing the lake in that storm is one of the sillier things I've done. Fortunately, the energy of the storm was released in impulses rather than as a sustained force. The wind and rain combined to beat the surface of the lake down instead of lifting it into breaking whitecaps or we would have been in trouble. Dave, chortling because he was no longer a rescuer, remarked that if there was anybody in the mountains, my day was not over. I wasn't much worried. This storm was severe enough that the most desperate vacationing climber with one day left on his vacation and fifty weeks of being chained to a desk facing him, could not pretend that it was a passing summer shower. It was not only violent, it was cold. There was a smell of the Gulf of Alaska about it. You could tell that an Arctic air mass had penetrated south.

I looked forward to a few quiet days in the ranger station as Dave and I walked and hitch-hiked back to Jenny Lake. The climbers would be out of the mountains and the campers would be heading for motels or the desert. The back of the ranger station would be warm, full of climbers drinking tea. The guides would be in, looking at our photographs of the peaks, planning one more climb, swapping stories.

When we got to the ranger station I was told that the other ranger on duty, George Kelly, had been sent out to check on an overdue party of ten from the Appalachian Mountain Club. This was an annoyance but couldn't be serious. Ten people can't just vanish in a range as small as the Tetons.

The failure of the Appies to return as they had planned was irritating to us. People often get benighted in the Tetons in circumstances like those attending this climb: a large party, composed of people of varying experience, climbing a route that is reputed to be easy but is seldom climbed. In fact, those circumstances are guaranteed to produce a bivouac. At the ranger station we would normally give the party plenty of time to extricate itself from the route and get back before we did anything dramatic. Often there was another party in the same general area who would spot the late party. From where they were last seen, we could make a reasonable guess of how long it would take them to get back. If the missing party exceeded our estimated time of return, as well as their own, then we'd set things in motion. Even then we wouldn't scramble a full scale search. Our first action would be to send out one ranger, or two if there was to be technical climbing, and combine the search with some other activity such as a patrol, if possible. We might also pass the word around to one or two key rescue types that such and such a party was overdue. What that meant to them was that they'd be where they could be easily reached and maybe pass up the second beer until the word went about that everybody was out of the mountains.

Sometimes the worried family or concerned friends who were waiting in the valley would take exception to this stalling for time. But there really is no other way to do it. If we'd scrambled a full-scale search and rescue operation every time a party was overdue, the expense would have been enormous but, most important, tremendous pressure would be put on the party in the mountains to get back in the time estimated and the result would be many more injuries and deaths.

In the case at hand, we actually did not stall as long as we normally would have. There were a lot of people in the Appalachian Mountain Club encampment who were concerned enough to bring down word to us of the overdue party. They certainly expected a response from us. Second, the storm increased the possibility that the party could be stuck for some time. One detail was worrisome, the party was not well equipped for cold weather. So, very soon after we were notified, Ranger George Kelly was on his way into the mountains on a patrol. He would stall by organising a search party from the Appalachian Mountain Club encampment. It's not that we didn't worry. We always worried. Worrying was a major component of our work. It is not difficult to imagine the worst, even after a hundred repetitions of one's imagining's turning out to be worse than the reality. We worried, but we had learned an orderly, logical procedure to follow in these cases and kept our imagining at a distance.

The leader of the party was Ellis Blade, not himself an Appie but a recognised leader. Blade was not really what Europeans would regard as a guide. Americans do not hire guides in America, they hire authorities. Glenn Exum, the founder of the Exum Guides, has a kind of genius for spotting young men who carry an aura of personal authority. And that is part of the reason for the success of his guide service, a success which is unparalleled in America. The Exum Guides at that time ranged in age around late twenties to early thirties. Blade was in his fifties. The rest of the party varied greatly in experience. Steven Smith, quite young but a good rock climber, was the assistant leader. The other able rock climber was Lester Germer, who was sixty-five. Charles Joyce was a good recreational rock climber, very respectful of the Western mountains because his experience had been mainly on the cliffbands of the East. Janet Buckingham was an experienced hiker, with Lydia and Griffith June, Charles Kellogg and John Fenniman in various stages of learning rock climbing. Mary Blade, Ellis's wife, was also along and was an experienced mountaineer. The route they were to climb was known as the Otter Body Route, after the shape of a snowfield in the middle of the east face of the Grand Teton.

The party got off as planned at 4.00 am Thursday morning, a good sign.* There had only been a couple of minor problems in the days prior to setting out. Blade hadn't been able to generate much enthusiasm for conditioning climbs. The time to get the party into condition had been scheduled, but things hadn't

* For many details of events, I did not personally witness, I am indebted to James Lipscomb's account in two issues of *Sports Illustrated*, 1965, "72 Hours of Terror", June 14 and "Night of the One-Eyed Devils", June 21.

quite worked out. This is not surprising in view of the fact that the encampment was the size of a tribe, but one with random membership. Going into the wilderness to set up a new society is an American passion, but it takes a lot of energy just to eat, sleep and talk in a situation like that. There are new people to meet and hierarchies, liaisons and enmities to be established before the group can truly focus on its stated purpose. It requires the genius of a leader like Shackleton to select team members who accomplish the settling-in work quickly and in such a manner that the resulting organisation is the one that's needed to do the job.

The problem, other than conditioning, that Blade might have had on his mind at 4.00 am that Thursday morning was that Steven Smith, the young assistant leader, was suffering from an attack of no confidence. He didn't like the looks of the weather. He had vomited the evening before, and had confided his doubts to Charles Joyce. Blade was fifty-four and Steven Smith twenty-one. They never became co-leaders in any meaningful sense. It was Joyce who broached Smith's worries to Blade. If there was to be any rapport established between these two, it would have been up to Blade to establish it. Presumably part of his responsibility was to train the next generation of leaders. It is also true that mountaineering in America was undergoing a tremendous growth in rock-climbing skills; hundreds of good young climbers were, within three years, learning to do moves on rock routes that older climbers had thought only feasible on boulders in campgrounds. Blade would be an unusual man indeed if he did not feel his authority somewhat undermined by this new generation.

As for Smith, it's possible that he had a touch of the 'flu or had picked up a bug from the water. It happened to me at least once a season in the Tetons and to all the guides and climbing rangers I know. Whatever the cause of Smith's loss of confidence, the events of the first day conspired to keep it that way. They did however make an early start.

Four and a half hours later, at 8.30, they started up Teepe's Snowfield. A pace twice that fast would be regarded as slow by most climbers. Blade had plotted the climb with a five-hour margin of daylight. Half of his margin was gone before the party roped up.

Janet Buckingham broke out of her steps in the snow, and although Smith held the fall easily, Janet's feet flailed away at the snow uselessly. Anybody who has taught climbing beginners is familiar with the scene. The student or client literally loses contact with his/her feet and thrashes away hoping that a miracle will occur and one of them will stick. Perhaps Smith didn't know how to deal with the situation, perhaps he hadn't the chance. It was Blade, leaving his own rope, who talked her back into confidence in her steps again. The incident with Janet would have been soon forgotten by all involved except that disturbing incidents began to accumulate.

The lead rope of five made it to the top of the snowfield half an hour before noon. The second rope, Smith's, didn't join the lead rope at the top before lunch. They stopped on an outcropping about three rope lengths below. This area is scarred by debris fallen from the cliffband and two snowfields above. This detail did not go unnoticed by Joyce at least, and he was the one who spotted the falling ice first and gave the warning yell. One block carried away Fenniman's ice axe. Another glanced off Kellogg's foot. Joyce had two blocks to dodge and only managed to dodge one. He was hit hard and knocked into the air. Though briefly stunned, he was uninjured.

To this point, Joyce, though he was Smith's confidant, had been maintaining a neutral stance on the question of whether the climb was advisable or not. After being hit, he still wasn't as shaken as Smith, whose hands were trembling, but he was now of Smith's opinion that this was an ill-fated climb and they ought to go down.

Blade had gone down to check that everybody was all right and then quickly climbed back up to his rope, before a discussion could ensue. The lower party, wanting to get out of the track of falling debris even more than they wanted to go down, followed quickly.

While they were getting underway, Joyce said to Smith, "Let's get out of here." Smith replied, "He'll kill us all."

As the entire party reached the top of the snowfield, a storm hit. It was noon. This was not the familiar late afternoon thunderstorm but the arrival of one that had been threatening since the previous evening. The party took refuge in the moat between the top of the snowfield and the rock which at least sheltered them from the wind. Smith finally confronted Blade with his desire to retreat. Blade responded that the snowfield was hardening and had become dangerous. As the heavy rainfall and hail from the first huge cumulus cloud passed and the rain moderated, Blade gave the word for everyone to put on their packs and start moving up. Joyce sought out Smith.

"What's he doing? Is he nuts? We've got to go down. You're a leader. Tell him we've got to go down."

Eventually it would be Joyce who would take command and make the decision to go down, but that was to be two days hence.

The party traversed the top of the snowfield to the base of a rock couloir. Blade sent Germer ahead to scout the route, asking him to report "how it would go". The wording is significant. Phrased that way, it is not the same as asking "Ought we attempt it?"

This couloir, carved in the interstice of the east face and the east side of the Grand joins the Otter Body Snowfield to Teepe's Snowfield. It is rather alarmingly free of the debris which packs the bottom of most Teton couloirs. It is too steep, too water, ice- and rock-washed to hold anything much in it for long. Obviously the rock is not particularly sound which is why a couloir developed. Griffith June saw the couloir first as a bowling alley and then found in his mind the inscription from the *Inferno*, "Abandon hope, all ye who enter here." Wet, cold, late, tired, with weather threatening and tension in the group growing, it can not have been a cheerful party that geared themselves up for rock climbing.

Germer returned with his report which he recalls thus: "I told him it looked easy. I know now he was asking for advice, and I gave him a rock-climbing opinion. It was easy rock climbing. I was not considering the safety of the party. The camp had chosen Blade as a leader, but I should have said something." Possibly there was something else at work here. The opening sentence in the description of the route in Ortenburger's, *A Climber's Guide to the Teton Range* (1956 edition) is: "Petzoldt (who did the first ascent) ranks this as one of the easiest routes on the Grand Teton." Twenty-seven years after the first ascent, an Eastern cliff climber of Germer's stature could not in good conscience rate this climb as more difficult than the first ascent party found it to be. Unless Blade had reason to think that he was seriously off route, which was unlikely, he knew what Germer's reply was to be.

Ellis Blade retorted when Smith once again said that they ought to go down, "I've been on that glacier before in weather like this. It's as hard as ice. If we go down, someone will get killed."

Smith pressed the point. "We can't climb the mountain now."

Blade's response was, "You keep your mouth shut."

"Well, I'm assistant leader of this group," said Smith, "and I think my opinion should be considered."

"Well, don't you forget that I am the leader and I know it is safer to go up."

In the hours that follow, they all got soaked, Lydia June had a shock from a lightning bolt, Smith avoided a rock avalanche only by leaping across the couloir into the arms of Griffith June, and Kellogg was hit by a rock which drove his crampons through his pack and into his back. Griffith June considered leading a splinter group back, a serious responsibility. He had the authority within the AMC organisation, but not as a mountaineer, and they were very much in the mountains now. He urged Blade to lead them back but Blade replied that they were committed.

Blade now climbed quickly and well, getting the party three-fourths of the way up the couloir. Griffith June arrived at a huge boulder two pitches from the top, big enough for them all to sit on. Joyce secured them with pitons and they all bivouacked there except Blade who had reached the wide ledges and easy slabs at the top of the couloir. There was no reconsideration of Blade's decision. There were complaints, perhaps fewer than there might have been had Mary Blade not been part of the group. A decision to go down would have been a decision to abandon Blade on the mountain.

Three inches of wet snow fell during the night. They had no down garments, no dry clothes, and virtually no food. In the morning, Germer asked Smith what he thought, Germer didn't like the rotten rock and had been weakened by the bivouac. Smith replied that he didn't know the route.

It took all of the next day, Friday, to get the party up the remaining two pitches to the top of the couloir. Joyce and Fenniman climbed up to Blade. June slipped on the ice just below the point where the angle of the couloir eased. He tried repeatedly and fell repeatedly. He cut steps, almost made it, and fell again, this time further and over an overhang. There was danger of his being strangled by the rope. Smith muscled him over to the bivouac pillar where June collapsed exhausted.

Germer then went up and set up an intermediate belay position where he stayed until all six remaining climbers were up the couloir. (This was during the time when Dornan and I were being driven from Mount Moran a few miles to the north.) Though fit enough, Germer was in his sixties and this was too much; he had lost all reserves. His hands were claws; he clutched a piton in each and made it up the ice. Blade moved on but was called back. Germer announced he was dying.

Blade assessed the situation and had a new plan, but not a new direction. There can be an infinite number of situations, tactics and explanations but there can only be one conclusion. He, Joyce and Smith would go up. They might find climbers at the top. If not, they'd go down the Owen-Spaulding Route and get help.

There was twice as much snow above them as they climbed on Teepe's Snowfield and beyond was another cliffband.

When duty ranger, George Kelly, got to the AMC camp at the Petzoldt's Caves, there was no word of the missing party. By the time he radioed this news down, we were back in the ranger station and instructed him to organise a search. We were getting a little nervous. The search was to a certain extent window-dressing. These people couldn't be sent up on any difficult terrain. In other words, any place they could be allowed to search would be a place where the missing party could get out of by themselves. What they could do was to look and listen. They did and what they saw was three members of the party up on the Otter Body Snowfield.

The need for a plausible explanation for what was happening with that party was increasing by the moment, while the prospects for getting such an explanation were decreasing. At their present rate, it would be two days before they got to the top. We were at first inclined to believe that these three could not be from the party we were seeking, but a review of the facts available to us convinced us that they had to be three of the ten. There was no way to make sense of it. It was hard to believe that if there had been an injury, accident or a fatality someone couldn't have gotten out to tell us. If there had been some kind of horrible disaster and these were the only survivors, that would explain why we hadn't heard from them, but not why they were going up. Only one thing was clear, we had to get serious about finding out what was going on.

There had been a short rescue the evening before involving a client of the guide service. The guide service had provided most of the manpower for the rescue. Barry Corbet was one of those who had helped. He was to take a group up the Grand on Saturday but another guide had taken his party to the high camp at the Lower Saddle earlier in the day while he got some rest. He was on his way up to join them when he met George Kelly and was pressed into service. As they followed the track of the party up the snowfield and into the couloir, the storm renewed itself. Barry was equipped and George wasn't. They were, as we later determined, within 400 feet of Blade's group when they turned back, Barry to join his party.

Doug McLaren, a district ranger and member of the rescue team when it was originally organised a decade earlier, was our supervisor, though no longer an active climber. It was he who organised and co-ordinated rescue activities. Doug ordered a pack team to move as much equipment as we could reasonably muster up to Garnet Canyon. Garnet Canyon is the cirque rimmed anticlockwise from north to south by Disappointment Peak, the Grand Teton, the Middle Teton, the South Teton and Nez Perce. Doug, Sterling Neale, Jim Greig and I left in the advance party at 7.00 pm. Rick Horn and Mike Ermarth, the remaining strong climbers on the park team were to follow with more equipment. All the available Exum Guides volunteered, Jake Breitenbach, Pete Lev, Fred Wright, and Al Read; and they were joined by four other volunteers, Dr Roland Fleck, Bill Briggs and Dave Dornan, who were soon to become guides, and Peter Koedt, who later helped me in organising the Jackson Hole Mountain Guides until the Vietnam disaster forced him into Canadian exile. These guides and volunteers were to come up in the morning. Another guide, Herb Swedlund, was holding at the Petzoldt's Caves, awaiting developments. The majority of the professional mountaineers in America at the time were to carry out this operation.

The four of us got a little sleep at the end of the horse trail about an hour's climb below the encampment at the Caves and started up around 4.00 am. We arrived at the top of the snowfield at about 10.30. Here I made a serious mistake in route-finding. The party had to be either on the cliffband between Teepe's Snowfield and the Otter Body Snowfield, or possibly at the top of the Otter Body just above the point where the three climbers had been spotted. There were two obvious routes up the cliffband. One was the couloir to the right of the cliffband, dark, wet, rotten, and the other was a nice sunlit rock line straight up from where we were.

I'd never been here before, but I'd been nearby six weeks earlier looking at it from a col about 400 yards to our left at the southern edge of the snowfield. I had come to take a look because the climbing pressure on the standard routes was becoming such that I was interested in finding another easy way to the summit to recommend to those climbers who mainly wanted to get to the top of the mountain. What I had seen in June was far from being the easiest route on the mountain. The sun reflected off the snow into the couloir to reveal a mass of contorted ice, as if a section of rapids in the Grand Canyon of the Snake had been instantly frozen and set up vertically in this evil-looking crevice in the mountain. Debris, both ice and rock, cascaded out of it. It seemed the picture of unpredictability. There was no pattern other than a headlong, downward plunge. The mountain seemed to be saying, "Here I keep no pacts." At the same time, I did note the comparative warmth and orderliness of a sunlit route up an open chimney just to the south of the icy corner. I had decided this was the route Petzoldt had gone up and though it may have been easy for him, it wasn't easy enough for the type of climber I had in mind. I descended from the col without bothering to traverse the snowfield to take a closer look.

Now the ice was gone and water poured down the couloir. My comrades were of the opinion that the route went up the couloir. I said that was impossible, anybody could see that that was no place to be. It was not a place for people. My memory of my first look at the couloir in June coloured my present perception of it considerably. Thus I persuaded them to follow me up the route I had seen, which is in fact not the Otter Body Route but the Smith Route.

The discussion had planted enough doubt in my mind that I wanted to make sure the climbing went as easily as I had claimed it would. I've never worked harder to find the easiest possible line. I scanned the rock almost frantically and climbed with as nonchalant a motion as I could. However, the climbing, while easy, was not trivial and at the point which in the guidebook account of the Smith Route is described as "the difficult overhanging portion", the climbing became seriously non-trivial. As we paused to deal with this shocking appearance of fifth-class climbing on what was supposed to be a third- and fourth-class route, we heard voices unmistakenly coming from the top of the couloir.

We rappelled down and decided that only two us would go up to investigate, partly because of the rockfall danger and partly because the voices we heard seemed to be singing! Sterling Neale and I had travelled together, worked together and climbed a lot together. I wanted him to stay at the bottom with Doug because it looked like that was going to have to be the organisation point. I didn't know what the tremendous barrier was between where we were and where they were, but there must be something keeping them from descending. Sterling could practically read my mind and I wanted him where he would be in a position to do something if things got complicated. Also, Jim Greig was bigger and stronger than either of us and there were at least seven of them up there someplace.

Angry because of my mistake, I climbed carelessly and managed to break my hammer soon after we got underway. I remember the climbing as being more difficult than does Jim. The last two pitches, bypassing the overhang and crossing the ice, could be psychologically intimidating to a climber, or a party, not in good form.

The route lay up the right-hand or east side of the ice at the top of the couloir. The party was on the slabs at the "tail" of the Otter Body, about thirty feet above and half a rope length in distance. There was about seven inches of snow on the ice almost heavy and wet enough to adhere to the ice while bearing our weight. We weren't able to protect the pitch in a manner which could stop a fall short of the overhang. We had neither ice pitons nor crampons. A rope from above would be just the thing.

For the first time, we turned our attention fully to the party we'd come to rescue. They seemed surprisingly calm. Did they have a climbing rope? They did. Would they toss us an end? They would. The young man Fenniman stiffly approached the lip of the ledge with a rope. He seemed a bit perplexed. We instructed him to give the coil a healthy swing and toss it down to us. He swung the coil back and then forward but failed to release it. He did the same thing again. And then again. And again. There was something odd about the motion. He wasn't swinging the coil to get up momentum, but swinging indecisively almost as if he wasn't sure he wanted to cross over to them and disturb the calm which reigned there. The swinging motion became mechanical. He'd forgotten that he was not only to swing the coil but also release it. We hadn't told him that he had to do both. We told him. The coil, released in the middle of the swing instead of at the end of it, dropped in front of his feet. Jim and I exchanged glances. Perhaps if he climbed down the slab to the next ledge toward us?

"I won't! I won't!" He spoke not directly to us but first to the air at our left and then to the rock at his feet.

"Stay where you are!" we said in one voice we just managed to keep from rising. We were in for it, no doubt about that, we'd really gotten into something which promised to be very strange.

Jim "went for it" and we made it across and joined them on their ledge. They undoubtedly had been badly frightened and were probably making an effort to recover their wits. Possibly they were somewhat embarrassed. The resulting impression on me was of an unnatural calm. It seemed to be an effort for most of them to acknowledge our presence. There was a polite smile, a curious, almost disinterested gaze, the sort of thing I'd experienced in New York subways. Mary Blade seemed positively cheerful. They'd been singing, she told us. She also told us that Lester had been having a difficult time. Lester wanted to know if we'd brought any strawberry jam. We hadn't. We should have. According to Lester that's what we were supposed to do, bring strawberry jam and tea. He was a little put out with us and seemed doubtful that we knew our business.

I was offended. My first thought was, "Jesus Christ, Lester, if I knew what we were going to find up here I would have brought the Tenth Mountain Division!" I had just enough presence of mind to realise that I was feeling defensive and said nothing. The Grand Teton National Park Rescue Team was and still is the best rescue team in the country. Where did Lester imagine he had gotten the authority to lecture us? From a book, a book on European practice? I had a picture of the members of these large climbing organisations sitting around in their meetings *imagining* rescues with the old New England obsequiousness toward things British and Continental. The European teams were unquestionably better than ours. Gary Hemming used to urge me to go to Europe and learn from them and I wished I could. But what we'd been able to glean from books we found unadaptable to our circumstances. There was a more immediate reason for my defensive response to Lester's suggestion that we didn't know what we were doing. What were we going to do?

I signalled to Jim. Under the pretext of moving to a better radio transmission site, we climbed up to the next ledge and walked behind a boulder to talk.

"What in hell are we going to do?" he asked.

Jim later told me that I calmly lit a cigarette and replied, "We're all going to die, that's what we're going to do."

I guess I had to say it to get it out of the way. I'm glad I did. Life doesn't provide many opportunities to deliver a line like that. Anyway, the notion was not that far-fetched. The radio wouldn't work and we'd managed to get off without taking an extra battery. I restrained myself from throwing the radio down the mountain and satisfied myself with shouting into it, cursing and shaking it.

Eventually, by moving about from rock to ledge to chimney and bouncing our voices off the walls on the East Ridge, we found a place where we could shout out of the couloir and have some words heard and, we hoped, understood by Sterling and Doug. All we could tell them was to stay out of the couloir. What we wished to have been able to tell them was that we would be setting things up, up here, while they organised the equipment and men coming up from below. At some convenient moment, we would freeze all motion in the upper couloir while they set up belaying and lowering positions below us. Then we'd have a bucket brigade of various techniques, fixed ropes, maybe a litter or two, rappels, belays and so forth, depending on the terrain and condition of the members of the party. It could have been very elegant but it was not to be. Jim and I would just have to start moving the group down the mountain any way we could until we were back in communication with our team-mates, or until they could see what was needed and we could see that they could see what was needed.

We started. There was a ledge big enough for the whole party below us but it was further than the two short pitches Jim and I could manage with the equipment available. Could Fenniman, the only one of the party who was reasonably ambulatory, help us? He'd have to. The fact that we had to use Fenniman in the shape he was in gave me a feeling like what I imagined the French Existentialists meant by the absurd. A little ironic repartee crept into the conversation between Jim and me, something of Hemingway, a bit of Camus' Stranger. Jim would lower one to me, I'd lower that one to Fenniman, he'd belay them to the ledge.

I had anchored Fenniman to a slab about thirty feet above the big ledge and gave him very precise instructions about what to do which I repeated several times. While doing so, my sense that things were absurd became a feeling that things were desperate. The entire operation had to funnel to and through this eighteen-year-old youngster just out of high school who was headed for Dartmouth. I'd once been a kid just out of high school headed for Dartmouth and couldn't imagine what I'd have been able to do if I were then in the position he was now in.

He had been there, within a stone's throw of this place, for two nights and now nearly three days. He was in what must have appeared to him as the most precarious position he'd been in during the entire nightmare. He was, in fact, quite securely anchored, but he had only my word for that. It would not be surprising if he had come to doubt the word of people who claimed to know better than he the position he was in. He might have been bound to a rock over an abyss by a strange god or demon for all the events of the past three days might have taught him.

It was no wonder that I wasn't quite sure if I was talking to the whole Fenniman or to a messenger the whole Fenniman had sent to hear me out. The messenger seemed reliable, even heroic. I felt that Fenniman would get the job done, but had the odd thought that I'd like to meet him some day. It occurred to me that he might untie himself from the anchor and step off the mountain. That had happened a few years before to a guide with a head injury on this same peak, three ridges to the south. I moved the knot tying him to the mountain around behind him, where it couldn't be reached accidentally as he tied and untied the people we sent down. I made my instructions simple, precise and routine and tried at the same time to speak to him as a peer who could of course do what we were asking of him.

It worked. He did it exactly as I instructed; exactly the same way every time. When I had seen him swinging that coil mechanically back and forth when we'd asked for the upper belay some part of my mind had registered the potential in those precise movements and the potential in his "I won't! I won't!" There must be a way that he could be made to say "I will! I will!" There was, but as the sequel was to show, something very different might have happened.

We first assumed that they could provide their own motive power and set the pace of the descent if we belayed them down a fixed rope. The least experienced of them would not have found the first pitch at all troublesome under normal circumstances. Now people were falling down on flat ledges, falling into a stream two feet wide and three inches deep and spending thirty seconds trying to figure out how to step over an eight-inch rock. Sometimes you see this in a beginners' rock-climbing class when the client is really frightened. There are ways to deal with it. But these people did not look frightened. What we were seeing on their faces and hearing in their voices wasn't fear but confusion, as if the problems of balance and motion were intellectual problems entirely. We had to give up trying to talk them through the moves. We were becoming exasperated at the ineffectiveness of our explanations and instructions and knew that our exasperation would only make things worse.

Tactfully at first, and then less so, we relieved them of their autonomy. Staggering, slithering, stumbling, as long as they kept descending, they could pick their one way down. If they stopped too long, a tug, a nudge and finally steady, unrelenting pressure kept things moving as the sun got lower.

After the first of them had gone down the snow-covered ice, it was snow-covered no longer and all pretence of down-climbing was abandoned. They got soaked; sliding down the ice and water and I shivered for them. Speed was becoming imperative. Fenniman caught on. I overheard someone explaining to him that they had lost a foothold. To which Fenniman replied insistently, "They say you have to keep moving."

Speed under these circumstances is a relative term. We who were trying to imagine that we were in control of things were tying, untying, handling the rope with one hand, gesticulating with the other and talking and thinking as fast as possible. Those who were being controlled were rudely precipitated off a pitch, tied to an anchor and then left to a shivering halt of a half hour or more before it was their turn again.

Once down on the big ledge, things seemed better. Perhaps the ledge they'd spent so many uncomfortable but relatively safe hours on had been difficult to abandon. There was less of a feeling of us and them. There was some conversation. We found out all we could about what had happened as the opportunity arose. I began to learn their names and to take account of them as separate people. I noted that the Junes seemed to be holding together. That doesn't always happen to couples under stress in the mountains. I wondered if Germer was recalling warm summer days rock climbing in the Shawangunks. Janet was the wettest, coldest, seemed most out of place, but I was impressed by her endurance. I wondered if Mary Blade was worrying about Ellis, and if so would she be more concerned about his safety or the repercussions that seemed obviously destined to come to him. Kellogg appeared to be not too badly off, something like a nice young man just recently embarked on a course of dissipation.

There was little time for these thoughts. Above all was the fact that we could make a mistake and kill one of them, or not make a mistake and still have one of them die. Lester Germer was the obvious candidate, the one everybody was worried about, but there were others. And what of the missing three? We had to take Mary's word that they were in pretty good climbing shape, but what did "pretty good" mean? The best we could hope for was that they would be spotted by Barry who was on the summit today. The trouble was, Barry would be down by now. Perhaps Doug and Ster already had news?

I chafed at our slow pace. My earlier route-finding mistake had cost us about two hours and that was going to make the difference between day and night in this gully, between warm sun and 32° granite, between wet pitches and icy pitches, between snow you could heel down and snow as hard as ice. My mistake had the appearance of meaning the difference between life or death for one or more of these people. Once you parade yourself in the world as a rescuer and once you take charge of the party, everything that happens after that is on your head.

We made another effort to communicate with Doug and Ster. We tried to impress on them the mass of equipment that would be needed and reiterated the point about them staying out of the gully. It was frustrating for them, and we could see that some of the guides had arrived too, to watch the shadow of the Grand move out over the valley at an increasing rate, while we appeared not to be moving at all. But the rock falls we were setting off were fairly convincing. The main thing we wanted to happen was to have the snowfield all set up for lowering so that as each of the party arrived at the top of the snowfield they could be lowered quickly from anchor to anchor.

Just before dark, Jim called down to me the news that two of the missing three were coming down from above. The significance of the fact that there were two, not three took hold slowly. I couldn't imagine how the third could be rescued. If we stopped everything to bring a litter and eight climbers up through us, I was sure somebody would die of exposure, there would be rock fall both above and below and there'd be nobody left to help us get these seven down. I also found myself fervently hoping that I wouldn't have to go back up the mountain.

When Blade got to me I interrogated him fairly fiercely about the condition of the third. It was Smith and he was dead. I was in danger of feeling relieved and that made me ruder. Also, it was difficult to believe. "Are you sure he's dead, because if you're not, somebody has to go up. How did you check? How long did you wait before leaving him?" Blade told me that the body had started to get stiff. I didn't believe that but whether he was dead when they left him or not, he was certainly dead by now. I sized up Joyce. He was clearly in better shape than anyone else. It was a little startling to see a normal person apparently unaffected by this place.

I had pulled Blade aside to question him. I could imagine what the impact of the news that the strongest member of the party had died of exposure might do to their will to survive. Furthermore, if someone else was going to die it was unlikely that they'd do it quickly and allow us to go on. I had a horrible image of being immobilised there in that gully helplessly watching a slow chain reaction of dying. I ordered Blade not to talk about it.

He moved across the ledge and gathered everybody there around and made a little speech about how we were trying to help them and they'd have to co-operate with us. I found that astonishing and a little amusing. Astonishing that he still was functioning as a leader and amusing as I tried to imagine how they could not co-operate with us. Then I had an awful insight.

What from their point of view would we be doing if we were not trying to save them but kill them? I was a little ashamed of my rough treatment of Blade. I had my own mistakes to worry about.

Janet got soaked again. She lost her footing while being lowered, swung into a waterfall and was too stiff and cold to roll out of it without help. I began to feel that she might not make it and I had to do something personally to give her heart. The distance the rescuer maintains between himself and the victims makes stepping out of it a more effective gesture.

I made her squeeze in behind a flake which would not only protect her modesty if that was necessary but mainly protected her a little from the cold evening westerly pouring down on us from the snowfields above. I made her take off her Levis, lectured her about the fact that denim was the worst possible material to wear in the mountains and wrung the water out of them as much as I could. They were new and stiff. I imagined that she'd bought them down in Jackson, in honour of her visit to the West. I gave her some food I'd been saving for someone it might make the difference to, including possibly myself. Then I took my favourite sweater out of my pack and made her put it on. I tried a little levity. I told her that it was a twenty-five dollar sweater and she'd better not get it dirty! She took me seriously – so much for levity. Whatever was going to happen was going to happen without interference from me.

There were shouts from below. They were coming up and we were to be careful about rocks. It was worth being a climber to feel the cameraderie that I felt then, an emotion that embraces much more than mere bullshitting around a table in a tavern.

First to arrive were Pete Lev and Al Read. Lev is the picture of earnest strength. Read is a man in command of himself. Witty, quick to perceive the ludicrous as the ironic, he is a natural leader and an unobtrusive one. Lev is very compassionate and was taken aback by what he saw, including me and Jim. Jim and I were emotionally numb by this point and I saw concern in their faces. But suddenly it seemed possible that most of us might escape from this place. Suddenly the mountain seemed covered with people who knew what they were doing. Herb Swedlund was down there, Swedlund who would joke with the Devil. I couldn't wait to get down to hear him say something like, "Sinclair, you're quaking like a dog passing peach pits." Rick Horn was down there, probably performing great feats of strength and daring while screaming. "The world is contrived to drive us insane."

The next pitch below ended in the middle of a slab which bulged out from the base of the couloir. Every rock that came down the couloir had to hit that slab. Jake Breitenbach was at that anchor. When I got to him, I was afraid for him, a fear that seemed familiar. Then I recalled the boulder in the great ice gully on McKinley that seemed to pursue us. He, however, was ebullient, as he was most of the time in the mountains. For him, this was what it was all about. How often do you get to have fun like this, up here in an interesting part of the mountain with practically all your climbing and guiding buddies? He was good for the people we were rescuing too. He told them, as he prepared to send them down the vertical slab below, "We always arrange to have these rescues at night so you won't know what you're stepping off of." He picked them up and kept them going. For one or more of them it is likely that Jake made the difference.

The man I was most eagerly waiting to get to was Sterling, because once I got to him and passed below, he would take charge.

I asked Pete and Al if they'd set up the snowfield. They hadn't. It turned out that the guides, Jake Breitenbach, Al Read, Pete Lev, Fred Wright, Dave Dornan and Herb Swedlund, Mike Ermarth and Rick Horn of the rescue team and Dr Walker from Jackson had arrived at the base of the couloir just minutes after Jim and I reached the top of the couloir. Even if the radio had worked, the word that we needed masses of gear would have gone out too late. Again, the critical two hours I had lost. There went my hopes that things would soon speed up. It had taken Jim and me five hours to get the party down five pitches. It was another seven hours to 2.00 am when the last victim was to reach the top of the snowfield. Just two more ropes would have cut that seven hours nearly in half.

Al and Pete tactfully suggested that Jim and I go on down to the snowfield, they could handle matters up here. They received no heroic protests from us.

My last image of the gully is of Horn working on the pitch exiting the couloir. I was rappelling down a steep slab and Horn came racing up by me, foot over hand it seemed, to help someone who'd gotten hung up on a ledge. He was muttering to himself and lunged to the ledge just as I realised that he was climbing unroped. I asked him if he thought that was wise. He didn't, but there weren't any more ropes.

At the top of the snowfield, a huge platform was being cut, large enough to hold all the rescued and some of the rescuers. I described the situation above as best I could to Sterling after telling him he looked good enough to me to kiss. I told him that it wasn't at all clear they all were going to make it. Lester Germer had expressed a sentiment to be left alone to die. I'd be tempted to let him and was glad it was out of my hands. Actually the fact that Germer had the whole party dedicated to keeping him alive certainly gave them a badly needed focus for survival. Germer was, I believe, in some degree conscious of this because, as we later found out, he had spotted the rescue team coming up Teepe's Snowfield and had said nothing to his companions.

Jim and I stood around on the ledge until the first victim arrived on it. There was some debate about whether to set up a series of anchors down the snowfield a rope-length apart or fewer super anchors to which we would just add ropes. I tried to join in the discussion and realised that I couldn't think very well and that it was no longer our show. Jim and I decided to go down.

I got as scared as I've ever been descending that snowfield. We were without ice axes and crampons. The surface was so hard that we couldn't kick steps deeper than half an inch. The rock hammer and pitons we had to stop a fall weren't convincing. I couldn't judge the surface either by sight or touch. I had difficulty keeping my body balanced over the pitiful footholds we were kicking because there was no elasticity left in my legs. At any time I could have moved on a marginal hold to a place where I quickly needed a good hold to find that I was on water ice and that would be it. All the way down my thought was, "And I said we wouldn't need crampons. You stupid son of a bitch, if you fall you'll deserve it."

In those circumstances we paid little attention to the commotion going on above us except cynically to remark that we hoped our mates didn't bomb us with one of the victims.

At this point we shall leave Pete Sinclair for a while and let Al Read take up the story:

Pete Lev and I had climbed up several leads in the late afternoon and were the first to meet Pete Sinclair and Jim Greig who were coming down from the Otter Body Snowfield lowering the helpless people, all suffering from hypothermia. We did not reach them until late afternoon or dusk as I recall. Pete and I were quickly joined by other rescuers and we all participated in the lowering process down the rock wall to the top of Teepe's Glacier. We were all wearing headlamps and the shadows of the victims and the rescuers against the walls were quite dramatic. I remember Jake Breitenbach (killed on Everest the next year) strapping one man to his back and rapelling down. Some were in very bad shape and two, it seemed at the time, rather near death. Anyway, there was no time to wait for litters because it was still snowing and all the victims were absolutely soaked through.

A crew lower down at the top of Teepe's Glacier had hacked out a large platform just below the rock walls and were receiving the Appies as we lowered them or brought them down on our backs. All finally were sitting on the snow tied to a number of ice axes driven in to the hilt just above the platform. The snow was extremely steep and quite hard. A slip would have meant a 2,000-foot slide down the glacier (really more of a steep snowfield but technically a glacier) into the rocks of the moraine below and certain death.

We all were very concerned we would have more hypothermia deaths unless we got the people down to the rescue group waiting at the bottom of the glacier with medical attention, soup, sleeping bags, etc., and the helicopters which would be there at dawn (no chance of pickup at the top of the glacier). We decided to lower everyone – really just slide them – down the glacier from our top stance to a lower stance several hundred feet below. Here we decided to make another platform from which a final lower could be made to where the angle of the snow eased and the Appies could be carried or dragged to the edge of the glacier and assistance. Herb Swedland and Jake went down to make the lower stance – perhaps 500 feet down. Meanwhile, Peter Lev, Sterling Neale, Rick Horn and I tied five loops in a climbing rope and placed five Appies in them. Each victim was tied about ten feet apart. We belayed this expeditious arrangement from two ice axes driven into the floor of our platform. I stood on one and let out the rope while Sterling watched the system and prepared to add additional ropes. Pete Lev (wearing crampons) descended to assist the Appies as they were being lowered. We slid the victims one by one off the platform and began lowering. They were heavy and I wished we had had a better belay.

Suddenly Pete yelled up to stop. He said there was an empty loop. There were only four people on the rope. Obviously one had fallen out of his waistloop. Dead, we thought! But after yelling down to Herb and Jake, nobody had seen or heard a body whirling by. Because everyone was working in the fall line, obviously a falling person *would* have been noticed. Pete then saw someone in his light about fifty feet to the right. He yelled at him. No response. He ran over to him and told him to return to the rope and safety. Pete immediately began to cut a platform as the person was wearing no crampons – only his mountain boots. Of course he had no ice axe. Pete told him to follow him back to the rope. The victim, John Fenniman, said nothing but looked as if he understood. Pete began cutting steps back to the rope, which we had by now stopped lowering. Rick Horn was preparing another climbing rope to throw down to Pete, so he could tie in the victim. We all knew he could come off at any minute.

As Pete began cutting steps back to the rope, Fenniman ignored him and went the other way instead. Pete stopped and climbed back to him, Pete insisted he follow him. Then Fenniman suddenly grabbed Pete's ice axe and they began grappling and struggling. Pete yelled up to us for help.

Rick Horn, also wearing crampons, who had by then readied a climbing rope, quickly lowered himself down and diverted Fenniman's attention. Pete scampered away, still retaining his ice axe. From behind, Rick managed to tie a quick bowline around Fenniman's waist and get away. He quickly returned to our ledge and put a belay on Fenniman. We all looked down at him with our headlamps. He began slowly to climb up towards our stance. I was still holding the remaining four Appies on belay through the two ice axes.

As Fenniman approached our platform his eyes were bulged out. He was ashen and looked as if he had gone mad. He had! He said very slowly. "You are the Devil. You are taking me to Hell" – or words to that effect. I could hardly believe what I was seeing and hearing. All at once he jumped up on our ledge and began hitting us. We believed he was trying to reach the several ice axes still stuck in the snow behind us. I remember thinking, as his fists were banging into my face, that I might have to let go of the belay to keep myself from being thrown off the platform or hit by an ice axe if he ever got hold of one. I remember yelling to Rick, "Kill him if you have to!" One of the Appie victims still on the platform yelled back, "No, no, don't kill him!" It was all quite incredible.

Rick finally managed to give Fenniman a shove and he went over the edge, but was caught at the lip by the belay, secured by Rick, who yelled we were only trying to help him. But when he continued to resist, Rick had to knock him out with a kick to the side of the head. The frontpoints of his crampons missed by a fraction. Fenniman went limp, Rick dragged him over to the rope, tied him in, and sat on him. The lowering was renewed.

Coming up from below, Jack Turner describes the scene as first seeing four people being lowered out of the darkness – limp and facing every direction, some upside down. Suddenly he saw a victim being ridden by Rick. Rick was hitting him with his fists and gagging! What was happening was every time Fenniman showed signs of coming round, Rick had to put him out again without actually killing him, and the tension and desperation of the experience had nauseated him. According to Turner this remains as one of the most amazing scenes he has ever witnessed.

The rest of the victims were lowered without incident and all fully recovered. I saw Fenniman later that morning being carried in a litter down to the helicopter landing site. He remembered nothing and could not have been nicer or more thankful. He simply had momentarily lost his mind and was trying to protect himself. I rather imagine he had thought he was dead or dying and that we indeed were trying to take him to Hell.

Pete Sinclair and Jim Greig had spent twenty-two nonstop gruelling hours on their vital first part of the rescue. But the next day something had to be done about Steve Smith's body. Pete Sinclair takes up the story again:

We didn't want to bring the body down. The Chief Ranger, Russ Dickenson, and the Superintendent contacted Smith's parents and asked for permission to bury Smith on the mountain. I don't know how they found the words to ask them and I don't know how the Smiths found words to grant it, but they did. I felt awful about it, as if we were violating the code that Achilles violated in refusing to allow Priam to give Hector a proper burial. Achilles relented, we didn't. I knew the Smiths would probably recall that Steve had loved the mountains and might wish to be buried there. That might have been his wish had he died in the heat of action. But life had not ended in glorious action for Steve Smith, it had oozed out of him, sapped from him by an insidious worm of self-doubt that had gotten lodged in his soul, giving him no opportunity even to struggle.

On Monday, Rick, Jim and I were transported to the Lower
Saddle by helicopter. The weather looked lousy. Soon it started
to snow. We stayed in the guide's hut, lounging on several
layers of sleeping pads and drinking tea, chocolate and soup.
Rick told us about his adventures with Fenniman. He still
hadn't quite recovered from that experience and obviously
didn't relish the task at hand. Our plan was to go up the
Owen-Spaulding Route, cross over the top of the mountain
just south of the summit and descend the snowfield to the
shoulder of the Otter Body where Smith's body lay, bury him,
and descend the route taken by Joyce, Blade and Smith and
then on down the evacuation route, cleaning up as much of the
debris as we could. The snowstorm was not an auspicious
beginning. This was turning out to be one of the worst climbing
seasons in memory. Jake used to say that the Owen-Spaulding is
both the easiest and the most difficult route he had climbed on
the Grand, easy under normal conditions, difficult under the
conditions currently prevailing. That worried me some but that
wasn't what was worrying Rick, much the strongest climber.
Every hour or so Rick would inquire as discreetly as possible as
to what we thought *he* would look like when we got to him. It
dawned on Jim and me that his was to be Rick's first corpse, and
I have to confess that we laid it on a little. We weren't
unsympathetic but we knew that nobody can help you through
that experience. The best you can do is to gain what distance
you can by finding what humour you can, not laughing at the
death but laughing at what your imagination is doing to you.

It snowed throughout Monday night and for much of Tuesday and then began to clear. We would leave for the summit
before dawn on Wednesday. It was not an unpleasant prospect.
We were well-rested, in good physical condition and we'd spent
most of the past four days high in the mountains.

The Owen-Spaulding Route is on the shaded side of the
mountain. It was bitterly cold for midsummer that Wednesday
morning and the whole upper part of the mountain was completely iced over. It might have been November. Jim and I
climbed slowly and cautiously, protecting every high-angle
pitch but Rick found that maddening. He seemed almost frantic
to get to the summit ridge, out of the cold and into the sun.

Over the crest of the ridge we found a beautiful summer day

in the mountains. Not hot of course because we were in fresh snow above 13,000 feet, but the sun opened our down jackets and eased into our tensed muscles. We called a halt for an early lunch. The partially mown hay fields made squares of light green between the darker green willows along the Snake and the Gros Ventre rivers and the greenish-grey and light brown sagebrush flats of the valley. The snow was clean and too bright for unprotected eyes. We had passed from winter to summer in the space of a few moments and a few yards.

We moved at normal pace now, picking out a route with caution in the couloirs we had to cross to reach the snowfield and then descended with an occasional belay down the East Snowfield to the rock above the body. Some scrambling and a short rappel brought us to Steve Smith. Near him was an empty matchbook, the matches lay scattered about. Each one was tried, none had lit. Much later, we heard the story of how at Smith's death Charlie Joyce rebelled, took Blade by the shoulders and told him that they were going down, all the way down.

We took what personal effects we thought his family might like to have, tied a rope to the body and manoeuvred it over the moat between the base of the cliff and the Otter Body Snow-field. Getting it adequately protected was something of a problem. We looked for a place near at hand where the snow pack was thickest and least likely to bare the rock in even the driest year. Rick was above anchoring the body. From a stance a few feet above the corpse I guided the rope to a position where it would drop directly down a small chimney to the debris at the base of the cliff. Jim straddled the rope at the body with his knife out.

"Well," said Jim, made the sign of the cross over Steve Smith and cut the rope. I had forgotten to bring a Bible. We covered the body first with small rocks, in case there were any carnivorous rodents up there, and then with larger boulders.

Long Haul on La Perouse

Norman Hardie

At the beginning of time, according to Maori legend, the children of Rangi, the Sky, came down to earth and Aorangi, one of the sons, set off to explore in his canoe with three of his brothers. The canoe ran aground forming the South Island of New Zealand and the four children became four great peaks of the Central Alps. Aorangi, which means "sky-cloud", is now better known as Mount Cook (12,349 feet/3,764 metres) though the old name is still used by the Maoris. The South Island does indeed look like an upturned canoe, with the spine of the Central Alps running up the centre. Though these mountains are not so lofty as other ranges on earth, they are heavily glaciated, with the ice creeping down to 2,000 feet above sea level. They also get more than their fair share of precipitation. The moist air sweeps across the Tasman Sea, sucking up moisture like a sponge, only to wring out its soggy clouds over the western flanks of the Alps. Higher, like a good wife's washing, it is a uniform white at the colder elevations. To the south-west in Fiordland the peaks are rain-washed, vertical and smooth; in places even the all-pervading jungle cannot cling. While to the east of the Alps the rainfall is slight, the ground parched and the country baked brown. Indeed, it is a memorable experience to travel over Arthur's Pass, on the road or rail link between the two coasts and witness these changes. As one drops down to the western seaboard, the encroachment of the bush is felt. It is everywhere, elbowing in, the offspring of the 200 odd inches of rain per year. It is varied and picturesque country, with tree ferns, cabbage trees and lancewood, to name but a few of the junior members of a lofty family with such big brothers as rata and rimu trees.

The main chain of the Central Alps forms a baffle wall between two great seas, the Pacific to the east and the Tasman to the west. It is from the latter that the violent storms sweep in, usually preceded by their advance packs of hogsback clouds, sure get-back-to-the-valley signs, recognised and feared by all Kiwi climbers.

A range of mountains which provides possibly the best Himalayan training ground in the world must inevitably be a rough, tough place. It is. The mountains are both dangerous and difficult. There are inevitably accidents.

During my stay in New Zealand I got to know several of the mountain guides who were employed by the New Zealand Government Tourist Board. Harry Ayres was then chief guide at the Glacier Hotel at Franz Josef and together with Mick Bowie and that earlier generation of founder guides, Peter and Alex Graham, they had a fine tradition and safety record. It was Harry who gave me a job after an abortive gold prospecting trip on the West Coast in the early 'fifties.

The New Zealand guides have never been exponents of Grade Six climbing. The emphasis in their training was on knowledge of the peaks, basic mountain craft and the well-being of their clients. They could cut steps for twelve hours a day and Mick Bowie would still have enough spare energy to puff away at his pipe whilst doing so! One wonders how many modern "tigers" would stand up to such physical exertion?

It was with this backbone of guides, Mick Bowie and Harry Ayres, that a rescue was successfully completed from close to the summit of La Perouse which will probably never be equalled in sheer protracted effort. Over the years I've witnessed the transition from sweat and toil rescue to the quick whisk by helicopter. I can't say that I regret this change – it's a lot easier – yet something has been lost. Before, it was team effort, where men worked as a closely knit unit, often exposed to danger themselves, always subjected to the grinding, arm-stretching work obligatory in taking a casualty off a mountain. But with this hardship an understanding and compassion was generated which isn't a part of the clinical and remote evacuation by a helicopter.

The accident on La Perouse was before the days of helicopters in New Zealand and from the men on that rescue a powerful nucleus of Himalayan climbers was born. The name of Norman Hardie will be forever linked with that hard core of Kiwi climbers that explored the remote area to the south and east of Everest. In that fascinating wild country our paths crossed on several occasions, in the depths of the Hongu valley and in the steamy Choyang, but I met him first in Christchurch. Norman, like his colleague, Ed Hillary, is an unassuming man. Here he gives his account of the La Perouse rescue of Ruth Adams, still vivid to him over the intervening years, and an enduring monument to the determination of a small group of men:

The peaks near Mount Cook are named after Pacific navigators. Some, such as Tasman, Drake, Torres and Magellan preceded Captain Cook in time, and others came after him. Among the latter are Vancouver, Hicks, Dampier and La Perouse. On the ridge to La Perouse are three peaks named after British Admirals, Sturdee, Beattie and Jellicoe who were not Pacific navigators.

At the beginning of 1948 Mount Cook had been climbed seventy-four times and La Perouse merely twelve. On 6 February the South Ridge of Cook was ascended for the first time by Ruth Adams, Ed Hillary and the two guides, Mick Sullivan and Harry Ayres. (Through Ed's inability to get leave at Christmas, when most amateur New Zealanders do their mountaineering, he had made several climbs with Harry). Three days later the same party set off at 4.00 am to climb La Perouse. The normal route in those days involved three hours' travelling from Gardiner hut, up the Hooker Glacier, then over Sturdee, Beattie, Jellicoe and Low before the ice ridge to the main summit. It is generally a long hard snow and ice climb, with several big pitches of fragile rock on the buttresses of the British admirals, and on the slopes to Low. Mount Low was named after R. S. Low of the Scottish Mountaineering Club, who was in the party that made the first ascent of La Perouse in 1908.

These four made good progress on a fine morning until they encountered an ice wall on the descent from Low to the last col before La Perouse. Hillary and Ayres got down the wall but, on finding it far from easy, called to the rear pair to divert round the end of it. Ruth and Mick cramponed to a steep slope and were working their way down this when Ruth slipped. She slid down the ice slope out of control, passed the position where Mick was firmly placed and, to his horror and that of the two spectators, their rope snapped in what was really not a major fall. Ruth slid onwards about sixty feet, dropped over a short cliff and was stopped by a projecting rock – the only obstacle which could have prevented her going a further 4,000 feet.

Mick had been given that rope by a client from Europe in 1938, and he regarded it so highly that he locked it away for safekeeping on the outbreak of war, bringing it out again in 1948 for the special climbs which he and Ruth undertook that year. Although the rope looked in good condition, it had apparently rotted in the damp atmosphere of the West Coast.

The three climbers rushed to Ruth, secured her to the slope, and made their assessment of the situation. She appeared to have a broken wrist, possibly a damaged back, and definitely bruising and concussion. Clearly without further assistance the party could not carry her over the long tortuous route they had ascended. In 1948 there were no helicopters in New Zealand and no climbers carried radios. Getting the news out, and assembling the rescue team in this remote site was to be a major effort. The injured woman was a long day's march for a climber from the first telephone; and Christchurch, the nearest centre for mountaineers, was a further 170 miles away.

Ed Hillary stayed with Ruth, and spent most of the day cutting an ice cave and lining its floor with rock slabs, to give some security for the night. His patient regained consciousness and although cheerful, was quite unable to walk. The two guides had rushed back down their ascent route to Gardiner hut, where Mick picked up food, a cooker, two sleeping bag covers, a bag for Ruth, and climbed solo back up to the accident scene, doing the last hour in the dark. They all sat in the cave, ate a bare meal, and huddled together for the night, two without sleeping bags. In fact, Mick Sullivan spent the subsequent five nights without a bag. Meanwhile Harry had run on down to the Hermitage Hotel at the foot of Mount Cook and reported to the chief guide, Mick Bowie. Immediately a call was put through to Christchurch, so that late on the night of the accident a strong group of climbers received the bad news.

Mick Bowie was nearing the end of his distinguished guiding career. He had been chief guide for many years. He had once led a mountaineering expedition to southern China and had spent several war years with the New Zealand Army in Egypt and Italy. Mick led the whole rescue operation. Also at the Hermitage were three trainee guides whom he brought in from other climbs, as they returned to the hotel in the dark. Equipment was packed for an air drop. Before dawn they all set off for the climb to Gardiner hut and then right on to the accident site, which they reached as darkness was falling, on the second night.

During that day a single-engined plane had dropped three loads in accurately placed positions and with minimal damage. Thus the patient, Ed Hillary and Mick Sullivan received a stretcher, a tent, food, fuel, a long rope and another sleeping bag. Apart from receiving this equipment there was very little they could do for the day.

On this same complex day the Christchurch party drove to the Hermitage in the dark hours of the morning. I was then a junior engineer at a hydro-electric construction project on the way to the Hermitage. At 5.00 am Bill Beaven, from one of the Christchurch cars, woke me vigorously and said, "The Mount Cook South Ridge party has had an accident on La Perouse. Can you come?"

"I've got a busy day. But Bill, you appear quite cheerful for a search party member!"

"Well, yes. It should be an interesting trip. If we act quickly everyone should get off safely – and it's a good team."

"I'll try my best. Start without me, and I'll catch you if I can."

I rushed to the Chief Engineer's house, explained the situation as I saw it. He said he would drive me to the Hermitage, but first he had to eat. I then ran to the rooms of two of my work mates and handed to them the duties that were to have been mine for the next few days. My climbing gear took just a minute to gather.

In this early morning activity the local policeman, who was not a mountaineer, was woken from his slumbers. As the police had just been given the responsibility for rescue operations, he announced he was also coming. Ted Trappitt, a good friend of mine, is now in one of the senior police posts in New Zealand, but on that occasion I felt his presence on such a technical climb could be a great embarrassment. The policeman, my boss, and I, drove with some speed to the end of the road. For the last few miles La Perouse became visible – a great ice peak towering above multiple shining cliffs. Between the cliffs are steep gullies, and even from fifteen miles away I was able to point out the great cones of avalanche debris at its base. Ted Trappitt became silent.

At the hotel we obtained more information. Harry Wigley, the pilot, had read a message stamped in the snow when he made his air drops, and it stated, "O.K. all well." He also reported, the three on the site were about a hundred yards on the west side of the main divide.

Ted looked at me, with a brief smile, "That hundred yards is a relief. The accident is outside my boundary of operations."

Carrying as little as possible, I set off alone, some two hours behind the Christchurch party. Fortunately for me, the long car journey in the dark had taken its toll on the others and I was able to overtake them before I became committed to any really technical climbing. Some were passed, returning, having decided they were not fit enough, straight from office desks, for this type of major rescue. Our Christchurch party had now Harry Ayres, the guide, at its head. He had replaced broken crampons from his run down the glacier the previous day, stolen a few hours sleep, and was on the way up again. The whole tourist and climbing operation from the Hermitage was to be left without any climbing guides for a week.

We were astonished to find a long line of steps cut up the face of Jellicoe, not to Harper's Saddle, the normal route. Mick Bowie had made a new direct route to save time and all of us followed these widely spaced footholds in the fading light of the second night after the accident. Darkness overtook us as we were working our way up the icy face. Our group scattered in pairs on this unknown territory, and I was relieved to be roped to Bill Beaven who had been one of my main climbing companions for several years. We pressed slowly upwards assisted by the light of one feeble torch. It was bad enough, looking after our own safety, recognising the correct positions for our boots and ice axes, but every few minutes we were alarmed by the whistle of rocks passing over us, like cannon fire.

"Bill, that mountain is mighty loose up there."

"We should stop at a crevasse lip every time they start. Each climber ahead is 'gardening' when they reach that hundred feet of black rubble at the crest of the ridge."

"Yes, a good idea."

But when the next group reached the rocks we were not near a protective crevasse. There was no option but to keep climbing. Needless to say, strong words were hurled up the slope as each rock barrage descended. I heard later that Mick, leading his three new guides up that first ascent took time off to give just one command to those further down the rope.

"No bloody mistakes here."

At midnight, at the crest of the ridge, our group of eight unrolled sleeping bags on the ice and slept until daylight. Two were still on the face and they spent the night there. With the weather remaining fine so far, the absence of tents and snow caves did not matter. Breakfast was a slender snack in swirling mist. We struggled along the crumbly ridge and then there were stretches of guide-cut bucket steps, until at 10.00 am we were at the accident site.

Thus, forty-eight hours after the fall the team was fully assembled. In total we were sixteen climbers and one patient. Among the climbers was Dr Gerry Wall, now a Member of Parliament, who had been a student at medical school with his patient, Dr Ruth Adams. His examination revealed no alterations to the original diagnosis by Ruth's climbing companions. She was put securely in a stretcher, given sedatives and prepared for the long journey. We rummaged among the air-dropped supplies and it appeared that Ruth would have all that she was likely to need, but it was more than evident the sixteen climbers were destined for a very hungry journey.

Mick Bowie had given much thought to the two known routes off the mountain. The one we all knew by then, over Low, Jellicoe and Sturdee, was long and steep, involving many risks from further accidents with such large numbers moving about on great areas of rotten rock, and much New Zealand rock is very treacherous. The weather seemed to be deteriorating, and on that route there appeared to be the likelihood of two more nights on the ice at above 9,000 feet.

The alternative was to descend to the West Coast side where the route off the mountain was technically easier, and by the second night the party should be at the Gulch Creek Rock, an enormous glacial erratic which could shelter the party under its overhangs. There would be alpine scrub for fuel there and we would be secure, but still some three days of trackless forested gorge from civilisation. In the interests of getting everyone off

the mountain safely, as fast as possible, Mick chose the West
Coast route, down to the shelter rock and then out via the Cook
River. La Perouse at that time had been climbed only three
times from the West, but in our party was a man who had been
on one of these climbs. Doug Dick had been in a trio, including
David Lewis, later known for his solo yachting, that had
climbed La Perouse in 1938. For this expedition-type climb
no real tracks had been cut through the bush, and for ten years
no one had returned to the Cook River. Carrying the stretcher
in this country would be a formidable task, but there would be
fewer risks of a fatality by this choice of route.

To reach the North-West Ridge of La Perouse it was necessary to climb a further 500 feet, to a point not a 100 yards along
from the summit before beginning the descent. That climb was
hot and frustrating, with ropes being trampled, big packs
having to proceed forward and three vertical ice walls to be
scaled. In the morning the guides had gone ahead, cut steps and
put ropes and belays at the worst places.

It soon became apparent that the six, or sometimes four,
handling the stretcher could not also carry their full packs. Nor
could they be roped together and hold coils of slack rope.
Progress came to a halt just 200 yards from the accident site.
Men on each side of the stretcher, working on very steep snow,
bumped their heads into the packs of those ahead. Crampon
spikes tore into climbing ropes. Previously silent complaints
were now sometimes murmured. We halted. The guides approved the removal of the climbing ropes, and delegated jobs to
most of us. Some without packs were to do the stretcher work.
Others were somehow to manage the additional packs and be
available for a turn on the stretcher carrying, sliding and pulling. Consequently there was much travelling back and forwards
for packs and equipment; some climbed with two rucksacks. In
weather which had earlier been threatening, seventeen people
emerged at 4.00 pm just beside the summit of La Perouse. No
one seriously considered diverting to bag that rarely climbed
peak.

As the clouds dispersed it was comforting to hear Doug Dick
telling Mick, "When we came up in 1938 we used this snow
ridge ahead. One can't go to the end of it. We have to go down a
steep face to the west to avoid the enormous bluffs which drop

away from the ridge end. It's all rather steep but reliable for quite a distance. But lower down there is loose rock where we had troubles ten years ago."

For the descent along the ridge, new techniques had to be tried and adopted. Our giant leader, Mick, tied 400 feet of air-dropped rope to the stretcher. He established a firm anchor and the carriers moved on to the extent of the rope and then rested, as Mick walked forward to anchor for a further move of 400 feet. In the late afternoon the slope steepened and by winding in and out of a crevassed area we eventually reached temporarily easier ground. As the light was fading we emerged on to an exposed but rocky terrace at about 8,000 feet. Here we stopped for the night.

Throughout the day I had been hungry and I had frequent misgivings about our food supply. As each of us scratched a groove for laying out a sleeping bag, Mick came round and issued us with a slice of cold corned beef, two slices of bread and a portion of tinned fruit. This was washed down with water from the ice-cold pools, only feet from our stopping place. Very little was said that night and few had a sound sleep. Several light showers fell on the mountain, but there was no severe wind. I dozed off several times, and eventually I came to full life with Mick's gruff voice beside me, "Wake up, Hardie. The day's half gone. The sun will burn a hole in your arse."

I opened my eyes, and it wasn't daylight yet. But the clouds had gone and the full extent of our exposed eyrie soon became apparent. The almost totally unclimbed Balfour Range was across the La Perouse glacier from us. The sun later touched Tasman, Malaspina and Vancouver far to the east. But to the west, far below us, the still scarcely lit bush on the Cook River cliffs promised much gloomy struggling before the journey ended.

We had been cramped on a tiny hard and damp terrace, with a tent for Ruth, and saturated clouds for us. At one stage Neil Hamilton rolled over and committed a terrible crime. He crushed Mick Bowie's pipe! Mick, always a heavy pipe smoker, surveyed the damage as he was putting on his boots and said drily, "I had hoped this rescue would have got through without a disaster." Neil, the only other pipe smoker in the party, unveiled his own, and handed it to Mick, who puffed on it at every stop.

Breakfast consisted of another slice of cold tinned meat and two of plain bread, again without a hot drink. The hard work continued and it took a full day to get down to the Gulch Creek Rock. First there was a long descent of a loose rock couloir, and the only way to handle this was for climbers to go down in pairs, using the long rope as a handrail, then scrambling clear at the bottom. Eventually the stretcher was lowered, being guided by two men to avoid injuring the rescuers. Another hazard was the likelihood of sharp rocks tearing the fabric of the stretcher.

Gerry, the doctor, did much of the attending to Ruth. She was tightly strapped in with just part of her face visible. For most of the travelling she was heavily sedated, so there was very little conversation with her, and discussions about the look of the next downward hazards were held away from the likely range of her ears.

It was not until nearly lunch time some three whole days after the accident, that there was a general acceptance that the operation would be successful. We stopped on a terrace by a small tarn, munched the normal slender ration, and more openly discussed the prospects. Before leaving the Hermitage, Mick had sent a message to people on the West Coast, requesting a team to cut a track through the bush for us, if we were not seen descending the ice slopes on the east side. Mick now seemed confident the track work would have started and he said, "For a strong party not carrying much, it is possible to struggle through without a track. In fact we might even see someone tonight."

There is a lot of difference between a man pushing through hard country alone, and six men carrying a stretcher with a patient whose injuries required delicate transportation.

In the afternoon we carried and slid the stretcher down a further 2,000 feet of loose rock and snow grass, aiming all the time at the vast sheltering rock which had been visible most of the day. At 4.00 pm sixteen tired and very hungry people struggled through the first small patches of alpine scrub, and lowered their loads at the rock. Here at last under the overhangs there was shelter, and, what seemed more important, fuel was available for the first time. Great billies of tea were produced, damp gear was put out to dry, and Ruth was temporarily released from the cramp and heat of the stretcher.

Mick Bowie's forecast was right. We were still settling in when four men appeared from the moraine which gives access to the Cook River.

"Are you carrying a body or a patient?" was the first question.

"She's alive and not too bad, but she'll have to be carried all the way."

"Anxious relatives, and hordes of reporters are down at the highway, desperate for news."

The four new arrivals emptied the food they were carrying into the joint pool. They hadn't brought very much, as they had come up in a hurry, and they had to bring their own sleeping bags, climbing gear, a tent, and clothing.

"We had no idea you were short of supplies. From all reports, the outside world thinks tons of it were dropped from the plane when you got the stretcher."

Within an hour two of them set off for the road, carrying the news of Ruth's relatively satisfactory state, confirming our outward course, and requesting food to come up the fast forming track.

One of the four who came up the Cook River was Earle Riddiford. This was the first time he met Ed Hillary. These two were subsequently on three Himalayan expeditions together and it was Earle and Eric Shipton who in 1951 first broke through to the crest of the Western Cwm and confirmed the easiest way to the Nepalese upper slopes of Mount Everest.

After numerous introductions Earle joined Bill Beaven and me. His first remark to us was, "This new track will open up some great climbing for our four next season."

Bill said, "We've had exactly the same thought."

For several years we three, Earle Riddiford, Bill Beaven and I, had been part of a highly successful group which climbed in the more remote valleys of New Zealand, accomplishing many first ascents, from places where we would have to carry loads for a week, before putting in a base for an expedition-type climb. In fact our group was to use this new Cook River track ten months later, when we completed the climb of La Perouse, and several other mountains.

At the Gulch Creek Rock, Earle, always one for looking ahead and planning ambitious schemes, said, "What's Ed Hillary like on the mountain?"

I replied, "This is the first time we've met him. But he seems very good to me."

Then Bill added, "He's fit and he worked really hard on the mountain. You know he's also got expedition ideas for the Himalayas."

Earle had been pressing us for years to set our eyes on the Himalayas, but the giant problems of costs, sponsorship, permission, oxygen and publicity appeared forbidding. We never did all join forces in the Himalayas, but within seven years, three of us, and of course Ed Hillary, each made first ascents of peaks above 23,000 feet.

The warmth of dried bags and the lower altitude gave everyone a better night at Gulch Creek. But Mick, who for the whole journey had been pressing us with the gruff command for an early start, now added to the previous strong words, "There'll be some streams to cross and some likely wading in the Cook River. It'll be low in the mornings, and high each afternoon with the melting snow." From the rock we all scrambled to the moraine which covers the lower few miles of the La Perouse Glacier, before the Cook River begins. Like all moraines, it is a jumbled mess of sharp rocks, steep slopes, mostly bedded on ice. Fortunately, the further down the glacier one goes the less ice there is visible. Gradually, the going improves.

In mid-morning, when the worst of the moraine was past, a single-engined aircraft was heard, and then seen, coming up the valley. A tiny homemade parachute dropped out and landed safely near us. I looked up. "That doesn't look like much of a food drop." Tied to the parachute was a brief hand-written message. "Wave a parka if Ruth is safe." Evidently last night's messengers had not travelled in the dark. We waved. The plane departed. Again we picked up our burdens and struggled onwards.

Soon the plane returned, did several circuits round the group, and another parachute dropped out and opened. It also looked small. Someone collected it and returned with a big carton. It was eagerly opened and inside was a giant fruit cake. What a joyful sight! Ruth's father, Ernest Adams, runs New Zealand's main cake bakery.

After a big cake morning tea, the team performed better. Soon the valley closed to a steep-sided gorge and we were forced into an area of enormous river-washed boulders, originally dropped there by the glacier. With the roaring river lapping their sides, it was usually necessary to climb over them. Where this was done the route was through the bush. As soon as we entered it we could see that the first upward helpers had at least cleared a slender track for our outward passage.

But the difficulties were enormous. There would seldom be fifty consecutive yards of normal stretcher carrying. The total width of men on each side of the stretcher was too wide for the initial narrow track cut through the trees. Great tree roots, thousands of boulders, steep bluffs where ropes had to be used, wet moss-covered rocks and a raging river had to be negotiated. Frequently the stretcher had to be moved from hand to hand, in circumstances where men were unable to move with the main vital load. Those coming behind, having their turn at relaying the pack loads, or carrying two packs at a time, had fewer problems, as the bushmen's route was better suited to persons travelling singly. But it was still extremely hard work.

As time went by, more helpers came up the valley. They included Ruth's three brothers. More bushmen were working on the track and there were obvious improvements the further west we travelled. Also food began to arrive in great quantity. But still it took us three days to get out from Gulch Creek to the West Coast road.

At one camp, in the depths of the humid rain forest, we were sitting round a fire, shortly to crawl into our sleeping bags, when one mountaineer spied an axe, picked it up, and began to chop firewood. Immediately an enormous bushman with immense arms bulging out of a black singlet leapt up and grabbed the axe. He looked at the keen edge as a professional golfer may inspect his putter. Then he took a heap of logs, laid into them with immense skill, and sprayed us all with showers of great chips as he rapidly produced a stack of firewood. I sat in wonder, and one of my new associates whispered in awe, "He's the toughest man on the Coast – won last year's Australia and New Zealand downhand chop. No one can ever touch his axe."

It was on the seventh day since the accident when Ruth was transferred to the greater comfort of a car. Soon she was flown to Christchurch – and eventually she made a full recovery. In fact she completed a medical degree, married a doctor, had three children and went into medical practice in Melbourne, Australia.

The rescuers and ever willing bushmen were given a great welcome at the small town where they emerged. After an enormous feed, a thorough clean and a good sleep, I stated I intended walking back to my work at the hydro dam. This meant a two days' walk on tourist tracks and a crossing in snow of a 6,500-feet pass, emerging at the Hermitage, where I could easily arrange a ride to work. The guides were horrified at this. Yet another crossing of Copland Pass meant no great joy to them. One came to me and requested, "Keep away from the bosses at the Hermitage and don't say where we are. We've been offered a ride through by car and train to Christchurch. We'll get back to the Hermitage a day after you."

They enjoyed their comfortable journey the long way round, and they certainly deserved the rest.

A Long Way to Kinabalu

Dan Carroll

This is one of those cases of going downhill, rather than up, to perform a search and rescue mission, but before this descent, the rescue team had to travel half way round the globe to the island of Borneo and climb the highest peak in South-East Asia. This is probably the longest call-out ever, a distance of 10,000 miles (a close second is a Mount Kenya call-out, also recorded in this book).

Dan Carroll is team leader of RAF Leuchars Mountain Rescue Team in Fife, Scotland. RAF Mountain Rescue goes all the way back to 1943 and was founded principally for the location of crashed aircraft and the evacuation of their crews. Their responsibility widened over time to rescuing military personnel engaged in mountain activities, and hence to civilian walkers and climbers. It also expanded its remit to back-up local rescue teams, often pressed for manpower and resources. RAFMR moved with the times and all the teams are well equipped and well trained. Team members are volunteers within the service, with day jobs as aircraftsmen and other military trades.

Dan was the climbing leader of the successful RAFMR Everest expedition in 2001, and summitted the highest mountain of the world by the difficult North Ridge. Here he gives an account, a story of skill and dedication, of how their team descended into the deepest depths of one of the most notorious gullies in the world.

It was 15 March 1994. "This isn't a wind-up Dan." Jim Smith, the team leader of RAF Kinloss Mountain Rescue Team, sounded serious. I listened intently as he explained that ten Army personnel had gone out to Malaysia on an Adventurous Training expedition to attempt the first complete *descent* of a steep gully on a 13,455-foot (4,101-metre) mountain called Kinabalu. The party had split into two groups of five which had become separated on difficult ground. One party had major epics and, after eleven days, eventually made it to safety. The other group were still missing in the gully! The Malaysian rescue services were not capable of operating in the steep gully at that altitude so, unbelievable as it sounded, the RAF Mountain Rescue Service had been tasked to go to look for five missing soldiers 10,000 miles away!

Alister Haveron, the Chief Instructor of the RAF Mountain Rescue Service, decided to take a total of seventeen troops from (at that time) six RAF rescue teams in the UK. He liaised with the Ministry of Defence, who were investigating the background of the missing five and attempting to find out about the mountain, as well as organising civilian flights and equipment.

Kinabalu is an awe-inspiring mountain, rising in splendid isolation above the steaming northern jungles on the vast island of Borneo, east Malaysia. The lower half of the mountain comprises near-impenetrable tropical forest, while the top half is bare granite carved into wild peaks and ridges, smooth slabs and vertiginous faces which rise uninterrupted for over a kilometre above the jungle. Local tribes have named the mountain Aki Na, Home of the Spirits of the Departed It's the highest mountain in South-East Asia and, on first sight, it's easy to comprehend the fascination that the mountain holds for mountaineers. Almost all of the visitors with the intention of climbing Mount Kinabalu ascend by the tourist route with a local guide. On the first day they climb to a rest house situated at the top of the forest at 11,200 feet. They leave the rest house early in the morning to climb to the summit for sunrise. By mid-morning, the mountain is shrouded in mist and swirling cloud and there are often heavy tropical downpours in the afternoon.

That was all we had to go on. No detailed information about climate or conditions; we didn't even know if there was snow in the gully and a few of us packed axes and crampons "just in case"! We had two hours to sort out kit, get vaccinations and, to top it all, my passport was out of date! Luckily, I was based at RAF St Athan in South Wales at the time, and soon got a new passport from the agency at Newport. Similar scenes of un-hurried preparation got under way at five other locations throughout the UK as the RAF responded to this unusual call for long-haul assistance from halfway around the world. The RAF Kinloss team members arranged to borrow a Nimrod aircraft to take them to RAF Brize Norton – stopping off enroute to pick up some of the team from RAF Leuchars and RAF Leeming. A SAR Wessex helicopter from RAF Valley flew the Valley MRT troops over to Brize Norton, whilst the Stafford and St Athan troops travelled by road.

This was a highly unusual deployment for the RAF teams, but it went incredibly smoothly, probably due to the fact that every member had been on previous overseas expeditions and could envisage the requirements and foresee pending problems. One was ready cash! We were unsure how long the rescue would take and twenty members could get through a lot of money buying food, accommodation and equipment. At that time, RAF rescue teams only had access to cash funds and we ended up taking several thousand pounds in cash and relying on the British military when we ran out. After this call-out Team Leaders were each issued with a company credit card to cater for such emergencies.

Eventually, all seventeen of us were assembled at Heathrow. In addition we were joined by two jungle survival instructors from the RAF School of Combat Survival, an ex-Royal Navy Outdoor Instructor (Lieutenant-Commander Mike Elesmore) who had first-hand knowledge of Mount Kinabalu and an Army doctor (Major Tony Williams). We boarded a Malaysian Airlines 747 to Kuala Lumpur, then onwards to Kota Kinabalu. Total travelling time was twenty-two hours from leaving Heathrow. At Kota Kinabalu International Airport we were met by the Malaysian Army and taken to a rather pleasant five star hotel in the middle of town. Unfortunately, we were not to see much of the hotel during the next two weeks!

Immediately after arriving we were briefed on the situation by Lieutenant-Colonel Tony Schumacher, commander of the British Army jungle warfare training team in Brunei. Due to the size, complexity and media interest involved with this incident, he was appointed by the military as the on scene search and rescue commander. After this briefing, most of us got our heads down for a few hours. The remainder were invited to a briefing by two of the surviving soldiers – the other three were in hospital! They had set off to descend the gully twenty-one days previously. Their story was told matter-of-factly, but it was apparent that they had been through great hardships.

At 0200 hours on 23 February 1994 ten soldiers, led by Lieutenant-Colonel Robert Neill, set off from the rest house at 11,200 feet, intending to make the first complete descent of the steep uncharted Low's Gully. The expedition members had ascended the tourist route some days previously. Some of them had climbed to the summit of Kinabalu and they had all carried out some rudimentary abseil training before making the climb over a col at 12,500 feet into the gully itself. The gully starts in an enormous slabby amphitheater surrounded by several 13,000-foot peaks and then it plunges via waterfalls, narrow ravines and vertical cliffs to the jungle floor thousands of feet below. Each of the ten men had taken approximately eight days' rations. Despite their training, some of the younger, fitter personnel had reservations about the competence and capabilities of the others.

From the start, it was clear that the five who had escaped were a young, fit, strong group, mainly of non-commissioned officers. The missing group comprised two older officers and three inexperienced Hong Kong Military Service Corps personnel. The survivors described very steep ground, abseils down cliffs that were more than 800 feet high, hacking their way through dense jungle, wading and swimming through deep pools and abseiling or jumping down waterfalls.

Initially, the survivors had waited for the rear party, who were very slow but, without radios and lacking any formal contingency plans, the groups soon lost contact with each other. They had last seen the rear party at about 10,500 feet on 2 March. The survivors said that after about eight days of descent, they had come across a huge waterfall that they were unable to descend or pass. To escape the gully, they were forced to cut across very steep and slippery slabs covered in loose vegetation. Then they descended high-angled ground cover to the jungle below, where they spent several days wandering through uncharted jungle, getting progressively weaker and weaker. This group split again before they came across a village. It was 12 March – seventeen days after they first set foot in the gully for their planned eight-day descent! Even then, due to a national holiday, it was very difficult to get a message to the outside world of what had happened.

The survivors were obviously glad to be out of the gully alive. They had described a terrible ordeal that they thought would never end. They had all been bitten by leeches and their feet were rotting after having been wet for most of the time. They had lost most of their equipment in the waterfalls and one had taken a serious fall whilst crossing the steep slabs to escape from the gully.

All in all, it painted a bleak picture for the missing soldiers and a serious scenario for the rescuers! The Army expedition had set off to climb Kinabalu on 22 February, the survivors' briefing finished at 0200 hours on 16 March. We were aware that we had no time to waste.

Utilising Mike Elesmore's knowledge of the area around Kinabalu, and taking into account the fact that there had been, thus far, no search effort on the mountain itself, Lieutenant-Colonel Tony Schumacher requested that the RAF deploy as soon as possible and concentrate on a search of the gully. The Malaysian Army also volunteered the services of approximately a hundred troops and Tony Schumacher indicated that, due to their familiarity with jungle operations, they search up both banks of the river which flows out of Low's Gully.

The town of Kota Kinabalu is at sea level. Our immediate plan was to split our group into two; a fast party would leave in four hours (at 0600 hours) to ascend the tourist route to a rest house at 11,000 feet. There they would spend the night acclimatising and resting before ascending to the 12,500-foot col, at the start of Low's Gully the next day. They would then descend into the gully and make a reconnaissance of the ground. The second party would organise equipment and provide the second wave probing deeper into the gully.

We intended to drive to 6,000 feet at the start of the tourist track. This would leave us 5,000 feet of ascent in five kilometres, usually an easy task for the RAF Mountain Rescue, but after travelling for more than twenty-four hours and having little rest during the previous two days, it was a daunting prospect! At this point Brigadier-General Hussain bin Yussof of the Malaysian Army offered to give us a lift to 11,000 feet in his helicopter. We accepted. In our jet-lagged condition we had

forgotten the two golden rules of RAF Mountain Rescue troops
– never rely on helicopters and only trust officers as a last resort!
We paid the price in precious time being wasted.

After three hours of flying round and round Mount Kinabalu
at 2,000 feet in a Sikorsky with a bad hydraulic leak, we landed
in a kampong (village) in the jungle. The mountain was swathed
in thick cloud that showed no sign of lifting. However, the
General had something else in mind for us. He took control of
the village school (a windowless barn) which had a blackboard
and ten chairs. The General's aide gave some chalk to Corporal
Graham Stamp and told him to teach the General all about
search and rescue in the UK! Stamp started by describing the
responsibilities of the police and where the RAF rescue co-
ordination centres and coastguard fitted into the picture. He
then described the UK's voluntary system of mountain rescue
and the part played by the RAF MRTs and the SAR helicopter
flights. With much prompting from the General, Stampy then
talked about training and call-outs and reaction times and
equipment. Meanwhile we sat in total disbelief at this complete
waste of time whilst the General's aide was taking copious
notes. It turned out that his intention was to glean as much
information as possible from us, with a view to arranging a more
formal approach to SAR in Malaysia.

After a couple of hours of SAR lessons by Stampy the
weather had cleared enough to take off again. Unfortunately,
the hill was still in cloud but we eventually managed to persuade
them to drop us off, this time near a road where we managed to
scrounge a lift to the Park HQ and the start of the tourist track.
There we were allocated a guide and two porters to help carry
some of the ropes. We were off up the track with 5,000 foot of
ascent and five kilometres ahead of us. Despite lack of sleep and
heavy bags we made good time and made it to the Pana Laban
rest house at 11,200 feet about two hours after nightfall – and
only eighteen hours after our arrival in the country. We ate well
and slept soundly in a rat-infested shed salubriously named
Burlington House.

First light on 18 March and we started the climb up through
the mist, across easy-angled slabs to the col at 12,500 feet. We
fixed rope across these slabs to facilitate both descent and to
mark the route for reinforcements. On the other side of the col

we had our first breathtaking sight of Easy Valley which leads directly down to Low's Gully. The top of Easy Valley was made up of wide slabs. In Jim Smith's words, "Easy Valley was like a monstrously huge, black and foreboding amphitheater. The dark and domineering walls reaching for thousands of feet above your head made you feel claustrophobic. Whoever gave Easy Valley its name obviously had a sense of humour!" We could see some of the route ahead. After the slabs, it went less steeply through a vegetated section to a point known as the Lone Tree at about 10,500 feet. After that the route dropped steeply out of sight. From the col, we picked our way carefully across steep, slippery slabs fixing some rope as we went. Then we hacked through thick vegetation, then over the tops of waterfalls that flowed to unseen drops. At the Lone Tree we made a couple of abseils until we could see, through the trees and mist, some bigger cliffs below. Carefully we inched closer to the slippery edge but from the top it was obvious that longer ropes were required. It was getting dark and we decided to leave equipment at the Lone Tree and ascend, over the 12,500 foot col, and back to the rest house at 11,200 feet. Later that night the other team members arrived from Park HQ with 500-feet ropes, jumars and other equipment. We spent another night in the rat shed and on the floor of the rest house which became our forward operating base for the next week.

Next day, before first light, our second group went up to the col and down to the Lone Tree. In order to maintain communications it was necessary to leave a radio link at the col and this was maintained throughout the search. The second group set up an advanced base at the Lone Tree, then fixed ropes down an initial 150-feet vertical section. A trail which had been hacked through the jungle by the Army expedition led to another 150-foot drop, then a series of 500-foot near-vertical sections. The first two volunteers, Bren Dunn and John Roe, abseiled down through waterfalls and searched below these cliffs but found nothing.

The time was now pushing on and the mist had given way to heavy rain. Not wanting to be caught in the gully in a flood, the pair started to jumar up the ropes. Going up through the waterfall couldn't be avoided and was really cold, wet and strenuous. The whole group eventually made it back to the

Lone Tree, which was located in relative safety, on top of a small ridge. They had a damp bivouac with rain and mist as companions.

The rain continued overnight and throughout the next day. The corrie at the top of the gully acted like a gargantuan funnel, gathering water and sending it cascading down the waterfall sections which were now flowing too fast to be descended. The group climbed back to the rest house where Alister held a briefing and decided that, while the rain continued, we could not descend past the Lone Tree. Meanwhile, on the northern side of the mountain, the Malaysian Army helicopters had managed to make some searches of the lower part of the gully. They estimated that they had searched up to approximately 7,000 feet.

On 22 March the weather improved slightly. Over the past days, we had discussed likely scenarios and most of us were of the opinion that the missing soldiers had probably had an accident, perhaps whilst descending one of the cliffs, due to an anchor failure or a fall on the steep slimy slabs. We envisaged that the survivors of the accident had become trapped, unable to ascend the vertical cliffs or to descend further. We had additional doubts about their chances of surviving after twenty-eight days out in poor weather with less than eight days' rations. Indeed, after our initial forays down the gully, some of the rescuers made the judgement that they could not justify the risk to their own lives and they decided that unless there was some sign of survivors, they would not go below the Lone Tree.

We had a group planning meeting and decided that we would use four rescuers who would take all the available rope to make a fast lightweight push as far down the gully as possible. The rope would be left in place all the way down the gully to allow the four to escape by jumaring back up and it would also allow additional manpower to descend if required. We would have a group of six at the Lone Tree ready to descend if necessary and a further six at the col and the rest house who manned the radio link and acted as reinforcements.

We all knew that it would be a mammoth task to get casualties from the gully. The prospect of attempting to evacuate any injured up the vertical cliffs and across the col at 12,500 feet was unthinkable, and we decided that when we found the missing party we would attempt to stabilise them where they were while an evacuation route downwards was being prepared. We hoped to get the casualties down to a location suitable for a helicopter lift.

There were plenty of volunteers willing to make the descent and it was decided that Jimmy Clethero, Graham Stamp, John Roe and I would provide the correct level of technical climbing abilities and first aid skills. It was also important to leave personnel at the top who were capable of organising and effecting the rescue. Ten of us left at first light, making the ascent over the col and down to the Lone Tree in record time. Four of us then continued down, past the previous low point, fixing rope as we went. Fifteen hundred feet below the Lone Tree we found a bivouac site with RLC (Royal Logistics Corps) marked out on top of a slab in pebbles.

We continued as fast as the steep ground and slimy rock would allow. As we descended, we found other signs of the passage of the Army expedition: sardine tins and wrappers, old campfires, bivouac sites and, occasionally we followed tracks where the moss had been scrapped off the rocks of the gully bed. The last of the rope was used up just as darkness fell. We had descended to about 8,200 feet at a point where the gully had narrowed to an immensely deep gorge approximately 100 feet wide, and with walls that seemed to us to be thousands of feet high. We made a bivouac on a relatively flat rock in the middle of the river and spent a cold, noisy night, too tired to worry about the danger of floods.

We needed more rope to continue safely and we drew straws to decide who would ascend part-way to meet the troops bringing down more rope and who would be the lucky couple to wait behind and descend further when the ropes arrived. Jimmy Clethero and Stampy drew the short straws, so before first light the next day, they set off at high speed back up the gully to meet Jim Smith and Carl Van Der Lee who had descended from the Lone Tree with ropes. They arrived back at the bivouac site with 500-feet of rope at 1300 hours and John Roe and I immediately set off down. Speed was of the essence – not only for the casualties' sake but for our own safety – we were in a narrow gorge thousands of feet below a huge catchment area and if the rain started again (which was most likely), we would be in a most precarious situation.

We carried nothing but the rope, a radio and a head torch each, fixing ropes only on the steepest sections to allow an escape to be made. In the interests of speed we were forced to wade sections of the river and to make detours into the vegetated sides. It was very cloudy right down to the gully bed but en-route we found several clues, campsites and tracks. However, there was nothing to suggest that the missing soldiers were in trouble – the campsites had been left tidy (apart from a few Hong Kong sardine tins). We found a climbing rope which had been cut into two and left in place over two steep drops for abseiling, again there was no sign of problems.

By 1615 hours we had descended a further 2,000 feet and had used up all the rope. The gully continued ahead for a few hundred metres with some small drops before what sounded like a big waterfall out of sight round a corner. We were now at an altitude of about 6,300 feet and the Malaysian Army helicopters had claimed to have searched up the gully to 7,000 feet. We came to the conclusion that the missing soldiers had made it down to the jungle, which was not far below us. After blowing whistles and shouting, we reluctantly decided to turn uphill. After the decision was made to turn back we went fast, there was not much daylight left and we had lots of jumaring, hauling, wading, scrambling and climbing over slimy rocks and boulders before reaching the relative comfort of the slab. We debriefed Alister, utilising two separate radio links at the Lone Tree and the col, and then collapsed into sleep, no longer caring about the continuous roar of the river.

Next morning dawned grey and overcast, threatening rain. The four of us at the slab awoke stiff and cold but we had some 2,500 feet of slipping, sliding, scrambling and jumaring to ascend to the safety of the Lone Tree. Then, together with the remaining team members, we continued up the last 2,000 feet, over the col and down to the rest house.

With the information gleaned by the search of the gully, Tony Schumacher decided to withdraw the troops from the gully and to concentrate the search on the lower section from the jungle up to the base of a big waterfall. British Army Paras and SAS troops had been brought into the area and were in the process of making a reconnaissance flight, with a Malaysian Army helicopter, to find an insertion point near the waterfall.

During a low-level fly-past, a British troop on board the helicopter spotted the message "SOS" laid out on a slab in pebbles. After another pass, the missing soldiers were spotted. Miraculously, after thirty days in the gully, all five were still alive!

They had started to abseil down a steep section but didn't have enough rope to reach the jungle floor and were trapped in a relatively safe position but unable to go up or down. The previous day John Roe and I must have stopped only a few hundred metres away from them! Although it was cold in the misty gully, they had some shelter under an overhanging rock and plenty of water. During their ordeal, they had made several dangerous attempts at escape but the steep, vegetated terrain around them thwarted their efforts. They had managed to make less than eight days' rations last eighteen days. There was no natural food available and they were faced with eating medical supplies – throat pastilles indigestion pills etc.

As a result, they were malnourished, extremely weak and mildly hypothermic, but thankfully still alive. Some rations and a medic were dropped off for the casualties but due to the terrain and weather, they couldn't be evacuated by helicopter until the next day.

Postscript: In 1998, a strong and very well equipped British expedition, including one of the young survivors of the Army expedition of 1994, returned to Mount Kinabalu and made a successful descent of the whole gully.

Accident – Empress Hut

Hamish MacInnes

In 1955, when I was climbing down near the base of New Zealand's South Island spine in the Darran Range, I met a colleague whom I hadn't seen for years. This was John Hammond who, together with Chris Bonington and me, had started his winter climbing career in Glencoe in Scotland. I arranged to meet John a week or so later at the Hermitage Hotel. But when I arrived, I discovered that John and his companion had fallen on the western side of Mount Cook and their bodies had not been recovered.

Some time later, when making a solo attempt of Mount Cook from the other side, I reached the Haast hut late one evening. There was no-one there and though it was possible to get a weather report from the Hermitage using the hut's two-way radio, which had a hand cranking generator for transmitting, I realised that I was too late for this. After a spartan meal of dry biscuits and a can of beans, I snuggled into my sleeping bag, resolved for an early night as I intended being off by three am.

I can't say why I later got out of my warm bag and switched on the radio receiver. It was operated by a spring switch, so that it couldn't be left on, thereby running the battery down. During those few seconds that I depressed the switch there was a crackle of static, then the weak hum of a carrier wave. A faint voice, but it was definitely a voice, crackled from the small speaker.

"Accident – Empress hut, urgent . . ." Then there was silence.

I was dumbfounded. With those few words the sender had

imparted to me his desperation. But had I been hearing things? No, I told myself, I was quite awake. I wasn't conscious of any telepathic message, but still, for no apparent reason I had put the radio on although I knew there could be no possible traffic on that frequency. But as I pondered, I wondered why the message was so brief, why wasn't it completed? I sat astride the generator seat of the transmitter and started to hand crank the generator. It had a double handle which required quite an effort to turn to give sufficient power to operate the set. Usually two people use the transmitter, one to give the message and the other to provide power via the treadmill, or rather the handmill. I didn't get any response from the mystery operator. However, I continued and somewhat out of breath, managed at last to contact the Hermitage and told them of the weird message. I also said that I was quite convinced that something terrible had happened on the other side of the mountain at the Empress hut. Fortunately, they believed me.

Mick Bowie who had put the Ruth Adams La Perouse rescue into motion was still chief guide at the Hermitage. He was a big man, quietly spoken, who, you felt, could bare your soul with his glance. As soon as he got the message he guessed who had sent the distress call. Two Australians, Cooper and Murphy, of the Sydney Bush Walking Club had asked him a few days previously if Mount Cook was in condition. Mick had told them that it wasn't and warned them against attempting it. I had also met the two Australians at the Unwin hut close to the Hermitage a few days before and had spoken briefly with them, but of course I had no idea of their objective. Despite Mick's warning they went up to the Empress hut on the west side of the mountain with the intention of attempting Mount Cook by Earl's Route.

On 25 February, 1955 at 3.00 am they left this refuge in overcast calm weather and reached the low peak of Cook at 7.00 am. It's about a mile between the low and the high peak. They reached the main summit and returned to the low peak by midday. A wind had now sprung up from the west and it was this wind and the poor snow conditions which had deterred me from making an ascent of the mountain. Thick cloud and rain came in on the back of the wind and visibility was poor. They were descending the steep couloir leading towards the Hooker

Glacier when they slipped on snow-covered ice. The snow avalanched with them, for it had virtually no anchorage due to the thaw, and they were both partially buried. Cooper was killed in the fall and Murphy suffered back and head injuries as well as breaking his wrist, but he managed to dig himself out. Due to his injuries, he couldn't dig down to his friend, but after a great effort managed to reach the Empress hut by descending a rock ridge. It must have been a gruelling experience.

When he reached the hut he collapsed on the floor and it was two days before he was able to move. It was on the third day that I providentially received that weird weak signal from him. Due to his injured arm he hadn't been able to operate the generator properly, indeed it was difficult enough for a fit person with full capabilities, as I had discovered, and it was that short message, about four seconds long, which I had intercepted that saved his life. Murphy was taken down in a distressed state by Mick Bowie's rescue party. The body of Cooper wasn't recovered.

I also had a frightening experience in that same couloir down which the Australians fell. The next year I made the first ascent of one of Mount Cook's ridges with two Americans, Dick Irwin and Peter Robinson. When we had finished the climb, we took the rope off and soloed the last section to the summit of Mount Cook. On the top we met a party of two guides from the Hermitage and a client. It was the first time that two parties had met on the summit. As they had ascended from the Empress hut by Earl's Route, we decided to return that way. It was, they said, in good condition. They, on the other hand, were going back down the normal way, by the Linda Glacier, also making a grand traverse. Still travelling unroped, we started to descend the couloir that had proved to be the downfall of the Australians when Peter Robinson caught his crampons on his trousers and hurtled head-first down the ice. With amazing ability he managed to arrest a 300-feet fall with his ice axe and, being only bruised, he managed to continue, though much more slowly than before, and with the rope on! We had to bivouac above the Empress hut that night, as we were caught by darkness.

Mick Bowie would have been able to observe our early progress through a telescope and was no doubt going to be annoyed that we had thrown precaution to the wind and gone unroped up that final section of the mountain. When we arrived at the Hermitage the next day I saw Mick standing outside smoking his inevitable pipe and in all probability waiting to give me, as ringleader, a piece of his mind, so before he could take his pipe out of his mouth I hailed him.

"Hello, Mick, we did the climb, the new ridge, and we've decided to call it Bowie Ridge. I hope you don't mind?"

Later, Mick, when he was guest of honour at a dinner, related this story and concluded, "How could I give the blighters a telling off when they named a ridge of Mount Cook after me?"

Buried on Mount Cook

Karen Gazley

There have been countless dramas enacted on the great stage of the Central Alps of New Zealand. Even today, though helicopters and modern rescue methods assist the evacuation of climbers, they don't prevent accidents. As long as there are mountains there will be accidents. Paul Gazley, a talented young man, a pilot with the Royal New Zealand Air Force, was a national springboard diving and squash champion. He and Karen were married only seven and a half months when he was tragically killed in the second of two freak accidents. In the first he was buried for twelve hours under one of the biggest avalanches ever to come off Mount Cook. The second he didn't survive. Karen and Paul tell their story.

At home in Auckland I was bursting forth with all the news of my first South Island trip. I was so thrilled to see the family again and still highly exhilarated by the wonderful adventures I'd experienced during my discovery of the South. Three girlfriends and I had toured by car and thoroughly enjoyed some tramping in Fiordland, but Mount Cook particularly held a strong fascination for me.

By chance I had met Paul for a few minutes in Hokitika on the West Coast just as his party was departing by bus for Christchurch after their three strenuous weeks of tramping and climbing in the Southern Alps.

Now, a week later, the magnetism of those mountains still overwhelmed me. The prospect of returning to work the following day was far less inspiring and brought me abruptly back to earth, but I also realised that there was a lot more to life than just working.

It was while listening to the 11.00 pm radio news that I first learnt that something was very wrong in those mountains. Paul Gazley and Olly McCahon had been caught in a massive avalanche off the South Face of Mount Cook at 5.00 am that morning. Olly had managed to free himself and had raised the alarm and by the time I heard the news broadcast Paul had been found. Certainly, I had been spared earlier anxieties, as I had been driving for most of that day from Wellington to Auckland.

Suddenly, my world seemed shattered! Feelings of utter loss, despair and anguish seized me. I seemed so helpless and detached, being hundreds of miles away, not really knowing what was happening except that Paul was alive; these thoughts tortured me for the rest of the night. I prayed fervently for him.

It was 5.00 am on 14 January when Olly heard a cheerful call, "Look at that," from Paul who was in their bivouac above the south side of the Noeline Glacier where they had spent the night. It was an ideal site, a horizontal rock-rimmed platform with fresh water a short distance away trickling down the rocks. They were now making preparations to climb Nazomi (9,716 feet/2,961 metres), overshadowed by Cook's glistening South Face.

Paul had been stuffing his gear into his tiny climbing sack when he looked up and saw the top cliffs breaking off the South Face of Cook 1,500 metres above. He yelled to Olly who was some distance away.

Paul later wrote:

> When I looked back, the plummeting ice hit a shelf part way down the face and exploded like a bomb. Powder snow was thrown high into the air and in front of me thousands of tons of it began crashing on to the glacier. Huge hunks of ice, as big as houses, began smashing themselves to pieces. I dismissed the thought of it sweeping half a mile across the glacier and burying us because we were too high, but I crouched down behind the rocks securing myself against the expected wind blast.

Olly was fifty metres from the bivvy site attending to nature's wants. Crouching comfortably he raised his head as Paul called out. Olly recalls:

I looked up. The South Face of Cook was shedding its top
ice cliffs directly opposite and above us. The avalanche
grew huge as it thundered down, hit the bottom shelf on
the face and exploded across the glacier. I crouched,
staring fascinated, as it filled the whole sky and the world
became a roaring wilderness of white, crashing, crushing
snow bearing down on my head and shoulders. Hard
things smashed on to my right hand and hit the back of
my bare head, squashing me helplessly into a huddle on
the rocks.

Paul's last impressions before he was buried were:

The blast came and scattered our gear over a wide area.
Then it happened – what I hadn't counted on, being
bombed from above. I tried to stand up, but try as I
might, the onslaught was too much. I was crushed into the
snow, completely immobilised.

I tried to move, but it was impossible. I was jammed
down into a kneeling position with my chest on my knees,
my right hand caught up by my head, and my left hand
down by my side. Air was essential; I had to be able to
breathe. I began to call for Olly, thinking that his position
would be far worse than my own. Then I began swearing
at myself, calling myself every name under the sun and
struggling in vain to free myself from my icy tomb.
Somehow, although I don't remember how, I managed
to free my left hand and, by clawing away at the ice,
cleared a small hole in front of my face. By reaching out as
far as I could, I was able to reach within about fifteen
centimetres of the surface. At least I was now able to
breathe.

My left hand looked dreadful. The fingertips were
missing and bleeding, steadily staining the snow red. I
was determined not to scrape with them any more but soon
found myself doing so. I then began punching at the snow
but it was frozen solid and the effort was useless.

Meanwhile, Olly had been partially buried:

The world was hushed, no sound broke the awful stillness. Where there had been warm, red rock there was now a desert of hard-packed snow and nowhere could I see gear, bivvy or Paul. Shocked and dazed by a blow on my head, I was buried up to the waist, my smashed right hand was spreading blood over the snow.

Panicky, desperate digging and heaving got me clear and the resulting freedom helped me fight off my new and overwhelming fear of the South Face towering over me. Inspection of my right hand revealed smashed knuckles and a badly cut palm. It looked as though I could write off my first finger. Closing my mind, I wrapped the hand in bog paper and a handkerchief.

Above, the South Face was now showing grey ice and bare rock where there had been ice cliffs. The whole width of the Noeline was a jumble of blocks with great slide tracks sweeping off down the glacier. Around me the scene was almost unrecognisable, especially as I had partial amnesia and had to concentrate hard just to remember where I was and who I was with. Dread of the South Face stimulated my efforts to climb up to the bivvy site. I was soon well above it, although it was some time before I realised this and came down again. Finding the bivvy brought little joy for everything was buried.

I could see no sign of Paul, although I guessed he must still be there. But it was now at least an hour after the avalanche and with one hand and no gear I couldn't dig. After some desolate soul-searching I left him for dead and headed for the Gardiner hut. Obviously the best way back was to follow Saturday's tracks, but they were across the glacier under the South Face. With my heart in my mouth I scrambled across the debris, in terror of a repeat performance. As I reached the other side and turned down the tracks I heard a crump and looked round to see a little avalanche coming down further along. Fear lent me wings and I headed down the glacier at a very rapid trot.

Signs of the avalanche were everywhere. To my left the glacier was heaped with avalanche debris and where I was travelling the snow had been swept bare by the blast.

Things went well until I reached the steep slopes above Gardiner and there, in sight of the hut, I found my way blocked by slopes of very hard snow. How I longed for ice axe or crampons and I wasted some thought on which I would rather have before deciding that crampons would be best.

Fortunately it was now quite late, and the slopes further over were in the sun and presumably softened, but between lay the steep hard snow, criss-crossed with slots. These turned out to be the solution to my problem for I found that I could balance along the lower lip of one, then scramble down to the next using a pocket knife as an ice dagger and then repeat the performance. After that it was O.K. and with the sun warming my back I hurried down to Gardiner and the radio.

At 10.35 am on 14 January Barrie Thomas, chief ranger at park headquarters, received an urgent message from Olly McCahon at Gardiner hut. A practised rescue procedure swung into action. Senior rangers Irwin and Thorne aided their chief, now field controller. Fortunately there was an Iroquois helicopter at Tekapo, fifteen minutes' flying time away. The helicopter left park headquarters at 12.22 pm and carried a team of R. Whitely (leader), M. Dorfliger and Eric Saxby. Olly was collected from Gardiner and they flew over the search area. The wind was increasing and the weather was fine and hot. The high temperature caused such lack of power at 2,600 metres that the helicopter could not chance a landing at the bivouac site. There was no sign of life below. So the search party was unloaded at Gardiner hut at 1,700 metres, some one and a half climbing hours to the bivvy.

At 2.15 pm the helicopter flew a second rescue party to Gardiner. This consisted of Paul von Kanel, Colin Monteath, Etienne Kummer and Hans Muller who followed the first team up the Noeline Glacier. The helicopter now flew Olly to park headquarters. Suffering from shock and in need of medical attention for his hand, Olly had remained with the rescue teams for as long as he could be of use. At headquarters, he was attended by Dr Anne Hall and Dr Jock Staveley who were both holidaying in the park and, as soon as the accident was reported, had told headquarters of their willingness to help.

Paul, still trapped under the avalanche, continues his story:

I decided the only way to free myself was to try and turn over so that I could push the ice off with both hands. To do this I had to free my right hand and I began desperately yanking it back and forth trying to free it. Every time I pulled it, I scraped a little more skin off it leaving an ugly raw area. Finally, when I freed it, the fingers were too cold and useless even to pull back my parka sleeve to look at my watch. In vain I began using my left elbow as a hammer, smashing it against the ice, trying to free my knees so that I might have been able to turn over. I could not give up hope. I had to keep trying. I didn't even know that Olly was alive, let alone that anyone was searching for me.

I had no idea of time, but resigned myself to the fact that if I ever did get myself free then I would most likely have to spend the night there as it would be too dark to walk down the glacier. My feet were getting cold and I began wriggling my toes to try and warm them. My right foot was the worst. I couldn't even feel it. The prospect was frostbitten feet.

At 2.30 pm the leading team reached the area where Paul was believed to be buried. What had been so clear from the air was entirely different from the ground. Snow had melted and there was no sign of blood from Olly's gashed hand which might have helped in pinpointing the location. Olly's and Paul's climbing gear was spread over a wide area, such had been the force of the windblast created by the avalanche. All likely places in the vicinity were searched, but to no avail. Then the searchers climbed up to some rocks where they had seen a sling and karabiner. They decided these had been swept down from above as the sling was not tied.

On the arrival of the second team, the searchers combined their efforts. Two climbers searched towards the head of the Noeline Glacier, while the others concentrated on the area above the previous search site. It was in vain. All seven searchers converged on a convenient spot to eat a hurried lunch while they discussed further search plans. They decided to ask the Air Force to fly Olly back to locate the burial spot more precisely. Two searchers were sent to Gardiner to call them. Meanwhile, the others resolved to concentrate their efforts at a higher level and in closer groups. Here they noticed some tracks made by Olly on his way down to summon help.

Eric Saxby left the searchers to pick up some surplus gear he had unloaded at a lower level. On his return he stopped at the lunch spot to drink from a rock pool. As he bent to scoop water into his hands, he heard a faint shout for help. He was immediately alert to the possibility that one of the two returning to Gardiner had fallen into a crevasse. He straightened up and called,

"What is it? What do you want?"

"Over here! Over here," returned a muffled shout. Eric scrambled over the rough terrain towards the call. He stopped, puzzled. There was no sign of anyone.

To Eric's anxious cry, "Where are you?" there came from beneath his very feet the quiet answer, "Don't tread too hard, you are directly above me."

Eric dropped to his knees and frantically dug away ice and snow with his ice axe and hands, calling to his companions while he did so, but they were too far away to hear. He uncovered fingers issuing through the ice some thirty centimeters below the surface. Eric dug deeper. He could now see part of a head. He uncovered it, a metre below the surface of hard-packed snow and ice. It was now 5.00 pm.

Paul recalled:

> During one of my bouts of scraping, hammering, punching, yanking and twisting I heard voices. I recognised one of them. I yelled as loudly as I could. There was an instant reply. I yelled again but this time there was no reply. My heart sank. I began yelling again as loud as I could. Then came a reply from right on top of me. At last a hand came through the snow.

Eric had been unable to make himself heard to the other searchers. He left Paul for a brief period to rush to them and yell exultantly, "I've found him! I've found him! He's alive! He's OK!"

Disbelief gave place to relief, then to ecstasy. The five whooped deliriously as they raced to the bright, relieved voice and grin from the hole in the ice. Eric continued digging. As the other rescuers arrived they began to dig, prepare the stretcher, arrange a safety line and unpack food. A radio message was sent to the hut-bound pair to request the return of the helicopter.

Half an hour's digging was still required to release Paul from the rock and ice that had imprisoned him for twelve hours. He could never have freed himself alone. He was lifted out and a jersey laid out for him on the snow.

Paul said: "I remembered very little of the whole operation. When freed, I tried to stand up but my legs just collapsed under me and I fell in a crumpled heap on the snow."

Attention was given to his left hand and he was fed some peppermint chocolate. The rescuers dressed him in warm clothing and placed him securely on a stretcher for the long haul down the glacier.

Paul recounts: "They had to sledge me down the glacier. This was done with celerity but it seemed an endless journey for me. My whole body was cold and my hands were freezing. I stuffed them down my trousers to try and warm them but there was no warmth in me at all."

The condition of the glacier and its ever-present risk of avalanche, the gathering darkness and the need for speed in man-handling the heavy stretcher demanded consummate skill from the rescuers – particularly as much of the route was taken at a run.

On the way down the glacier the helicopter flew above the returning party and made radio contact, but conditions prevented it hovering and winching up the stretcher. So the downward haul continued. At Gardiner hut, Paul was given hot tea but his hands could not hold the mug, nor could he sit up to accept it. Here, his hands were bandaged and he was wrapped in blankets.

At 8.30 pm the helicopter came back up the Hooker Glacier to determine whether or not a pickup was possible. Darkness was rapidly falling, but the crew knew the urgency of the occasion. Firmly supported under each arm, Paul stumbled up the rocks as the helicopter was landing. He was hurried aboard and made secure by the loadmaster.

When Paul arrived at park headquarters, he was in a state of severe shock. He was conscious but hypothermic and pulseless, with frostbite to both hands, left elbow and left knee. Dr Hall and Dr Stavely decided he should be treated on the spot. They set up a drip bottle on the end of a broom to supply intravenous Dextran to help counteract the shock. Park rangers hugged him to raise his temperature by direct body heat. His feet, which were very white, were immersed in a bedpan of warm water. Dressings were applied to the frostbitten areas.

After two hours, his pulse could be felt and his body temperature had risen to near normal. At 1.00 am he was given Bactrim capsules and went to sleep on a mattress between two electric blankets, which Barrie Thomas had borrowed from private houses. Dr Hall stayed with him through the night. Her main concern was the acute kidney damage that could be expected from the crush injuries and the low body temperature he had suffered.

The next morning Paul was transferred by helicopter to Christchurch Hospital. He was minus the tips of his index, second and third fingers of his left hand and was frostbitten on his right hand, left elbow and left knee. Initially, he was treated for acute renal failure which had resulted from both muscle crush and disintegration of striated muscle fibre. Other factors considered important were hypothermia, dehydration and a degree of hypoxia (abnormally decreased oxygen supply). A week later he was transferred to the plastic surgery unit at Burwood Hospital and for the next seven weeks was treated for the frostbite damage, particularly involving two serious operations to his left hand.

One had to admire him for his cheerfulness amid physical discomfort, immobility and the knowledge that his future held so many uncertainties – was this the end of his flying career? However Paul recovered completely and, despite a pinned ring finger on his left hand, was able to return to diving, squash, tramping, climbing, skiing and flying.

Paul's remarkable survival appeared to be something of a miracle. The medical world attributed much of the complete recovery to his extreme fitness. But was he now living on borrowed time?

We eventually married in December 1974, a few weeks after I had qualified as a medical laboratory technologist at Middlemore Hospital, Auckland, and we then very happily settled in Blenheim. Paul was stationed here as base adjutant and pilot for RNZAF, Woodbourne.

19 July dawned as a Saturday morning with prospects of a reasonable weekend; certainly a full one so typical of the life we had been living. My morning was taken up with working in the lab at Wairau Hospital and general lassitude was sweeping over me by the time I returned home; probably increased by the knowledge that the inevitable end of week housework had still to be done. The previous day Paul had run in a cross-country marathon at Trentham with the Air Force and was exhausted – not only did he appear weary, but actually admitted it. Regardless, he was playing in another squash tournament on both Saturday and Sunday in which Blenheim was host to Nelson and, as I was unable to watch the Saturday match, I promised to watch him play on the Sunday.

It was while baking that afternoon that an excruciating stomach cramp suddenly pierced my system with such violence that I almost collapsed on the kitchen floor. The pain remained as a constant throb and on awaking on Sunday morning I felt dreadful. However, I had a strong urge to attend mass. I mended some Dachstein mittens for Paul which kept me occupied for a while before stirring myself for the 11.00 am mass at the Catholic church at the end of our street. I hadn't been for ages, as many other things had temporarily assumed equal importance. I may as well not have bothered. The priest's words I did not hear. I felt detached and alone. Voices thundered in on me and washed over me. Eventually the mass ended and once again I was caught up in the surging tide, everyone moving towards the door. Then it happened. As I walked out of the church I experienced what I can best describe as a premonition. I looked down at myself as a message flashed through my brain, "My God, you're wearing widow's clothes." I immediately erased this from my mind and didn't think anything further about it until three days later, but that morning I had worn my favourite slacks suit – black slacks, black and white woollen jacket over a red skivvy and complete with red accessories.

The same day I watched Paul play one of his most dynamic squash games. He was a very strong player with particularly powerful shots and his superb fitness allowed him to spring across the court with such agility that it appeared effortless.

Paul's mountain experience was invaluable to the Air Force and he was asked each year to assist in the training on a particular Air Force survival course. He was to instruct a party this week, an aircrew from No. 40 Squadron Whenuapai, which flies Hercules aircraft to Antarctica. He took a considerable time packing his old faithful canvas pack.

"I'm going prepared for anything," he assured me, putting in plenty of warm clothing and several pairs of mittens, as his hands readily suffered from the cold since being frostbitten two and a half years previously. My baking was not only to be a special treat, but more important, was a survival "stand-by".

Monday morning at work was a struggle. Finally, I had to acknowledge that I could no longer persevere and so biked home at lunchtime. Sadly, I had just missed Paul who had been home earlier in his lunch hour after being refused a warrant of fitness (or test certificate) for our Fiat. However, the necessary arrangements were made for me to take the car to a garage the following day. We had a brief chat over the phone and by mid-afternoon Paul was on his way to Wigram, Christchurch. How I wished I was going with him – just to be there. Paul seemed uneasy about going alone, even pleaded with me to join him – but we knew this would be impossible on an Air Force exercise. I was so grateful when he rang me that night from Christchurch.

The 9.00 pm news on TV featured heavy snows in Christchurch. I immediately and somewhat anxiously thought of Paul, but realised of course that he was fine. I had only just been speaking to him and had confidence he would take every care. Before leaving he had emphasised that he would be prepared if they were caught in a storm. After all, he had experience, fitness and the equipment.

Little things started to go wrong the following day. Trivial really, but still big enough for me to wish Paul was home again. Then, the next day, 23 July, 1975, seemed to be a continuation of trouble. It started with further complications in getting the car through its test – now it was a headlight – later the day merged with night in one shattering nightmare.

I noticed someone dressed in black as I walked out of work at 5.00 pm that evening. I was anxious to check the Fiat which the mechanic had delivered. I saw the car parked under nearby pines. Relieved to see that I now had a new warrant of fitness sticker displayed, I leapt in, then remembered the headlight and just to be sure it too had been replaced, decided to take a quick look. The black figure materialised beside me as I bent over. It was the Rev. Dick Simpson, an Air Force padre, and he told me that Paul was involved in an avalanche at Mount Cook.

"I couldn't take a second one," I murmured to him almost disbelieving what he'd just told me.

Paul had spent Tuesday night at Ball hut at the foot of Mount Cook with the rest of the instructors and students. On the Wednesday morning they had all climbed the ridge behind the hut to do basic snowcraft, self-arrest with the ice axe and generally skylarking in perfect snow conditions. Their final task for the day was to dig snow caves at the head of the Ball Glacier and sleep in them overnight.

The avalanche struck all twenty-five of them just before 4.00 pm. Some rode it and swam furiously to keep on top, some were buried with shovels in their hands and even succeeded in digging themselves out, but those who were actually excavating the snow caves at that time were engulfed.

John Moore, Dick Strong, Howard Conway and Olly McCahon had been instructing the climbing on the Mueller Glacier, together with ranger Martin Heine. They returned to HQ to be met by Barrie Thomas, the chief ranger, who told them that several people had been buried in an avalanche on Ball Pass. An Iroquois helicopter which was in the area as part of the course would fly them in as soon as possible. They all piled out of the Land Rover and raced off to pack their gear. When they returned the Iroquois was waiting and avalanche probes, radios, spare headlamp batteries, food and shovels were being loaded. The rescue team were airborne by 4.45 pm. First they flew down to Unwin hut (the Alpine Club hut at Mount Cook) where the air crew were based and landed on the road outside to pick up a doctor. Then they flew up the Tasman Glacier to Ball

Pass where they landed by 5.00 pm. As soon as they were on the snow, equipment was ferried to the avalanche tip. Once there radio contact was established with HQ and avalanche probes assembled.

Just below the avalanche debris were a few men in sleeping bags. They had been dug out, shaken but uninjured.

In Olly McCahon's words: "I went uphill with a load of probes and handed them around, then returned for more and met Martin Heine who said that Paul Gazley had been dug out and looked pretty bad, but was still alive. It was a grim moment and my first reaction was a desire to cry, but there was no time, so Mart and I just looked at each other, muttered a few inadequate words and got on with it."

Over the next few hours the Air Force men were organised into probe teams and dug anxiously for those who had been located by the probes. Now the search party relieved them of the digging for these members of the avalanche party were near exhaustion. Theirs had been an emotionally and physically demanding experience and without much direction they had worked as a close-knit rescue team.

A food box was uncovered some six feet down. Then another buried man was located, whereupon Olly and Howard Conway were called over to assist in digging him out. Meanwhile, the rest of the Park's Board team had arrived and now had a probe line operating in an endeavour to locate the remainder. By then the survivors had gone down to the base of the slope and were provided with a well-earned hot meal and then directed to bed in a snow shelter. For them it was to be a night of terror – an overwhelming fear of yet another avalanche taking them in their restless sleep tormented them until daylight. As it was almost dusk it was decided that the helicopter would come in after moonrise to take out the most shocked of the survivors and the body of the man they'd just found. The rest of the night passed slowly in increasing cold, probing the snow and taking breaks for cups of tea and soup until they found another and finally the last body just after midnight on the last attempt before they had decided to give up. There were three dead and Paul who was critically ill – or so they all thought until they learned the next morning that he had died at the Hermitage, despite every effort to save his life.

Olly wrote later: "I can't even pretend to understand why Paul's and my paths should have come together on these two occasions or why I should live and he die. All I can do is to remember him as he was; fit, brown and happy on his way up the Hooker and then so cheerful and courageous in hospital afterwards . . . I remember him as he was and I'm grateful for what we shared in the mountains and what I gained from those experiences."

The weather was good so the helicopter was able to operate, first lifting the survivors. Finally, the search team flew out to Park HQ with two bodies.

When the Rev. Dick Simpson told me that Paul had been involved in another avalanche, I was absolutely numbed of any emotion and I drove home, parked the car in the garage and then went with Dick to his place and didn't for one moment think the worst. It just couldn't happen twice! Minutes seemed endless as we waited for news. At 6.00 pm I was relieved to hear that three of the four missing had been found and Paul was one of them and was being flown to Timaru Hospital. At this point I phoned both our families. More waiting. The phone rang. Dick answered it in the hallway as I sat anxiously in the lounge already planning my journey down to Timaru.

Then there was an ominous silence! A firm hand rested on my shoulder; I turned to hear the agonising words, "I'm sorry, Karen."

Every bodily emotion erupted as I sat screaming No! No! in utter horror and total disbelief. My hopes had soared so high. Now crushed so cruelly to a pulverised nothingness. That dreadful phone call was to report that Paul was dead. Shock froze every fibre within me as the world helplessly looked on.

Storm on Peak Lenin

Paul Nunn

Paul Nunn and I had known each other for more years than we cared to remember. In 1970 we were fellow members of an expedition to the Caucasus, that stark upthrust between the Caspian and the Black Seas, a cradle of civilization and now a playground for mountaineers. Paul, Chris Woodall and I completed a climb up the forbidding face of Pik Shchurovskiy and at our second bivouac, Paul, usually a human power house, with an exuberant enthusiasm for life, came dangerously close to being an exposure victim. It was probably a blend of two dangerous ingredients which fortify this death cocktail: altitude sickness and exposure.

In the following account Paul's role is reversed and it was he together with others who set off from their base camp in the high Pamirs to attempt to reach Soviet women climbers, encamped and trapped on the summit of one of Russia's highest mountains. All big mountains are potentially dangerous; like fast cars they must be treated with respect. Yet if one uses common sense they can be traversed and enjoyed with impunity. The two popular ranges in the Soviet Union, the Caucasus and the Pamir, are high and subject to violent storms. Also being marooned in a vast land mass they can be grippingly cold.

The Russian climbing bureaucracy appeared somewhat ambiguous in its policy. On the one hand they were acutely safety-conscious and enforce a control time. Before setting out a party was allotted a number of days or hours to complete their climb. The route itself must be approved by a panel of Masters of Sport, experienced senior mountaineers. This panel and the climbers agreed on a reasonable time for the expedition. Should the party fail to return at the specified time, a rescue party sets off im-

mediately, unless of course the overdue mountaineers have managed to advise base by radio or some other means that they have been delayed. It was also necessary to have a simple medical examination before setting off on a major route. To western climbers all this was an anathema, although I can see the point of it in such dangerous mountains. But what I can't reconcile it with is the Russians' press-on-regardless policy, which advocated that the objective, ie. the summit, should always be reached. I can remember on a previous trip to the Caucasus in 1965 being told off for turning back when we had retreated in the interests of safety, on a relatively low peak, due to adverse conditions. After all, I climb for enjoyment not for death-dicing thrills. It will be interesting to see how the freedoms which came with the break-up of the Soviet Union extend to the climbing scene.

In the 1970s the Russians ran organised climbing camps in both the Caucasus and the Pamirs and in this way mountaineers from all over the world have had the opportunity to climb in the Soviet Union. I received an invitation to climb in the Pamirs in 1974 from the Federation of Sport, but couldn't make it. However, many of my friends, including Paul, did and for them it was an experience they won't readily forget.

There was little hesitation for me in joining the British Pamirs expedition of 1974. Every member knew me and I them, while some were among my oldest friends. Fourteen years before Clive Rowland and I had a first weekend climbing together in the Lakes, dreaming up Overhanging Bastion and the steeps of North Crag Eliminate, and Kipling Groove on Gimmer Crag in Langdale next day. Our ventures together were always successful. The same could be said of previous experience with Doug Scott and Paul ("Tut") Braithwaite, particularly in our ascent of the North-East Pillar of Asgard on Baffin Island in 1972. Guy Lee impressed by his wide experience, Speedy Smith by his enthusiasm and ability on rock. It was the most able group of climbers ever to leave Britain for the Soviet Union, and also the most piratical in appearance.

There had been only one British expedition to the Pamirs since 1963, when Robin Smith and Wilfrid Noyce died and relations became strained for some years. In 1970 Hamish MacInnes, Chris Woodall and I climbed a new route on Pik

Shchurovskiy in the Caucasus in one push. In 1974 the objectives were ambitious – nothing less than an alpine-style climb up the East Face of Peak Lenin (23,400 feet/7,134 metres) seemed satisfactory, with all the seriousness and difficulty of commitment at high altitude.

The Soviet Mountaineering Federation had made a huge effort of organisation in drawing together climbers from many nations in a huge meet in the Achik Tash valley of Kirghizia. Under the great domes of Peak Lenin and her neighbours they built a tented village for more than 150 foreign climbers and many more from the Soviet Mountaineering Federation. The climbers came in relays from Moscow after meeting there in early July. While they flew in from all over the globe, our contingent chugged across Europe on the London to Moscow express, drinking endless glasses of *chai* (tea). After only a day or so in the hurly burly of the capital, a whirl of circuses, meals, intense conversations and meeting both our hosts and other national groups, we flew south-east from the great plains to the dry lands of Central Asia, to Osh on the old trade route to Peking and at last to the Alai Valley. As the climbers spilled from the plane into Asian heat and the red dust there shimmered a dazzling wall of mountains which spanned the whole horizon to the south. A few hours jolting by lorry led us to Base Camp at over 10,000 feet, tired and yet elated by the journey from Moscow in less than twenty-four hours. Dinner came in a great military tent only twenty miles or so as the crow flies from Sinkiang, China.

The Base Camp was run by the Moscow psychiatrist, Michael Monastyrski, a small weather-beaten individual who could put on a stern look of disapproval if things went badly. In practice he proved a sympathetic and likeable man, for whom the International Meet held many trials in store. Michael organised the logistics of the camp and was responsible for the smooth running of the establishment and of supplies which had to be ferried either from the Alai airfield or from Osh, a twelve-hour dusty road journey.

Mountaineering was arranged in liaison with a small group of prominent officials of the Soviet Mountaineering Federation, including the veteran of numerous first ascents, Vitali Abalakov, and the urbane one-time secretary of the Federation,

Eugene Gippenreiter. Both Eugene and Michael spoke excellent English, making our visit far easier. Also, each group was asked to develop a special relationship with an adviser, a prominent Master of Sport who would comment upon plans made and volunteer as much help as possible. There were a few days settling in, medicals of a simple nature, waiting for gear to arrive and checking on plans. This was all to the good for acclimatisation aided by short walks towards Peak Lenin across grassy meadows or to the yurts of the Kirghizian shepherds tending their flocks of sheep and goats.

Eventually all the formalities were complete, the various climbing groups moved off towards a variety of objectives and we drew our food from the stores, packed our sacks and set off for the Krylenko Pass, 19,095 feet, which had to be crossed to reach the base of the East Face of Peak Lenin. There was quite a crowd on the 5,000-foot north slope of the pass. Apart from the British, who broke the trail up through deep snow in three days, eleven American, three or four Soviet climbers and a team of Japanese were moving in the same direction. Though there had been negotiations about precisely which objectives the various groups were to try once the pass was crossed, the eventual outcome appears to have been left to fate and the relative speeds at which the parties moved. Doug and Tut were first up the slope, unsurprisingly as Doug had only recently returned from over 27,000 feet on Everest South-West Face, while Tut generally goes well at altitude. In contrast Speedy and I found 19,000 feet for the first time a terrible graft, but eventually we all made it over and down to a camp on the Saukdhara Glacier at about 17,000 feet.

It was a marvellous but remote spot, ringed in by a line of major peaks and opening up vast views of glacial wastes and more distant and little explored snow mountains. Like a huge Brenva Face of Mont Blanc, the East Face of Peak Lenin looms across the head of the glacier, a mass of hanging seracs and soaring ice ridges. Ever energetic and impatient, Doug and Clive set off late in the afternoon of our arrival on the Saukdhara, to plod out a path through the deep snow towards the face. Doug was some hundred yards from the tent and unroped when he suddenly disappeared from sight. Clive cautiously peered into the crevasse to find him ensconced on a bridge of snow less than twenty feet below. He fed down a rope and Doug emerged snow covered but fortunately unharmed. The plan was that we should push straight on to the face the next morning, moving lock, stock and barrel up the mountain. It was very ambitious and in retrospect likely to succeed for only a couple of members of the party who were better acclimatised. In any case it was not to be.

That evening two Estonian climbers who had come up via the Saukdhara in support of an attempt on the Hiebeler Route on the East Face distracted me from some serious thoughts as we fed them tea and tried to converse. Soon after dark, snow pattered on the tunnel tents, each crowded with three inmates and already white rimed in frozen condensation.

As the third day of the blizzard dawned in the tiny gauze window of the tent, my head ached and my guts seemed wrenched with exhaustion. A pervasive and nauseous chill crept into every cell of my body. Despite excellent equipment, prolonged inactivity and increased dampness was clogging my system and destroying bit by bit the indispensable insulation upon which all depended. The aches from continued overcrowding in the tent were abominable, while deep and constantly falling snow pressed in the walls and roof. An incessant wind depressed the spirits and was isolating in the extreme. Even Guy's endless fund of wit froze, while Speedy had long stopped speaking. Only Doug and Tut remained in adequate physical condition, while everyone else had some form of altitude headache. Our nights were disturbed by the jolting of the glaciers, as huge earth tremors twisted the geological substructures through which they carved. Through the black nights and driving snow great echoing roars thundered all too near. Though we saw nothing, the shaking earth hurled off slabs of snow, sweeping the Estonians from the Hiebeler Spur to their deaths and burying an American party on a new route on Peak 19.

I peered out of the tent, moving slowly in the logistics of high altitude brew-making, into a third morning of complete white out. There was no sign of the high peaks, or of anything more than a few yards away. Ambitious plans had dropped us into a trap, as Abalokov had feared. The way up was barred, food was becoming slender and we had to get out. To go downhill would lead via the Saukdhara, close to China, though how close or how far it was we did not know. After some shouted deliberation it had to be the Krylenko again, two miles away and 2,000 feet above. Some of the equipment would stay behind for the next attempt, so the crossing had to be as fast as possible to avoid a tentless night out.

Unhappily, we had assembled in the driving snow outside the tents. Doug and Tut shared the lead, plodding in calf-deep snow at the front of the long rope of six. As we set off into the opaque haze, painfully tramping towards the Krylenko, the Estonians were dead or dying a mile or two away and Jon Gary Ullin was deep under the snow of Peak 19.

After a couple of hours of glacial tramping the caravan stopped for the fortieth time. Through the murk ice cliffs barred the way. "We've missed the upper glacier, have to go back, youth," came from Doug. So down it was, and then up at last into the ice corridor leading between Lenin's East Ridge and its eastern neighbour. Mercifully, the snow abated and about midday the sun shone for a little while, but the snow softened and dehydrated bodies protested. Doug and Tut still went well, but everyone else suffered headaches. Guy plodded on self-contained but tired, Speedy lost psychological clarity so that urgings made no impact, while I remained mentally lucid but found my knees folding frequently. Clive took up an effective rearguard position and chaperoned us to the Krylenko and a view of the Achik Tash as massive black clouds swept up the valley and boiled into the basin of the descent route. It was six or seven hours after leaving camp with only five more hours of daylight.

From the col the rope split, and while the others sped ahead I remained roped to Speedy, and Clive kept us company on the descent. Only a few hundred feet below the col a great wind-slab avalanche had broken away to a thickness of four feet and several hundred yards wide. Vast areas of slab remained hanging on all sides of the upper basin and, tired as we were, we moved down as fast as possible, so that our enthusiasm led us to go too low at one point, and there followed a painful pull back uphill to reach the crevasse in which we had left eleven Americans, four Russian climbers and a tent a few days earlier. The site of the camp at 17,400 feet had seemed protected, or at least more nearly so than anywhere else on the 5,000 feet of climbing to the col. The overhanging lip had proved only just sufficient defence. From mounds of snow only a few broken tent poles and tattered rags emerged. Speculation about the fate of the residents seemed pointless. Doug scraped around for morsels of food and found Molly Higgins' diary. There was little knowing whether this tough little blonde was alive or dead with her companions under the compacted avalanche debris. After more despondent pokings around there was no alternative but to continue down, as our cooking equipment, tent and food had shared the fate of the Americans.

With very few hours to darkness the urgency became the greater as we lacked tents and even down jackets or sleeping bags in some cases. The bank of battleship-grey clouds enveloped everything and in premature dusk we fled very fast as altitude diminished, hopping crevasses and sliding through avalanche debris with manic energy, with no time for ropes or delay. In only minutes I slid down a huge avalanche runnel a thousand feet to the edge of a steepening in the slope, every moment conscious of the recent high temperatures above, ears cocked for a roaring in the mist as the Krylenko discharged its next bombardment. As I peered down, Clive shot out of sight down another avalanche runnel into the gloom. Speedy was close behind, so I did the same, sacrificing caution to speed. Once I turned upside down in the massive careering swoop down the icebacked runnel, but so much deep snow abounded below that the eventual landing was deep and soft. In the mist I could hear voices and, staggering with fatigue, I joined the others as the snow blew in and the temperature began to plummet. Speedy was still to come and there was a small icefall to negotiate before the glacier which led to a place where we hoped some French tents remained.

The minutes ticked by and our bodies froze. We cursed and muttered at the delay and eventually Tut, earliest down and thinly clad, preferred to go back on to the slope to find our companion. In not too long he returned with Speedy. We had gravely miscalculated in leaving him alone as he, unlike everyone else, had not regained mental clarity as descent proceeded. Only a little way up the slope, after making the slide, he had stopped, at a loss as to what to do next. We roped and in the last light negotiated the icefall and in a black night groped down the lower glacier. To my relief as the site of the old camp on Krylenko moraine came in view there was a light, and soon we found ourselves in an American pyramid tent eagerly swilling brews.

Al Steck and Mike Yokell were resting there after escaping the avalanche in the Crevasse Camp above, at the cost of cracked ribs and a battered knee. From them we learned that all seven Americans there had survived, though it had been a close call. Bruce Carson, Fred Stanley, John Evans and Al Steck had been hit by the same avalanche as they fled the Crevasse Camp, and Steck had almost been buried, while all were lucky not to die. Sleep came with the deadness of relief. Masses of snow fell overnight and even the interminable moraine heaps leading to the Pass of the Travellers and Base were heavy going next day.

An earth tremor had started the great avalanche. The Americans had been prevented from crossing the pass on their second carry by the bad weather and were left to the mercy of the Krylenko slope. It almost caught them. The Japanese party had not yet committed themselves to the slope and merely lost gear dumps low down. In the same earthquake a four-man party on Peak 19's North Face was hit by a similar avalanche and despite frantic efforts to dig him out Jon Gary Ullin died.

After that storm no one dared enter the jaws of the Krylenko, as avalanches streamed down in procession. A mountain of valuable equipment was lost on the slope while we could not get back to the East Face. All subsequent planning was conditioned by tent shortage and by dreadful snow conditions. The Soviet advisers were now acutely worried and understandably anxious there should be no more accidents. At Base Camp there was an atmosphere of pessimism and exhaustion as we rather frantically tried to get permission to get back by a low level route to our equipment, and the camp directorate concealed their grief and preoccupation at the loss of the Estonians. The weather was very bad and a little multi-national group could only ease into black nights with the aid of the national beverages of Scotland and Russia. It seemed justifiable, despite the health rules.

After days of bad weather the shortness of our month long visit pressed, the routines and food of Base palled, and we persuaded our adviser to let us look at the Krylenko again. There was just a possibility of reaching it by the traverse of a 20,000-foot peak to the east and by that circuitous route reaching the camp on the Saukdhara Glacier. It boded ill as we plodded the Pass of the Travellers in driving rain and crossed the miserable and characterless moraines to Moraine Camp.

Early next morning Doug and I tramped up the glacier, but the avalanches on the Krylenko proved no more attractive at close quarters, while the crossing via the spur of Peak Lenin's outlier was a major venture in itself. Time was short and we needed action, which fortunately suggested itself in an elegant snow ridge of no great difficulty which eventually merged with the East Ridge of Peak Lenin itself. Three Scots, Bruce Barclay, Alan North and Greg Strange, had intended to join us in crossing the Krylenko and now, as a nine-man British party, we changed our plan. The ridge provided a route from below 16,000 feet to the summit of Peak Lenin. It had not been climbed, but ran parallel to a narrower ridge which a French party had ascended while we were on the Krylenko, eventually joining it and the classic Lipkin Route up the main summit. A baking day was spent in making the few preparations, for we had little equipment and only two tents for nine climbers, though we were lacking in neither food nor fuel.

The crocodile of climbers set out early next morning, climbing solo across initial ice slopes on to the ridge and then beginning the most formidable soft ridge plod that I have ever encountered. Almost everyone took turns to make steps, knee- or thigh-deep in the crusted snow. One thought only of the next ridge top, which might be reached in a three- or four-man lead, or of the next few steps upwards, firmly placing the ice axe, no rope, no insurance. At least there was not too much to carry. Gradually the ice jumble of the upper Achik Tash fell below, the sun rose higher in the sky and by late morning a small tower loomed ahead. Doug and Tut ploughed an insecure route direct, while Clive and I also used a rope to outflank its steep section. In such a large group there seemed scope for variation. Above, Clive took the lead on the deepest snow yet, waist deep, softened by late morning sun. No one could sustain more than a couple of hundred feet leading in such stuff.

At last, as the subsidiary peak of Lenin began to look nearer, everybody stopped for a brew, a few sweets, and a slice of smoked sturgeon from the yellow fillet which hung from my rucksack lid. After plodding in front lower down, Clive, Bruce Barclay and I spent about an hour in the afternoon in semi-slumber, while Alan North, Greg Strange and the others pressed on up the upper ridge. As the sun slipped behind the peaks to the west the snow solidified a little and we followed the tracks up small steep steps and round crevasses serrating the upper peak to a shoulder which offered a safe camping place.

The caravan had kept going from dawn to dusk, through morning frost and midday sun, gaining over 3,000 feet and considerable distance in bad snow conditions. It was reason for satisfaction as Doug, Guy, Clive and I all hacked away at the snow cave in which two of us would reside to relieve the tent shortage. There was a bitter wind which urged on the outdoor activities and Clive and I were glad to slide gingerly inside, trying to avoid the tendency to knock crusts of snow on to down gear. Clive snuggled into his duvet, with only a blue hat and hooked nose emerging from the down cocoon, as I resuscitated fingers frozen in the efforts with a snow shovel. With all hands on deck the five-foot cave had taken two hours of breathless effort and it was almost dark when a hot brew attached to a long arm emerged from the tent.

Overnight it was fine, bitter cold and deep frosty, and the dawn a brilliant blue, with magnificent views east into Sinkiang and north across the arid yellow foothills of Central Asia. A cup of tea again emerged and eventually we struggled from the powdery hole. As always it was difficult to get going. It took an hour to get rigid boots on to cold feet, frozen gaiters on to stiff boots. Speedy poked a nose from the tent he shared with big Bruce Barclay, Greg Strange and Alan North. People just wandered off up the ridge, knee-deep and breathless still, as they were ready. After a few hours a minor summit found the whole party sitting thawing in the sun, brewing and gnawing without conviction at the salted sturgeon.

A few steep little gendarmes of rotten rock decorated the crest of the continuation ridge which would lead to the Lipkin Route up Peak Lenin. The tottering pinnacles looked difficult and time-consuming, and Clive, with a quick eye for a feasible route, led on to a long evasive traverse across unstable slopes of snow. We crossed them before the sun destroyed their cohesion by the same techniques as before, with those out in front who had the energy to gasp and plough through deep snow. At last the ridge broadended and the whaleback leading onto the Lipkin stretched ahead. Leaders changed more frequently as fatigue took its toll and midday haze and heat wore down our tired bodies, but still the weather held. There was more tea and a long stop after an especially tiresome rise, while the site of the camping place on the Lipkin was visible a mile or so away. Most people were feeling the altitude and each progressed at his own pace through the deep snow and patches of afternoon mist.

I stopped hurrying on this relatively safe ground, as there was no tent to arrive at on the spur. Tired and in a reverie I looked across the séracs of the North Face of Lenin, above which the Lipkin Route threads a traverse of almost two miles. It was all very big, but curiously rounded and superficially inocuous, deep plastered in new snow everywhere except where avalanches had already swept down after the recent bad weather. Apart from ourselves almost all the climbers in the Achik Tash had been channelled onto the Razdelny and Lipkin Routes up Peak Lenin. It had not appealed to our group at all, and I was pleased with our variant which twinned admirably with the Eastern Rib ascended the previous week by Vincent and Benoir Renard and their friends.

The last pull to the camp seemed hard work. I still felt the weight of the Krylenko exhaustion as I slackened my boots and the others climbed into the tunnel. It was a stony, bare, windy place, with little tent platforms. Clive and I slid into a bivouac sheet as the easterly wind battered at the tents. Tea and food filtered from the overcrowded tent as the wind hammered away at the slopes. Fine powder snow got into the top of the envelope and swirled wildly inside, sticking to Clive's beard and getting even into the top of our sleeping bags, making us cough and suffocate. I failed to get my toes back to life as the wind howled through the darkness. Clive and I had shared many a dangerous and icy night travelling by motorbike. But this was a miserable night. Neither of us said much about it.

In the morning my feet would not revive, and I remembered the months it took before they came back after the Caucasus Shchurovskiy climb in 1970. The two bivouacs on that were the worst that I have ever encountered, desperately uncomfortable, wet to begin and frozen solid by morning. I was not prepared to go so far again, even with better equipment, although the summit was only 2,500 feet above. Clive was in better condition and seemed to be standing the altitude better. I did not want more nights over 21,000 feet without a tent. It was windy and cold but the sun was coming. I announced my decision to Clive, put on outer boots and spoke briefly to those in the tent. Of our group I thought I was now weakest, though judged most of the other tent less able to continue. Without many words, wishing everybody luck, I set out slightly uphill on the first leg of the Lipkin Traverse, across the North Face to the safe descent spur.

The shelf of the Lipkin Route is about a mile wide, cutting across the North Face of Peak Lenin and traversing over a long band of ice cliffs. There was little loss of height before it merged into a steeper ice and snow slope. As I trod out a deep rut, resting frequently to catch breath, a mysterious row of masked figures slowly came into sight. There was not an inch of human face to be seen, but they all appeared very short in stature as they slowly pushed their upward furrow to meet my descent. "Good morning," in English evoked the same response, and a pleasant female voice went on to tick me off for wandering the big mountains alone. They explained the whereabouts of their ice cave camp of the previous night. Tired and still chilled as I was, I felt better, though I was still near level with our miserable bivouac. Later I was to become familiar with this morning lowpoint at altitude and with the subsequent recovery. The eight masked Soviet women turned away and began to climb on very slowly and steadily, and I headed out onto the vast avalanche-rutted slope leading down from the mountain. It took time to get crampons fixed but then the loss of altitude was rapid and the deep snow of the lower slopes of the Lipkin occupied me for the rest of a morning.

There were two more meetings. Above the ice cave Eugene Gippenreiter and two other climbers appeared. He produced an apple and told tales of his fall on Chimney Route on Clogwyn du'r Arddu in North Wales, while I swallowed half of it – the apple, that is. After a few jokes we parted. Eugene was going up to try and keep count of the climbers on this route. I aimed for lamb stew at Base Camp. The sun made the 5,000 foot descent to the glacier very tough, but on a lower plateau Al Steck's tanned face and twinkling eyes peered from the underside of a gnomic hat which he never seemed to take off. With Jock Glidden and Chris Wren he was intent upon reaching the summit, despite an earlier avalanche injury. Loaded with great pack frames which I thought must be full of down, they laboured up through softening snow.

Ironically, after crossing numerous crevasses, I came near to being pipped at the post. A curious man-sized hole gulped me in within yards of the Lenin Glacier. Fortunately, as it appeared bottomless, my arms shot out and I stopped, nor was it particularly difficult to escape. The glacier and the Pass of the Travellers I took at full speed. Flowers carpeted the meadows below and I was in Base Camp for supper 10,000 feet below the spartan purgatories of the ridge.

The remaining eight British climbers moved up with their two tents onto the harsh plateau of Peak Lenin on the day of my departure. Clive, Doug, Guy and Tut reached the summit the following day after an early start, but Alan North was the only member of the other foursome to do so. Leaving later than the others, he almost lost his life on the return as cloud and high wind obscured his retreat. As the eight came down the Lipkin two more Britons, Graham Tiso and Ronnie Richards, were among a number of groups reaching the summit via the Razdelny Route to the west. The Soviet women met them from the east and camped on the summit, intending to descend the Razdelny next day and make the first female traverse of the mountain. Now a major storm was forecast and the wind rose, clouds scudded across the high peaks and the temperature dived even at 11,000 feet. Over fifty climbers remained scattered over the two standard routes. Japanese, Soviet Ladies, and Steck's group of Americans were all very near the summit of the mountain. Very large groups were also high on the Lipkin Route and at the Razdelny Pass.

On 5 August the Base Camp radio had advised all groups remaining on the mountain to retreat as an exceptional storm had been forecast. Next day in atrocious weather came a radio report that the International Women's group were in difficulties high on the Razdelny route. One of them, Arlene Blum, had already gone back in deteriorating conditions the previous day with Jed Williamson to Camp 3 on the Razdelny Col. The weather was now extremely bad with very high winds and blizzard conditions, as a small party led by Pete Lev moved up to help the remaining three down. They met the Bavarian, Anya, retreating after the night of violent storm and she was escorted down by Michel Vincent of the Grenoble group. François Valla and Jed Williamson went on to find the other two women, Eva Eissenschmidt and Heidi Ludi, unable to move down as Eva had collapsed with symptoms of advanced hypothermia. They were at about 21,500 feet in a very exposed position. Lev and Valla decided that there was no alternative but to attempt to move Eva down, and after trying to get her to drink, wrapped her in a tent and lowered her down the ridge with great difficulty. In practice they had to make a sequence of diagonal lowers along the north side of the ridge in a wind of about eighty miles an hour. After a series of such lowers a Bavarian, Sepp Schwankener, came up from Camp 3 alone after retreating earlier because of the bad conditions. With his help it was possible to lower her a little further through deep snow, but only at the cost of getting further and further out on to the North Face rather than keeping to the ridge. Tired and worried about both the women, they stopped and Valla went to Camp 3 with Heidi Ludi to get more help. Eva had stopped breathing and Sepp Schwankener and Lev gave her artificial respiration but despite considerable efforts breathing could not be restored. As the place was dangerous they secured her body and escaped from the slope on to the descent route, meeting Jed Williamson and others coming up to try and help. All then retreated to Camp 3 where some of the lighter tents were destroyed by the wind.

Meanwhile, Jeff Lowe and John Roskelley had at last completed the American Route on Peak 19 where Jon Gary Ullin had died in the earlier attempt, but there was little respite in the Achik Tash. So many parties of such varied experience were on the mountain and in conditions so bad that it seemed inconceivable there would not be trouble.

The eight Soviet women I had passed on my way down remained camped overnight from 5–6 of August on the very summit of the mountain. Initially, while the attempts to rescue Eva were going on, Elvira Shataeyeva contacted Base to say that one member of her group was sick and that their tents were unable to withstand the ferocious winds. Though they had been instructed to retreat like everyone else, they had initially persisted in their long prepared plan to descend by the Razdelny. But after an exhausting night they set out back down the Lipkin Route as directed, taking the sick woman with them. It appears that one woman died of exposure belaying the rest of the group down and the whole group stopped only a little way down the slope. By the evening of the 6th several more of the climbers were suffering the symptoms of exposure. The leader contacted Base in the evening and was instructed to continue down, even if it meant leaving those unable to go on. The weather remained diabolical, and late on the evening of the 6th only five of the eight women remained alive.

Help with a rescue party was volunteered by French, Americans and British. Our hosts were desperately anxious and understandably wanted to handle this cruelly evolving tragedy themselves. Four strong Soviet climbers were already at Camp 1 below the Lipkin intending to render assistance. But so many people were still on the mountain and exposed to risk, at Camp 3 on the Razdelny, or very high on the Lipkin Route where there were embattled groups of Siberians, Japanese and Americans, that it made little sense not to put more experienced helpers back into the field. The senior Soviet climbers agreed and also called for help with helicopters from Dushanbe. But everyone who threw together gear for a rapid departure on 6 August knew that there was little chance of the remaining Soviet women surviving even if the conditions improved. At best we might save one or two survivors or help other climbers in trouble on the mountain.

On a sleet-driven grey afternoon the rescue party plodded off across the Achik Tash towards the Pass of the Travellers. Cloud hung in great banks over the foothills and Lenin was shrouded totally. The path down to the Lenin Glacier was muddy red, soaked with rain and snow in the days of storm. As the group of English, French and Americans reached the Lenin Glacier a harsh November-like wind swept down the moraines. Sleet became snow and Bernard, a tiny animated Chamoniard, donned a huge cape which covered him and his rucksack. This silver grey phantom, hunchbacked and bizarre, produced a few wry laughs even in these grimmest of circumstances. We were all quite fit, everyone had done their bit of mountaineering, so a few days after climbing the ridge, here we were, hiking across expanses of glacier to the foot of the Lipkin, a route down to which the French had skied, by Lenin's North Face, only a short time before. At the camp below the spur three Russian climbers waited amid the bedraggled tentage. The snow swept in great curtains down the glacier and there was a pervasive damp chill. Clive crawled into a soaked tent and we brewed and rehydrated American steaks one after another.

As darkness fell the others heard Elvira, the women's leader, speak from over 8,000 feet above. "Another has died. We cannot go through another night. I do not have the strength to hold down the transmitter button." In fact this was one of several transmissions which our Russian companions had received. Their faces were riven with frustration and grief at being able to do so little. Three of the women appear to have been alive on that storm-blasted plateau, with winds approaching a hundred miles an hour at over 22,000 feet. Later in the evening as we went through the seemingly empty motions of preparing to climb the mountain to their rescue, they came on again. Only two remained alive. By 9.00 pm the storm blew out to be replaced by a frost so bitter that we shivered in our best down so many feet below them.

Early next morning Doug, Tut, Guy, Clive and I, Jeff Lowe, Vincent and Benoir Renard, Bernard and two other Frenchmen moved off early with Boris and the other two Soviet climbers, trekking all day in fine weather up the great slopes leading to the Lipkin Spur. Above, Al Steck, Jock Glidden and Chris Wren emerged from a prolonged bivouac within a short distance of a Japanese party which had adopted similar chrysalis tactics and they all struggled to the summit. They found the women, spread along the ridge leading back from the summit, most of them together in the ruin of their fatal final camp. The Americans, who had known nothing of the tragedy, reported their news on the radio carried by the Japanese. The latter had an inkling of the situation from their companions at Base and had once tried to fight the elements in an effort to find the women, but with no success in the maelstrom.

In late afternoon the final slopes to the ice cave at 17,500 feet were swept by a cold but relatively innocuous Lenin wind. In its depths, still several thousand feet below the plateau, the report of events above was received. Everyone was now in retreat, with Americans coming back by the Lipkin, Siberians far on the descent of that route, and the beleaguered Camp 2 on the Razdelny relieved by John Evans and others from the American party. There was not a lot more to be done by us – in death it became a domestic tragedy. Guy Lee and I remained at the Lipkin ice cave for only an hour or so. The cave was crowded and the necessity which had brought us back dissolved. Several of the French had turned downwards already and while Tut, Doug, Jeff, Vincent, Bernard and the Russians opted to stay up for one night to plough a path with the Masters of Sport to meet the retreating parties, we turned back towards the valley, speeding down in a few evening hours to the camp from which we had emerged with so much toil that day. Next morning we fed tea to the groups fleeing from the Razdelny, storm-battered, shocked men and women – Heidi Ludi with blackening finger ends. In the late afternoon Tut and the rest came down and we quitted the Lenin Glacier for the last time, crossing the Travellers' Pass, strolling down the Achik Tash Pamir past goats and flowers into Base.

It was the worst storm within living memory in the area. High wind and a bare terrain threatened even the most modern tents on Peak Lenin. The wooden poles and zipless doors of the Soviet Ladies' tents stood no chance so near the summit, despite the strength of the materials. Tactics, too, were a problem. The Soviet approach to climbing insists not unreasonably on the unity and cohesion of the party. The ladies had moved up Peak Lenin quite slowly, acclimatising gradually. Even in a team of eight this might have assured a successful traverse in less adverse weather. But the plateau is very high and long and to remain there long is risky for any party. In bad weather it is potentially highly dangerous, not least because of the possibility of losing the way, if the party has to move, and with risks of sickness, deterioration and even death if the group is caught in a storm. The ladies had been ordered back by Vitali Abalakov. They stuck too rigidly and bravely to their planned traverse in the teeth of ferocious weather. Nor would they consider leaving the summit with the last groups descending the Razdelny as the storm lashed into the mountain, after the fatigue of their ascent with loads to the summit.

Possibly that was the critical point. Once one or two members became sick in the first day of the storm, only quick descent might have saved all or some of the party, as their equipment would not enable them to survive. Their commendable team spirit prevented them doing this as individual members weakened. Bluntly, descent would have meant leaving someone behind. They could not do it even when ordered to do so from below. Perhaps it was already too late and few would have had the strength to cross the plateau in such a blizzard. The likelihood of them meeting Japanese or Americans embattled in their tents on the lee of the peak was not great. About the entire event there was a fearful logic.

As the tragedy unfolded in Base Camp emotion ran high. In particular there was a belief that helicopters might have speeded rescuers up the mountain with a hope of being effective. In practice this was not likely to have been of much real help. High winds, even low down, combined with poor visibility, could easily have caused a helicopter to crash at these altitudes. At most it might have taken a group of rescuers the day's walk to the Lenin Glacier. Probably the main hope was that the lost Japanese might have found the party when they heard of the plight of the retreating group. But tough and resilient as they were, it was a condition of their survival that they did not stay out searching long or they, too, would have lost their way back and with it their lives. Even had they found the women, they might have had neither the strength nor the numbers to get them back to their camp, nor the equipment to shelter so many.

The official inquest seems to have reached a similar conclusion. It was a bitter finish to a disastrous summer. Yet as always new things grew out of the wreckage. Speedy Smith married one of the Dutch contingent, a good number of the Americans turned towards the Himalayas where John Roskelley made an oxygen-free ascent of K2 in 1978, while Tut led the upper Rock Band of the South-West Face of Everest and Doug reached the summit in 1975. If one survived that bleak summer and the will to climb remained, what was there in the world that would destroy it?

As for Paul, he was to be killed in 1995 in a sérac fall in the Karakoram.

Death in the Everest Icefall

Hamish MacInnes

I first met Doug Scott in 1972 when we joined forces with Don Whillans as members of Dr Karl Herrligkoffer's European Everest expedition to the South-West Face of the mountain. To say that the expedition was a fiasco would be an under-statement. It started with waves of suspicion amongst the rival factions and ended on the open sea of hostility. Though Herr-ligkoffer didn't particularly want us as members of his team, he wanted the money which I had been promised by both the BBC and the *Observer*. We were quick to rename the doctor Ster-lingscoffer when he was out of earshot.

My opinion of German efficiency declined early on in this expedition when there was an obvious lemming-like rush to get to Base Camp and a disregard for the need to acclimatise. The main group survived this, but Horst Vitt, a German diplomat who was on his way to visit us, died of pulmonary oedema. Professor Huttl also fell victim to the altitude on his way to Base Camp to conduct physiological experiments and had to be evacuated to Kathmandu, then back to Germany.

Despite international differences, we three were eventually established at Camp 4 at approximately 24,000 feet with the purpose of establishing Camp 5 some 1,500 feet above. It was here that we had what is probably the highest high-altitude quarrel in history. The so-called Big Four, Werner Haim, Adolf Huber, Leo Breitenberger and Felix Kuen, argued the toss with us. Felix as the climbing leader didn't give us much choice.

"You must down go" he pounded the edge of a box platform

with his ice axe to give extra emphasis to his words and only added over and over again, "I vont give one millimetre . . ."

The Big Four had returned to the fray as they felt the summit was looming closer in good weather; they were determined to be at the sharp end from now on. For the past week they had been whooping it up at Base Camp where they had gone to welcome their leader, Karl, who had just returned from a flying visit to Munich to collect down clothing for the Sherpas. The Sherpas had refused point blank to go above Camp 2 without it. When Karl returned with his feathers he helicoptered as far as Pherichi at 15,000 feet. On arrival at Base Camp it was found that he had suffered a mild heart attack. Full use was made of the helicopter flight for Leo Breitenberger was sent back to Kathmandu as he was suffering from pleurisy. Hans Berger had gallstone trouble and Peter Bednar, who had been suffering from a cholera injection gone wrong, both retreated to Base Camp, but later returned to Camp 2. A Persian, Mischa Saleki, who was a member of the expedition (making its working title something of a misnomer), had been constantly bullied throughout the trip by the Big Four and now decided he could stand it no longer. According to a German press report, he stowed away in the helicopter at Pherichi, an extremely difficult thing to do, especially at 15,000 feet when even the passenger seats have sometimes to be removed to lighten the machine.

On such an expedition you get to know your companions well. You live in close proximity for months, get used to each other's smells and habits and share danger and pleasure, be it a super-cold high-altitude view with peaks standing out as if fresh from a mould, or a piece of well-travelled cake which somehow escaped the hungry gauntlet of climbers in lower camps.

Well, the Big Four, or rather the Big Three, as Haim injured a knee near Camp 3 and had to be evacuated down the Western Cwm by improvised stretcher, didn't get up the South-West Face. Felix, poor chap, later committed suicide back home in Austria. We didn't have many laughs on the Herrligkoffer expedition; it wasn't that sort of a trip. But an amusing incident happened on the bleak ice of Camp 1. One of the Big Four who suffered from constipation – an uncomfortable affliction in the cold of high altitude – was squatting in solitary splendour on the glacier close to camp. Imagine his dilemma when a crack appeared in the ice between his boots.

Doug, I discovered, is an idealist, a great companion on a big trip. He trained as a physical education teacher and taught in his home town, Nottingham, for ten years. His long hair didn't endear him to the crewcut Germans, but it was inevitable that eventually they respected him.

We had acquired an assortment of rather useless items of clothing from the Base Camp coffers. Doug amassed a large pile of this jumble, not in the least suited for use on the mountain. No doubt it had been donated by well-meaning hausfraus back in the Fatherland. Realising that there was a ready market amongst the Sherpas for such draperies, Doug negotiated with a wily Sherpa called Dorge. Dorge, like most of his tribe, is a born trader. For example, on the steep wall between Camps 4 and 5, at over 25,000 feet, we had watched him wander nonchalantly over the face retrieving tatty bits of Japanese fixed rope, remnants of a previously unsuccessful expedition. A Sherpa, I concluded, who went to so much trouble to find tethering for his yaks was obviously a formidable business man. He cornered Doug's clothing market by offering slightly higher prices than his companions on condition that the clothing was left with him at Base Camp and the money was collected from his wife at Ghat, a small village south of Namche Bazar.

On our way to Kathmandu when Doug called at Dorge's house, his charming spouse confessed that she didn't have a rupee in the place. Somewhat disconsolate, but philosophical, Doug shrugged his shoulders and said that he'd call later.

We had only been back in the UK for a week or so when Chris Bonington asked Doug and me to join his expedition to the South-West Face of Everest. He was due to leave in about four weeks. We didn't hesitate. We both felt that we had a score to settle with that prodigious heap of rock and ice. After all, we thought, it would be a pleasant change to be on a properly organised trip. Chris doesn't leave things to chance – or leave the Sherpa's down clothing back home. Chris's expedition now gave Doug a heaven-sent opportunity to visit Dorge again on the way back to Everest. But heaven had taken more than Doug under its ample wing. Dorge had gone into retreat, his wife told

Doug when he called this time; he had taken up the god business and was going to be a lama. Once again Doug went away philosophically. It wasn't until we went back to Everest again with Chris in 1975 that Doug at last caught up with the elusive lama. Tut Braithwaite and I were with him when we called at Dorge's quaint house above the river. Dorge was at home. He had returned from his cave of meditation. He certainly seemed pleased to see us and we felt the same way, for we had shared hardships high on the South-West Face. He didn't have any money now, he told Doug, but he had good *chung*, would we like a glass? We would, then another and another and eventually parted in good spirits, Doug telling the impecunious lama that he could forget about the long-standing debt.

The highest point reached by our 1972 expedition was no higher than that reached by the Big Four, or that other ill-fated assault, the International Everest Expedition of 1971, which was even more infamous for its discord, rocks and verbal abuse flying in rarefied air. When the Bonington expedition was defeated in 1972 we remained good friends after a great fight in hellish conditions of high wind and temperatures of –40°C.

When we started to clear the mountain, Dougal Haston and I went down ahead of Chris and Doug. It was 16 November when we left Camp 2. Mick Burke had descended the previous night so that he could get some film of us arriving at Base Camp. The Icefall was particularly dangerous. Earlier in the expedition Dougal and I had spent many cold mornings fixing ropes and placing ladder bridges over crevasses. We would set off at 3.00 am to do this work as the Icefall seemed to doze at this time of day and we were usually back down at Base Camp in time for a second breakfast. One section of the Icefall was so treacherous that I had put up a sign urging anyone crossing the area to clip on to the fixed rope which Dougal and I had secured across this passage of horrors. The ice seemed to be constantly moving, albeit slowly, but its groans resembled those of a great snake writhing in its death throes. Séracs leaned like Saturday night Glaswegians and we sneaked under these. When we had enough energy, we passed them at a run, not easy at almost 20,000 feet.

When Dougal and I came down that day at the end of the expedition this passage was worse than ever. I had spoken with

Colonel Jimmy Roberts about it. Jimmy was Deputy Leader and in direct charge of the Icefall porters. I had told him that I thought the area would collapse in less than a week. Now over sixteen days had passed and it was complaining, with its belly-aching rumbles, even more persistently than before.

Dougal and I angled down on to the home straight to Base Camp, with only the minor worry of an avalanche from the Lo La to trouble us, peanuts compared to what we had just come through, and I said, "Thank Christ that's behind us."

"Aye, Jimmy," said Dougal, "it's no the place to dither about."

Tony Tighe, a friend of Dougal's, was just setting off for Camp 1 when we arrived. Tony was an Australian, a warm-hearted lad who had been working as a barman at the Vagabond Club in Leysin in Switzerland where Dougal lived. Though he wasn't a climber, he was fit and had unbounded enthusiasm. He had been doing thankless jobs at Base Camp for the past two months and though he wasn't an official member of the expedition and not supposed to go above Base Camp, Chris had agreed to allow him to go up to Camp 1 so that he could see the Western Cwm. We all thought this was the least that could be done to reward Tony for all his chores. There were about twenty Sherpas going up as well to collect loads from the camp. Though the Icefall was highly dangerous in places from falling séracs and subsidence, technically it was easy with all the crevasses bridged and ropes in the trickier sections. It was in fact as safe for one person to go up or down as fifty. We wished Tony a good climb and with a wave he was off, a colourful figure. He had been pestering Chris for weeks to visit Camp 1 and this was his big day. Unfortunately, it was also his last and he never saw the Western Cwm.

Chris and Doug met him as they came down. Despite his fitness he lagged behind the Sherpas, who with the end of the expedition in sight had wings on their crampons. At Base Camp we had our first wash for many weeks and were sitting in the main tent when I said to Chris, "Well, thank goodness it's all over safely, Chris."

He flared up, a look almost of fear on his face. No doubt the memory of Ian Clough's death on Annapurna was still fresh on his mind. Ian, a good friend of both of us, had been killed in literally the last hour of the expedition by a falling sérac.

"There's still some to come down that last bit!" Chris said tersely.

He was right of course and I wonder if just then he had a premonition. A short time later there were murmurings from the Sherpas. Though we hadn't heard anything at Base Camp the Sherpas suspected that there had been a big collapse in the Icefall. This was confirmed presently by Phurkipa, our Icefall sirdar who had just returned. He told Chris of the subsidence.

An hour or so later Barney Rosedale, our doctor, came into camp. He and Tony had been the last Europeans on the mountain. He looked distraught and told us he had managed to get round the collapse by a dangerous diversion. He had seen no sign of Tony. Phurkipa, it transpired, had been the last person to see him. We tried to piece together the information we had on Tony's movements and came to the reluctant conclusion that he must have been caught in the fall of ice. Barney told us that he had heard a deep-throated graunching noise at about one o'clock at Camp 1. This had been followed by a great mushroom cloud of ice particles. Some Sherpas had just left Camp 1 to go down to Base Camp and had almost been caught in the fall. An ice ridge on which they had been walking had collapsed beneath them. They came rushing into Camp 1 saying that Ang Tande, one of the Icefall porters, was hanging on the safety rope which Dougal and I had installed. He was swinging seventy feet above the new and equally unstable floor of the Icefall. It was fortunate that the Sherpas had made a point of clipping on to this rope and Phurkipa had duplicated my warning board in Nepalese for their benefit. Barney, acting decisively, managed to dash down to the scene of the accident with two good Sherpas and succeeded in rescuing the suspended porter. He then took all the Sherpas from Camp 1 down to Base Camp by a circuitous and hazardous route. He saw no sign of Tony Tighe on the way, however, and he didn't think that there was another route through the chaos. It was obvious to us all that Tony had been buried.

As Mick Burke and Dave Bathgate were the freshest of our group they volunteered to go up and conduct a quick search. It was already late but they set off with some Sherpas. The Icefall was bathed in moonlight when they arrived at the scene. Crazy shadows reached out from the séracs and the crevasses were black slits. In the moonlight they could see that some of the séracs were still in a critical state, leaning Pisa-tower-like, which to any experienced mountaineer spells death. There was no sign of Tony, only the ominous grinding of the mills of the Icefall. Mick Burke said afterwards that being amidst that scene of destruction was the most frightening experience of his life.

Though Barney had taken all the Sherpas from Camp 1 down with him to Base Camp the previous day, there had still been fourteen Sherpas at Camp 2 doing a final clear up. They had now reached Camp 1 and somehow they had to be taken down. Also a further search for Tony was required in the stark light of day. Doug Scott and I volunteered to do this; Dougal had taken Tony's death badly and had gone down to Pherichi to be on his own.

The scene at the lonely hanging rope was one of devastation. It was as if the immediate area had been subjected to saturation bombing. As Dave and Mick had reported, some of the ice towers were ready to fall at any minute, but when we picked our way under these, we tried to take our minds off the danger and made as systematic a search as possible. We had taken several Sherpas up and they were obviously terrified. So were we, but we tried not to show it.

As we neared Camp 1 Doug complained of a headache and pain in his eyes and I thought he must have got snow blindness. Eventually, we reached Camp 1 to be greeted by the remaining Sherpas who had spent the night there, having arrived after Barney and his group had left. They had tried to go down through the fall, but had turned back at the site of the danger.

We quickly made up loads to take back to Base, leaving all but the most essential equipment. The Sherpas, who normally leave nothing of even the slightest value on the mountain, raised no objection. I was concerned for Doug; his sight was deteriorating and I tried to contact Base on the walkie-talkie but without any luck. I thought extra manpower on the lower stretch of the Icefall would help us.

We retraced our route through the great blocks of ice, a valley of death. I remember at the time thinking that it looked like the destruction of a city of glass. Though we also searched on the descent there was no sign of Tony. There was no question of his being alive under such debris; the smallest of the ice blocks must have weighed several tons. We threaded our way down under a broiling sun, for the Everest Icefall can be one of the hottest places on earth in mid-morning.

Two years later we were back again, with Chris's 1975 expedition to the South-West Face. Now we were successful, with Doug and Dougal first to reach the summit, but tragically this time it was Mick Burke who lost his life. Mick was always a prickly customer, but it was Mick who, with Dave Bathgate, had unhesitatingly gone up to look for Tony that night and it was Mick, too, years before, who had played his part on the dramatic rescue on the West Face of the Dru in Chamonix in the French Alps.

Dougal was later killed in a skiing accident close to his home in Switzerland. Doug called at my house in Glencoe shortly afterwards when I was out, but he left a bottle of wine belayed to my front door handle. Attached to it was a note: "Take care, youth, there's not many of us left."

The Three-Hundred-Metre Fall

Marek Brniak

Polish mountaineers have a reputation for incredible toughness. Most of their high-mountain training is done in their native Tatras, a jagged range which they share with Czechoslovakia. Marek Brniak is a mountaineer, journalist and member of a rescue group which has been on many High Tatra rescues. Toughness is not a monopoly of the male climber, however, and in this tale we have a heroine. It is a story set in February 1977.

A hostile wind scoured the frozen lake below us. Swaying under huge loads, Jan and I staggered down in a maelstrom of driving snow, our clothing creaking and our beards encrusted in rime.

The great climbing days were at an end. Dim but welcoming lights from the Morskie Oko Refuge loomed ahead, inviting us to come and recharge our emaciated bodies with hot *bigos* and beer. Heads low into the blast, soapflake snow fluffing to our knees; a few more steps and we flung our heavy packs on to the floor of the log hut.

The place was packed and steamy, yet, tired as we were, we immediately sensed something was wrong. There was an unmistakably expectant tension. A shaggy-looking individual sitting at a nearby bench, eating soup with black bread, told us what it was all about.

"Something happened to a couple on Mieguszowiecki, you know. It's Eva and Tomek, they're on the North Face. Last night they were to signal from their bivvy to report progress and that all was well. When there was no signal we assumed that their torch had gone on the blink. But in the morning Eva's boyfriend was getting worried and went to the bottom of the wall. He could see nothing through the snow storm. About an hour ago, some hikers called in here to say that they had heard someone calling for help." He jerked his thumb in the direction of the warden's quarters at the end of the building. "The news has been radioed down to the rescue team in Zakopane. They're due any minute."

I took my place in the beer queue, always a respectable length at this time of day, especially with foul weather clamping in and little prospect of climbing. I glanced round the room again. On the surface everything appeared normal. There were girls in bright anoraks, men in warm climbing clothes, overweight hillwalkers and lean ones, some cheerful, others looking tired out. They were eating, talking, playing cards, reading. Someone was soulfully strumming a guitar. Fire danced in the stoves and the aroma of cooking mingled with the odour of wet greasy wool and the smell of wood smoke. Clothing and sleeping bags were drying, hung from the walls and draped over benches. Candle wax was splattered over the pine tables.

I had a feeling that these people didn't want to accept their misgivings, their fears that an accident could happen to them too. I know only too well that in situations such as this people often mask their true thoughts with boisterousness and an overstrained jollity.

Stawowy, the rescue team leader, appeared and was forming a party of volunteers to back up his own professional men, who hadn't yet arrived. The volunteers were out on the verandah sorting out equipment.

Jan and I had just realised our dream of *bigos* when we heard the deep throb of the rescue team's four-wheel-drive trucks approaching. In a few moments the white pencils of their headlamps swept the refuge and the verandah swarmed with the men of the Blue Cross.

The Blue Cross is the Polish Mountain Rescue emblem. They were an impressive-looking bunch, with neat matching jackets and breeches that gave them an almost military air. Most of them were Górale, the local highlanders, who are tough dedicated men. They take great pride in their profession, feeling that to be a member of the rescue team is a special honour. Their roots run deep in the Tatra rescue service, the association being one of the oldest of its kind in the world. At one time they were volunteers, now they are full-time professionals financed by the state.

Until now the High Tatra had experienced a fine winter, but the previous night the weather had deteriorated rapidly. It was snowing heavily and persistently, as though making up for lost time. Even worse, the *Wistr Halny*, a warm, penetrating snow-melting wind, had accompanied the snowfall. Now a mass of wet soggy snow was poised on the faces, making avalanches a major hazard.

We had retreated from our route not a minute too soon. Had we continued, the chances of finding a safe way down from the summit would have been minimal. But we abandoned our climb in the full realisation that discretion is the better part of valour.

Now in this insulated world of the refuge, sipping our beer in steaming clothes and feeling our frozen feet painfully awaken, we were well aware of what things would be like up on the North Face of Mieguszowiecki, a gargantuan massif looming over a thousand metres above the slate-coloured ice of Morskie Oko Lake. I didn't envy the rescuers their task. Helicopters couldn't fly in this weather and in order to reach the trapped couple they would have to climb a long steep couloir and then traverse along an extended system of galleries and ledges, now swept by avalanches.

We played poker, discussed politics and, inevitably, new routes that had been done recently and new ones to do. It was getting late and the benches at the tables were becoming vacant. The staircase creaked as people were filtering upstairs to get some sleep. The hut was overcrowded and people were having to sleep on the floors of the dormitories, so Jan and I decided to make ourselves comfortable on our benches downstairs.

Just before crawling into our still-damp sleeping bags we went out on to the verandah to see if we could pick out any lights, but the swirling snow prevented us from seeing anything. As we were turning to go inside again and grab some overdue sleep, it cleared for an instant and we could see the torch lights of the rescue party, like remote fireflies, on the opposite side of the lake, still low, stretched out in a vertical column.

"Not making much progress, are they?" Jan said. "They must be shitting bricks up there tonight – I would!"

As I was lying in my sleeping bag I could hear and feel the wind pounding on the walls. The hut shuddered in the gusts. Every muscle in my body protested after the exertions of our climb, making me fully aware that I was very tired, but, as is often the case when one is shattered, you can't drift off to sleep.

I lit a cigarette and contemplated the difficulty of surviving such a storm as this, the icy fingers of spindrift searching for cold flesh through every minuscule opening in your wind-proofs, the blast tearing at the two climbers high above, and at the rescuers, consuming their energy and their hopes.

I had never met Eva or Tomek in person. We had heard they were underprepared for such a serious climb. But the mountains act as a catalyst, giving our small climbing fraternity such a sense of unity that I had a twinge of guilt. I should have been out front with the rescue party. Granted, my presence, had I gone, wouldn't have produced any spectacular result, but somehow I couldn't help thinking that way.

Vivid voices and thuds on the steps of the verandah stirred me into wakefulness, for I must have dropped off to sleep at last. It was 3.00 am. "Why the hell are people going out so early?" I asked myself in a daze. "Isn't the weather ghastly?" I lay for a further couple of minutes snuggling deep into the down. But the realisation that this was the rescue party coming back percolated into my consciousness and my fingers groped for the zip of my sleeping bag.

The rescuers were a sorry sight, veritable snowmen, their faces masks of sorrow and resignation. I got my butane stove going and made them scalding mugs of coffee while they told me their story.

Crossing the open expanse of the frozen lake, the wind had buffeted their large rucksacks like sails. On the boulders of the scree slope beyond the gusts had stabbed at them so that they floundered into snow-covered holes, cursed, but kept going. It was well after 10.00 pm before they reached the foot of the couloir.

Jan Gasienica was speaking, an old hand in the rescue team, a big man with the hint of a pot belly. He came from an old Górale family.

"We entered the gully. It's quite easy going for most of the thousand metres, but higher we were fighting through waist-deep snow. I was sure that we were all going to be carried down. The conditions were very unstable.

"When we reached the bottleneck I was out in front. All I could see were the lights of the others below me and the reflection of their helmets. There was a thud. I was petrified. We've all had it, I thought, a bloody avalanche. But it wasn't; it was the wet snow cover settling. I drove a couple of pegs in a rock crack, put karabiners on them, and clipped in the climbing rope before carrying on. I'm used to rescue work, Marek, I'm not a timid bastard, but I must admit that just then my hands were trembling. I felt sweat trickling down my back. I had now almost reached the point where you leave the couloir and start the long traverse across the North Face. I was forcing myself on."

He paused for a moment, wiped his brow and took another gulp of coffee. "The snow was up to my armpits. I half climbed, half swam through it. I didn't pray, I just cursed that snow, willing it to stay in place and not avalanche.

"There was a huge cornice at the edge of the gallery; I don't know how I got through it, but I did. I saw rocks very close by. I could almost touch them. Then I felt something like an approaching train just above me. The avalanche swallowed me and I went with it faster and faster. I was in a vortex of snow particles, spinning, rolling and jerking wildly round and round. I felt the powder being rammed down my windpipe, choking me, and at the same time the snow round my neck was trying to strangle me. I was experiencing the horrors of a drowning man. Then there was this God Almighty jerk and the rope hauled me out of it just like a landed fish. I thought my back was broken, for it had taken the full force of me being hauled out of that wet heavy avalanching snow. I realised that I had pissed myself in shock and my clothes were stuffed solid with snow. What the hell did it matter? I thought. I was alive, just happy to be alive . . ."

Jan Gasienica took off his snow-encrusted gaiters.

"Everything was wonderfully calm and my senses were slowly coming back. I heard Kazek calling to all the team members to shout out their names to see if anyone had been swept away. Everybody called, the voices snatched away by the fury of the wind. Thank God, no one was missing."

The hut was slowly coming back to life with the accompaniment of the early-morning music from the bogs and the creaks and muttering from the upper floor. Then came the familiar banging of pots and tin plates from the kitchen. Now a maid bustled in to kindle the stove, her hair still awry. The rattle of coal being poured into the stove violated the last delightful minutes of that early-morning quiet.

At dawn the rescue party went out again, leaving us in a state of silent inertia, with the prospect of long hours of waiting. I peered at the world beyond the windows. The snow had stopped, but the wind showed no signs of abating. It howled round the refuge. Visibility was abysmal.

"This is going to be a bloody games day today. It's not fit for dogs out there!" grumbled my partner, jerking his thumb in the general direction of Mieguszowiecki's North Wall. "I wouldn't give them high odds surviving this lot, Marek. Last night in the gully the rescue team went beyond the call of duty, the risk factor was too high. I know it's courageous, but it's also silly."

People were playing cards – poker, pontoon, canasta – as if their very existence depended on the outcome. From time to time one or two would give a glance at the window facing the North Wall and look down at their cards again.

Somewhere up there, high on the windswept face, were two helpless people. Were they still alive? Were they still feebly calling for help? Help which couldn't come.

"What about going out for a walk, Jan? I need to stretch my legs," I suggested. My companion was shuffling a pack of cards. He had joined the poker school about an hour before but it was obvious that he wasn't paying much attention to the game for he had been losing steadily.

"Good idea," he agreed, "and a good time to pull out. Take my hand, mate." He gave the pack to one of the spectators and stood up.

It was warm outside. It always is with the *Halny*, but its strength had lessened somewhat by now. Clouds were rising and we could see the lower white skirts of the mountains. We spotted the rescue party, tiny orange dots, very low in the couloir, moving as if in slow motion. They were coming down.

We hurried towards them and twenty minutes later met them halfway across the lake. Kazek Byrcyn, the volunteer team leader, told us, "We intended to fix ropes the entire way up the couloir so that we would have a handrail, but it proved impossible." He looked depressed and exhausted. Indeed they all looked as if they had had enough.

"The couloir is worse than ever, a death alley for avalanches," he said. "They come down every few minutes. Also most of the cracks on the rock walls are jammed with snow and ice and you can't get pegs in. I think every one of us has been avalanched at one time or another in that bloody couloir today. It's Russian roulette. We're all soaked to the skin. I've radioed back to base that we can't go on in these conditions. I'm not prepared to expose the team to this sort of danger any longer."

We stood there, a shabby group on the ice. After Kazek's long speech nobody said anything for a while. It isn't an easy decision, forsaking climbers who still perhaps have a spark of life in them. You feel it's almost like passing a death sentence.

All of a sudden the face came into view. The clouds rolled up in the wind like a great roller blind. The last remnants licked the high ridges and surrounding peaks. The sun burst through in a blaze of harsh winter glory. One of the team members had his binoculars to his eyes and gave a gasp of astonishment. Immediately we all caught sight of a minute black dot spinning through the air. The body seemed to glide over the rocks and snowfields like a feather, over bands and down chimneys. It disappeared in a snow-filled basin, then took off into the air again, crashing down an icefall. It appeared to be going faster as it fell. It ricocheted off the bottom snowfield and came to a halt on the edge of the lake. We stared at it as if mesmerised, then all took off in a wild gallop in its direction.

It was alive. It was Eva. We could hardly believe our eyes. "So many of you . . . how awfully good you've come . . . Tomek's dead," she managed to mumble before she passed out.

Within an hour she was under anaesthetic and having her leg pinned in the Zakopane General Hospital, after a hair-raising journey down the hairpins on a snow-choked road.

What actually happened was this: on the brink of unconsciousness, Eva caught hold of a karabiner and accidentally pressed the gate open, which released her from her belay piton and precipitated her over 300 metres down the face. What is almost as miraculous as her surviving the fall was the fact that we were all there at the bottom to witness it at the very instant the cloud cleared, for she didn't cry out, and could have lain there at the foot of the cliff until the spring thaw.

A few weeks later a helicopter went back to the face, and Tomek's body was winched aboard. He was taken down on this his last journey to the sanctuary of the green flowering valleys. There at the helipad his mother was waiting.

The first crocuses were just blooming.

Self-help on the Ogre

Doug Scott

In 1977 Doug was a member of an expedition to the Ogre, a savage mountain in the Pakistan Karakoram. Doug's account of this trip, which is probably one of the most outstanding examples of self-help in the annals of mountaineering, is in striking contrast to the attitude of potential snow-holers and certified climbers who are churned out by institutions. Doug, like me, abhors this approach to mountaineering, which is after all basically a sport of self-reliance.

If I think back to the British Ogre Himalayan expedition 1977, one man stands out in my mind – the Balti porter, Taki, who, after carrying a sixty-pound box throughout a twelve-mile approach march, some of it over moraine waste, produced from the folds of his shorts, smocks and assorted rags thirty-one eggs, none of which was even cracked. How he did it I'll never know. Ostensibly he did it for thirty-one rupees and our favour, but how do you walk over a shifting chaos of moraine rock without breaking such a cargo? Well, I suppose, much more carefully than I could. Eight weeks later, eight more Balti came up the Biafo Glacier to Base Camp and, with as much care as Taki had for his eggs, carried me down some of the roughest terrain imaginable, with hardly a jolt to my broken legs.

Back in June, fit and full of optimism, six of us entered Baltistan, ready to climb the Ogre. The Ogre is the highest point in the Biafo Glacier region of the Karakoram. It was noted by Europeans in 1861, when Godwin Austen first surveyed the area, and again in 1892 when Conway came down the Biafo from the Hispar Glacier and named it. Then, during the 1930s, Eric Shipton and his friends carefully surveyed the whole region. The height of the Ogre stands at 23,900 feet (7,285 metres) and a local name was found for it – Baintha Brakk – but climbers seem to prefer the shorter and more intelligible "Ogre".

During the last six years, two British and two Japanese expeditions have attempted the mountain. All four attempts failed in the face of avalanching snow, steep rock and ferocious storms. The highest point reached was 21,500 feet, which was achieved last year when the Japanese explored the South-West Flank. Above their high-point there reared 1,000 feet of steep granite and, beyond that, sheer ice faces, long corniced ridges and a final 800-foot summit rock pinnacle. The technical problems would be quite something in the Alps, but here, at nearly 24,000 feet, the climbing would become a race against physical and mental deterioration in the rarefied air.

During the spring of 1975, Clive Rowland and I reconnoitred the south side of the Ogre. Our high point then had been 16,000 feet on the Uzun Brakk Glacier, where we stood bogged down in wet, sloppy snow, lost in amazement at the sight of the great lumps of rock, 8,000 feet high and liberally covered with snowy ramps and steep ice faces, that characterise the Ogre from the south. It is not a beautiful mountain from down there, being squat and having three small cones, like misplaced nipples, defining the summit, with the centre cone the highest. Yet there is one elegant feature, and that is the South Pillar, a prow of rock 3,000 feet high. While I was excited about the prospect of climbing that, Clive was clearly attracted by the South-West Flank, where there was a possible route up ridges and snow-fields that looked the most likely way to the summit area. As a result of this divergence of interest, we put together an expedition with these two routes in mind.

The expedition finally resolved itself into a party of six: Tut Braithwaite and I were to try the South Pillar, while Chris Bonington, Nick Estcourt, Mo Anthoine and Clive attempted the South-West Flank. We were, mercifully, without a leader. The inclusion of such a personage would have been laughable, seeing that all members of the team had had so much expedition experience that they could easily arrive at decisions communally. For some this was their first leaderless expedition and they no doubt found it stimulating to work things out for themselves, while former leaders perhaps found it restful to be without the burden of total responsibility.

Despite an apparent lack of organisation, we had worked hard preparing for our respective routes, but these well-made plans foundered in our case when a big rock smashed into Tut's leg at the start of our South Pillar route. After two weeks of waiting for a large blood clot to move, Tut could still not use his leg for rock climbing. Laboriously, we recovered all our food, equipment and a special hanging tent from the base of the pillar (at 19,000 feet). So ended a two-year obsession – an obsession which had caused me to catch my breath a few times at the thought of taking off to climb with just two climbing ropes and none back down to the ground. But for me, at least, there were still alternatives, while Tut had no choice but to sit the trip out in Base Camp. For someone as active as he is, that wait must have been one of the most frustrating periods of his life.

"Mountain one, climbers none," as Mo put it.

Round Two had already begun, with Chris, Nick, Clive and Mo busy climbing and fixing ropes up the ice rib leading to the West Col. In less than a week they climbed from above Advance Base, at 17,000 feet to 20,000 feet on the col. At the end of this period, Chris and Nick took off for the top, with about five days' food. Finding themselves suddenly alone, the other two descended – Clive because he wanted to reconnoitre a different way via the West Ridge, and Mo because he felt they needed more supplies and more time to acclimatise. Nick and Chris pushed out from the col along a ramp and round on to the South Face. Up to a point above the South Pillar they had followed a line pioneered by the 1976 Japanese expedition. Four days later, they returned, having failed in a very bold attempt to reach the summit. Faced with depleted food stocks and lack of climbing equipment, and suffering from the effects of altitude, they had not felt up to climbing the 800-foot summit cone. They did, however, traverse up on steep snow to the West Summit, before reversing their route of ascent. They set off back down to Base Camp, but on their way came across Mo, Clive, Tut and me at the West Col. We were in the process of making an attempt on the West Ridge which started with a 1000-foot rock pillar. This rekindled Chris's ambition for the top, and he persuaded us to return to Base to give him a rest and also to collect more food.

A few days later, on 6 July, Mo, Clive and I returned to the col and went up to a smaller shoulder, about 1000 feet higher and just under the 1000-foot pillar, where we made a camp. Tut and Nick (unknown to us at the time) had decided not to rejoin the attempt, as Tut's leg seemed to be getting worse and Nick had still not recovered from his attempt with Chris. Chris therefore started out alone, knowing we would be waiting below the pillar. As we put the tents up at Camp 2 on the top shoulder I would have given anything to have been at home. Half an hour later, inside my tent supping hot tea, I looked out of the entrance as the sun set and decided that there was nowhere else I'd rather be but up there at 22,000 feet, watching that sun dipping down, silver lining strands of cloud strung out over Snow Lake and the Hispar Glacier beyond. Range after range of bristling mountain peaks stood out silhouetted against each other, the nearer ranges sharply and darkly defined, while those in the distance faded into the sun's diffused haze of yellow light. Above them all, some 150 miles away, Nanga Parbat caught the last of the sun, whilst everywhere else was plunged into gloom. We zipped up the tent against a strong wind and snuggled content into our feathers.

I thought of the morrow, when we three would at last get on to rock. I looked forward expectantly to covering what ground we could up the pillar, going along hopefully lapping up that granite rock, on the way to who knows where exactly.

During the next two days we got to work on the 1000-foot pillar. This provided some interesting climbing on both faces and in cracks, all carried out at a height of about 22,500 feet. We then descended to the tent to wait for Chris, having equipped the pillar with 450 foot of fixed rope. The four of us eventually took off on 11 July, reclimbing the 1000-foot pillar and continuing to about 23,000 feet, where we dug a snow cave just below the final rocks of the West Summit. During the next day, Mo and Clive took over the lead and went across some very steep ice (65°), made all the more difficult by a thin coating of powder snow. They then continued up to the West Summit Ridge, via a steep couloir. After a stop for a brew, we slowly climbed the ridge and traversed over the summit. We brought the day to a close by digging a big snow cave just below the long ridge connecting the West Summit with the Main Summit. The snow was thick here, but it was lying at about 50°–55° on ice, giving grounds for concern. Even when we had dug right into it, the thought crossed our minds that the whole South-East Face could easily avalanche and take our snow cave with it. We did dig a bit deeper and a position at the back of the cave was more often sought after than one at the front, but our main hope lay in the face not avalanching, which it didn't until we were off the mountain.

That night, within sight of the summit rocks, we cooked up a big meal of freeze-dried Strogonoff, rounded off with apple flakes and endless cups of tea. The cave was sealed off against spindrift and, despite the 23,000 feet altitude, we slept well. Chris and I set off next morning to break trail to the foot of the rocks. Mo and Clive were to follow later, as Mo wanted to take some ciné film for a BBC documentary he was making of the expedition's ups and downs. When Mo and Clive came up later, they were to be disappointed. Clive recalls, "When we reached the small col 300 feet below the summit it was obvious that we couldn't possibly reach the top that day as Doug and Chris were taking a long time on the final tower. At 3.00 pm we set off back to the snow cave, hoping to try for the top the next day, but fate had other things in store for us . . ."

Chris was feeling the effects of his previous attempt. He was moving well enough, but suggested that I led the rocks ahead, as I should be faster, being fitter. I greedily accepted and soon "lost" myself climbing two 150-foot pitches up a pinnacle and down its far side to a snow patch on the north side of the summit rocks. From the snow we followed a diagonal break right up to a seemingly blank wall. This turned out to be the crux of the climb, for a crack I eventually found and followed for eighty feet suddenly ended. From a wire chock wedged into the crack, I got Chris to lower me some forty feet so that I could make a pendulum swing across the granite wall. I swung first to one side then to the other, gradually increasing the arc by a sort of gallop against the rock, until I could reach over to another crack which looked climbable. I was just placing a chock when my feet slipped off and away I clattered across the rock. Chris continued to hold his end of the rope firm and, after another session of galloping about, I regained the crack, banged a piton into it, clipped my étrier to that and stood up from the peg, gasping for air after these exertions at nearly 24,000 feet. Chris let out the tension in the rope and by leap-frogging the aid up the crack, I was able to reach a point higher than before. Here the wall relented and I was able to free climb to a point fifteen feet above the pendulum swing, to where a crack went through an overhang to the top of the wall. I climbed this using direct aid from chocks and the odd piton and, just as the 150-foot length of rope adjoining us together had all been run out, I arrived at the top of the wall. Chris then jumared up the rope to join me, and from there we traversed down seventy feet and climbed an overhanging corner into the summit gully.

This final 100 feet took up the last hour of the day, for when Chris had arrived on the top of the Ogre the sun had gone down over the Hunza. As he had my camera, I had been able to sit on the top and take in the new perspective of Snow Lake and the hundreds of snowy peaks stretching off in all directions, without, for once, having to fiddle with camera stops and speeds.

Not having any bivouac equipment, Chris and I were very anxious to get down to the snow cave. However, it had been a good climb, at least above the fixed rope. There had been so much variation – a veritable magical mystery tour of a route, taking in steep rock and ice, a climb over the West Summit and then a traverse across and up to the Main Summit.

We worked our way down a ridge of soft snow to a block of rock. We put a nylon sling round it, threaded our two climbing ropes behind that, and threw both down in the direction of the 150-foot wall. To regain the peg crack, I had to push myself well over to the left as I abseiled, but eventually I got to the crack, just as I was reaching the end of the double rope. I leaned across to fix myself on to a peg, pressing myself over with my feet. I stepped my right foot up against the wall but, in the gathering darkness, unwittingly placed it on a veneer of water ice. Suddenly my foot shot off and I found myself swinging away into the gloom, clutching the end of the rope. Mo saw the fall from below and they then knew that there would be no summit for them the next day.

I couldn't imagine why the swing was going on and on. I had not realised how far left of the abseil sling I was. And all the time I was swinging, a little exclamation of awe, surprise and fear was coming out from inside me, audible to Mo some 2,000 feet away at the snow cave. And then the swing and the cry ended as I slammed into the opposite side of the gully, 100 feet away. Splat! Glasses gone and every bone shaken.

A quick examination revealed head and trunk O.K., femurs and knees OK, but – Oh! Oh! – ankles cracked whenever I moved them. The right one felt very peculiar: Pott's fracture, I diagnosed, without much real idea – left one, too, but perhaps it's just the tendons. So that was how it was going to be: a whole new game with new restrictions on winning – it was curious to observe my own reactions. I had no fear then, there was too much to do. I banged a peg in, put a couple of wire nuts in, tied off direct from my harness and hung off them while Chris came down the abseil rope.

"What ho!" he said, cheerily.

"I've broken my right leg and smashed the left ankle," I said.

"We'll just work at getting you down," he replied, airily. "Don't worry, you're a long way from death."

Too true! – the thought that I might have major problems of that kind had not then entered my head. I felt extremely rational, remarkably clear about what to do.

We continued our descent as far as we could that night. Chris abseiled down to a large patch of snow on a rock slab. By the time I reached him, he'd hacked a step out in the snow and, for the first time, I put my body weight on my legs and ankles. They both collapsed, the right leg cracking horribly. So I got on my knees, with my lower legs stuck out behind, and kneed across the ledge with no trouble at all.

"So that's how it's done," I thought. And that's how it was done over the next seven days, with a little help from my friends – Chris, Clive and Mo.

Chris and I hacked away at the snow patch, producing a passable ledge on which we could lounge back in a half-lying, half-sitting position. Most of the time we sat facing each other with our bare feet stuck into each other's crutch. Every half hour or so we would reach down and rub a bit of life into each other's feet, a lesson learnt whilst bivouacking on Everest two years before.

Mainly I cursed the night away, moaning and groaning at the cold, wishing I'd brought a sleeping bag and a duvet, afraid that internal bleeding might cut off the blood going to my toes. That thought kept me grabbing at Chris's toes which I would rub furiously, hoping that he would take the hint and rub mine, which he did with gentle pressure. The night passed in these little flurries of action. At 5.30 next morning we abseiled four more rope lengths down to the snow basin of the South-East Face.

Mo and Clive didn't keep office hours either. As Clive noted: "Mo and I went off at first light and passed Chris on the snow slope. Mo went to Doug who was behind and I stopped about two or three hundred feet short of him and hacked out a platform so that I could make him a brew. The rest of that day was spent in returning to the snow cave."

We spent that night in the snow cave and ate the last freeze-dried meal, leaving ourselves with only soup and tea. It was with some concern, therefore, that we found a howling blizzard raging outside the snow cave the next morning. We had to get down to Advance Base to get food and even lower to escape the debilitating effect of the lack of oxygen. But first we had to climb up 300 feet to gain the West Summit. Clive tried first, but after climbing for three quarters of an hour he had only gained eighty feet and packed it in as his goggles, eyelashes and everything else froze up. Mo tried next and returned in ten minutes. As Clive wrily pointed out, "Mo isn't as daft as I am." There was so much snow in the air it had become impossible to see, and the wind made it difficult to stand up, let alone climb steep snow.

The next day, 16 July, there was less wind and we all set off out into the heavy snowfall. Clive took the lead, slowly kicking his way up desperately deep powder snow, angled in places at 60°. Mo went next up Clive's rope, then I, then Chris. It took Clive three hours to climb 400 feet to the West Summit and seven hours for all of us to reach there. Mo then took over the lead, rigging all the abseils, as well as two horizontal sections where I was hauled over on ropes. Clive took up the rear. We eventually reached the snow cave where we had spent the night of the 11th. The weather was terrible – cold and violent. We had to dig out snow that had drifted into the cave, but as it was dark when we arrived no one felt like waiting around in the storm whilst the digging took place. So we ended up with cramped quarters and an inadequate entrance. Mo and Clive already had damp sleeping bags, and these became quite wet during the night with snow drifting in on to them. It was the worst night of all: no food, wet, still above 23,000 feet and me slowing them all down with the 1,000-foot pillar still to come. There was only one way for me to tackle a big, complex problem like that, and that was one day at a time, keeping the broad idea hovering around in my mind that I'd got to get to Base Camp, but each day thinking no further than that day's objective, confident that if each day's climbing was competently executed then the whole problem would eventually be solved.

Next morning, Mo stuck his head out of the cave and announced that the storm was now, if anything, worse. He went off, followed by Clive, then me, then Chris – all of us bent on reaching the tents, for there we had left a pound of sugar, which was something we had not had for two days. That seemed to be a number one priority. But also there was no real resting place between the snow cave and the tents – so we had to make it. It was a nightmare descent. Whenever there was a ridge of level ground, I found crawling painful, seeming always to be catching my legs on protruding rocks. Only on steep, snowed-up rocks did I feel comfortable, for then Mo would have fixed up the abseil ropes and I could slide down with my body making contact with the snow and rock, whilst my feet stuck out, out of the way of obstacles. Clive stayed right by me during the descent, making certain I was belayed, hacking out the occasional steps for my knees and checking my maudlin tendencies. I was apt to moan a lot and lose my temper with myself at which point Clive would come in with "You're always moaning!" and "Who needs legs?" and other punny remarks which brought me out of myself. In this fashion we started to descend the 1,000-foot pillar.

Unfortunately, on the way down, Chris abseiled off the end of one of the double ropes. Luckily, Clive had tied the other off to a rock, so Chris fell only about twenty feet or so, but he still broke two ribs and painfully damaged his right hand. Cold and getting colder, he had no alternative but to continue the descent. Mercifully, he did not at once start to experience the pain in his thorax that was to dog him later. It was a sorry little band that made the tents. Mo was the first and he had to re-erect them, as they were both flattened under three feet of snow.

The rest of us were happy to crawl straight in out of the tearing wind and into our sleeping bags. For me, it was a long and painful process removing gaiters, boots, inner boots and socks. But it had to be done so that I could rub my frozen toes back to life, for circulation was somewhat restricted by having my legs permanently bent at the knee. More serious, though, were my frozen finger ends. Crawling about so much I had no opportunity to keep my gloves dry, and not much time to stop and warm my hands when they started to lose sensation. I hoped that things would improve now that we were losing height, and we all kept thinking that the storm could not go on for many more days.

Mo came into the same tent as Clive and me, to warm up, as his sleeping bag was now reduced to a useless clump of wet, soggy feathers. We played cards, hoping the storm would finally blow itself out during the morning, so that we could move the tents down to the West Col later in the day. Chris was now in a bad way – coughing, his throat hoarse, his voice down to a whisper, and every cough increasing the pain under his ribs. He burst into our tent during the morning, announcing that he really must go down as he thought that he had pulmonary oedema. We discussed this with him, but he did not seem to have any of the gurgling noises one hears about. It was probable that he had mild pneumonia which wouldn't have been helped by spending the day out in the swirling spindrift. Neither did the three of us fancy the sub-zero temperature and harsh wind, for Mo announced that he had not felt his toes for nearly a week and Clive's digits were also numb. Despite it being our fourth day without food, we decided to give it one more day. At least now we had enough sugar for the next dozen brews of tea. We had been taking tea without milk or sugar for breakfast and half a curried meat stock cube for dinner, and we were lacking in energy, but now noticed a slight change for the better with the sugar.

It was still blowing hard the next morning as we roped down to the South-West Col. By now I had become quite expert at knee-climbing. I found that being on my hands and knees was actually an advantage in particularly deep snow, and I did a bit of trail-breaking. Mo unearthed some old Japanese ropes, and we slid down the first 500 feet to the West Col. We went across to our former camp site and dug around until we uncovered a waste bag, in the bottom of which was some boiled rice mixed with cigarette ash, which we ate. We rummaged around some more and found an ounce of milk powder and, in another bag, three packets of fruit sweets and two packets of cough sweets. We shared them out when Clive and Chris arrived.

We moved off to the top of the fixed ropes that would take us to Advance Base the following day. I carried Clive's sack as he had to go and recover a tent that had fallen off his sack higher up. There was now about a mile to go across soft snow, but at last the clouds were rolling back to reveal the mountains all around covered in fresh, sparkling snow down to the glaciers. My arms kept sinking deep into the snow with the weight of Clive's sack pressing down over my neck. Despite following Mo's footsteps, I took many rests, flopping down flat out in the snow. Expeditions are usually good times to sort out a few things in the head – times to drop down a level or two – but it occurred to me then that since my accident I had brought such an iron will to bear on every moment of the day that I had not given such matters a thought. But there had been some compensations, for whenever I shut my eyes I went off into a hallucinatory world of lilac and purple colouring, incredible shapes and forms, caricature people and stylised views of distant times and places. It did not make a lot of sense, but it was one way to while away a few minutes and recover enough to take a further twenty or so crawling paces through the snow.

Mo and I dug out tent platforms, put up one of the tents and then the other when Clive arrived with it. Chris came in very slowly, coughing up a rich yellow fluid from his lungs.

Chris and Mo set off at first light for Advance Base. Clive and I followed four hours later, for by then the sun would be up to warm our frost-bitten hands and feet. Also, Chris and Mo would have had time to cut out big steps at various key places.

Abseiling down fixed ropes was no real problem for me, so I was able to descend 2,500 feet in four hours. Crawling over soft snow down to 17,000 feet was also relatively easy, but after that the snow became thin, and I had to crawl over hard, sharp glacier ice.

We arrived at last to find that Advance Base was no more – either blown away or taken away by Nick and Tut – so there was nothing for it but to follow Mo and Chris down to Base Camp. Clive gave me his down trousers and over trousers, but I went through these after another mile. The next section was the most painful of the whole retreat. The distance was about four and a half miles from the end of the fixed ropes. About one mile was on soft snow, two and a half on ice and one on moraine. Clive was worried.

Just before dark it was evident no one was coming to help us. We didn't want to bivvy on the ice again, so I rushed off to Base Camp to get a torch and some food. I found Chris asleep under a boulder. He told me that Mo had gone off in hot pursuit of Nick who had that same morning given us up for dead.

Nick had left us a note which said: "If you get as far as reading this, then it presumably means that at least one of you is alive", and added that he was going down to fetch Tut from Askole and form a search party. There was no torch in camp so I got Chris to lie in his pit on top of the moraine ridge above Base with a gas stove burning to light the way for us off the glacier. I then grabbed some food and set off back up the glacier to find Doug. It was pitch dark, but after about an hour we found each other by shouting and whistling. After eating the food it took Doug about three hours to crawl the rest of the way, all the time the little beacon getting closer and closer.

At 10.30 that night (20 June), I crawled over the last of the moraine rocks. My legs were very swollen from knocking them countless times. I stopped to examine them and was horrified to find that I had worn right through four layers of clothing and that my knees were numb, bloody and swollen.

One last bank and I was on the triangle of moraine that surrounded the thick green grass of Base Camp – a little oasis amongst the chaos of shifting rock and ice. I crawled to the old kitchen site. I thought when I saw the meagre supplies that had been left that the others must have really thought we were dead. However, it was good to eat Purdy Cake with a cup of milky tea and then to fall asleep on that little meadow.

Next morning the sun shone on to our wet sleeping bags – you could feel the warmth come right through into the murky interior. Pulling open the draw-cord from inside, putting my head out to see the grass, the flowers and the stream running across, then getting out, brewing a mug of tea, eating a powdered egg omelette and feeling the sun burning my skin: beautiful memories these.

For four days Clive looked after Chris and me, and still there was no sign of the porters that Mo should have sent. On the fifth day, however, when we were down to soup and Tom and Jerry nougat bars, Nick arrived with twelve porters to carry me down, together with the remnants of our gear. Mo, in the meantime, had gone off with Tut and our Liaison Officer, Captain Aleem, to Skardu, in order to dispatch a helicopter for arrival outside Askole on 28 July.

When Mo arrived in Askole, Tut had already been there a week and had made good friends with the headman and many of the villagers. As each day passed it had seemed to Tut and to the Baltis that our chances of being alive were growing increasingly slim, especially when Nick arrived alone. Thus, when Mo walked in, they were all overjoyed to discover that we were safe, if not exactly one hundred per cent. The headman sent off to other villagers to ensure that we had twelve strong and able porters. And that was exactly what we got.

In three days they carried me down to the Biafo Glacier and then along to its snout and on to a flat field near Askole, where a helicopter could land. It was a remarkable journey on a homemade stretcher constructed of juniper wood poles, a climbing rope and sleeping mats. Never once did they look like dropping me, and I seldom felt a jolt. It was good to lie out, listening and waiting as they made decisions as to route finding, choice of camping place, who should fetch wood and water, who should take the heavier part of the stretcher, and so on. They inevitably made the decision after a gentle murmur had gone round the motley band – no one ever shouted or became excited. Their voices blended into a sing-song melody which seemed completely in tune with the rhythm of their village lives. They knew just what to do. And I for one have nothing but admiration for these hardy people, who are all very individualistic and full of character, yet are easily capable of working to a common aim in complete accord. That is how good expeditions can work.

It was sad to be suddenly plucked away from them by the noisy helicopter. Unlike Taki with his eggs and the eight stretcher-bearers with me, the helicopter was not so gentle: coming into Skardu the engine cut out, and we suddenly plummeted twenty feet to the ground some hundred yards short of the helipad. As a result Chris had to wait for a week in Askole while the helicopter was repaired, but eventually he, too, was flown out to Skardu.

Three days later, after fine hospitality at the British Embassy and a first-class flight home, courtesy of Pakistani International Airlines, I was being plastered and pinned in Nottingham General Hospital.

After the expedition, when I heard of Doug's crawl back to civilisation, I sent a note to him at the Nottingham General Hospital: "Take care, youth, there's not many of us left."

The Rock Wizards of Oz

Alan Sheehan

The motto of the Australian rescue service should be "No Worries" for they are an efficient and compassionate bunch of lads – and sheilas. Many climbers assume that this flatland continent has little to offer the mountaineer. They may be right in respect to major ice routes and high-altitude problems, but Australia does have mountains, snow (at least for skiing) and rock climbing, with an abundance of canyons which have catapulted the sport of canyoning into the top league.

Wherever nature provides the raw material for adrenalin release, you inevitably get the associated problems that go with climbing and, in canyoning, the added ingredient of hypothermia (yes, in Australia!) and navigational embarrassment through these rocky labyrinths, in other words getting lost! So it's refreshing, and comforting, to note that the diverse rescue groups that operate in Australia work so closely and efficiently together for the welfare of the injured bushwalker, rock climber and canyoner.

Alan Sheehan, who is a rescuer and Senior Vertical Rescue Trainer in Oberon, NSW, is also an engineer. The partnership of rapidly assessing and then implementing the mechanics of a difficult technical rescue is an essential qualification for today's rescuer. Alan describes some incidents on his patch.

Within two to three hours' drive from Australia's largest city, Sydney, lies the Kanangra Boyd Wilderness Area. With abundant rugged beauty, solitude, and its close proximity to the city, Kanangra's the place for outdoor adventure activities. With this popularity comes an increase in searches and rescues. Australia's not synonymous with large precipitous mountains, but the area around Kanangra is nevertheless challenging. A challenge some find irresistible, but can't always handle.

Kanangra Walls are the primary feature of the Kanangra Boyd National Park. The tops of these and the Boyd Plateau sit between 1,000–1,200 metres above sea level with peaks throughout the park and the adjacent Great Dividing Range reaching over 1,300 metres. Certainly not large mountains by international standards, but not trivial in terms of ruggedness – to coin a phrase there are "more acres per square mile" in Kanangra than most places. The Boyd Plateau to the west is predominantly hard granite, while the Kanangra Walls area to the east is softer sandstone, leading to the development of large canyons between 500–1,000 metres deep.

The Kanangra Canyons are predominantly open canyons with big faces and pitches and spectacular views, confined generally. Not much wonder why it's such a popular area for canyoners (enthusiasts who descend canyons). The canyons of the nearby Blue Mountains are different again – narrow, tight and generally confined.

The rock at Kanangra is not well suited to climbing. It's poor and very variable in strength with unreliable holds; most slopes are steep and loose. Few climbers play in Kanangra when the reliable rock of the Blue Mountains is next door. Climatic conditions vary from typical sub-alpine at the top, with the usual changeable weather, to rainforest conditions in the deeper canyons. Several limestone lenses throughout result in a profusion of wilderness and show caves – the most famous are the Jenolan Caves.

While police retain the combat role for Land Searches and Rescue in Australia, the State Emergency Service (SES) often provides the skilled volunteer manpower for many of the search teams. In the case of Kanangra, the nearest contact for know-how and assistance is the Oberon Unit of the New South Wales State Emergency Service. In Oberon's case, knowledge of the area also means Oberon State Emergency Service is an important source of search intelligence for the police.

SES is a voluntary organisation. Every state and territory in Australia has a State or Territory Emergency Service. New South Wales has over 6,000 volunteers across the state. For example, Oberon also takes part in general rescue, road crashes, land, and in some cases vertical rescue. This unit is small, about a dozen keen volunteers, and about the same number we can call in when "it" starts getting too close to the fan. Most of the volunteer members are or were avid bushwalkers, climbers, canyoners and cavers who know the Kanangra area intimately like their own back yard.

Land searches are the most common rescue with an average of twelve to fifteen a year, many for overdue bushwalkers and canyoners in the Kanangra Boyd Wilderness Area. Others can develop into full wilderness or vertical rescues. The most popular canyons in Kanangra can be done in a day, but there's many that require two or more days and some involve a couple of days' hike before the canyon is even started! Not surprisingly, helicopters get used whenever possible and, as one would expect, most real ground-based call-outs occur in bad weather.

Over the years Kanangra has taken its toll. Most of these unfortunates underestimate the terrain or the weather, or suffer an illness or injury. Navigation error is the next most common factor resulting in search and rescue calls, followed by separation of members from the group. Around five to ten per cent of rescues are for people who have done everything right, but a minor incident has caught them out. Like Roy, a bushwalker who fell on a sloping part of the track below Smith's Pass at the eastern end of Kanangra Walls. Leaf litter on the track caused him to slip, the result, a fractured ankle. Oberon SES and Oberon ambulance officers responded, applied first aid and arranged a helicopter to evacuate Roy to a hospital in Sydney – the heath on Kanangra Tops was too thick to reasonably consider a stretcher carry unless it was absolutely necessary.

There are many stories of misadventure associated with Kanangra. In recent times a bushwalker died, apparently in his sleep, while camping at Dex Creek on Mount Cloudmaker. Kanangra Canyon itself has been responsible for two lives lost, both the result of falls. Kalang Falls, Kanangra's most popular canyon, recently claimed a life, also a fall. On Margaret Falls, Christy's Creek also claimed the life of a girl stuck mid-rope attempting to pass a knot through her figure eight descender on a 138-metre abseil in the early eighties. In recent times two experienced leaders from a mountaineering club died on a rope in remote Carra Beanga Canyon. There have also been several air crashes in the area. Two young men died 2.5 kilometres from their crashed aircraft in 1993 – they survived the crash, but for how long was open to conjecture and the coroner made an open finding. It wasn't until twenty-one days after the crash that their plane was found by a bushwalker, despite an intensive air search. Such is the rugged nature of Kanangra within a few hours' drive or a twenty-minute flight of Sydney.

Sometimes in a place like Kanangra seemingly insignificant events can result in disaster. The following is an account of a for real rescue that interrupted a cave rescue exercise.

On 19 April 1997 Oberon State Emergency Service's annual cave rescue exercise was in full swing when the call came in: "an authentic vertical rescue on Kalang Falls – a fallen abseiler on the fourth pitch. How soon can you respond?"

Kalang Falls is the most popular canyon in Kanangra Boyd National Park. They descend a total of 500 metres into Kanangra Deep, in eight or more abseil pitches. The canyon is open, typically steep loose sandstone. Key members were called out of the cave and the exercise aborted. Gear was collected while they all made their ways out of the cave, among them Mark Windsor, Bathurst City SES, and Matthew McMahon, Oberon SES, both vertical rescue instructors and very experienced in Kalang. Between Mark and myself we had enough gear to access the casualty and start the rescue. Matt would wait for David King, senior vertical rescue instructor from Hawkesbury SES, to get out, then they would follow to complete the hasty team. The rest of Oberon's crew would follow once the gear was packed up and, if necessary, the rest of the participants in the cave rescue exercise would be called.

Mark and I arrived at Kanangra Walls just as the Westpac rescue helicopter was landing and preparing to do the job. We donned wetsuits and prepared for a night rescue in the event that the chopper couldn't finish the job. The helicopter located the injured man and dropped in their medical crew and two SCAT (Special Casualty Access Team). They also lifted out the injured man's companion who had been with him all day. Matt and David arrived. While the medical crew stabilised the injured man, the chopper left for refuelling. Meanwhile the rest of Oberon SES's crew arrived and others manned a radio relay at Gillespie's Lookout to call the remainder of the rescuers from the camp at Dingo Dell if required.

The Westpac rescue helicopter returned after dark. From Echo Head, we watched it disappear between trees and rock walls 200 metres below. It returned to Kanangra Walls with the injured man, who was transferred to an ambulance while the chopper went back to get the rest of its crew. The pilot made several attempts at retrieving them but was forced to abort – the hazy mist had developed to the point where there was not sufficient visibility. The crew had to spend the night in the canyon. The chopper then flew the injured man to hospital in Sydney, and returned in the morning to pick up their crew.

Apparently the injured man stumbled and fell on steep ground approaching a small waterfall (known to us as the Little Tree Climb) below the fourth pitch at about 10.45 am. It took several hours for two men from his party to complete the canyon and raise the alarm, but the casualty died with severe head injuries. He was not wearing a rock hat. Apparently there had been a mix up with rock hats and he had declined offers to go back to camp for another one.

Sometimes things happen which are nobody's fault, an attack of appendicitis, or a conspiracy of nature that can confound the most experienced. The following is an account of a big wall vertical rescue from the main face of Kanangra Walls – the result of a day which should have been routine for the people being rescued, but Kanangra wanted to play . . .

It was 9.30 pm on a Sunday night, 26 September 1999 and the crew was standing by at the headquarters waiting to commence a search for a despondent elderly woman who had just viewed the body of her son that day. She had previously lost her husband and her son had taken his own life just a few days previous. The phone rang. "She's turned up! Cool! We can go home." Or so they thought. The sergeant said, "Now that I've got you here, we can look at this other one."

It was an overdue canyon party, three males in their twenties, super fit and experienced. In fact, they were all abseil instructors at the Australian Defense Force Academy, one each from the Army, Navy and Air Force. We discovered that the informant wasn't directly in contact with them, so the answers to a lot of our questions were a bit rubbery.

It transpired that they were doing a reconnaissance trip down what they called Kalang Main Falls canyon. To us this could be either Kanangra Main or Kalang Falls. There are real differences in equipment, lengths of rope, time and skill required to negotiate these two specific canyons. Kalang's very popular; descending some 500 metres with between eight and thirteen abseils, depending on the mix of abseiling and scrambling you want to do. It can be done dry or wet comfortably in a day. Kanangra on the other hand also descends about 500 metres but in bigger pitches. It starts with the main waterfall, a 186-metre drop, usually done in two or more pitches ledge to ledge. All the pitches are over fifty metres in height. Kanangra can also only be done wet and it's a really big day.

The more we dug for information, the more we realised we needed hard information from someone who knew the facts.

The weather was, of course, lousy! Overcast, rainy, no chance of using choppers with the bad forecast. We planned to send the crews home to prepare for an early start in the morning. Meanwhile, a team of four of us drove to Kanangra Walls car park to gather some better intelligence. Myself, Matthew McMahon, vertical rescue instructor, and two vertical rescue operators, Jim Young and Craig Gibbons, comprised the team.

Our trip to the walls was delayed by increasingly heavy rain and fog as we moved east from the Great Dividing Range. Classic easterly weather! We met three personnel from the ADFA at Kanangra, including the CO of the overdue canyoners. They were co-operative, giving straight answers. "They're doing Kalang Falls; one of them has done the canyon before." We gathered that they were well equipped and capable. Their protocol was that if one got injured, they would stay together as a group. We suspected the problem was with the weather. It was apparently fine early that day, and the change hit sometime in the afternoon. Either the wet conditions had slowed them significantly, or caused an injury, or they were unable to navigate properly due to reduced visibility. We also discovered that one of them was prone to hypothermia.

We scouted from the tops to get a better idea of the weather situation. Visibility in the rain and fog was down to ten metres, even with pit lamps and a 1.5 million candlepower portable searchlight – the beams got defused. There was so much water going down the falls that it was clearly impossible to make voice or whistle contact with anyone below, but we tried anyway. Then we tried at a spot which normally allows a view into nearly every pitch of the canyon, and afterwards moved round to Seymour Tops to cover the possibility that they'd gone astray on the way out. There was no response.

Given the new information we decided to bring forward our start time. Rendezvous at HQ at 5.00 am, at Kanangra by 6.30 am. We got home at around 2.00 am and packed food and did a final "check and sort" on our kits, and decided to place Hawkesbury State Emergency Service Vertical Rescue Crew on standby.

We arrived at Kanangra Walls shortly before 6.30 am. There was no sign of them walking out during the night. No improvement in the weather either. While Matthew McMahon and his team of Peter Howard, Craig Gibbons and Chad Sheppard prepared to enter the canyon, Jim Young, Dave Walther and I did another quick search from Echo Head. We called and listened . . . no response. Once again, this time with three blasts on a Fox 40 whistle. Bingo, we got three blasts back – and not from a Fox 40, so it wasn't an echo! They were apparently in Murdering Gully, the exit route from the canyon. This gully climbs some 500 metres in 500 metres. There's a maze of tracks in this place, mostly on the east side – not all of them make it out!

Dave and Jim and I started down into Murdering Gully, from time to time calling and listening. Meanwhile the canyon crew was ready to go to Echo Head to assist with calling/ listening and communications. As we descended, calling, echoes played games with our calls, then, about halfway down (about 300 metres change in altitude), we got replies, free of echoes. They were above to the east, in the cliff ledges.

We redirected the canyon crew to follow the base of Kanangra Walls east, and dispatch a team from Bathurst City State Emergency Service across the top of the walls to locate the overdue party from there. Meanwhile we started the climb.

The slopes below the main face of Kanangra Walls are steep, loose and heavily vegetated. As well as climbing we also had to traverse eastwards. The surface here is a mix of loose soil – sometimes mud, scree, small cliff steps and obnoxious but friendly vegetation – typically lomandra (cutty grass), hawthorn bush and wait-a-while vines under a broken canopy of trees.

By 10.00 am we knew where they were within 100 metres. My team and Matt's canyon crew met up about 50–100 metres below them. The Bathurst Group were directly above the missing party and were able to communicate with them after a fashion. They estimated that they were about fifty metres below them. We knew, however, that there was nowhere on this face where main wall, above the cliff steps, was as little as fifty metres. We gathered that the party were uninjured but suffering from hypothermia. The fog ruled out visual contact. After several attempts to get them to descend, it became apparent they weren't going to move. They *knew* they had hypothermia, they also *knew* they were uncoordinated as a result and were not prepared to risk a mistake under the circumstances. A fair enough call, we considered.

We decided to access them from the top. The difficulty of the climb and the subsequent evacuation from that point was not the best option if they didn't feel confident enough to abseil to us anyway. Without knowing how far down from the top they really were, we immediately called for Hawkesbury to roll, to back us up. If we required to set up another vertical rescue system down the face, we'd need them to drive the system at the top. While we navigated out of Murdering Gully, Army cadets, who had been on exercise in the area associated with the overdue instructors, began carrying our rescue gear in to the location.

On the walk in the Commanding Officer was telling one of the Oberon crew about how fit and capable his blokes were, but that they didn't know the area. "Just the opposite of our guys!" was the tongue in cheek reply!

Once above, we spent some time trying to determine where exactly the cragfast party was located. If we picked the wrong spot to commence operations, we might not be in line with the right ledge. With good fortune we had a small break in the fog and were able to get a brief glimpse of where they were. It looked as if they were on the second ledge down. This part of the Walls is renowned for a lack of suitable anchors on the top of the plateau. Recreationally it is not uncommon to use small heath bushes as anchors, but for a rescue we require something beefier. A large natural rock bollard suited our needs, situated about fifty metres back from the edge, and a couple of smaller rock formations closer to the edge would form the basis of our anchor system.

Normally we would dispatch a first responder to access the casualties by abseiling. With some doubt as to whether a 200-metre rope would reach, we opted to rig a full V3 system. This was made up of a load line rigged through a rescue descender for lowering, a removable haul system, and a reversible safety to allow the load line to be held while the haul system was reset. With this set-up we could lower a rescuer, rather than have him abseiling on a rope which might possibly be too short or directionally misplaced. Abseiling could also mean a lengthy prusik back up. The extra time in rigging would make it far easier to handle any error of height or position. Another factor that we kept in mind when making this decision was that of suspension syndrome. Prusikers are at risk most of suspension syndrome when performing long or difficult ascents when stressed, fatigued, hypothermic, dehydrated, etc. Given our subjects were too hypothermic to risk a descent, we didn't want them perhaps considering a prusik out as a way to save face and build their body heat.

The loadline was 200 metres of 11-mm kernmantle. Edge management was provided by a Larkin rescue frame. This would cut down on friction over the edges and give more control. The power was eight Army cadets. Craig Gibbons was lowered 120 metres to the party below, fifty metres of this was overhanging. Matthew McMahon was edge manager, I was team leader. The ledge between ourselves and the overdue party was not a ledge at all, just a steep sloping band of rock face. As a result we were able to raise the first two men solo, returning the rope to the bottom each time using a spare rope pack on the end for weight.

Around 1.00 pm Hawkesbury rescue crew arrived, just in time to see the successful rescue of the first of the overdue canyoners, and assist with the remaining rescues and derigging. By 2.00 pm, all of them were on top of the walls and the system was derigged. They were checked out by ambulance officers but suffered no injuries apart from hypothermia and embarrassment at being rescued.

Talking with them later, we found that the weather had closed in severely about 3.00 pm on Sunday afternoon. With poor visibility they had relied on the canyon guide book which advises to bear left when the gully gets too steep. This and the omission of any mention of the side gullies feeding Murdering Gully (which, though normally dry, were now running due to heavy rain), and the lack of visibility to allow for any checking and correction, resulted in them going approximately 800 metres east. It's not uncommon for parties negotiating Murdering Gully to do this, finding themselves in the rock steps at the base of the main face of Kanangra Walls. This is indeed the cause of the plethora of tracks leading to nowhere, which results in further confusion.

Twice the canyoners realised they had made navigational errors and descended to attempt a correction. Finally, with their determination to get out and not be the subject of a search and rescue, they pushed hard up into the rock steps below Kanangra Walls before spending the night camped in a small overhang on the face of the main Wall. Most of the climbs up the rock steps were free climbed by the Army instructor, who then belayed his companions as they ascended, several of these pitches being completed in the dark. Gutsy moves to no avail!

Kanangra may not be a Kilimanjaro or K2, but just a short drive from the city, it quietly challenges thousands of adventures of all walks of life and abilities each year. It's a place of rugged beauty. Awesome. Inspiring. Luring. Potentially treacherous to the ill-prepared, and sometimes to the well prepared! A place that demands respect. Kanangra is the type of place where almost anyone can push themselves to their limits, on a good day, and still be within 1.5 kilometres of the car if they want to! On a bad day? Well, when you're doing what you love, is there any better place to have a bad day?

Lucky Joe

Hamish MacInnes, Joe Simpson, Simon Yates

Joe Simpson fell the best part of 2,000 feet in the Alps in an avalanche on the North-East Face of Les Courtes. "I didn't have any helmet on. Only my legs were buried when I finally came to rest, and apart from a cut head and bruising, I was otherwise unhurt . . . I was bloody stupid and I deserved to die."

Joe Simpson had already had one dramatic demonstration that someone somewhere was keeping half an eye on him when climbing the Bonatti Pillar in 1984, and in 1985 he was to survive an even more spectacular climbing accident on the other side of the world on the West Face of Siula Grande in the Peruvian Andes.

But first the Bonatti Pillar.

Joe and his climbing partner, Ian Whittaker, had virtually finished the climb and managed to get to a bivouac ledge in gathering darkness and swirling cloud. Probing the corners of their lair for the night with the aid of their headlamps, they saw that it was in fact a huge pedestal which formed the right wall of a high-angled corner they had just ascended. Above the pedestal there was no continuing corner, only a vertical smooth wall. There was no way up there, so they counted themselves lucky that they had come across this providential ledge when they did.

Joe found an old piton above the ledge, which he decided to use for a belay, but this wasn't much good for protecting Ian, who was further along. Ian tied a belay rope to a rock flake which was close to him and passed the end to Joe who secured it to the peg. The rope now acted as a sort of handrail between the two of them. Joe also found an additional spike behind him and put a couple of slings over this to which he tied himself for added security, then he clipped on to the handrail and settled in for the night, the great void beneath them masked in the darkness. Joe had zizzed off when he heard Ian's voice.

"Do you think we're safe from rocks here? I was going to sleep without my helmet on."

"Safe as houses," Joe returned, for above them were great overhangs and any rocks falling would be well out from the face and their ledge. "But," he continued, hedging his bets, "I'll keep mine on just the same." In the light of his headlight Joe watched Ian take off his helmet and place it beside him, then clip himself on to the handrail in case he literally dozed off during the night.

As if on cue there was a frightening noise, a sort of groaning followed by a violent tug on both their safety ropes. They were falling, cocooned in their bivvy bags. Then they jerked to a halt on their handrail rope, both hanging like socks on a clothesline. The old peg and the rock spike had fortuitously held. The ledge, now disintegrated, crashed 2,000 vertical feet down the face to the couloir, then bounced another 1,000 feet to the glacier.

Presently in the anonymous darkness all was quiet. Joe wondered about his companion, he seemed to recall a cry. Had Ian plunged to his death? But Ian's reassuring Lancastrian accent floated out of the night. He was all right and needed a drink! He had a head injury and, hanging there, Joe examined his scalp by the light of his headlamp. It wasn't too serious. They were grateful to be alive. Had the ledge collapsed only five minutes before, when they weren't belayed, they would now be mutilated messes on the Dru Glacier.

Gradually they took stock of their position and found that they had lost all their gear, even their boots. Joe in fact still had one and he now disgustedly tossed this useless item in the wake of the rock fall. Ian had even lost one of his socks and had to utilise a woollen climbing mitt in lieu.

With the beam of Joe's headlamp they saw that their climbing rope, their lifeline, was shredded by the fallen rocks and hung uselessly down the corner below them. The two young men then examined their belays with some trepidation. They saw to their consternation that the spike which Joe had put the slings over as an added safety precaution had disappeared, though the karabiners were still clipped to his harness. The slings must have parted when the ledge went. Joe next examined the old ring peg to which they were attached at his end of the now V'd handrail. He observed that it had bent and then, pulling sideways on it to get a better look, he saw to his horror that it moved. On Ian's side the case was no better. The other handrail belay, the spike, had sheared off at the bottom with the ledge but somehow still held, even though they saw splinters of rock still falling out of the gap surrounding it.

The climbers were now in an unenviable position, unable to move, with a loose peg at one end of the rope and a shaky spike on the other. They had no gear left to help safeguard themselves and any violent movement could send them both crashing down the face. Even to climb up the rope would involve too much disturbance and anyhow they were still trapped in their bivvy bags.

Joe and Ian hung on their line for twelve hours, frightening themselves when they had to move to overcome cramps. They were both forced together at the bottom of the V in the rope. It was like Russian roulette where any movement could trigger off the vibration which would dislodge the peg or loosen the flake further.

They shouted throughout the night and signalled with their headlamp to the Charpoua hut, for it was in line of sight from where they were. In the cold light of dawn the frightening drop they could now see below worked overtime on the imagination. Salvation came in the form of an Alouette III helicopter. Their distress signals had been seen. It eased its way towards the face until it hovered like a giant humming-bird not fifty feet away. The two climbers pointed at their stockinged feet, then held their arms up in a "V" to indicate that they required help. Possibly the understatement of the year. The pilot took all this in and after giving a thumbs up he swung down towards Chamonix.

Members of the Chamonix rescue team were dropped by helicopter on a ledge above the pair and set up a hand winch. Some time later a guide came down on the steel winch wire to evacuate them. After they were both taken up to the ledge, the

Alouette came in and they were picked up on a helicopter winch and lifted up into the cabin.

Joe has since speculated on his rashness in throwing away his remaining boot, for he heard a few days later that a French climber had found a climbing boot in the couloir at the bottom of the Dru and it worried him to think that this may have been the other one of the pair.

The scene changes to the Peruvian Andes in 1985. Joe's companion is twenty-two-year-old Leicestershire-bred Simon Yates, then living in Sheffield. Their objective was one of the highest unclimbed mountain walls in Peru, the 6,360-metre (17,447-foot) West Face of Siula Grande. They set up their Base Camp at 4,500 metres at the top of the high Quebrada Sarapoquoucha, a superbly isolated place.

After one abortive attempt on the wall, driven back by bad weather, they set off again on Tuesday, 4 June. They were now on their own, in a remote spot and on a serious climb, their only contact with the outside world being non-climbing Richard Hawkins, down at Base Camp.

They climbed to the high point of their first attempt and found the equipment they had cached in a snow hole. The snow hole itself had been destroyed in an avalanche and Simon and Joe were lucky to recover their gear. In view of the avalanche danger at this spot, they dug out a safer snow cave to the south, which was also closer to the face.

The route began up an avalanche cone which was fortunately consolidated. The climbing proper then started with a bang. It was unrelentingly steep and an icefield which they ascended was a constant 80°. They slanted to the right as they climbed and the angle eased to about 65–70°, then got through a rock band via a steep twenty-metre cascade pitch of ice.

Difficulty after difficulty presented itself, often with avalanche risk. To the right a 300-metre yellow rock wall dropped to the base of the icefield. Their problem was to get across this wall by a ramp, access to which was blocked by séracs. It was dark by the time they got to a very steep fall of ice at the foot of a secondary ramp line.

But there were no bivvy sites, so Joe carried on up this. It started as overhanging honeycombed ice for about eight metres, and thereafter was hard ice leading up through a galaxy of large icicles. This pitch was vertical in places and exited in a frightening funnel pitch on to a snow gully. Simon came up then and led through. They were amazed to see on the left of the gully a twenty-metre-diameter "golf ball" of snow just stuck on to the face, apparently defying the force of gravity. Fate smiled on them now, for they found a huge natural cave inside.

In the morning the difficulties continued unrelenting. From the cave they traversed right and fought their way up another cascade of ice at a high angle. After a further pitch, they at last managed to get on to the main ramp, their key to the higher part of the route.

The ramp was in fact an enormous hanging gully with fortifications at each end in the form of séracs and cornices. Getting there had been desperate and by the looks of things getting out at the other end would be equally exacting. Now they did a rope length to the right, followed by 250 metres up the left side of the gully. This wasn't so steep, between 50° and 60°, by far the easiest climbing so far.

They stopped to take stock of this next problem: the exit from the gully ramp. There was a broken rock wall on the left with a nasty icefall running down parallel with the gully. This looked just possible if they avoided some large icicles on its left, but the snow and ice looked like unstable nougat.

It was Simon who started up this pitch, thrutching up the rotten snow which was plastered at a high angle, but he had to give up after fifteen metres and abseiled from an icicle – not the most reassuring anchor. He next moved left on to the rock face in the hope that this would get him high enough to make a traverse into the gully beyond the ice. He managed to insert a Friend, (a cam-type device which he used as a running belay) and was about three or four metres above it when both of his handholds came away and he peeled off the rock. It was his good Friend which possibly saved his life.

The two young men were now faced with the last option in this dicey trinity. They would have to climb the icicles direct. With care, Joe took the lead up the overhanging ice, and soon it eased to vertical, when he paused for an instant, hanging by the wrist loop of his ice axe. With his other hand he put in an ice peg called a Snarg. It was then a matter of smashing a mass of icicles to enable him to get over this crux. Whilst engaged in this risky occupation he cut his chin. He made a rush to climb the remainder of the steep section which was strenuous and hard. Beyond lay an eighty-metre ice funnel which led to a ridge, a ridge both sharp and airy.

Simon came up and Joe then led on, traversing once more to the right, looking for a way through to the top. It was hair-raising stuff, the basic material for future nightmares. He was back on rock now, it was loose as well as being covered with crappy snow. Tantalisingly, he could see the summit cornices less than 300 metres from him, but en route were ghastly steep powder snow-flutings, like a ploughed field, huge furrows tilted at a ridiculous angle. They found that once in a chosen channel it was almost impossible to change lanes. Just a hundred metres of this took all of five hours!

They felt like high-altitude navvies, forcing a trench up the trough in the flutings. Darkness overtook them and it was two tired, worried climbers who excavated a snow hole on the side of their chosen "flute". It had been a frustrating and dangerous section, possibly worse for the second man who could do nothing but sit on his insecure bucket seat excavated from the loose snow and be covered in a cascade of spindrift sent down by his partner, who struggled up to his armpits forging the deep trench.

They were forced to spend the night in their unstable snow hole, hoping that it wouldn't collapse beneath them: to go any higher that night would have been suicidal.

The next morning was 7 June. They were poised for the push to the summit which was only 150 metres away, but despite starting just after first light they didn't top the summit cornice until 2.00 pm, relieved to be off those horrible flutings.

They stayed on the top for half an hour, taking photographs. Then gathering clouds to the east told them that it was time to move. They studied their way down, by the North Ridge. As this route had been first climbed by a German party in 1936, Joe and Simon had assumed it would not present them with too many difficulties but, seeing it now, they knew better. It looked horrendous, sweeping away to bristling cornices overhanging the West Face.

They set off down but were soon enveloped in thick cloud.

Simon takes up the story:

Shortly after starting the descent we were engulfed in cloud and
snow, and lost contact with the ridge. At this point I became
completely disoriented and was trying to lead Joe in totally the
wrong direction. Fortunately Joe's argument to go the other
way prevailed and after a lot of nasty traversing through flutings
at the top of Siula Grande's East Face, we saw the ridge again
through a break in the cloud. I led up towards it and when I was
about thirty feet from the crest an ominous cracking sound
filled my ears. This was instantly followed by a falling sensation
and the thought that we were both going to die. After what
seemed to be a very long time the falling stopped and I was left
hanging upside down with an unnerving view of the West Face
beneath me. It didn't take long to realise that I'd stepped
through a huge cornice. I climbed back up and informed Joe
that I'd found the ridge! The event only served to emphasise the
dangerous and unstable nature of our chosen descent route.

The ridge continued to be an assortment of snow mush-
rooms, steep flutings and occasional crevasses. The stress involved in descending it was immense. The fear was suppressed
slightly by the concentration required for this technical down
climbing and it left me with an uneasy feeling. The day came to
an end with about a third of the ridge behind us. The wildest
bivouac on the route, a snow hole in a near vertical fluting, did
little to relieve my uneasiness.

Joe was in the front now, leading down the ridge, and he
describes what happened:

I had thought that the worst of the ridge had been completed
but soon found that this was not the case. It became very
tortuous with large powder cornices and steep knife-edged
ridges. It was not possible to keep below the line of cornices
owing to the fluted and unstable powder slopes on the east side.

We descended roped together fifty metres apart. The climbing was never technically hard but always extremely precarious
and very tense. Towards eleven o'clock the worst was past and
the ridge now formed large solid broad whalebacked cornices.
Simon was out of sight as I contoured round the first large

cornice and approached the second one. Beyond the ridge dropped to our West Face descent point.

I was surprised to find an ice cliff on the other side of the cornice. This was about fifteen feet high at the crest of the ridge and nearly forty feet high further down the East Face. It wasn't possible to abseil, as the snow on top was unstable and the ridge too dangerous to attempt. I therefore began traversing the cliff edge looking for a weakness, an ice ramp or a crevasse, by which I hoped to get down the cliff.

Suddenly a large section of the edge broke away beneath me and I fell twenty feet on to the slope of the East Face, and then somersaulted down. I knew I had broken my leg in the severe impact as my crampons hit hard ice.

Simon knew that Joe had fallen by the tug on the rope and he was worried:

The reality of the predicament did not come home to me until I had done the precarious abseil to where Joe was. I got out some painkillers from my rucksack and gave them to him. His right leg was quite obviously broken. My immediate thoughts were that the situation was quite hopeless and that Joe was as good as dead. But eventually I realised that I would have to make some kind of effort to try and get him off the mountain.

I traversed back towards the ridge and saw that reasonably angled snow slopes led down to the Col Santa Rosa. Fortunately Joe's accident had occurred on the last technical part of the ridge. After returning to him, I then climbed up to free the abseil ropes which had stuck. While I was doing this Joe managed to traverse towards the ridge on his own.

Getting back up to the abseil point was for me the most frightening part of the epic. It involved climbing the ice cliff at its lowest point. This place, unfortunately, also happened to be on the corniced edge of the ridge. Climbing the ice solo took a very long time with terrifying views of Siula Grande's West Face viewed through fracture lines in the cornice. When I reached the anchor point I made sure the doubled rope would now run freely and abseiled again. There was no trouble this time and the rope pulled down easily. I then caught up with Joe who was making slow and painful progress.

I'm not exactly sure whose idea it was, but a system for lowering Joe was devised. The two fifty-metre ropes were tied together. I sat in a seat-shaped platform dug out of the snow and started lowering Joe through a Sticht plate, a friction device. After fifty metres the knot which joined the two ropes together reached the plate. Now Joe took his weight off the rope so that I could swap the knot to the other side of the plate and lower him a further fifty metres. I then down-climbed to him and as I was doing this he cut a platform for me to belay from for the next lower. While I was lowering, Joe would lie on his left side to stop his broken right leg from being jarred. Even so it was obviously very painful but I only stopped lowering him when the pain was intense, because of the urgency of getting him off the mountain.

Joe recalls:

Simon was very much in control and all I had to do was cope with the pain and execute any manoeuvres as safely as possible. We both began to feel optimistic about getting to the glacier and the sanctuary of a snow hole that night. We worked well as a team and made steady progress down the 650-metre face. Already Simon had lowered me 200 metres to the col.

By nightfall we reckoned we were only two and a half rope lengths from the glacier. On what should have been the second-last lower, disaster hit when I was lowered accidentally over an ice cliff. The situation suddenly changed from possible to hopeless. When the lowering ropes reached halfway point at the belay plate I was hanging free fifty feet above a huge crevasse!

Simon, who could not now see Joe, was also in a desperate situation:

After about fifty feet the rope came tight, and I knew Joe had gone over a steeper section. I carried on lowering until the knot in the rope came up and gave tugs on the rope to tell Joe to take his weight off the rope.

Joe did not respond. I carried on tugging at the rope and screaming for Joe to do something. As time went by my screaming became more desperate. I was getting very cold. My already frostbitten hands were getting worse, my legs were going numb and the snow seat was gradually collapsing.

Back to Joe:

This, I thought was the end. I was exhausted and very cold, and felt cheated, as if something was determined to finish me off, irrespective of what we tried to do to prevent it. I was giving up the ghost.

In darkness, with avalanches pouring off the cliff edge above, a strong biting wind and a temperature of −20°C, I felt too numbed to attempt anything. My efforts at prusiking failed as one of my frozen hands dropped a loop and I felt too shattered afterwards to do any more.

I distinctly remember thinking of Toni Kurtz who was left hanging on a rope from an overhang on the North Wall of the Eiger. He froze to death. I thought that at last I knew what he must have felt like. Approaching death wasn't as bad as the books led me to think. I tried and failed – tough shit! I was spinning from my waist harness, too weak to hold myself upright, and I could see in my mind's eye that horrific old black and white photograph of Kurtz's corpse on the rope with long icicles hanging from the points of his crampons. My legs were numb and I was grateful because I could feel no pain now. I wondered if Simon would die with me and if anyone would ever find us.

The longer I hung there, the more relaxed I felt about everything, even feeling quite calm about knowing I was going to die fairly soon. In a lazy sort of way it didn't really bother me, seemed to have nothing to do with Joe Simpson. It was just a fact of life – of death.

Simon must have had a terrible time on the slope above struggling to hold on to me and realising his belay seat was collapsing beneath him and all the time being in the full force of the avalanches.

Simon's predicament was indeed desperate. He realised that if he didn't do something soon they would both perish.

I remembered Joe had given me his Swiss Army knife for cutting abseil slings. After getting the knife out of my rucksack I cut Joe's rope. It seemed a very rational thing to do and I did it very calmly.

On the end of the rope Joe must have known that what was about to occur was the only logical solution:

When I felt myself slip several inches I realised what was about to happen. I wondered whether he would be able to cut himself free in time. I looked down and knew I wouldn't survive a free fall into the crevasse.

I was looking up the rope when I suddenly felt myself hurtling down. I wasn't scared, more confused. I hit the snow roof of the crevasse very hard and twisted sideways as I broke through it, then accelerated down again. I couldn't see but felt all the snow roof cascading past. Further down I hit a snow bridge in the crevasse on my side – very hard – and banged my knee, which made me cry out.

It took me a long time to recover and sit up. I think my left hip had been dislocated because when I moved it popped back in. I could only feel my knee at the time.

Simon had now to act quickly or he could freeze to death on the exposed face:

I immediately set about digging a snow hole as it was necessary to get into my sleeping bag as quickly as possible. Excavating the hole took a very long time. My mind was full of quite bizarre thoughts. At first they were speculative: what had happened to Joe? I knew we were nearly on the glacier and hoped Joe had not fallen on to the avalanche chute leading to this. I wondered if the fall had injured him further and if he could survive the night. Eventually I became convinced that my action was bound to have resulted in Joe's death. I got into my sleeping bag and felt terrible. My mind was working at an incredible rate, jumping from one subject to another. Occasionally I would smell the water in the surrounding snow and wish for a drink. Eventually I had a little sleep.

Joe, after his fall:

That Sunday night in the crevasse was the worst thing I've ever experienced in my life, for I suffer slightly from claustrophobia. The first thing I did was put an ice peg into the side wall of the crevasse and tie myself to it. Then I looked around with my torch. There seemed no way out but up. The roof I came through was about fifty feet above. It was impossible to climb up there but in desperation I tried four times before giving up.

I'm sure I went mad from about 11.00 pm to 3.00 am and I was convinced that Simon thought me dead. I had no reason to presume this, I just felt it in my bones. It was a living nightmare, a turmoil of thoughts ricocheting within my head. I reckoned it could take me days to die in that crevasse. I've never felt so isolated and abandoned in my life. I seriously thought of untying and jumping down the hole to my left into the bowels of the ice, but I knew I wouldn't be able to do it. I just huddled up against the ice wall like a frightened child and cried, shouted, moaned and generally felt very sorry for myself. I then tried to rationalise, thinking that we all have to die some time and that this was just my time, this was my way. I wondered how many others had died in a similar way and what they had done and how they had coped. It felt strange to think I was now just another one of those reports you see in Mountain Accident statistics. I had now an awful realisation of what all those tales of climbers' deaths in the mountains really meant. I felt sad for all of them.

This went on and on, recurring thoughts, getting nowhere. I had deliberately not got into my pit – my sleeping bag or my bivvy sack. At about 3.00 am a wave of anger and resentment swept over me and I made a resolute effort to control myself. I decided, fuck it, I've got this far, why give up now? Maybe in the morning I'll see a way out. I never once believed that Simon would find me or get me out. It was as if I had banished him from my mind. When I did struggle into my sleeping bag it was with the greatest difficulty. The pain was intense but eventually I did get some disjointed sleep.

I awoke about 6.00 am and at once started screaming, "Simon . . . Simon." I felt dehydrated and it was difficult to shout. But no sign of Simon, perhaps he too had fallen? He wouldn't be able to see me where I was and maybe my voice was too weak.

Dawn for Simon wasn't a bed of roses either:

When I awoke it was still dark and I began to think about getting down to Base Camp. This made me very afraid. I was quite convinced that I would be killed as a form of retribution. When it got light I packed my rucksack and geared up, very slowly and meticulously as though it was a sort of peculiar last ceremony.

After getting out of the snow hole I saw the slope beneath ended in a cliff edge and below that the avalanche chute led down on to the glacier. I traversed rightwards above the cliff towards a couloir that I could see would bring me down on to the glacier. Once in the couloir I had to abseil and as I went down the doubled rope I could see across to the ice cliff that I had lowered Joe over. At the bottom of it was a huge crevasse. Joe had obviously fallen into it. I shouted, "Joe, Joe," while abseiling, but I was totally convinced that he was dead, and didn't bother going over to the crevasse.

Walking back across the glacier was tiring due to the deep snow and my general condition. Only when I reached the moraine was I convinced of my own survival. I began thinking then of how to break the news to Richard at Base Camp. I realised that I could fabricate a less controversial story to tell him and later other people, but I dismissed this idea immediately, knowing that I was simply not capable of it.

Coming over the final moraine before Base Camp I met Richard on his way up to look for us. I told him Joe was dead and explained how it came about. In a very subdued mood we went back to base.

Joe in the bowels of the ice decided to get to grips with his situation:

Look around, I told myself, see what it's like. Is there a way out? Not up, impossible, not left, not right. Hang on. I can see a ledge. Is it a false bottom to the crevasse eighty feet down? There's light on it. Maybe there is an exit from down there, I rambled on. No. Can't go down deeper, don't want to go down. But what if that snow floor is just a thin cover? I'll never get back up to this ledge again.

I pulled the rope down from the blocks of snow in the roof above and saw the frayed end of nylon fibres. Seeing it sort of made my mind up for me, as if it confirmed the situation that I was in and forced me to face facts. If there was no escape down there then it would make no difference to me now. I was going to die if I stayed here so what difference would it make if I did so eighty feet lower? It was Hobson's choice but I still cringed from going down. It might mean a quick death if I fell and I wasn't as prepared for that as I had thought.

In the end I weighted the frayed end of the rope with karabiners and abseiled down. Once on this lower snow bridge or platform, I was delighted to find that the floor was reasonably solid though I didn't detach myself from the rope.

I could see holes going deep down on the outer side of the crevasse, so obviously it continued beneath what I was lying on. The floor must have been made by avalanches pouring in from above and they had formed a powder cone rising right up to the roof which began about twenty or thirty feet in front of me. At the top I could see a small circular hole, head width, with a column of gold sunlight angling in on to the back wall of the slot. Seeing this gave me the most incredible lift. All the time I was in the crevasse and especially then at its deepest point I had the most overwhelming sense of isolation and of being completely cut off and abandoned. It was the eeriest feeling, all light blue and shadowed, everything totally lifeless, like being in a crypt, where nothing living had ever been or would ever come again.

That shaft of sun however dispelled all this and gave me a link with the outside world, even though I had great doubts if I would be able to climb the slope, knowing how hard the climbing had been for me up above.

The angle was about 50° at the bottom, gradually steepening to 60° near the roof and in the region of twenty-five feet wide at the base and six feet broad at the top. I crawled over to it, still tied to the abseil rope fixed to the ice peg eighty feet above. It was very soft powder and after much faffing around I sorted out a system by which I could tackle it. I cut out then stamped down a small platform-step with another step just below it to the right, then I hefted my bad leg into this and with axes and armpits buried deeply above, executed a big hop to get my good leg on to the platform, then I lifted my injured leg up to it as well and started all over again.

The pitch was about 130 feet and when I got higher the abseil rope hung almost horizontal behind me. The steeper it got the more precarious and strenuous it became to step up. Several times near the top I very nearly fell off.

After six hours of this hell I popped my head out through the roof exit and saw before me all the world. My world. The feeling of exultation was quite indescribable. I couldn't believe that I had done it. I could see the glacier about 150 feet below me and the route back to camp. I was yelling and shouting like a mad thing, just shouting for no reason except perhaps relief. I wanted to cry but couldn't.

It was about 12.30 pm on a bright sunny day. When I reached the glacier, I knew that Simon had returned presuming me dead. I saw his tracks and started to crawl after them. The rest was just crawling. For another three days I clawed my way down, getting weaker each day. Despite being out of it a lot of the time, hallucinating on the glacier, talking to myself, shouting then shouting some more, I just kept going mechanically, detached, like an automaton. I was very methodical about it. I am surprised in retrospect how controlled I was, fixing stages to reach, not thinking beyond them, snow holing and bivouacking when I wanted to keep going on yet knew the weather would kill me if I did. I know that if I had been in that situation at eighteen, I would not have survived. There was a lot of experience in me that made me do the right thing at the right time.

By far the hardest thing was being alone, having no one to talk to or to encourage me. The great temptation was to just lie still and say sod it, I'm going to sleep for a while. It was so hard to fight on my own. This was especially so the two days on the boulder field when I fell a lot; I always seemed to be lying still, waiting for pain to subside.

I had continuous conversations with myself as if I were talking with another person. On the last day, 1 June, I saw Simon's and Richard's footprints in the mud and was convinced that they were with me. There was an uncanny sense of someone else following along quietly. It felt very comforting. I was absolutely sure for about three hours that Richard was in front and Simon behind, out of sight because they didn't want me to be embarrassed by my condition, but encouraging me along. When I fell over and it hurt badly they didn't come to help. I thought it was because they wanted me to do this thing by myself and that seemed all right, really. I was just glad that they were there and someone knew I wasn't dead.

Suddenly the bubble burst and I knew they had never been there and that I was alone and dead as far as they were concerned. That came as quite a blow to me mentally.

Until halfway through the third day dehydration was very bad. I had had no water or food since Sunday night. It now was Tuesday and I felt terrible. I couldn't raise saliva and my tongue was swollen and dry. I had trouble breathing evenly, always being excessively out of breath. When I got to water I drank litres and litres. It tasted like nectar and at once I began to feel stronger and had less trouble breathing.

I knew having no food was bad but didn't miss it and I was very much aware that I was getting progressively weaker and slower. That last, usually ten-minute, walk to camp took me six and a half hours! I could just shuffle a bit and then lie back shattered. I've never felt so fucked in my life.

Simon and Richard were meanwhile packing up camp:

The night before we had arranged to leave, just as it was getting dark, I heard a distant cry that sounded like "Simon". I thought little of it as there had been a few locals about tending to their cattle. But Richard and I were awakened shortly after midnight by a clear call of "Simon, help me."

We shot out of our sleeping bags and dashed outside the tent. It was an eerie sight that greeted us. The night was misty with gently falling snow. Joe was slumped on a rock about fifty yards from the tent. He was in an appalling physical state. His face was incredibly thin, his eyes sunken, he was covered in mud, stank of fleas and urine, with a smell of acetone on his breath from starvation.

Joe said later:

I believe that was as far as I would have got. When Simon's and Richard's torches came bobbing across the snow everything seemed to drain out of me; all the fight which had kept me going evaporated. There was no longer a need to boost myself, now others would help. I felt myself just give up and pain came rushing in, the exhaustion, everything. I sometimes wonder if that wasn't the point at which I was most at risk, whether I could suddenly just have keeled over and died. I felt like death, and no doubt smelt like it as well.

At this point a helicopter would have been an answer to prayer, but this was not the Alps or Glencoe. It was one of the remoter corners of the High Andes, and evacuating Joe Simpson involved a tortuous haggling first with muleteers, then with police in the nearest town, followed by a truck ride to Lima with an obliviously drunken driver, before Joe was deposited in hospital three days later. He was not yet rid of the trauma of his ghastly experience and in hospital during pre-sedation had one more of those weird dreams he had suffered during the long nights and agonising days after the accident.

Joe:

I was back in the crevasse again and a passage from Shakespeare's *Measure for Measure* came to mind where a condemned man contemplates execution. I had had to learn it about fifteen years before and hadn't seen or even thought about it since. It was a dream with words. When I woke up I wrote it on my plaster cast:

Death is a fearful thing . . .
. . . To die, and go we know not where;
To lie in cold obstruction, and to rot;
This sensible warm motion to become
A kneaded clod; and the delighted spirit
To bathe in fiery floods or to reside
In thrilling region of thick-ribbed ice . . .

The Bogus Commander and the Y-fronts Rescue

Hamish MacInnes

I find it intriguing that the most memorable rescues are not those reminiscent of trench warfare scenes, with a victim's brains splattered over rocks or limbs distorted by a horrendous fall. The mind seems to have the ability to filter such horrific sights, at least to reduce the focus of memory. Only a few rescues are fun and the jokes and events are recalled with clarity and nostalgia.

The Y-fronts rescue was one such. It certainly was unusual and had an added element of farce about it. Also the weather was balmy, which always helps. We weren't involved in struggling up avalanche-prone slopes looking for buried bodies, or subjected to running the gauntlet of falling rocks, invisible in the dark.

The Y-fronts call-out still resides in that compartment of our memory labelled Fun things: instant recall, whereas many tragedies are fortunately blurred and seemingly of another time and place.

Its chapter companion, the tale of the bogus Commander, though not X-certificate, is remembered for the frustration it generated, and the precious time wasted. It too is unique in its own perverted way and is an interesting study of human behaviour.

It was Easter weekend 1987 that the Glencoe Mountain Rescue Team was called out to an incident on Stob Coire nan Beith, a mountain on the south side of the glen. It towers above Loch Achtriochtan and resembles a hurriedly assembled pyramid, as if created just before the Almighty's coffee break. Severing its flanks of red rhyolite is a gully deep and straight, rising steeply from scree at its base to the very summit. It was down this defile, Summit Gully, that a climber fell 1,000 feet and suffered fatal head injuries. His companion miraculously survived and hobbled down to raise the alarm. Easter weekend normally presages the tail end of winter, though it can also be a time of snap frosts as it was on this occasion. The gully resembled a slick high-angled bob sleigh run plunging down to rock-studded snow slopes at the base.

I had asked for a helicopter for the call-out, as the carry down to the A82 through Glencoe is both boulder-strewn and arm-stretching with a loaded stretcher.

By this time we had gone up through the steep narrow mouth of the corrie before we received a radio call from Police Constable Stewart O'Bree at our base truck. The truck was parked close to the Elliots' cottage at Loch Achtriochtan.

"Base to hill party, base to hill party, Sea King helicopter ETA forty-five minutes."

"Copied that, Stewart," I replied.

Meantime we had located the fallen climber, partly buried in snow debris. We lowered him to easier ground, then, putting him in a body bag, strapped him on to the stretcher.

The day was cold and wintry with a stiff south-westerly curling over the ridges high above. The blast collected confetti-like snow particles and infused them into the clear air. The corrie, which often doubles as nature's centrifuge, a virtual wind generator when a strong south-westerly blows, is a nightmare for chopper pilots. Flying conditions weren't good and I remembered that the wind direction had veered to the south-west overnight. When the Sea King arrived and tried to nudge its way into the corrie it was as if the big yellow machine was being repeatedly struck by a huge invisible hammer. We realised with resignation that it was now a case of all hands on shafts and shanks's pony to base. However, as usual, there was the happy prospect of a pint at the Clachaig Inn some 2,000 feet below after our toil.

What unfolded next was the strangest series of events ever to befall the Glencoe team. It started with a garbled message over the RT.

"Hello, Glencoe base, this is Navy 71, Navy 71 . . ."

This was followed by the flak of static. We didn't receive

Stewart's reply to this as we were now in a blind spot close to the stream which plunges out of Coire Beith, beside the waterfall known as Ossian's Shower Bath.

"Come in, Navy 71, this is Glencoe base."

There was a long pause.

"Base to hill party, base to hill party. A brief message has been received reporting a further incident to a naval party of eight persons. As far as I can gather there's one casualty – a broken leg. Can you advise on procedure please?"

"Got that, Stewart. Also heard a bit of it direct. Try and get more info on their location. But they'll have to wait in the queue. We'll have the dead climber down in about an hour."

"Roger, I'll try and raise them again, out."

"Hello, Navy 71, this is Glencoe base, please identify yourself."

In a few minutes Stewart relayed to us the reply.

"Hello, Hamish, the naval Commander says he's not sure of their position as the only map they have is in a rucksack with the cadet who's fallen. They can't get down to him. He also asked if it's possible to pinpoint their position using a radio detection finder. I told him the team doesn't have one."

"Thanks, Stewart, we got that."

Then came a call from the 202 Squadron Sea King of RAF Lossiemouth. It was being driven by Flight Lieutenant Stephen Hodgson, his co-pilot was Flight Lieutenant Harry Watt. They too had intercepted the cryptic message identified as Navy 71.

The tone of these messages confirmed the Commander's military background, the procedure was impeccable, the accent English and clipped, and there was that bona fide call sign, Navy 71.

Two other members of the rescue team had arrived at base. Walter Elliot with his brother Willie and their father before them had been engaged on rescues long before we had an official rescue team in the area. With him was John Hardie, then a climbing instructor. Walter with a shepherd's intimate knowledge of the glen tried to get a more accurate description of the location from the naval caller but was frustrated, both by the failure to get a sensible reply to his questions, or even an acknowledgement. The only clues he got were: "As far as I can determine my party's reached the fourth peak on the left after the National Trust for Scotland Centre."

When we heard this from Walter on the radio, we came to the conclusion that this probably put the location of the accident on the south side of the Aonach Eagach Ridge.

The question about the location detector was curious, to say the least, and we discussed it as we negotiated the steep rocky descent, for it was an unusual thing to ask and Stewart's accurate but negative reply that we didn't have one may have escalated the following sequence of events.

We arrived at base with the fallen climber and the ambulance reversed up to the truck to collect the stretcher. As I watched the body bag being slid into the vehicle I thought another mountain rescue statistic which never considers the trauma of a young life lost and the destitution and grief of the relatives. He had been a social worker from Devon, taking in Glencoe for the Easter break. Meanwhile the Sea King had landed close by on the field in front of Achnabeitach, the Elliots' cottage.

In the poor light and squalls Willie Elliot, Walter's brother, with his stalking telescope, or glass as he calls it, spied a group of climbers near the west end of the Aonach Eagach Ridge across the glen. They were invisible to the naked eye. This was a chance for us to use our secret weapon, a beefy directional amplifier system which echoes round the crags like a sonic boom. We managed to contact the climbers 3,000 feet above and a mile or so away. Base was of course too distant to hear any replies, but the climbers were asked to make arm signals in reply to our specific questions. In this way, with powerful binoculars, we established that, despite traversing most of the ridge, they had seen no sign of another party. Willie Elliot, with the solemnity of a Highland seer, was the first really to cast doubt on the authenticity of this latest call-out.

"Aye," he said, sliding his glass closed in one deft movement and putting it back in its case, "it seems a funny business to me!" I learned later that those at base felt that they were being watched, for it was uncanny how the calls from the naval party seemed to synchronise with movements at base.

We had a quick fix of lemonade and Mars bars at the truck, then rustled up a hurried search plan. Within a couple of hours of receiving the first call from the naval party we were once again, like the Grand Old Duke of York's ten thousand men, only rather fewer, toiling up the mountain opposite.

Despite the negative message from the climbers on the crest, we concentrated our search on the Aonach Eagach Ridge which is on the north side of the glen. We knew that due to the steepness of the face much of it isn't visible from the top. This ridge stretches in four miles like a great jagged barrier reef. It is the narrowest ridge on the British mainland and a popular venue for walkers to fall from. Now it had shed most of the winter's snow and the black rock pinnacles above resembled unhealthy molars in the fading light. In this setting it was easy to visualise it as a remnant of the power of the last ice age. Even to this day there are erratics poised on the summit crest.

We also sent four of the team, Davy Gunn, John Hardie, Bob Hamilton and Peter Harrop, to search the narrow ridge of Gearr Aonach, which is one of the Three Sisters, so called by the tour drivers who can't pronounce the Gaelic names of these aloof rocky maidens. This ridge too was exposed to the icy blast.

All the team was now out, as well as some volunteer climbers. There was no further response from the phantom caller, however, despite repeated requests from base or from the team walkie-talkies at their higher elevation. The trouble was, we realised, that the distress call could have come from anywhere over a wide area and it would take many more rescuers and volunteers than we could muster to search every valley, gully and buttress within walkie-talkie range. It was a daunting task.

There was an unusual report of a naval officer being seen at Clachaig Hotel by Doris Elliot, Walter and Willie's sister. She saw this official looking figure operating a walkie-talkie and he seemed to be spasmodically driving about in a naval vehicle, as if trying to get a better signal. Naturally she didn't think anything of it at the time as there are often military parties in the area.

Meantime PC Stewart O'Bree, now relieved by Willie Elliot at base, was making official enquiries at road level, trying to glean more information on the naval party who must be staying at some centre or camping in the region and have at least one vehicle.

A frigid twilight had given way to inky bodges in hollows which spread to envelope the slopes of the Aonach Eagach and merged into a uniform blackness. By the time we had descended from our various search sectors it was 1.00 am. Our headlights formed pinpricks in the night and on the A82 vehicle headlamps stabbed the darkness, creating long arcs of light on the corners. There was still no sign of the missing cadets.

We were now highly sceptical of the radio calls. First there was the question asking about a radio detection finder at the very start of the scenario; then the convenient uncanny silences when specific questions were asked. Also it is very difficult to make eight aspirant sailors vanish into thin air, even in such a vast area as Glencoe.

When I got back home there was little chance of grabbing sleep. Despite our deepest misgivings we had to continue the search. An extra helicopter, a Wessex from RAF Leuchars in Fife, was scheduled for dawn, together with an RAF Mountain Rescue Team and three civilian teams. This made a total of a hundred rescuers.

Next day we continued searching; we consoled ourselves with the fact that hoaxes in the realm of mountain rescue are rare, and the knowledge that you just can't take impetuous decisions to abandon an operation prematurely when lives may be involved. The media inadvertently assisted. The story had captured the headlines. Mystery coupled with possible tragedy is irresistible fodder for the tabloids.

Further down the glen, at the Forestry Commission campsite, some progress was made. It was discovered that a man in naval uniform had spent the night at the camp. He had since vanished. Stewart O'Bree, now back at the local police station, had received a telephone call via Police Headquarters in Fort William from a Mr McCubbin who operated a small store at the Forestry campsite – only about a mile from where our base truck was parked. He gave a statement to Stewart that both he and Robert Fordham, the camp warden, had been told by campers about a "naval person" who had been acting strangely. The naval officer had bought provisions at the shop and had paid for them by cheque, signed "A. Wilson". This, we realised could be our bogus Commander.

Despite the escalating evidence of a hoax, dawn saw us combing the gullies and crags and this went on until late evening. Everyone was shattered. We had used the two helicopters most of the day. Some volunteer climbers who had assisted the team since first light couldn't be contacted as they didn't have walkie-talkies and were even later in returning to base, despite the fact that we fired pre-arranged signal rockets to inform them of the stand down. They then faced a drive back to their homes in Glasgow, Edinburgh and even to south of the border.

A scaled down search was conducted the following day by one of the RAF teams and a few Glencoe members, but this was abandoned at 1.00 pm when nothing further showed up. It was later estimated that the cost to the taxpayer for the two helicopters alone was £43,765, and of course there was well over a thousand man-hours clocked up by the rescuers. We had no alternative but to scale down search operations. The case of the bogus naval Commander was put on a back burner; there were real human beings to rescue.

A report in the national newspapers was to shed light on the mystery. The Commander's eventual detection and arrest had a Gilbertian quality to it. After broadcasting the hoax message he had hot-footed it to nearby Fort William. But, let us go back twenty-four hours, the day after the hoax call-out, 18 April, when the Commander and an Army sergeant met at the Glen Nevis campsite near Fort William.

The genuine military man was Sergeant Thomas McKay, the Edinburgh District gunner, who fires the one o'clock Castle gun and is known to thousands of tourists the world over as Tam the Gun. The Sergeant was awaiting the arrival of a party of officer cadets from Heriot Watt University in Edinburgh who had been hiking the full length of the West Highland Way, a long-distance leg-stretcher which runs from Glasgow to Fort William.

The Commander drove into the campsite in a staff car which had the words Royal Navy emblazoned on the sides in white lettering. The Sergeant noted that the vehicle had official naval number plates. There were in fact two men in the car, the Commander who introduced himself as Mark, and his companion, a Belgian naval officer on attachment to the Royal Navy. Tom invited them for a cup of tea, adding that he was awaiting the arrival of the cadets and that they would be going to a pub later. The Commander asked if he could join them, saying that he was expecting a party of naval ratings from HMS *Drake* the next day; they were going to take part in an exercise on Ben Nevis.

In due course Tom's officer cadets arrived, glad that their five-day hike was at an end, and after grabbing some food, they all adjourned to the Argyll pub in Fort William. It appears to have been a happy evening; in the words of the Immortal Bard, "Wi' reaming swats, that drank divinely". The cadets after their route march had perhaps more pints than caution dictates.

Tom, who returned to camp a short time later, was taken aback to see Mark with the cadets on parade, bollocking them for their exuberant behaviour. Tom made it clear to him that he was the senior member of his group and that Mark had no right to speak to the cadets in that manner. Mark took the rebuke calmly and apologised.

Next morning Tom discovered that the Belgian had left. Mark said he had gone to meet up with the naval party. Before he hit the road, Tom said that if Mark was ever down in Edinburgh to look him up at the Castle and he'd show him round. On the A82 south the Army party passed two Royal Navy four-ton trucks which they assumed were Mark's group heading for Ben Nevis.

The following Tuesday Tom was back in Edinburgh and was driving down Castle Street when he saw Mark again – he was conspicuous, still wearing combat trousers and a naval pullover. They greeted each other and Mark told the Sergeant that he was shopping for new boots. Before they parted, Tom invited him to his house that night for dinner.

After the meal Tom asked his wife to put on a video he had recently bought on the Falklands War. Mark had previously mentioned that he had served in the campaign. As they watched the tape, Mark said that he was on the ship when the film was being shot and to look out for the officer who would start to cry. He appeared to have a detailed knowledge of the film. This more than anything diminished any lingering doubts that Tom had of the Commander. Mark refused the offer of a bed and opted to camp on Castlelaw Ranges on the edge of the city. He said he liked to bivvy, but promised next day to go on a tour of Edinburgh Castle with Tom. He also asked where the nearest barracks was as he required petrol. The Sergeant saw various items of equipment inside Mark's car, including walkie-talkies.

Next day they met up as arranged at the Castle drawbridge. Mark rebuked the sentry on duty as they entered, asking him why he didn't salute an officer of the Royal Navy. He was then given a tour of the historical artefacts in that famous fortress that has been sacked by both Edward I and Robert Bruce. But Tom was puzzled when they were looking at a Second World War naval officer's cap and Mark commented that the crown on the badge was now different. Tom knew, as Mark should have known, that the crown on cap badges changes with the reigning monarch. This was a bit odd, Tom thought. His doubts were shortly to be substantiated.

Mark had a free lunch in the officers' mess and afterwards had the temerity to complain to the mess steward as to the quality of the food! He was lucky that he wasn't shown the same hospitality as guests at the infamous Black Dinner of 1440 when the Douglas heir and his brother were hauled from the table in front of King James II, and beheaded.

Later, leaving Mark at the gunners' hut, Tom went to collect his mail at Brigade Headquarters. He glanced at a copy of the *Daily Record* and saw an article on the mountain rescue hoax in Glencoe – the police were appealing for information on the naval perpetrator. In a flash he realised that the description of the bogus naval Commander fitted Mark precisely.

The Sergeant reported the situation to the Royal Military Police stationed in the Castle who went to the gunners' hut and asked Mark for his ID. He produced this and they then took him to an interview room.

After a short time he went back to the gunners' hut, to which Tom had returned, and asked what was going on. "It's just routine for all non-tourists," Tom told him. "Your staff car attracted attention. After all, the Castle is a military base."

As they were chatting the phone rang. Tom picked it up; it was the Special Investigation Branch. They wanted Mark back at the interview room. They also told the Sergeant that Mark's staff car had been blocked off on the esplanade by a military police car to prevent him making a get-away. One of the SIB officers who had served with the Royal Navy had noticed that Mark's ID card was the wrong shade of blue. Mark was arrested.

During interrogation regarding an alleged hoax call-out of

mountain rescue teams in Glencoe, Mark made references to the IRA and the Prevention of Terrorism Act was invoked. We knew nothing of these goings on in the backwoods of Glencoe, nor did the public at large and it was only when the case came to court that the story began to unravel. Mark came up for trial at the High Court in Inverness at the end of July 1987, presided over by Judge Lord MacDonald. I was cited to attend to give evidence with several team members.

During the trial a can of worms was revealed to the public. When Mark's car was found parked on the busy Castle Esplanade it was suspected that it could have a bomb on board, but none was found. It was also alleged that at various places in Scotland, including at Fort William on the Glen Nevis road, he was recruited by the IRA to enter military establishments disguised as a naval officer; that caches of arms and explosives were buried in North Wales, the Lake District, Redford Ranges, Edinburgh, and in a wood near Fort William for use against military bases. He denied all this and further denied that in pursuance of terrorist activities he and Benjamin Claus gained entry to Redford Barracks and Dreghorn Camp, Edinburgh, in disguise, to put to the test an identification card and disguised vehicle, and stole a quantity of paper. He was also standing trial on two fraud charges; three charges of theft; using false naval number plates on a car; a contravention of the Uniforms Act by wearing a naval uniform (which he had got at a jumble sale) to which he was not entitled. He also denied calling out the Glencoe Mountain Rescue Team and other rescue agencies.

After a trial which lasted six days the verdict was summed up: "The twenty-nine-year-old accused was convicted of public mischief by broadcasting an Easter weekend distress message that he was a naval commander and that one of his men was lying injured in the hills. As a result two helicopters and a hundred men carried out a search over two days."

Mark was also convicted of pretending to military and civil police who arrested him for the hoax that he was a member of the IRA and knew where explosives were buried. This caused the police and bomb disposal squad to waste time and public money in fruitless searches. And he was found guilty of stealing six walkie-talkies from a rescue centre in North Wales.

The court heard that on nine occasions, dating back to 1973, Mark had twenty-eight convictions for dishonesty, deception and fraud. In 1982, he was sentenced to six years imprisonment, being released only the previous October. Lord MacDonald went on to add: "Notwithstanding what has been said on your behalf and in the reports and letters, I am clearly of the view that you were perfectly sane and fit to plead and knew what you were doing. You have committed offences of such gravity that they merit very severe treatment indeed."

Mark was sentenced to six years.

As I mentioned at the start of this chapter, not all rescues are tragic – or false alarms! Let's return to sunshine and underpants . . .

I think that I had had a glass of home brewed silver birch wine before turning in the night before the Sunday morning I received the call from the police about a missing man in Glen Etive. That may have been the reason for the brief delay in answering the telephone; after all it was 3.00 am.

The desk sergeant in Fort William was on the line and told me that a short time before a group of climbers had returned to Glen Etive in their old van after a sortie to the Clachaig Inn, where they had attempted to allay their drooth (thirst) with a few pints of natural ale. It had been a scorching day. The midges of Glen Etive were waiting in ambush.

They had unrolled their sleeping bags on the floor of the van and settled in for the night. The trouble with beer is that it later has to be disposed of, often at inopportune moments, and one of the party, a twenty-five-year-old janitor from Edinburgh (whom I will call Dave) was on his first visit to the mountains. He had to relieve himself at about 2.00 am. It was cold, the heavens alive with a myriad of stars, as they often are when a large area of high pressure anchors itself over the Highlands. The only other place I've seen such stunning clarity in the heavens has been in desert regions.

Nearby the River Etive was glinting in the moonlight. Dave was dressed only in his underpants. When he didn't return after what seemed ages, one of the girls sleepily looked out but couldn't see any sign of him. She thought he must be having an inordinately long pee but she awakened the others.

They searched the general area pretty thoroughly, calling out for him and also checking the nearby bank of the Etive, but there was no sign. This far north it doesn't really get dark at this time of year and they would certainly have spotted him had he been sitting somewhere, but they realised that it would be easy to miss someone lying amongst the heather or rocks. It was then that they drove up to Kingshouse Hotel, which is on the fringe of the Moor of Rannoch, and contacted the police. Hence my wake-up call.

When we arrived at the lay-by where their van was now re-parked we questioned them about their missing friend, but they just couldn't shed any further light on the incident. We then started a more detailed search of the general area, deciding (wrongly) that the missing man wouldn't get far without boots or clothing, for the pre-dawn air had a cold bite to it. Also the Glencoe terrain isn't conducive to walking barefoot, other than on the main highway. Above, to the west, the massive bulk of Buachaille Etive Mor dominated the lightening sky and on a hillock a short distance away I could see the outline of a stag, like a cardboard cut-out, still as the rock above it.

After combing the area thoroughly, we returned to the van and questioned the climbers once more. Apparently, the previous day Dave had been abstractly throwing stones into pools in the river. Some of these are deep and when the river is in spate they can be dangerous. Now it was tranquil, like quicksilver in the half-light of dawn, but we knew that some of the pools were over ten metres deep. Ruling out any long-distance barefoot hike on Dave's part, we opted to search the river thoroughly.

Midges like their breakfast as soon as it warms up and a naked man would represent a midge's conception of paradise. We didn't think that he would have taken to the A82, as there's no civilisation to speak of for about twelve miles. His friends had already checked that he hadn't gone to Kingshouse Hotel. Also none of the police or our team en route to Glen Etive had seen any white-skinned apparition on the road. But just in case he had opted to walk down the narrow single dead end track which masquerades as the Glen Etive road, I asked Willie Elliot to take his National Trust van down the glen just to make sure. We all agreed, for the moment, that we would concentrate on the river and, as several team members were professional divers, they went off to collect their dry suits and air bottles.

By now it was daylight and the sun squeezed up over the edge of the Moor of Rannoch like a great fresh custard pie. I reflected that serious accidents don't come on sun-drenched days, but usually with bad weather. The odds are stacked against the victim then. Big storms and avalanches are accessories for nature's misdeeds; but not today I thought. This could be a falling off day, not an exposure one. The water had a hypnotic effect – possibly as it had on Dave the day before? The rocky pools have been meticulously gouged out of the red rock by the great ice cap thousands of feet thick which had covered the Moor of Rannoch aeons before, and since the great thaw the rhyolite has been assiduously polished by the water of Etive.

There was almost a holiday atmosphere about the call-out. John and Richard Grieve, two divers in the team, had only to look beneath the surface of the water to see right down to the perfectly formed spherical stones on the river bed. They would have spotted a one pence piece on the bottom, such was the clarity.

All good things come to an end; the section of river was given a going over in an hour or so. The net was now about to spread as back-up rescue teams arrived from various corners of the country, also Search and Rescue Dogs, an RAF Sea King and a Wessex helicopter. There were over seventy rescuers already assembled and I'm sure that we all felt that this was better than felling trees, diving for scallops, cleaning the toilets of B&B guest houses or, in the case of the law, booking speeding motorists.

We had already set up base and the area was divided into search blocks, over a wide sweep, taking in the whole of Buachaille Etive Mor, which comprises three mountains on a humped-back ridge of some three miles, forming on our side the easterly flank of the Buachaille.

We reconsidered an earlier discarded theory that Dave could have walked up to the A82 and there hitched a lift, perhaps concocting a story that his clothes had been stolen. But it was most unlikely that anyone would have stopped to pick him up in the middle of the night. It's difficult enough to get a lift in broad daylight when reasonably dressed, such is the mistrust of modern society. I did however suggest the police enlist the help of the BBC with an appeal for information on their news bulletins. After all, I argued, he wouldn't be easily forgotten by a passing or charitable motorist. "Would any driver who saw a man wearing only underpants on the Glencoe section of the A82 last night please contact their nearest police station . . ."

But the diced caps at Police HQ must have thought it too frivolous for a Monday morning. It's true there can be embarrassing circumstances in making appeals or even enquiries as to the whereabouts of allegedly missing climbers, particularly when one assumes one is dealing with a married couple and finds the wife answers the home phone!

Meanwhile the search for Dave had really got into swing and within an hour or so the helicopters, working on a grid search, had covered the large expanse of the east face of the mountain. But there were dozens of gulches and crannies where someone could remain undetected. On the positive side, reports started to pour in for, being such a brilliant day, the hills were alive with the crunch of boots. The rescue team members questioned these climbers. One report by radio to base stated that a party had seen a solitary figure high above them very early in the morning. They were climbing the wide angled gully, Coire na Tulaich, which is the tourist's highway to the summit of Sgurr Dearg, the first and most dominant peak of the Buachaille Etive Mor massif. They said that the man didn't appear to have much clothing on, but they hadn't thought this odd for already, even on the north side of the mountain, it had been rapidly getting warmer.

If this indeed was Dave it seemed remarkable, for to get to Coire na Tulaich from where the van was parked in Glen Etive meant a hike up to the A82 and along this westwards to gain access to the corrie. His alternative would have been to cut round the rugged base of the mountain, thereby avoiding the roads, then, without footwear, climb the long escalator of the corrie with its flint-like scree which would have tested the soles of a fire-walker. It seemed a way out possibility when he had a perfectly good pair of boots back at the van!

Those at base were now soaking in some sunshine and enjoying a brew of tea. The helicopters had gone off to refuel and were now back parked close by the road. They had had no luck as there were so many people on the mountain, including by this time over a hundred rescuers, most wearing the bare minimum of clothing, so looking just like the elusive Dave! It was difficult to differentiate one specifically scantily clad individual from another. It was obviously now a job for the more personal touch of ground parties.

I had been pondering for some time how Dave managed to traverse round Buachaille Etive Mor, then ascend Coire na Tulaich on his bare feet. And according to the latest radio report relayed from the summit of the Buachaille, he had been spotted on top of this mountain at dawn.

I decided to call an old friend, consultant and expert in sports medicine, Donald MacLeod. "Could there be a psychiatric explanation for this strange behaviour, Donald?" I asked, and added, "Is he in any other danger than falling over a cliff?"

"I think that's possible, Hamish," said Donald slowly, "but, hold on, I'll give a colleague a ring. He's an expert in this sort of behaviour. Your missing man may be on medication, or even drugs, which doesn't always agree with alcohol."

It transpired that I knew Donald's colleague, Dr Martin Plant, who was also a climber. Our suspicions were confirmed by Martin.

"Yes, in certain circumstances someone with a specific mental condition, and under medication, and having taken alcohol, could be more or less immune to physical pain and quite capable of taking the unusual hike."

Though this theorising didn't help us much, it did put another slant on the dilemma. A fine heat haze was forming; Glencoe was unusually busy with an assortment of groups and individuals heading up Coire na Tulaich and other routes to the summit of the Buachaille. Some continued over the three main tops running from north-east to south-west.

At 1.45 pm came what we thought was a positive sighting. A man fitting Dave's description had been spotted heading south to the second peak, Stob na Doire. How this came about was as follows: members of the Glencoe team who had ascended the long drag towards the summit ridge were fanned out across the vast expanse of the eastern wall of the mountain, checking every likely and unlikely depression and boulderfield. Bob Hamilton, a fisherman by trade, spotted a couple above, dressed in black motorcycling leathers, an even more bizarre sight than someone sporting only Y-fronts in a heat wave!

Bob has a charming apologetic way of asking questions, but I think he probably surprised himself when this one came out as, "Are you wearing underpants?" He realised that this was a pointless enquiry, considering the heavy neck to riding boot apparel of both riders. But before he could rephrase things one of the men responded as if it was a perfectly common question to be asked on top of a mountain.

"If it's underpants you're after, there's a chap up above wearing only Y-fronts."

That's when an embarrassed Bob came on the radio and alerted us at base. From our truck I relayed this message to all rescue teams, some on other frequencies. The helicopter crews pricked up their ears – action at last.

Shortly afterwards, Ronnie Rogers, dressed only in white shorts, a rucksack and climbing boots, who was above Bob and to the south a bit, spotted Y-fronted Dave about half a mile ahead on the summit ridge. With renewed effort he set off in pursuit. Ronnie's fleeting figure was then seen by another member of our team, Peter Weir, who at the distance mistook Ronnie's shorts for Y-fronts. Peter then too shifted up a gear and started running along the wide easy crest. At this point Dave was out of Peter's sight as he had dropped into a dip on the ridge. David Cooper, a local business man who helps the team from time to time in search operations, also joined the pursuit.

Ronnie caught up with the genuine Y-fronts at last and, to his relief, saw that Dave appeared uninjured, even his feet seemed fine. Dave was under a rocky outcrop when Ronnie, swiftly followed by Peter and then Bob and David, reached him. He had his hands on a large slab of rock when Ronnie, ever polite, asked, "What are you doing, Dave?"

"Having a shower – give me a hand!" was the immediate retort.

"Where did you spend the night?" asked the incredulous Ronnie.

"I had a terrible time," Dave blurted out. "There were monstrous cats going round me all night, some of them had huge heads . . ."

"How's your back?" a breathless Peter asked, for he saw it was an angry red with sunburn.

"Oh, I slept in the snow last night. It was cool, my back was burning."

Others soon joined them, but Ronnie couldn't contact base to give us the glad tidings as they were in a radio blind spot. David Cooper went up to a higher point and from there was able to get a signal out. A helicopter was fired up. The Sea King landed on the ridge close by and Dave and some of the rescuers were picked up. On the way down to base, Dave, who had been given a headset by the winchman, told the crew, "This is the best trip I ever had."

When he landed he was quickly checked over and there was no sign of serious injury other than sunburn. I gave him the loan of a jacket and a pair of overtrousers for his flight to the Belford Hospital in Fort William. It surprised us all when Dave was released later that day.

Windy Mountain Epic

Alison Osius

The following story is of two young men who, with hindsight, could be accused of acting foolishly and of not observing the basic rules of mountain safety. It is always easy to be wise after the event and there is always a battery of armchair experts ready to point the accusing finger. However, we all make mistakes, especially when young and in the mountains, where often experience is gained through errors. Sometimes these are minor and go into one's memory bank for future use, occasionally they have far-reaching consequences, as they did with Hugh Herr and Jeff Batzer. They will have to live with their mistake for the rest of their lives.

A friend of mine, Paul Ross, was a member of the rescue team involved in this incident, and he was also one of the principal actors in our 1958 excursion on the Bonatti Pillar.

Alison Osius worked for Paul in his mountaineering school as a climbing instructor and she knew many of the rescuers as well as the two rescued men. Paul suggested to me that she could write an unbiased report of what was a very controversial incident.

Thirty feet up a rock wall, nineteen-year-old Hugh Herr presses hard with the three fingertips he has fitted on to a quarter-inch quartzite edge, and reaches right to pinch a sloping pebble. He thrusts his upper lip out in ferocious concentration, then swiftly moves his feet up on to two crystals jutting out like small thorns. He slaps left to palm a dent in the rock.

His last piece of protection is below his feet: if he falls, he would drop in a "winger" of at least ten feet before his rope pulled taut. His left hand crosses over to a three-quarter-inch hold, his right to one bigger yet, and he cruises to a ledge.

With an exultant whoop, Huey ties himself to metal wedges he inserts into the rock, the climb over: a new 5.12, virtually the top level in rock climbing, in the Shawangunks, New York. Such ratings depend on strenuousness and the size of the holds, regardless of the route's length. Huey, his face tense with excitement, brings three other climbing experts up the route one by one; they all take falls but eventually join him. A fourth, strength spent, gives up halfway.

Huey rappels to the ground, his purple-striped pants and multi-coloured Spandex top astonishing against the grey-brown rock. He rests his left foot on his knee, takes an Allen wrench from his pack, inserts it into a hole in the bottom of his artificial limb, and efficiently unscrews the foot. The wood and rubber foot is painted with an amusing parody of a Nike sneaker. The fibreglass leg is blue, with pink polka dots.

He tried to climb this line on the cliff a few years ago, before he lost both his lower legs.

"But I was doing it all wrong then," he comments, screwing on a different foot, its purple paint slightly peeling. "It's all in the footwork."

Before the accident, Huey was called the Boy Wonder, or Baby Huey (after a cartoon character who doesn't know his own strength). He was a competitive gymnast on his high school team and arguably the best rock climber in the east. Today he is called the Bionic Boy and the Mechanical Boy. In March 1982 he had both legs amputated below the knees due to frostbite. Now, on artificial legs, he is climbing better than he was before.

He speaks haltingly of the mountaineering accident, when youthful optimism and misjudgment, things apart from his technical abilities, brought disaster. A volunteer rescuer died in an avalanche; for Huey, months of depression and pain followed.

Fiercely driven before, he became more so after the accident. "After all the efforts people made to save me, I felt I should make an incredible output to do well," he said.

Alone, he slipped out of his hospital bed to practise lifting his weight with his fingertips on a window ledge. The first time he tried to climb rock on his artificial legs, he cried because he couldn't stand up. Months of intense practice brought back spirit and superb ability: "When I knew it was possible to return to where I was before, the thought drove me nuts," he says now.

"I'd always had this incredible joy climbing. You're totally narrow-minded, zooming your mind into the rock, into the power of your hands, staying calm. Just calculating and going for it.

"I don't think I'll ever think I'm good at climbing. Ever think I've mastered the mental part of it."

He confesses to being turned on by risk. "A lot of climbers don't admit that. Placing myself into severe situations forces the best out of me."

Another Gunks (Shawangunks) regular, Russ Clune, said that when Huey was only fifteen he was not only extraordinarily strong but "the most balls-out climber I'd ever seen" when risking a long fall, even a "grounder", otherwise known as a "crater".

From Huey's father: "He is a fierce obsessive. Climbing for him was the greatest therapy in the world. He doesn't want to be the best handicapped climber in the world, though. He wants to be the best climber. Of the *homo sapiens*, period."

On Friday 22 January 1982 Huey Herr, then aged seventeen, and his friend Jeff Batzer, twenty, both from Lancaster, Pennsylvania, drove north to New Hampshire for a weekend of ice climbing on Mount Washington.

Mount Washington (6,288 feet/1,916 metres) is a formidable prospect in winter, its grim list of over a hundred fatalities making it as dangerous as mountains three times its size. The reason for the disproportionate number of accidents is the weather, which is considered as extreme as any on the American continent south of Alaska. Winds average forty-four miles per hour on its summit, where the Mount Washington Observatory frequently gauges wind velocities of over one hundred. In 1934 the observatory clocked a gust of 231 mph, the highest recorded wind speed in the world.

Huey and Jeff awoke at dawn in the Harvard cabin at the base of Mount Washington, where climbers frequently sleep. They were appropriately equipped for a day out. Each put on long underwear, layers of wool clothing, Gore-Tex parkas and outer pants, and mountaineering boots covered by padded Supergaitors.

The summit temperature was 9°F, and high winds and rapid weather changes were expected; it was already "snowing like crazy", as Jeff put it. Huey and Jeff, carrying a pack with rope, climbing and bivouac gear, were the first of seven climbers to leave the cabin. They told Matt Pierce, the hut caretaker, they intended to make a day trip up Odell Gully, involving about five hundred feet of technical ice climbing, an equal distance of snow hiking, and a descent via the Escape Hatch Gully. The two hiked about three-quarters of a mile to the base of Odell Gully, on the east side of the mountain.

Deciding that the pack and sleeping bag would slow their progress, they elected to carry only technical gear, and left their bivvy gear at the base of Odell Gully, to be reclaimed during the descent.

Huey later recalled moving fast and confidently up the four pitches of ice in Odell. He wanted to solo Odell, and he let the rope trail free behind him, enjoying the concentration required. At the end of each rope length, he would tie himself into ice screw placements to belay Jeff. Neither spoke beyond a few rope commands, nothing unusual for Huey, who is naturally quiet. The two raced up the ice section within an hour and a half, and began to trudge up the dry, loose snow above. The summit was about 1,500 feet further. The boys crouched behind a boulder out of the wind.

"You want to try for the summit?" Hugh asked.

"Think we could make it?"

"Well, we could just go a ways," Hugh suggested.

"We thought we'd sprint to the summit and spring right back," Jeff said later. "It was blowing really hard, but visibility wasn't too bad. It started out fun, really cold and windy, with ice crystallising on our faces."

The two boys are uncertain at what point they stopped. A Mount Washington rescue report compiled later estimates that they turned back when they reached Ball's Crag, less than half a mile from the top. Winds there were blowing at 64 mph, and gusting to 94; the temperature was one degree above zero.

"The weather was just horrendous," said Huey. "I said, 'Let's get out of here.' I turned back the way I thought we'd come." Having no map or compass, they tried to use the wind direction to get their bearings. "I guess it changed," he said.

In the wind and snow, the two crossed the auto road at least once without knowing it. This cuts a switchback up the mountain's north side.

For a while, they thought they had found a gully they remembered from the approach. Huey started run-stepping down it, elated. Jeff could barely keep up, and kept shouting to Hugh to slow down, in case he were nearing steep ice in the Escape Hatch.

The two were above treeline, and could see nothing of the terrain around them. They had descended the wrong side of the mountain, starting down the north-east ridge into the area known appropriately as the Great Gulf, and were moving down a water drainage run towards the trees.

"I realised for sure we were screwed when the gully just went and went, but going back up would have been death. It was the trees that saved us," Hugh said.

At first they trudged through a foot of snow, Jeff said, but well into the woods they struggled with snow up to their waists. Small fir trees, their branches interlocking, further slowed the boys' progress. Daylight faded.

Knowing they were lost, the boys dumped their hardware, rope and crampons, and slogged along the west branch of the Peabody River. Hugh broke through the ice, wetting his feet.

They continued to hike until perhaps 1.00 am, then found a granite boulder they could use for shelter, and cut spruce branches to lie upon and under. Hugh, exhausted, his clothes soaked and frozen, would cut a few twigs, then sit and stare. Jeff had more strength, and collected most of the branches. Hugh stripped his wet clothes off from the waist down, and put on a pair of Jeff's wool cycling tights and socks, then his own wool pants. That night, they kept fairly warm by hugging each other, and rubbed each other's feet for hours. The next morning, however, the boys could barely get their frozen leather boots back on their feet.

Hugh fell in the stream again the next day, breaking through to his chest this time. The water, two feet beneath the ice, surged over his knees. Gripped by the thought of being pulled under the ice, he shouted for help. Jeff grabbed a tree with one hand, extended his axe towards Hugh and slowly pulled him out.

At about 8.30 am they came to the junction of Madison Gulf Trail and the Osgood Cut-Off; signs pointed towards snow-covered trails to Pinkham Notch, Mount Washington Auto Road, Madison hut and Great Gulf Trail. Thinking they were saved, "We just stood there and cried," Hugh said. Unfamiliar with the area, the two set off towards the Madison hut, only two and a half miles away. What they did not know was that the Madison hut is both above the treeline and closed in winter.

"That's what really killed us," Huey concluded. "If we'd taken the right trail [towards Pinkham Notch, four and a half miles] we'd have walked right out of there."

They wasted waning hours and energy flailing up the steep, snow-covered trail, then turned back towards the intersection. Huey fell as they neared the signs, then again a hundred yards further, beside a boulder. This time he did not rise.

The boys crawled under the rock, pulling spruce branches about them again for warmth. When Jeff tried to take off his boots he found that the toes of his two pairs of socks had frozen to his boots. He inserted his ice axe into the boots, and sawed the toes of his socks off. Jeff wrapped his stockinged feet in his parka; Hugh put his mittens on his feet. During the night, temperatures dropped to $-17°F$, with winds continuing at about 50 mph.

At dawn on Monday, when Jeff tried to pull his first boot on, he found the tongue frozen stiff. He pried both boot tongues open with his ice axe, but then his swollen feet rammed against the frozen clumps of socks inside. He was able to pry the socks out of his right boot with his ice axe, and he and Hugh pulled together as hard as they could to haul the boot on to Jeff's foot.

"I worked on the other boot for two hours," Jeff said, "but I couldn't get the frozen sock out." (Two years later he reached into his old boot and found the wad of wool still there.) He kept elbowing Hugh, saying, "C'mon, get your boots on." But Hugh would lean forward, pause, then drop back. "His boots were horrible," Jeff said. "Covered with ice. He was delirious, hardly saying anything."

"I wasn't delirious," Hugh countered. "I was thinking about dying. I didn't have much to say."

That morning, Hugh said, "We'd have these contradictory surges: OK, we have to get out of this – then, we're gonna die."

He gave up on his boots and tried to walk with his mittens on his feet. "But I could only walk ten paces before I'd fall over."

Jeff mustered his last reserves, and made a desperate effort to hike alone to Pinkham Notch for help. He wore only one boot; he put an overmitt on the other foot. Several times he lost the trail, buried as it was. The blowing snow stuck to the trees and concealed the painted blazes. He found himself crossing his own tracks, reeling back and forth across the same area in search of a blaze. He finally fought his way back to where Hugh lay.

"Hugh, I failed," he said.

"That's OK," Hugh said simply.

The two felt their last chance was gone. "I totally relaxed then and let the cold engulf me," Hugh said. "I was completely numb. No pain. No hope. I'd fully accepted it."

Neither could stand now. They lapsed into long reveries as they lay still under the boulder. "I was mostly thinking about people, parents, how they're going to react," said Hugh. "It was terrible. So sad. Dying young – I felt cheated. I thought about my friends at the Gunks. I thought about all the routes I wasn't going to do there." Huey was hugging his friend for warmth, their legs overlapping. "Want to hear something I've never told anyone before? When I was lying there, I had to go to the bathroom and I couldn't move. I thought, I'm going to die anyway, and I just went. On our legs."

Jeff said, "I was thinking about my family, the dinner table. Sweet thoughts. Then about letting them down. It was so lonely. I thought about the chance they'd never find us. I thought about my mom, the closest person to me at the time. Then there were two things left. One was the thirst. We were so dehydrated. All I wanted was a drink. The other thing: I was really praying, out loud in front of someone for the first time in my life. And wondering what would happen to me when I went."

As evening approached, Jeff said, their extreme thirst was far worse than the cold. There was a hole in the middle of the frozen stream near them, but he knew he would break through the ice if he tried to walk on it. He made his way to the edge of the ten-foot wide stream and, using nylon runners, tied his ice axe to the end of a log. Pushing the log out, he was able to dip his axe into the water. The snow on the axe blade absorbed the water like a sponge. He ate the snow, and twice took a share up to Hugh before losing the energy it took to walk the three paces from boulder to stream.

Lying nearly still, they made it through the third night. On Tuesday morning the two knew they would not last another night.

Throughout that morning they spoke little. At about 1.30 Jeff saw a helicopter above them. He crawled out to spread his red parka among the trees, hoping it would be spotted from the air. When the helicopter continued on, he rejoined Hugh, desolate. An hour later they heard rustling in the trees.

"That was when I looked up and saw 'the most beautiful girl I'd ever seen!'" said Huey, referring to a quotation later attributed to Jeff by the *National Enquirer*. ("They made that up," according to Jeff.) "Know what?" Hugh said with a laugh. "I can't even remember what she looked like."

Melissa "Cam" Bradshaw, an Appalachian Mountain Club employee out snowshoeing on her day off, was north-east of Mount Washington in the area called the Great Gulf when she came upon an odd series of tracks. It was 26 January, the third day of a winter storm in which winds had been blowing over 50 mph and the temperature had dropped to $-20°F$. The tracks seemed to stagger, and crossed themselves several times. She began to follow them through the snow. An hour and a quarter later she peered beneath a boulder. Amid snow and cut spruce branches lay two boys, side by side. Their faces were ashen, with sunken eyes and cracked lips. They turned their heads and fixed her with dull gazes.

Cam Bradshaw was unconnected with the search and rescue effort under way on the other side of the mountain. In fact, Matt Pierce, caretaker of the Harvard cabin, had become concerned when the boys had not returned by nightfall on Saturday, and hiked out to the base of Odell to call for them. Visibility was only fifty to seventy yards even with a headlamp, and the wind was blowing 50 mph.

At 7.00 pm Pierce made a radio call to Misha Kirk, on duty at the Appalachian Mountain Club (AMC) hut in Pinkham Notch, who responded by contacting the New Hampshire Fish and Game Department, the United States Forest Service, and the Mountain Rescue Service in North Conway. It was too dark to start a search that night, so the operation was slated to begin at 6.30 the next morning.

Organisation efforts began immediately. Sergeant Carl T. Carlson of the Fish and Game Department called six officers who would be available with snowmobiles. Bill Kane of North Conway expected ten to fifteen volunteers. Two forest rangers, five volunteers from the AMC cabin and five AMC employees joined the roster.

The next morning, Sunday, Misha Kirk found the abandoned bivouac gear at the base of the Odell headwall. Searchers reasoned that the missing climbers could be injured and stalled anywhere along the 1,500-foot Huntington Ravine, from which Odell branches. They set out to search the most probable areas.

Paul Ross, one of mountain rescue's three team leaders, described his effort that day. He and several others rode five miles up the Auto Road in a snowcat, then set off and walked a mile further, heading for the Alpine Garden, which they intended to descend into Huntington. "But visibility was near zero and winds were so bad we were fighting to walk more than searching," Ross said.

When nothing more had been found by 4.00 pm, the search was suspended until the next day. The searchers had exhausted many possibilities outside of Odell Gully, but could not search the entire gully because of the severe conditions. With the help of the gear found in the discarded pack, Fish and Game officers identified the missing boys and phoned their parents.

"They could have been anywhere," Paul Ross commented. "It's a vast wilderness."

Only later, when the rescue was several days old, Ross added, did he learn much about the boys he was seeking and their crack climbing reputation.

As Ross's team mate, Mike Hartrich, observed, "We didn't know anything about them at first except their ages. They were obviously young – it reeked of inexperience. We thought they'd be in Odell or near it. If we had realised how strong they were, we'd have known they were capable of covering the distance they did. It turned out Herr was a very strong climber, and he'd gone up the gully in about an hour."

He did not guess the two might have pushed on to the summit. "No one goes to the summit in winter after a technical climb," Hartrich commented. "It's a long walk, cold, the terrain is nondescript, and there's not much to see up there in a whiteout. Of the thousand technical ascents from the Huntington side the mountain gets in a winter, probably no more than two parties go to the summit."

But even if the searchers had known the two had gone towards the summit, they would not have expected them to descend into the Great Gulf.

The following morning, Doug Madara and Steve Larson of the North Conway rescue team climbed up the right side of Odell Gully until they could see the top ridge. "We could see there was nobody lying there, so we came back down," Madara said. "We figured we'd done our job." He sustained minor frostbite: "I think almost everybody did."

Albert Dow and Michael Hartrich, high on the left side of the gully, found an abandoned karabiner and footprints leading up and out of the gully. They decided to continue up and right across the area known as the Alpine Garden, and descend on the Lion's Head Trail below it.

"We were following footprints, and could see where they'd made belays," Hartrich said. "You get a lot of traffic there, but we couldn't tell – could have been the boys. It was easier to walk across than try to come down through the rock and snow slopes on the side of Odell. You'd have to rappel, in that kind of wind." They lost the prints, however, in the blowing snow. The two started down the summer trail on Lion's Head, carefully avoiding potential avalanche slopes. Crossing the winter trail at an elevation of about 4,000 feet, they approached treeline.

"We were on a snow slope," Hartrich continued. "I glissaded down and was walking in the woods when all of a sudden I was swimming."

A two-to-three-foot slab of loose snow had avalanched off the 30°–35° slope. The sliding snow was approximately 70 feet wide and 100 feet long; it moved about 350 feet down the slope, trapping both men.

"I was carried probably a hundred feet – I was pretty much buried," said Hartrich. "The last thing I remember was snow piling around my head. I made a fist and beat at the snow, to try and clear an area around my head. If I just sat there it would have hardened up and I wouldn't have been able to move."

He had last seen Albert Dow a few feet above him to the right. Both men had been dragged through a forest of birch trees and firs; Hartrich remembered feeling several break as he hit them. He was able to reach an arm into his anorak pouch and retrieve the radio to call for help. "I couldn't move anything else," he said.

Bill Kane, eight other mountain rescue members and two rangers had started up towards the base of the Winter Trail in a Thiokol snowcat to meet Hartrich and Dow. As the minutes passed and the two men did not appear, the group became concerned and Kane tried to make radio contact; thus when Hartrich's voice on the radio shouted for help, the nine Mountain Rescue members fanned out to search immediately while the two rangers took the snowcat and raced to the first-aid cache in Tuckerman Ravine for shovels and avalanche probes.

Four others who had been hiking down from the Harvard cabin to Pinkham Notch set off to the avalanche site on foot.

Misha Kirk, who was on snowshoes, had contacted Hartrich and Dow by radio on his way to meeting them at the base of Lion's Head. He assumed the two were on the Summer Trail, approaching the Winter Trail. The search began there.

A few minutes later, Joe Gill skied across the Winter Trail and heard Hartrich shouting below. Descending, he felt movement in the snow mass and knew the whole area to be prone to slide again.

Joe Gill began to dig Hartrich out from the centre of the avalanche deposition toe at 2.25. He was joined five minutes later by Kirk and the nine from mountain rescue, then the rangers with supplies. The group started the search for Dow with a rapid probing technique known as a coarse probe, down from the top of the gully, checking the deposition debris and any snags, and then they began a fine probe.

They found Dow at 3.15, six feet from where Hartrich had stopped, and attempted to revive him for half an hour. Injuries to his neck and chest showed he had hit a tree.

The four who had been hiking up to the site arrived, to see Dow being taken down in a sled. Albert Dow was pronounced dead on arrival at the North Conway hospital two hours later.

The search resumed on Tuesday with a plan to break the area into grid patterns. An Army National Guard helicopter with a crew of four joined the search, lifting off from Pinkham Notch at 10.00 am. The boys were still believed to be holed up somewhere in the Huntington Ravine or Lion's Head area.

In trying to enter the ravine the helicopter met extreme turbulence, which forced it to fly 1000–1500 feet above the area being scanned. After an hour it landed to refuel before continuing for another two hours.

It was that day that Cam Bradshaw came across Jeff's muddled footprints and followed them to their source. She gave Jeff and Huey water, raisins, a vest and a wool shirt, and reassured them that she would return with help. Cam rushed off towards the AMC lodge, passing two hikers whom she sent to the boys by instructing them to follow her footprints. The hikers reached Hugh and Jeff and covered them with sleeping bags. At 3.20 Cam Bradshaw telephoned the AMC to report that the boys were alive.

Within ten minutes the helicopter was launched, and their families and Littleton Hospital in New Hampshire had been notified. Ground crews set off on foot along the Great Gulf Trail.

As the helicopter approached the site one of the two hikers caring for the boys ignited a red flare. The pilot, Captain John Weeden, hovered a hundred yards from the flare where the trees were only about twenty-five feet tall to lower Misha Kirk and another crewman on a forest penetrator hoist, a disk seat protected by metal flanges.

Kirk, a medic, evaluated the boys' condition and their location. Both were hypothermic and frostbitten; Hugh was incoherent, a stretcher patient. The rescue would be hindered by bad weather, rough terrain, fading light and the eighty-foot trees around them. Kirk remained with hot packs to attend the boys while the helicopter returned to Pinkham Notch to refuel for a lengthy hoist extrication.

Rescuers carried Jeff on a Stokes litter to the evacuation site, an awkward process due to the steep terrain and the three feet of fresh snow on the ground. He was hoisted aboard on the forest penetrator at 5.15.

Several ground crews had now arrived to help, but it was decided to hoist Hugh from where he lay rather than carry him to the evacuation site. This plan would be far more difficult to enact, but speed was now vital. It was dark, and all operations were by the light of headlamps and the helicopter searchlight.

Captain Weeden maintained the helicopter's position 110 feet above the site. Walter Lessard controlled the operation from the rear of the craft, lowering the hoist cable to the litter below. As the litter rose, it revolved so that the litter head was below the helicopter runners. Hampered by his gloves, Lessard took them off to straighten the litter, despite the sub-zero temperatures and the paralysing wind caused by the propeller blades.

"It seemed like he was struggling with it for five or ten minutes," Jeff observed. "Then it slid in." It was 5.45. Kirk and the ret of the party below began to hike out towards Pinkham Notch.

The boys arrived at Littleton Hospital at 7.00 pm, three full days after they were reported missing. Jeff's core temperature was 94°, Huey's, 93°. No one could tell what their temperatures were before they received aid from the hikers.

The mistakes the boys made are easy to identify. Their decision to try for the summit of Mount Washington got them lost when the weather worsened. They had changed their intended route, so that rescuers looked for them in the wrong places. Had they not ditched their bivvy gear, they could have shared it in relative warmth. Although unfamiliar with the area, they carried no map or compass. A trail guide would have told them that the Madison hut was above treeline and closed for the winter.

A sharp backlash of public and media opinion followed the accident. Martha Herr, Hugh's mother, summed up the reaction: " 'These dumb flatlanders come up and do this and one of our own died for it.' It got so we would wonder, can we buy the paper today or will it just depress us?" she said.

The New Hampshire people who were most critical of the incident tended not to be a part of the local mountain rescue service, Albert Dow's team mates.

"Certainly I don't resent them," Paul Ross of Mountain Rescue said. "We've all made mistakes. When I was very young, about sixteen or seventeen, I'd go blundering up mountains. Once I had to walk fourteen miles to get home. I never got bloody lost again!"

Michael Hartrich put it another way: "The boys did things

most people wouldn't have done. But they didn't do anything I haven't done. I just didn't do them all at once!"

Hartrich disclaimed credit for his own part in the rescue. "People say, you're so brave to be out in those conditions. But for an experienced climber they weren't extraordinary. The terrain was not very difficult technically. I don't think anybody felt they were sticking their necks out.

"It was chance that Albert hit a tree. If he'd ended up like I was, one of us might have dug the other out. We'd have brushed ourselves off and laughed about it."

Sixteen days after his rescue, Huey was transferred to the Presbyterian Medical Center of the University Hospital in Philadelphia. Circulation to his feet continued to be poor, and the tissue was infected.

Nine days after Hugh's transfer, Jeff entered Lancaster General Hospital. Infection was evident and circulation poor in his right hand and left foot.

On Tuesday 2 March Jeff's doctor was compelled to amputate the young man's right thumb and four fingers down to the first joint. Three days later he amputated Jeff's left foot. Jeff also lost the toes on his right foot.

Eight days after Jeff's amputations, about six weeks after the rescue, Hugh's doctor amputated both of the young man's legs six inches below the knee.

As we have seen, Hugh not only returned to climbing, he became better at it than he was before. Half a year after his amputations, he was climbing 5.11, and two years later he was climbing 5.12 more often and more confidently than ever. He is maybe the only amputee in the world to refer to his artificial limbs as an advantage: he is lighter now, so that his strength-to-weight ratio has improved. He has five pairs of feet, four of them for climbing different kinds of rock. One pair features pointed toes for crack climbing. Hugh's technical ice climbing too has improved; he uses rigid crampons shortened to about six inches for improved leverage.

He has difficulty walking on rough terrain, and when a trail is snow-covered, he crawls. Climbing steep ice is usually much easier than approaching it. Damaging the tissue on his legs one day can mean he must stay off his feet for three; the same applies to Jeff.

Hugh speaks of college, and perhaps of training to become a prosthetist, building artificial limbs. But for now, he confesses, "I'd rather get my slide shows and pants business going, and climb." He makes his living piecemeal: painting houses, sewing climbing gear for Wild Things Alpine Equipment in North Conway and sewing Lycra climbing pants of his own design in wild colours. He gives frequent slide shows to general audiences and handicapped people.

Jeff returned to his job as an apprentice tool-and-die maker, and his other sports pastime, competitive cycling. One year after his accident Jeff competed in a cycling race up Mount Washington. But more important to him now is his religious faith. He speaks to local church groups about what happened to him physically and spiritually during and as a result of his accident, and plans to go to bible college to train for the evangelical ministry.

Snow on the Equator

Oswald Oelz, Robert Chambers, Raimund Margreiter

This tale of a rescue on Mount Kenya is one of the most amazing in the annals of mountaineering. The rescuers had not only to combat the technical difficulties of the climb, but some had also to deal with the debilitating effect of altitude sickness. One rescuer was killed. The man they were trying to reach they expected to be already dead from his injuries. Several of the main characters in this high African adventure still feel, after seventeen years, that it was the most demanding and profound period of their lives.

Robert Chambers of the Mountain Club of Kenya was in charge of the rescue bid and he can still recall every detail of those days in 1970. Two friends of mine took part in the operation. Dr Oswald Oelz was one of the two Austrian climbers involved in the accident, it was his colleague who fell. John Temple was one of the rescuers who made a great contribution, especially in the early stages of the rescue. My recollections of John Temple are associated with balmy days in the Cuillins of Skye, warm rock and lumps of uncompromising commercial glucose as hard as gabbro, which caused temporary discomfort to my stomach and permanent damage to my teeth. John had an inexhaustible source of glucose, and Ian Clough, who was the third member of this happy rock-climbing trio, swore that the lumps would make excellent artificial chockstones from which to attach running belays. This was back in 1958 and the alloy chock had still to be invented. We enjoyed many routes together during that summer before John Temple left for Nairobi where he did some impressive climbs on Mount Kenya, some of them first ascents.

The first European to record seeing what later became known as

Mount Kenya was a resolute German missionary, Dr Johann Krapf, who looked northwards from a village in the Wa-Kamba district on 3 December 1849 and saw "snow on the equator". "It appeared to me," he wrote, "like a gigantic wall, on whose summit I observed two immense towers, or horns, as you might call them. These horns or towers, which are at a short distance from each other, give the mountain a grand and majestic appearance which raised in my mind overwhelming feelings." Though natives had spoken earlier of the mountain to explorers and missionaries, they were not believed, nor immediately was Dr Krapf. Indeed it was to be fifty years before someone climbed the mountain which gave the state its name.

The first recorded attempt was made in 1893 by Professor Gregory, whose loyal Zanzibari bearers made better porters than climbers and had an understandable distrust of snow and ice. One agreed to rope up with his master, but when a hold broke under him his nerve broke too and he addressed the professor: "That is all very well for Wajuuxi [lizards] and Wazungu [white men] but Zanzibaris can't do that!"

So the first ascent fell to the explorer Sir Halford Mackinder who six years later climbed Batian (17,058 feet/5,199 metres), the higher of the twin summits, accompanied, as was the fashion of those gentlemanly days, by two Courmayeur guides, César Ollier and Joseph Brocherel. The second summit, Nelion (17,022 feet/ 5,186 metres) was not defeated until Eric Shipton and Percy Wynn Harris climbed it in 1929.

Today the mountain and its satellites are within the Mount Kenya National Park. The plateau of moorland surrounding the peaks above 11,000 feet (3,351 metres) could be from the pages of Lord of the Rings. *Giant heather and groundsel grow like twenty-foot trees, while the lobelia stands as tall as a man, and below, the forest teems with a Noah's Ark of fauna, from rhino to leopard, who sometimes trespass on to this moorland.*

The twin peaks soar in splendid volcanic isolation over the East African savannah and while the area is a magnet for tourists and climbers, the ascent of Mount Kenya is by no means easy.

The two young Austrian doctors felt justly proud when they reached the summit of Batian by the hard North Face on 5 September 1970. I first met Dr Oswald Oelz two years later at the Yak and Yeti Hotel in Kathmandu when he was a member of an Austrian Manaslu Expedition. This is the start of Oswald Oelz's account of their amazing experience. After him various members of the rescue team contribute their own memories of an operation unparalleled on the mountains of Africa.

Dr Oswald Oelz

On 5 September at 1.30 pm my friend, twenty-nine-year-old Dr Gerd Judmaier, and I reached the main summit of Mount Kenya, known as Batian. This was our first trip outside the Alps and we were ecstatic to have reached our goal. We left the Kami hut at 5.30 am and found the climbing enjoyable, but difficult in places, due to ice in the chimneys. It was the first ascent from the Kami hut that season.

We stayed on the summit for a few minutes only since we were entirely in cloud and it had started to snow. To gain the descent point we traversed three pitches of the summit ridge to Shipton's Notch where I found two old abseil slings around a rock but used a new one to ensure a safe rappel down the face. Shipton's Notch is a comfortable place on the ridge and has enough space for several people to stand there. We were still roped up, Gerd was standing one metre to my left looking down the face and was holding on to a big rock block with his right hand. While fixing the abseil sling I suddenly to my horror saw the block breaking away and falling down the face together with Gerd. They both vanished. Somehow I managed to get the rapidly disappearing rope into my hands and tried to arrest the fall. My hands and fingers were burned immediately. But suddenly the rope snagged for an instant, interrupting Gerd's fall as he crashed diagonally down the face after a twelve-metre plunge. This enabled me to take a turn of the rope round my arm to stop him.

Immediately I heard him crying to give him some slack. I let him down another two or three metres. Writing this after all these years I still don't know how I managed to hold him.

He shouted up to me that he had an open fracture of his right leg. I quickly rappeled to where he lay, noting en route that our rope was severely damaged in several places by the rock fall.

Gerd was lying on steep loose rock on a ledge, and was bleeding from various head injuries, having lost his helmet in the fall. More serious, however, was the condition of his right leg where the tibia was sticking out of his stocking just above the climbing boot and a ten-centimetre splinter from the distal part of his tibia was lying quite separately beside him. This injury was bleeding severely. He had apparently also damaged the left leg. I applied a strong tourniquet around his right thigh and thereby controlled the bleeding.

Gerd was entirely realistic about his prospects for the immediate future: he calmly discussed three options for dying:

Shock and bleeding.

Freezing to death.

Fat embolism originating from his open bone.

Neither of us saw much hope in getting him down in time to obtain the vital medication.

He thought that his chances of survival were only a few per cent. I thought, but kept it to myself, that he didn't have any chance whatsoever. But we both resolved to fight, to fight as we'd never fought before.

I wrapped all our clothes around him and covered him completely with a bivouac sack. I also left our food supply, which was limited to 250 cc of whisky and one can of fruit. He asked me to say goodbye to everybody and said, "You know I had a good life." I told him not to give up, that I would get help in time, and I left hardly able to control my grief and tears.

I had to tie what was left of the rope together at several points so that I could now only rappel a maximum of ten metres on the descent. It was snowing heavily and I was full of remorse, knowing for certain that I would not find him alive when I came back.

It was almost dark when I arrived at the Kami hut. There were eight British and American climbers there and when I told them of the accident they immediately offered to help. The strongest of them, a Zambian British expatriate called Bert Burrage, climbed in the dark for two and a half hours to the Top hut at 15,700 feet where there was emergency first aid and a solar-powered radio. He got through to the police at Naro Moru, a village at the base of the mountain, and a rescue operation was then set in motion.

In 1970 the procedure for dealing with a major rescue on Mount Kenya was hypothetical, for until that year there had been no call for a serious evacuation from the virtual summit of the mountain.

Robert Chambers and fellow members of the Mountain Club of Kenya had speculated about such an emergency, and when it came to pass, like so many dedicated mountaineers, they did their damnedest to save human life and in so doing risked their own. Robert describes the situation and the events leading up to a spectacular rescue.

ROBERT CHAMBERS

In the Mountain Club of Kenya (MCK) in 1970, no one would have called our mountain rescue team strong. The club had perhaps a dozen people who could lead Severe or harder, and a dozen more with enough mountaineering and rock climbing experience to be of some use. We also had a few contacts in Uganda and Tanzania who were outside possibilities for help in a long rescue. Many of our members were expatriates on short-term contracts, which made it difficult to build up a team, or even to agree on and practise standard procedures. Every few months we would grit our teeth and force ourselves to devote the better part of a Sunday to a rather hazardous practice, usually at Leukenia, the most popular and accessible rocks near Nairobi, and actually owned by the club. After these practices, with their terrifying lowers of sporting victims, and their lively discussions about methods and procedures, I always heaved a sigh of relief that nothing worse had happened than the loss of climbing time. Our equipment was a mixture of the basic, two stretchers, and the avant garde, a cacolet (rescue litter), plus two 100-metre drums of wire for direct lowers. Every now and then we had call-outs on Mount Kenya, but usually for pulmonary oedema. The only really big climbing rescue before 1970 was not a true test of the MCK rescue team, because eight fit Germans happened to be already on the mountain and they did most of the climbing involved. Also the weather was good. We had never had to do a major rescue at altitude on our own. The one mock rescue we attempted on Mount Kenya was a dreadful thing. Many of the "rescuers" were more or less useless from mountain sickness.

Even less confidence was inspired by our "dry" rescues in the clubhouse. These were exercises in logistical fantasy, like military TEWTs (Tactical Exercises Without Troops). We would imagine an accident and then follow through our guesses of what might happen, hour by hour and day by day. No amount of beer made these anything but sobering occasions. Once we picked a really difficult place. We took one of the most inaccessible places on the mountain – Shipton's Notch on the West Ridge, just below the summit of Batian. This we reckoned would be harder than anywhere on the normal route. By the end of the evening, having allowed for mountain sickness and other contingencies, we could see no way the rescue could be completed. Hardly anyone could even reach the place. Despite the support of the Kenya Police and the Mountain National Parks, there was no way we could think to get someone off Shipton's Notch dead, let alone alive.

I used to daydream about mountain rescue. It added an edge to life to know you might be called out any moment for some dramatic excitement, and it was an exhilarating fantasy world to enter, with plenty of scope for seeing oneself in a heroic role. As long as it did not really happen. We had procedures and did practices, but we didn't have experience.

Jenny and I were lying in bed at home in Nairobi after a rather good Saturday evening and just dropping off into the deep and blissful, when the phone rang. There are moments for telephone calls, and this was not one of them. So I had to make the drowsy joke, "It's a rescue!" The phone crackled and a voice said, "This is Naro Moru Police Station . . ."

As convenor of the MCK Mountain Rescue Sub-Committee, I was automatically in charge of the climbing part of the rescue. Jenny and I telephoned around but could raise no other member of the climbing team, so we left the task to the Kenya Police Headquarters. I spoke to Bill Woodley, the Warden of the Mountain National Parks and a highly skilled pilot, and arranged to meet him at the Naro Moru airstrip at dawn. We then went to the Mountain Club, collected medicines and jammed the cacolet with difficulty into our Volkswagen Beetle. It left little room. I curled up as best I could to try to sleep while Jenny, pregnant with our first child, drove through the night, the 120-odd miles to Naro Moru.

The first question was whether the climber was still alive. After a night alone with a broken leg at that altitude, he might well not be. So we flew up to see, and also to recce a rescue route. We took off in the little two-seater just after dawn. It was one of those Kenya mornings so clear it almost hurts. We climbed slowly up over the forest, and then the moorland, and then finally breasted a col and ridge to the North Face and the summit. And there we could see a red blob on a ledge just below Shipton's Notch. And the blob waved. We flew right past and could see him well, lying there waving vigorously. I think that having seen Gerd Judmaier, as a person, alive on that ledge, was crucial for me in the days that followed.

As we flew round, I had a good look at his position. There were two possible rescue lines. One was along the summit ridge and down the North Ridge by the Firmin-Hicks route. The carry along the ridge looked to me out of the question, given our few climbers and the possibility of altitude sickness. And it was difficult to imagine our ever being able to complete the rescue down the long North Ridge which followed. Also any rescue along that line would take so long that Judmaier would be dead long before we got him off. So I looked at the alternative, so appealing from the air – a direct lower down the North Face, in two stages. It would need either our two drums of wire or perhaps two hundred metres of rope, but it looked feasible. If we could get the rope or wire, and the light cacolet to the Notch, plus three or four climbers, we would stand a chance of getting him down and off quickly. Or so it seemed to me, looking at it from the plane.

We landed back in Naro Moru. A few climbers were beginning to arrive. Judmaier's companion, Oswald Oelz, was also a doctor, and we got the message that the top priority was plasma to restore Judmaier's body fluids.

Meantime, high on Mount Kenya in the Kami Hut, Dr Oswald Oelz hoped to join the group who were going to try to get up to Gerd at dawn.

DR OSWALD OELZ

The others started to organise for the climb up to Gerd and prepared me plenty of hot sweet tea which was the only thing I could swallow. They were all suffering in varying degrees from mountain sickness and I didn't have high hopes for our ascent plan for the following morning.

Bert Burrage returned late in the night from the Top hut, having done a most remarkable job in alerting the police and the Mountain Club of Kenya. He also brought down vital painkillers and penicillin.

Carrying heavy loads, Dick from Los Angeles and I started climbing very early in the morning. On the more difficult pitches we left fixed rope. By 10.00 am it started to snow heavily and the climbing became increasingly difficult. I had excruciating pain in my fingers and hands which had been burned by the rope the day before. After reaching about 4900 metres Dick got very sick and exhausted from the altitude and could go no further, so we had to retreat and I lowered him with the aid of a karabiner brake, a method of running the rope through several interlinked karabiners.

I was utterly frustrated as I knew that Gerd was either dead or would be shortly and I couldn't help him. We reached the Kami hut at night, soaked with water and snow, freezing and exhausted. Four climbers from the Mountain Club of Kenya had arrived from Nairobi during the day. They seemed to be a little sick from the rapid ascent but had brought a lot of equipment. Unfortunately there were no intravenous fluids yet, which I considered the most important medication if Gerd was still alive.

ROBERT CHAMBERS

Much of the first three days was devoted to getting plastic containers of gear up the hill. That Sunday (Day 2) was hell, an awful long slogging walk up to Kami hut at 4400 metres (14,564 feet). We arrived to find that Oelz and an American, Richard Sykes, had tried to reach Judmaier that day and been driven back a few hundred feet from him by heavy snow. Oelz's hands were in a mess from holding Judmaier's fall and his clothes were soaked but he was very, very toughly determined to have another go.

I think it was the next morning (I am recollecting fifteen years later) that we held a crisis debate on whether to continue the rescue. Most of us were feeling dreadful, with varying degrees of mountain sickness and exhaustion, without even setting foot on the climb. In one view, to continue was irresponsible, Judmaier was probably dead already. We had learnt from Oelz how serious the fracture was. How could he survive two nights and a subsequent rescue with a badly broken leg? If we established contact with him, we would feel morally obliged to continue a rescue, although others were likely to die. Anyway we did not have the capacity to rescue him. The other view was that he might still be alive, and that a direct lower down the North Face could get him off the rocks really very fast. I was ultimately responsible for the decision.

To call off the rescue was simply not something I could bring myself to do. In fact, it did not all rest on my decision, there were some people in the party who were going to have a go anyway!

So Oelz and an MCK member, Silvano Borruso, set off on the Monday morning (Day 3) to try again to reach Judmaier. They took a radio. John Temple and Pradeep followed with the cacolet. The weather was cloudy and no pilot could see the Notch to tell whether Judmaier was still alive. I spent the day trying to acclimatise and gather strength at Kami. No message came back in the evening;

there was no radio contact. And it seemed to us that Judmaier was probably dead. Morale was very low.

Dr Oswald Oelz

Silvano, the strongest climber in the group, was coming back up with me. When we reached the start of the climb we met more people who had just arrived to help. We made rapid progress, impeded only by the heavy loads.

Although Silvano was increasingly suffering from the altitude as we climbed, he followed steadily. At 5.30 pm more than forty-eight hours after I left Gerd, I climbed around the last ridge that separated me from his ledge, twenty metres below Shipton's Notch. I saw the shape of a motionless body covered by the red bivouac sac. Desperately I cried, "Gerd, Gerd," certain he would not answer. But miraculously he moved the bivouac sac from his face and said in a soft voice: "Oh God, Bulle [my nickname] I didn't think you were still alive." He looked desperately pale and thin. I was over-whelmed and cried into my walkie-talkie to all the people on the mountain and the whole world that he was still alive and that we could save his life if we worked fast. However the damned walkie-talkie didn't seem to work for I didn't get any response.

Gerd was suffering terrible pain and I gave him first an injection of morphine. We also gave him some fluid for his desperate thirst. He could not tolerate very much and started to vomit. In the last forty-eight hours he had had a little sip of whisky and the canned fruit which he had to open with stones, since he had lost his knife. We all three were relieved to be together, but spent a miserable cold night on the slanting rock shelf.

The morning was sunny as always and if it wasn't for the injured man we would have enjoyed that beautiful location. There were several aeroplanes flying around which told us that the rescue was well under way and that the people of Kenya cared.

After I dressed and splinted Gerd's leg, Silvano tried to carry him on his back, while John Temple, who had arrived during the morning, and I tried to assist him with two ropes. But Gerd could not tolerate the pain when the injured leg was hanging down. At least we managed to take him to a flat space which measured two metres by fifty centimetres and belay him to pitons. Gerd was looking worse than the day before, he was dying slowly. He could not take enough fluid by mouth and I still didn't have intravenous infusions.

ROBERT CHAMBERS

The next morning (Day 4) Jim Hastings brought up plasma in a chopper, and landed above his normal ceiling using a saucer-shaped depression near the Kami hut. He had stripped his machine of all but essentials. Two climbing pairs set off. Dick Cooper was in one, and I was in the other. We both carried plasma. Dick was fitter and faster. I remember that Firmin's Chimney, the crux of the climb, was long and unprotected and difficult in icy conditions.

DR OSWALD OELZ

I was sitting on the minute ledge beside Gerd, my legs hanging in space. It had started to snow again. Gerd told me that he expected to die during the night. He thought that it was terrible that it took so long to die and complained that he could not simply go to sleep for ever. During the night he developed fever and asked me to unclip him from the pitons so that he could roll over the edge and fall down the face to a quick death.

(DAY 5) There was fog all around us and it was cold. There was also the noise of several planes and there was a new noise, the throb of a helicopter. Suddenly there was an almighty crash and after that there was no helicopter noise any more. We knew that it had crashed and our despair was now complete. Later we learned that the pilot, Jim Hastings, had died in the crash. Dick Cooper and another climber arrived and at last I got the essential intravenous fluids. Robert Chambers was just behind. After I set up the equipment on the rock face I injected one and a half litres. Gerd was now looking better. However, the injections started to freeze and during that night I held a Gaz stove underneath the injection bottles to enable me to give him more. From time to time I found myself thinking that it would probably be better if Gerd died now since we could not bring him down anyway. I desperately wanted to get away from this terrible place on this terrible mountain with its terrible weather.

(Day 6) The morning was very cold. There were now four climbers – John Temple, Dick Cooper, Robert Chambers and Silvano Borruso – as well as myself to help Gerd and we had enough rope to rig a cableway over the first difficult section we had to traverse. However, we failed once more to move Gerd as the pain grew unbearable when we tried. There was nothing to do but to wait for a stretcher.

ROBERT CHAMBERS

Preparations were being made for a North Face lower. From Nairobi Bob Caukwell traced 600 feet of nylon rope in Mombasa. The Kenya Police drove with it through the night over three hundred miles to Nairobi and then on to Naro Moru. It was loaded in a plane, to be dropped across the ridge. We were then to use it for the direct North Face lower. We watched the plane come, slowly excreting an extraordinarily long line, and it seemed so long it could not miss. But when released it curled and drifted and missed the ridge. So we were forced back on the wire, which would have to be dragged all the way up the long North Ridge route we had followed.

Those who had taken the stretcher to the base of the North Face reported heavy stone falls and were reluctant to bring the stretcher up by that route. The loss of the airdropped rope also meant that we would have difficulty hauling the stretcher up as we had proposed. So we decided it should come up by the Firmin-Hicks route.

Unfortunately this meant further delay, and much effort. We sent out appeals for any climbers anywhere in East Africa to come and help.

Meanwhile Dr Oelz had organised a primitive hospital ward near the summit.

DR OSWALD OELZ

I was again out of injections and painkillers and Gerd was getting rapidly worse. Covered by our bivouac sac and in the few clear moments between his fever dreams he talked about his past. He said that he had had a good life and that he was sorry to go. He complained about all the girls he had not had and all the wine he had not drunk. The snow storm in the afternoon was particularly strong and we got even more depressed. It was already dark when suddenly, like a *deus ex machina*, John Temple, who had gone down to meet the others, reappeared and told us that six Austrians were landing that night in Nairobi to help us. He also brought some plasma for intravenous injections. On my knees, partly in the open air, in darkness, with a bivouac sac that the snow storm was threatening to tear apart, I tried to insert a needle in a vein of Gerd's arm. My hands were open wounds and I couldn't feel anything but pain. I couldn't find a vein for the intravenous fluid, they were all collapsed due to the severe dehydration of my patient. After about two hours I finally succeeded in inserting the needle. I made injections throughout the night with the stove beneath the injection bottle.

ROBERT CHAMBERS

We faced a crucial decision whether to go ahead with the direct lower down the North Face. It would have to be done entirely from above, without support from below due to the stone falls which the descent would create. We debated what to do. Dick Cooper was in favour. Others were against. The party in Kami, with whom we discussed it over the radio, were strongly against. I remember sitting trying to make up my mind. The direct descent without support from below did look enormously hazardous. So we agreed on the much longer, slower and more strenuous, but safer route, along the West Ridge and then down the North Ridge, the way we had come.

DR OSWALD OELZ

Gerd had high fever and complained all the time. He asked me to make a fire and heard girls' voices, speaking

German. He also told us to start to work on his evacuation immediately and not to sit around.

ROBERT CHAMBERS

Different parties were now ferrying supplies up parts of the route. I worried that inexperienced climbers were going beyond their safety limits, relying on that extra verve and daring which rescues inspire. It seemed entirely possible that we would have another accident on our hands. Although Silvano Borruso was reluctant to go I sent him down. He had made a tremendous effort in the early stages of the rescue, and spent a night at 17,000 feet (over 5,000 metres) with only a shirt and anorak, having given his pullover to Judmaier.

At midday on Day 7 we finally got the stretcher to Shipton's Notch and five or six of us began to try to move Judmaier. The first part was uphill. Even with the stretcher suspended from a rope in a Tirolean traverse, it took us hours to do this. The carry along the shelves of the West Ridge that followed was exhausting, and belaying was a continuous problem. But by evening, we had Judmaier at the top of the North Ridge. From here onwards, it was steeply downwards. It was a very cold and bad night for everyone, not least poor Judmaier.

DR OSWALD OELZ

It was again desperately cold and Gerd was having weird fever dreams all night. He called us drunkards and demanded some red wine for himself too. I melted snow every two hours and tried to give it to him but he refused each time to take more than two sips.

On the Saturday (Day 8), Robert didn't think it possible for them to get Judmaier down the North Ridge.

ROBERT CHAMBERS

I had the idea of a direct lower down the Northey Glacier. We had enough rope, and the entire lower might be completed in less than an hour, providing we could organise lowering the joined ropes. I had climbed the

Northey ten years earlier, and knew it had two sections of steep snow and ice separated by about fifty metres of rock fall. But the Kami party who had now done a recce were adamant that the idea was crazy. They reported very heavy stonefall, and in my slightly paranoid state by then, I wondered whether they were exaggerating in order to prevent the plan. A stronger argument was that the Austrians were coming and preferred the ridge.

DR OSWALD OELZ

That morning (Day 8) Gerd was still alive and we started to lower him down the ridge. We got down several pitches by 11.00 am and then it started snowing again. I was standing with Gerd at the beginning of a sharp horizontal edge which was definitely impossible to traverse with the stretcher. While thinking about the solution to the problem I looked down the face and saw what looked like an Austrian climbing helmet approaching. I shouted down and there they were, our friends to help us. Werner Heim was first to arrive, pulling three ropes behind him. He looked so strong and trustworthy that I immediately felt that we would make it. Gerd had a moment of clarity and said, "If you don't get me down today you're wasting your time."

ROBERT CHAMBERS

I remember feeling that I had little left to give, and was marvelling at John Temple's resilience when there were shouts in German, and a concentrated ball of energy burst up through the mist and snow and, within seconds, as it seemed, had rigged up ropes for lowering the stretcher. It was Werner Heim. Others came up and in no time Judmaier disappeared on his spectacular descent.

The moment the main responsibility lifted from me, I more or less collapsed for a couple of hours. I have never been so tired.

The arrival at an accident scene of a mountain rescue team from so many thousand miles away is unprecedented. All were first-class climbers with vast rescue experience on the steep cliffs of the

*Austrian Tirol and Dr Raimund Margreiter was a professional
colleague of Gerd and Oswald. The other members of this group
were Walter Larcher, Werner Heim, Kurt Pittracher, Horst
Bermann and Walter Spitzenstatter.*

*Their assistance had been requested by Gerd's father, Professor
Judmaier, who had flown out to Nairobi from Innsbruck when he
got word of the accident. Upon arrival in Nairobi they first flew
round Mount Kenya in a Cessna charter plane to identify Judmaier's lonely bivouac sac close to the summit of Batian.*

*They then landed at Nanyuki, the nearest strip to the mountain,
and from there they went by Land Rover to the Base Camp. Now
with the help of porters they crossed two 4,000-foot (1,220-metre)
passes and in forty kilometres reached the Kami Hut. It was
exactly one week since the accident and they had still to climb
the mountain, 600 metres of Grade IV climbing and one chimney of
Grade V.*

DR RAIMUND MARGREITER

As Walter Spitzenstatter and I got to the foot of the face
we saw our friends already several rope lengths above us.
Walter had had a great deal of trouble with the altitude
during the ascent and we had spent a filthy cold night
some two hundred metres below the Kami hut. It was
clear to us that our friends would reach Judmaier long
before us and we decided, therefore, to put up a continuous abseil route as far as the Amphitheatre, in order to
guarantee the evacuation even during the night. The key
to this was a 200-metre rope which they had deposited at
the foot of the climb. It took a long time before we had
disentangled this, in order to fix it at the bottom. The
other end I tied round my waist and set off.

On a rock ledge at the end of the 200 metres we fixed the
rope with ten good firm pitons. After we had installed
three more abseil lengths of about forty metres, we
reached the Amphitheatre. The others had already
brought Judmaier as far as the upper end of the Amphitheatre, where I was able to attend to his injuries. He
was certainly in a very critical condition. As well as highly
efficient painkillers, I administered to him the principal
steroids. In order to guard against the so-called "rescue

death" which frequently hits a casualty at this point if he succumbs to the induced feeling of well-being, I tried again and again to demonstrate to him the seriousness of the situation and that he would only have to hold out a few more hours. I also gave Oswald a sip of whisky.

We continued down to the lower edge of the Amphitheatre without problem, then an abseil as far as the beginning of the 200-metre rope. Walter and I, being the last to descend, removed all the abseil points which we had only a few hours before so tiringly installed. As we came to the final abseil point at dusk it was like a nightmare: Gerd on the stretcher, surrounded by the rescuers: beneath us the endless ravine, only the first few metres of which could be seen on account of the approaching darkness. We were all aware of the risks involved on this lower and no one was keen to descend the last 200 metres with the casualty.

Werner Heim and I volunteered for this hazardous undertaking. The stretcher was attached simply to the fourteen-millimetre rope which had been untied at the bottom and pulled up; we had merely secured ourselves on to the bottom bar of the stretcher. We knew full well that on this very long descent communications were going to be difficult. Various rocket signals were agreed upon in case of emergency. And so with very mixed feelings we lowered ourselves into the darkness. To start with all went smoothly, but after twenty metres we couldn't shout up to our friends and the signalling code agreed upon didn't function either. So we had to carry the casualty to the lip of each ledge we came to. When the belayers above felt the rope go slack they eased the tension. When we then let ourselves down over the edge it meant a four- or five-metre drop each time – very unnerving. With increasing rope lengths these drops became progressively longer. Added to this, the rope dislodged stones, so that periodically a salvo would pour directly over us while we threw ourselves on top of the casualty to shield him with our bodies. The stones ricocheted off our helmets and rucksacks, which protected our backs to a degree. On one occasion the stretcher got itself stuck in a chimney, the back of which was a very steep smooth slab. As we had no footholds we could not free it despite our desperate efforts. We had a smoke and reviewed the problem, before giving it a final wrench which was rewarded with a rapid slide of a good five metres!

Fortunately for us the moon rose and improved visibility. There was however still a considerable obstacle to overcome: the eight-metre overhang at the bottom of the face. If we were to continue our abseil descent over this last pitch, we would all be hanging on the rope.

"Wait, and you'll see how safely an Austrian Army mountain guide can get you down," Werner assured me.

After twenty frustrating minutes when periodically the rope was slackened too much, he finally succeeded in hammering a special piton in three centimetres. From this peg he then belayed me – and the casualty – down the overhang. The peg held.

In order to tell those 200 metres above of our arrival we fired a rocket. It was 10.00 pm. Here on easier safe ground we were met by native porters and revived with tea. After a short halt Gerd was taken on to the Kami Hut accompanied by Dr Oelz. Slowly our friends emerged one after the other out of the darkness, all except Walter Spitzenstatter.

Apparently after the successful rescue he was shattered and still at the belay 200 metres above. Kurt was with him. As a rescue expert he had performed marvellously. I was horrified at the idea of having to climb up once more in the icy cold to help him through this sinister abyss. But after I had sorted out my gear I started the ascent again and eventually made contact with him by shouting. Walter was in a pitiable state and could scarcely stand. We had to support him as far as the hut, in the course of which we lost the path and unfortunately descended too far.

Robert and the other climbers were also shattered and even at this late stage there could easily have been another accident.

ROBERT CHAMBERS

For us there was now a great effort to keep concentrating and to get off the mountain safely. I had one more bivouac with two people who stayed behind. The next morning I nearly fell off on the last long abseil, which also caused others trouble.

Raimund and Kurt got back down with Walter ahead of Robert's party and Raimund was pleased to see that their effort was not in vain.

DR RAIMUND MARGREITER
In the hut Walter quickly recovered after receiving some oxygen. The rest of the night I spent caring for Judmaier: his leg appeared really bad. The still attached piece of fractured bone protruded far out of a purulent wound above the edge of the boot.

Oswald helped Raimund.

DR OSWALD OELZ
When we took Gerd's dressings off we were immediately assailed by the terrible smell of gangrene. The bone which was still protruding from the flesh was black. At first we were watched by several of the rescuers who quickly turned pale, then disappeared. Raimund and I were almost certain that Gerd would lose his leg.

DR RAIMUND MARGREITER
While I attended to his leg, Gerd celebrated his "rebirth" with somewhat too much whisky. The excessive reaction to this alcohol intake in his greatly enfeebled physical state was wrongly interpreted by the porters as mental derangement and a report of this was radioed to the valley. His condition next morning however permitted further evacuation.

Ruth, Oswald's girlfriend, had meanwhile arrived from Mombasa. She had first heard of the accident when she read the headline "Is he still alive?" in a newspaper. Oswald promised her that they would spend their next holiday at a beach – "which we never did".

DR RAIMUND MARGREITER
Gerd was now placed on the mountain stretcher and carried in relays by four blacks. We made speedy headway.

Towards midday it began to rain and the unfortunate
Gerd swam, so to speak, in the bathtub of the stretcher.
The wasted, bearded face with the gold-rimmed spectacles
reminded me of photographs I had seen of David Living-
stone: so must his natives have carried him through the
bush in his time.

*On Day 8 of the evacuation (13 September) Ruth and Oswald
took the long drag down to the beginning of the road. "However,"
Oswald said, "it was now very easy peaceful walking since I knew
that my friend would survive and I felt the fantastic high that
always comes after a big effort."*

DR RAIMUND MARGREITER

Aeroplanes repeatedly circled over us dropping messages: "Hang on, only another five miles, the whole of
Kenya is praying for you."

We were moved by this, the sympathy of a whole
country. In the late afternoon we reached the main camp,
where Gerd met his father who had organised the whole
operation so magnificently. The further journey by jeep to
the airstrip at Nanyuki, the flight to Nairobi, and the
medical operation had all been well prepared and thought
out beforehand.

*A farmer took Oswald and Ruth in his four-wheel-drive car
through the mud to his farm in the plains. Here, for the first time
in ten days, the doctor relaxed. Next morning they got the good
news that Gerd had been operated on in Nairobi and that he still
had his leg!*

*Robert Chambers considers the rescue in retrospect. It is the
summing up of a modest man.*

ROBERT CHAMBERS

We would have been faster if we had decided on the
North Ridge from the start: but then it would have been
harder to believe we could ever get Gerd off the mountain
that way and we might have given up. We would have been
faster if we had never relied on the cacolet stretcher; but

we did not know till we tried. Gerd would have been off quicker if we had called out the Austrians at the start; but it never occurred to us then that a team could come all the way from Europe. Jim Hastings the helicopter pilot would not have died if there had been no rescue bid, but in the event he did not die in vain, and there was no way there could have been no rescue. That was fate. The balance sheet in lives, at the end, was one for one, and it could easily have been worse. But to count lives seems wrong. Some things just have to be done. What I see now, and did not at the time, is how much we owed to the Austrians. If they had not come, I believe Judmaier would have died on the mountain, quite likely with some of us. His father expressed gratitude to us, but we should also thank him; for he and the Austrian climbers released us from the rescue, and perhaps in turn saved some of us.

The last words are with Oswald:

Ten years later we celebrated Gerd's "tenth anniversary" with a superb climb in the Tirol. The previous evening we enjoyed both the wine and the company of our girlfriends. It was an anniversary to remember.

High Winds in the Andes

Hamish MacInnes

Acclimatisation is possibly the greatest single factor involved in accidents on the world's highest mountains. If the members of the casualty's climbing party can be deployed, well and good, but if the rescue party has to come from much lower, the rescuers themselves are put at considerable risk from pulmonary or cerebral oedema, in addition to the danger of moving on difficult ground when suffering from mountain sickness.

This rescue story is from Chile, along the border with Argentina, on a mountain called Ojos del Salado, at 6,885 metres (22,590 feet) the second-highest peak in the Americas and the highest active volcano in the world.

I first heard about this accident from Bob Lyall, an expatriot Scot now living in Santiago. Bob is one of the prospecting bosses of the Anglo-American Corporation and has an avid interest in mountaineering. He called in at my home in Glencoe when on holiday in Scotland in 1985, and was telling me enthusiastically about a great volcanic complex he discovered when poring over NASA photographs taken from space. The company use these photographs for studying terrain with possible mineral deposits. The year before they had used them for a grimmer purpose. Bob told me the story.

It was in April 1984 when Louis George Murray visited Chile to see the Anglo-American projects at first hand. Louis was a geologist and a senior executive in the company, based in South Africa. He had a passion for the wide open spaces of the world and a talent for photographing them.

Both Louis and Bob Lyall were suffering from bad backs at

the time, legacies of countless miles in four-wheel-drive vehicles over rough and roadless terrain. With this in mind, Bob arranged for a helicopter to take Louis round the various projects in the mountains to the east of Copiapó, which is some 800 kilometres north of the capital, Santiago.

As Ojos del Salado was such a fascinating geological phenomenon, Bob suggested that it should be included in the itinerary as it could be overflown after a visit to Esperanza, which is the most northerly of the company's prospecting camps. The helicopter chosen for this flying visit was a Lama belonging to Helicopters Andes, a company whose pilots have vast experience of high-altitude work. César Tejos, an ex-Commander of the Chilean Air Force in Antarctica, was to be their "driver".

When César was asked if it would be possible to overfly Ojos summit with the helicopter, he consulted his tables and told Bob and Louis that it would be feasible with two passengers and a minimum supply of fuel, although a landing was out of the question. Even if a landing had been on, it would be unwise to leave the aircraft as anyone could collapse within a few seconds if suddenly deprived of the Lama's oxygen supply at that height.

Bob Lyall and Louis Murray started their inspection of the prospecting camps on 14 April and the following morning a pick-up truck was sent with Tomás Vila to Laguna Verde, a lake close to the mountain, with fuel for the Ojos flights. That same day the helicopter left Esperanza camp with Robert Schnell, Enrique Viteri, Louis and Bob on board. The mechanic was left at the camp to monitor the helicopter radio frequency.

Just after 8.00 am they located the pick-up at Laguna Verde and, after refuelling, Bob and Roberto set off on the first recce flight. Conditions were perfect and the Lama climbed high over the arid terrain, which is really the southern end of the Atacama Desert, and without trouble circled the summit twice and angled back down to the emerald-green lake. Though the weather was superb with clear, windless skies, it was confirmed that a landing on the summit was out of the question as the temperature was − 15°C, comparatively mild for the end of the South American summer.

In order to keep the helicopter as light as possible, it had been decided that Louis would do the second flight alone with César, and they took off at 10.20 am. The others at the edge of the lake watched the helicopter diminish in size until it was a mere speck in the azure sky.

When the Lama hadn't returned by 11.30 am they became worried, especially as they had no radio contact with the helicopter from the pick-up. At midday Tomás and Enrique drove west a few miles to get a better view of Ojos, but by 2.00 pm they returned having seen no sign of the Lama.

Bob Lyall had thought there was an outside chance that some minor mechanical fault had developed and César had considered it safer to return to the camp and his mechanic, rather than go back to Laguna Verde. So there was only one course left, to go to Esperanza, about 120 kilometres, to see if the helicopter had returned there. Once more Tomás and Enrique climbed into the pick-up and set off, while Bob and Roberto took up temporary residence in the old abandoned Chile–Argentina frontier post, constructed in natural caves by Laguna Verde.

At 4.00 pm the pick-up arrived at Esperanza and after speaking with the mechanic, who had had no radio contact with the Lama either, they realised that the helicopter was indeed missing. Santiago was then contacted and Helicopters Andes confirmed a First Stage alert with the National Search and Rescue Organisation of the Chilean Air Force. Some of the fittest personnel from the camp were mustered and arrived at the carabineiro post about 7.00 pm. Following in their tracks on the long dusty road, which climbs to over 15,000 feet, were other essential supplies and equipment: radios, food, bedding, generator, flares. Word arrived that a Cheyenne aircraft as well as the helicopter company's second Lama (Kilo Alpha) would depart Santiago 6.00 am next day to assist them. About to commence was the highest search operation ever conducted in the Americas.

On any rescue operation, especially in big mountains, there can be confusion and false leads to follow and eliminate, wasting valuable time. Such was the case for the ground party, led by Enrique Viteri, which set off to reach a mountaineers' refuge at 16,700 feet (5,100 metres), on the lower slopes of Ojos del Salado. This was a logical move, for one can't always rely on air search, especially at high altitude, and it was assumed that had the helicopter made a forced landing and the two men survived, they would have headed towards this known place of shelter. For to spend a night in the open without special clothing at such a height would be courting disaster. On the first flight with Bob and Roberto, César had pinpointed the yellow-painted refuge.

However, Enrique's party had trouble finding the hut in the dark. Previous parties had driven up there with four-wheel-drive vehicles, choosing whatever route took their fancy over the dunes, with the result that the place resembled a twin-tracked maze. It was not until they had radioed Eduardo Olmedo, a mountaineer who knew the area well, that they managed to locate the refuge at about 9.00 pm. On the way one of the party reported a white flare to the south-east.

Various flares were set off in reply, but there was no response to these. There was further confusion when the flares which they had fired were in turn reported as from the missing helicopter.

The white-flare sighting (it was established later that this must have been a shooting star) spurred the Ojos rescue team into setting off up the mountain from the hut at 10.00 pm. It was full moon and below them the vast expanse of open country was broken only by the white heads of the mountains. Laguna Verde lay in the shadow of a hollow between hills. They reached a height of 20,300 feet (6,200 metres) by dawn and searched into the next day, Sunday, without success.

As promised the Cheyenne fixed-wing plane arrived in the area at 8.00 am, but base at Laguna Verde had no direct communication with it. From the mountainside Enrique could make indirect contact by first radioing the Andes Lama helicopter, which was now airborne and heading up the narrow torso of Chile to Copiapó en route for the mountain. This way he could relay messages from base at Laguna Verde, where Bob Lyall and other members of Anglo-American were still ensconced in the subterranean guard post. The Cheyenne pilot was Pablo Pfingsthron, a man with 29,000 flying hours behind him and the co-pilot Jorge Lathrop, Director of Helicopters Andes.

Bob asked them to check out craters and fumaroles in the summit area, just in case they had landed safely and Louis's fascination with geology and photography had lured him to these features. The Cheyenne searched the summit area until its fuel was getting low then returned to La Serena to fill up. In the afternoon it again quartered Ojos, but still they didn't see any sign of the missing Lama, although false hopes were raised when they spotted red-jacketed figures on the mountain, to be dispelled when walkie-talkie and radio contacts established that they were, in fact, Enrique's team.

The Chilean Search and Rescue organisation were meanwhile deploying a Twin Otter and another Lama from the base at Antofagasta. Commander Heinrich was in charge of the official SAR and he asked José Miguel Infante, Helicopters Andes Operations Manager, to co-ordinate with him. But as José arrived in Copiapó in the company Lama ahead of the SAR group he refuelled and carried on to Laguna Verde where he touched down at 4.00 pm and managed one search mission before dark, covering the ground between the summit and Laguna Verde.

That Sunday night the rescuers got into their sleeping bags somewhat despondent and there was another false report of a flare, this time on the north side of Laguna Verde. The old frontier post was busier than it had been for years and the twin caverns echoed with the plans of the rescuers. Mixed teams of company men, carabineiro and police were selected to search on both sides of the border, but the Argentinian authorities would give permission only for civilian teams, so the next day an Anglo-American Company contingent under Tomás Vila was to cross the border to search the south-eastern flank of the peak. The police and army were ordered to Laguna Negro Francisco on the other side of Ojos to commence search operations there.

Up in the refuge the hope which the Anglo-American party had felt the previous night had now, after an exhausting day's search, been replaced with a numbness. They realised that Louis and César would have to be very lucky to be still alive. Their own situation was one of acute frustration. Though they were used to working at 14,000 feet or so, the extra altitude was telling. Acclimatisation is essential and in normal circumstances should be attained by slow degrees, not by a relentless push to over 20,000 feet. Every step had been an effort, yet colleagues in distress are a compelling incentive. However they could do no more good on the mountain and returned to base.

The next day, a Monday, was a day which the aircrews of the Ojos del Salado rescue won't forget. It was a day of high wind and turbulence.

José was airborne first in the Lama, with Enrique as observer, and checked out the wild country to the north and north-west of Laguna Verde. It was in this region that the flare had been reported the previous evening, but they found nothing. By 8.00 am the SAR Twin Otter started on its search pattern, while José in the Lama was on his second patrol of the day. Both aircraft were still operating within Chilean territory, but by 11.00 am permission came through to overfly Argentina and José immediately swung over the divide to concentrate his efforts on the south side of the mountain. Flying conditions were appalling – the prevailing westerly winds, warmed by their passage over the Atacama Desert, stream over the chain of high peaks which form the border, to descend in the notorious "mountain wave" on the Argentinian side. The turbulence behind the mountains was terrific, and José had to use all his skills to keep the Lama flying. At one point they were hurtled downwards at 4,000 feet per minute, and José wrestled the machine south towards the broad flat expanse of the Salina de la Laguna Verde, contemplating a forced landing, while Enrique radioed their position to Bob at base. However, conditions improved a little, and, all possibility of a systematic search having gone, José concentrated his efforts on solving their own predicament, and gradually worked his way back until he managed to slip over a pass some fifty kilometres west of Ojos del Salado, into the welcoming rising air on the Chilean side of the mountains, to angle back to base at Laguna Verde, exhausted by the tensions of what he later described as the worst experience of his flying career.

The press can be a mixed blessing on any protracted rescue. Often they get in the way, jam switchboards vital for communications and get the facts wrong. In all fairness, however, they often do good by publicising the plight of rescue teams in dire need of donations. On the Ojos del Salado rescue, however, the common radio frequency chosen by the SAR authorities for the emergency was Anglo-American's 7790. Once this was known, the frequency was monitored by radio hams and also by a broadcasting station. So Bob's contact back to the mining camps as well as SAR information was monitored and sent out for public consumption.

A report was made to the local Intendente in Copiapó that a helicopter had landed at approximately 11.00 am on the 14th close by Cerro El Gato, about 150 kilometres south-west of Ojos. Those at base were somewhat sceptical about this sighting, for it was doubtful if the missing Lama had sufficient fuel to get that far. Also the same helicopter had been working in that particular area a week previously. The sighting could have been confused. Nevertheless, after José's narrow escape that day such a possibility couldn't be discounted, for there was a stock of helicopter fuel at Aldebarán camp and José had spotted a pass which led there via Laguna Negro Francisco, which could provide a bolt hole for an aircraft in trouble. The Argentinians were now in action using a Hercules as a spotter plane crammed with observers. They had also a couple of Lamas standing by should they have any positive results. Help was now coming from all quarters and patrols were out to the north and west on the mountain, as well as Tomás Vila's group on the Argentinian side.

More oxygen for use in the Lama and climbing equipment arrived that evening, which meant that the Anglo-American party which was going back up Ojos now had better gear to tackle the upper regions of the mountain, and this time instead of using the Ojos refuge as an advanced base they pushed up higher and set up camp at 20,300 feet (6,200 metres).

On the Wednesday Bob Lyall returned to Santiago, leaving Enrique in charge on the spot, and he asked his second in command, Iain Thomson, to arrange photographic coverage of the mountain. Bob felt that studying enlargements might give them the best chance of locating the missing helicopter. This is a sound idea provided one can ensure comprehensive coverage from enough angles. For it is notoriously difficult and tiring to concentrate on searching what is often a hypnotic landscape in turbulent conditions from the air.

The photographic flight was set in motion but ran into such turbulence that most of the photographers spent the time being violently sick, and took two days to complete their assignment.

Meanwhile the Anglo-American party which had camped high on Ojos was not faring so well. One of the team was a small agile geophysicist and surveyor called Carlos Pérez and I was later to observe his ability as a natural mountaineer. Carlos' nickname in the mining camps is Darling, a word which he frequently uses to supplement his limited English vocabulary. With five colleagues Carlos had set off from their tents at 20,300 feet in an attempt to gain the summit. Now at 10.30 am and a height of 21,000 feet, only one other member of the party was fit to go on. The others had succumbed to altitude sickness. Above, after negotiating a difficult section on rock and ice, his remaining companion fell victim to sickness and exhaustion and Carlos told him to return to camp.

At 5.00 pm Carlos reached a cairn between the two summits and saw, close by a section of disturbed snow, a small weighted company pennant which Louis had prepared to jettison on the summit as they flew over. The objective of his climb was to search the summit and also to look down the east side, but due to a ferocious wind and driving snow he couldn't get to the eastern summit. He put the flag in his pocket, and decided to return to their high camp, but didn't reach this until 11.00 pm, so exhausted that he had to be carried the last few hundred metres to camp by his companions, who had heard him call for help. The temperature on the summit that day was −20°C.

Next morning, Friday, the photographic crew were airborne once more and completed their mission. By the evening all the material was processed and being studied in Santiago by Bob. There seemed to be two areas worth closer investigation. One photograph showed what looked like human figures close to an area of hot springs and the other showed skid marks on the snow.

Added to this, the news that Carlos had found the flag on the summit confirmed that the Lama had in fact reached the top of Ojos, probably a little over half an hour after take-off. This meant that, calculating from the Lama's depleted fuel reserves, the search could now be concentrated in a much tighter area round the mountain.

Iain Thomson made another flight as observer in the Cheyenne on Saturday the 21st and checked the two suspicious areas spotted in the photographs. Both proved negative.

That day, about lunchtime, Louis Murray's son, Michael, arrived in Santiago from South Africa and spent the remainder of the day and that night with Bob Lyall and family. It was arranged to fly him over the Ojos area the following morning to show him where his father and César went missing. At dawn the Cheyenne took off with Henry Stucke, Anglo's technical director for Latin America, who had come over from Sao Paulo, Iain Thomson and Michael on board. When they were overflying the eastern side of the summit the pilot Pablo Pfingsthron glimpsed a brief flash of light, on a patch of snow high on the mountain. They circled and Iain Thomson was able to recognise the missing Lama. There was no sign of life. SAR in Copiapó and the ground parties were advised of the find. The Twin Otter and the helicopters were scrambled and homed in on the location which was at 22,000 feet. As the Twin Otter tried to approach, closer than the Cheyenne was able, the wind was registering 100 knots and the plane was actually moving backwards at one stage. The helicopters couldn't get to the crashed Lama either, but they managed to report that the machine seemed more or less intact and there didn't appear to be anyone inside. This raised the hopes of the rescuers once more, for they knew that if Louis and César had managed to use the oxygen on board the helicopter, and get to the heat-giving fumaroles, they might just have survived the otherwise low temperatures. For the rest of the day flying conditions were desperate. Once Henry had described the location of the crash, "a snow patch like a map of South America, with the Lama in the position of Buenos Aires", Bob easily spotted the aircraft in several photographs, which goes to show that specialised knowledge is just as essential for interpreting aerial photographs as for on-the-spot search.

Flying conditions were better on Monday the 23rd, and the Twin Otter was able to make a near pass to the crashed helicopter and later a Lama flew close in. A figure wearing an orange jacket was still in the passenger's seat, but the exact position of Louis was difficult to establish.

Now all energy was concentrated on getting climbing parties to the crash and after a great deal of effort, between 27 April and 2 May, members of the Santiago rescue group, Cuerpo de Socorro Andino, under Alejo Contreras Stateding, together with Anglo-American personnel, succeeded in reaching the Lama. They had been instructed by SAR only to photograph the situation. In fact, the machine was so delicately balanced that there was a danger of it falling over if they had tried to recover the bodies. Both men must have died instantly in the impact, which had also sheared off the automatic electronic distress beacon.

There remained the formidable task of recovering the bodies of the victims, for early May is the start of winter in the area, with lowering summit temperatures, higher winds, and the possibility of severe snow storms. However, the Anglo-American team were determined to complete the task, if at all possible – they were fit and acclimatised, but lacked the technical experience necessary. So they engaged the support of four experienced Chilean mountaineers, led by Jorge Quinteros, and now, well equipped and organised, set out once again towards the summit. A bulldozer was called in, which cut a track suitable for four-wheel-drive vehicles from the refuge at the base of the mountain to a height of about 20,000 feet, and the bulldozer itself managed to assist in transporting equipment to Carlos' campsite at 20,300 feet. By 12 May the helicopter had toppled over in the wind and in two separate expeditions the bodies were recovered and taken down for burial.

As a tribute to Louis Murray, Anglo-American built the Louis Murray Lodge at 15,000 feet close to Laguna Verde on the wide-open desert country, and installed a new climbers' refuge, dedicated to César Tejos, at the end of the road up the mountain built during the rescue operation. It has never been established with certainty what caused the crash, but recently parts of the engine have been salvaged, possibly the highest salvage operation ever.

Middle Peak Hotel

Bob Munro

I first got acquainted with the New Zealand Alps in 1953 and spent two years mainly climbing and prospecting there. South Island is a wonderful place with a unique feeling of freedom.

This story is about an accident on Mount Cook, an enforced stay in a storm close to the summit. The peak was well named Aorangi, the Cloud Piercer, by the Maoris. Indeed clouds regularly envelop it and winds rush in from the Tasman Sea which is only a skip and jump away, to lash its icy flanks.

As a young man I often climbed unroped in the Central Alps on technically easy but exposed ground and was subsequently told off by pundits such as Mick Bowie and Harry Aires, two of New Zealand's great mountain guides. Nowadays such "rashness" is more accepted as a valuable means of saving precious time on long routes.

Despite my early misdemeanours I am still in close contact with these rugged mountaineers of the antipodes and this tale of Mount Cook was written by Bob Munro, a guide who worked for Alpine Guides and played an important part in this rescue operation. It illustrates the close ties that now exist between the helicopter and the rescue team.

Mark Inglis and Phil Doole flew by ski-plane into Plateau hut on the eastern flanks of Mount Cook on 15 November 1982 for a quick climb of this mountain during their days off before going back to work on the National Park alpine rescue team.

They actually returned two weeks later after doubling the record for survival above 10,000 feet (3,000 metres) in the Southern Alps, amidst the most intense media-generated public interest ever in an incident in the New Zealand mountains.

Inglis was a full-time mountaineer for the National Park after having given up a promising ranger training course to pursue his life in the mountains. Married, with a young daughter, he is small, almost frail-looking, but he had put up enough good climbs and been involved in rescue operations himself that he took over that season as the leader of one of two specialised alpine rescue teams based at Mount Cook.

Phil Doole, a qualified surveyor, was working his first season as a rescue mountaineer. Phil had already shown his capacity for survival in the mountains three years earlier during another alpine drama. An avalanche had claimed the lives of two people in an accident in the Upper Linda Glacier of Mount Cook. Doole and his companion were hurrying down to raise the alarm when his companion fell in a crevasse, the rope jerked tight and Doole was catapulted into the crevasse, breaking his leg and arm. With minimum clothing (the rest had been donated to the survivors of the first accident), he lay for two days in the crevasse and was finally rescued with thirty centimetres of new snow on top of him.

The climb the two had decided on is one of the classics of the New Zealand Alps. Rising in a series of sharp ridges to where it blends with the Caroline Face of Mount Cook, the East Ridge offers a lengthy snow and ice climb until it tops out at the Middle Peak right in the centre of the mile-long summit ridge.

The pair trudged over the Grand Plateau that first afternoon and spent the night in a crevasse at the base of the climb. They were planning a fast ascent and were lightly equipped. They had pile clothing and windproof outer garments but no bivouac sac, sleeping bags or stoves.

They began the climb at 5.00 am, finding that early in the season there was still plenty of unconsolidated snow on the ridge and hard ice conditions on the upper part of the face, making the going slow and painstaking. They could see as they climbed that the wind was starting to whip across the summit ridge but figured even if it was strong they would be able to force their way over the top and get quickly below the crest on the western side via Porter Col.

They weren't to know that they were at the beginning of one of the worst summers that region experienced. In fact a very unusual set of circumstances was developing that played the dominant role for the next two weeks in their lives and was part of a global weather imbalance. The Southern Oscillation index, a measurement of the relative strengths between two of the Pacific's most important weather balancing acts – the Australian-Indonesian low and the high-pressure system east of Tahiti – had begun one of its periodic shifts. Pressures rose in the centre of the low system bringing widespread drought in Australia, while the Central Eastern Pacific experienced devastating cyclones. The phenomenon "El Nino" affected most continents that year except Europe. The normally positioned Pacific high decayed until the pressure imbalance between Tahiti and Darwin was the strongest ever. In New Zealand this meant the establishment of a strong south-west jet stream in the upper air layers that showed unusual persistence.

Doole and Inglis started their climb just as this system was beginning and by 6.00 pm when they finally crested the summit ridge of Mount Cook they were caught right in the teeth of it. Mount Cook juts up 12,349 feet (3,765 metres) only twenty miles from the Tasman Sea, so any winds from the west are usually speeded up as they pass over this impressive barrier to their path. The East Ridge is ideally sheltered from these winds but there is no respite on the summit ridge itself.

Frozen from belaying each other and unable to make any progress against the wind, they crept into a small crevasse between the middle peak of Mount Cook and Porter Col, the gateway to safety. There is usually a good bergschrund in that area and it's often used as a planned bivouac. A guided party had spent a week in nearly the same spot three years before, trapped by weather, but also equipped with sleeping bags, and they emerged with only minor frostbite.

The bergschrund this year was small, about the size of a single bed – open-ended so that spindrift constantly blew through.

Over the next couple of days they made several attempts to get out, laboriously roping up then realising as they poked their heads out that there was no chance of survival beyond the bergschrund, and reluctantly being forced back inside to the feeling of utter helplessness at not being able to solve their predicament.

In the village concern had been growing since the first evening when they hadn't come on the regular 7.00 pm radio schedule at Empress hut on the western side of Mount Cook, their final goal from the top of the climb.

On the third day of their enforced stay they were obviously in trouble. That day at lower elevations a party of climbers had managed to get out from Gardiner Hut on the lower slopes of Mount Cook up the Hooker Valley, so if Inglis and Doole were in a position to move, that was the day.

As a precaution a park rescue team that had been training on the mountain range above the Mount Cook village was flown out in case it was needed the next day.

Most mountain search and rescue in New Zealand is undertaken by volunteer groups under police supervision but at Mount Cook specialised professional teams have evolved, largely to combat the serious and frequent nature of mountain search and rescues in the area.

While not tall mountains by world standards, the Southern Alps are rugged, heavily glaciated and with often dubious-quality rock. The weather changes rapidly and the storms can be as powerful as those in Patagonia or Antarctica.

Searches at Mount Cook are controlled by the Chief Ranger and usually involved helicopter support, either the air force with Iroquois machines or the local civilian pilot, Ron Small, with his Aerospatiale Squirrel. Small and his helicopter became the central piece in the unfolding drama.

The fact that the rescue received such intense media coverage was largely due to Chief Ranger Bert Youngman. In the highly emotive world of mountain accidents the press is usually kept at bay through irregularly issued reports via the police. At the beginning of this long search local television teams were allowed into the crew room during the operation, but as the waves of new reporters built up this was stopped, although press conferences continued. In fact the presence of the news media in such force and the gathering public interest in the events sometimes overshadowed the rescue itself.

By the Friday morning, Day 4 for Inglis and Doole, the park team were on full search and rescue standby. This meant that all other work was suspended and they had to be in full climbing kit with everything packed ready to go at a moment's notice.

The only problem was that because of the raging storm nobody was going anywhere.

The pattern that was to become so familiar over the next week established itself that day: getting geared up, doing the mental exercise that would enable the mind and brain to be roughly in the same place as the body might find itself being whisked to in this age of rapid helicopter transport. But the team just had to sit there. And sit there, like the runner being called to the blocks but never getting the release of the gun. The nervous tension builds up but is never channelled into action.

On the mountain by this time Inglis and Doole realised that they were past being able to help themselves. Mark Inglis wrote:

So much spindrift entered our alcove that it would have been very foolish to utilise our body heat to warm our feet. This resulted in the main complication of our stay. In my case, the frostbite started after the second night and was due mainly to excessive sweating during the climb, which drenched my inner boots and my two pairs of dry socks. Limited massage and elevation of our feet was as much as we could do.

A great deal of our time in the hole was spent lying, completely switched off. Every day we checked outside and each time we were nearly blown to kingdom come! Cold was with us all the time. Though seldom warm we only shivered after moving around, upon going outside or in the middle of the night. I am still convinced that in our situation, doing as little as possible was the best decision. From the first day we rationed food; not consciously – merely from habit. An average day was two biscuits and two or three spoonfuls of drink concentrate. Water was at a premium. Snow in the spare water bottle was melted by body heat under my clothing. This in itself tended to draw a large amount of heat from the body. I weighed 46 kilos (7 stone 3 pounds) on entering hospital, 13 kilos (28 pounds) lighter than normal.

The weather worsened through Saturday and Sunday. Snow fell to low levels and the Ball Hut Road from Mount Cook village to the Tasman Glacier lookout was closed because of the avalanche danger.

At Tasman Saddle Hut at the head of the glacier at 7,500 feet (2,250 metres) the recording anemometer was ripped off its bolts by the wind, landing 50 metres away.

There was the odd brief lull between the rapidly advancing fronts on the Sunday, and cloud had cleared back on the lower part of the East Ridge to enable pilot Ron Small to recce part of the route that the climbers had taken. No sign was seen but the rescuers got a nasty fright when cloud developed suddenly, completely enveloping the helicopter as it was hovering just above the rocks and snow on the ridge. A brief hole in the cloud allowed a narrow escape for the Squirrel's occupants.

During the next two days a widespread weather watch was begun, supplementing the meteorological service in Christchurch and with observers ringing the Mount Cook area, looking for the briefest opening to stage a search attempt.

The daily routine for the searchers involved a flurry of predawn activity followed by tense waiting through first light as this appeared to offer the best time for a respite from the wind and cloud. Then when nothing eventuated, ringing relatives to inform them of the situation and dealing with the ever-growing press corps.

Anything at all could have happened to the two climbers but if they were still alive after nearly a week out, then their only hope would have been the known bergschrund near the Middle Peak.

Arrangements were made to bring Dr Dick Price from Oamaru, 120 kilometres away, if they were found alive. Dr Price is a specialist in mountain medicine and frostbite, with experience of many New Zealand Himalayan expeditions.

By Sunday evening small progress had been made with the cloud lifting on the eastern flanks of the mountain, enough to enable two mountaineers to be landed at the Plateau Hut where they confirmed Inglis' and Doole's intentions from the hut log book.

On Monday 22 November (Day 7) the cloud base had lifted a little and just after 9.00 am Ron Small flew four climbers up the Hooker, hoping to land them on the white ice from where they could struggle up to Gardiner hut. He actually touched down on bare ice above the hut and as everybody clambered out his forward-speed indicator registered eighty knots! Helicopters have been taking the drudgery and hard work out of alpine rescue for some time now. The Squirrel was showing that it could function at the edge of climbable conditions.

That evening though, the wind briefly relented. Although great orographic banner clouds swirled out in the lee of Mount Cook, the summit ridge became visible for the first time in a week, and the rescue staff at Gardiner Hut reported patches of blue sky above them.

Ron Small was in the air again. Here is the rescue log for that evening:

1914 hrs HWW [call sign of Small's helicopter] have located one climber, red jacket waving from schrund to NW Porter Col.

1922 hrs Dr Dick Price on way to Mount Cook.

1932 hrs HWW – have lost drop bag. Request from Don Bogie to prepare climbing team to drop on lower Empress.

1935 hrs HWW returns to Park Headquarters.

1940 hrs Decision made to continue throwing out drop kits and then place four climbers at Empress.

2025 hrs Successful first drop, second and third.

2049 hrs Radio Call "This is Hotel Middle Peak. Mark lost feeling all toes, no food since Wednesday. Phil, two big toes frozen, sched in thirty minutes."

So they were alive! And still with a sense of humour.

The five toll lines out from the village were immediately jammed by the media and Park Headquarters had great difficulty in getting through to Dr Price, but the huge public interest that had people hanging on to every bulletin was working for the rescuers as well.

Dr Price was whisked by police car to the Oamaru Airport at speeds normally associated with the most dangerous hit-and-run cases. Over the next week repair men thought nothing of driving 300 kilometres to fix broken office equipment at Search Headquarters or oxygen equipment distributors travelling from

Dunedin, also 300 kilometres away, with some urgently needed gauges and cylinders.

But those minutes after the news came through that they were alive were hectic at Search and Rescue Headquarters. The first drop bag had been lost over the edge of the bergschrund and new ones hastily prepared as the light rapidly faded. One of the most relaxed people appeared to be Phil Doole's mother. Upon being rung in Wellington to be told that her son was alive, she replied that she always knew he would be and that he was good for a few more days yet, and she didn't want anybody taking any risks on his account!

Rescuer Ken Joyce explained later how they had spotted from the helicopter one person waving from a small bergschrund below the main Middle Peak bergschrund as Ron worked out how to ride the express train that was the wind pouring over the summit ridge. They tried dangling the drop kit out on a rope but the wind kept trailing it up towards the tail rotor. Next they tried bombing. Ken held the bag out the door and let go on Ron's command. The bag landed near the entrance to the bergschrund, teetered briefly on the edge then rolled off down the slope. Returning with three more kits they tried the same procedure. Ron put just enough bite on his blades to avoid windmilling them past the safety limit and with the engine barely idling they rode an escalator of wind up towards the bergschrund. Ken held the first bag out over the skids and let go when Ron called. The bag plumbed down right on target. Two more shots – two more successes – the last bag landed right on Phil Doole.

So they had been found and supplied with sleeping bags and food but the storm and the wind were back in full force the next morning so there was no hope of rescue. If the wind wouldn't allow a helicopter rescue, then it was going to have to be done on foot. So a plan was prepared in the event that they would have to be lowered off Mount Cook in a stretcher by ground parties. This would involve a lot of manpower, complicated rope work and again some respite from the weather. The prospect of bouncing those frostbitten feet, now susceptible to damage as they re-warmed in the sleeping bags, all the way off the top of Mount Cook, wasn't appealing either. Four alpine guides were brought in to swell the numbers of the rescue teams and a group of volunteers put on standby in Timaru, two and a half hours' drive away.

For Inglis and Doole, as they entered the second week of their stay, their ordeal was in some ways worse than the first. Up to the moment of being found they were engaged in the simple primitive art of survival. Once warm and fed and in radio contact with the base, their horizons broadened and they became concerned about the wider implications. What was going to happen to those frozen lumps at the ends of their legs? Would the rescuers carry things too far and a serious accident occur? Mark's wife Anne spoke briefly on the radio and messages were sent from Phil's family in Wellington.

These messages affected the climbers' morale, bringing in a flood of feelings that had been kept in abeyance during the bitter struggle to stay alive in a hole in the snow at 12,000 feet, lying on a thin mat with feet jammed into the bottoms of packs, as the thermometer dipped to $-20°C$ during that succession of long nights. When rescued Mark had a frostbitten finger from the constant pressing of the light button on his watch that measured the slow passing of each night.

But the weather that made 1982–83 such a freak season throughout the world, which enhanced the droughts in Africa and Australia and produced hitherto unknown hurricanes in Hawaii, continued in the same pattern; 200-kph winds from the south-west quarter lashed Mount Cook with rain and snow to low levels.

By now all New Zealand was following the drama via their TV sets and radio news bulletins. But there was so little to report. After two more days radio contact was lost with the pair. Although it was probably just battery failure, the lack of contact increased the anxiety.

By Friday 26 November, four days after they had been found and eleven days since they started climbing, a partial respite on the lower slopes of the mountain allowed the climbing team at Gardiner hut to be brought out, but that was all. Saturday the 27th was a repeat of all the other days but the forecast was for the south-west jet stream to weaken finally on Monday and be completely clear of the region by Tuesday. Dr Price gave two to four days' grace before any serious medical problems would develop.

The next day Bert Youngman decided to bring in an RNZAF Iroquois helicopter to help in ferrying climbers, as the option of having to do a long stretcher lower was a real possibility. It arrived just after 6.00 pm, when the weather began another one of those "race against the dark" evening clearances. The sky was still threatening to the south but the area around the top of Mount Cook began to clear back. So it was decided to establish a group of strong climbers on the Empress Shelf, a snow plateau about 1,500 feet (450 metres) below the stranded pair. If the rescue couldn't be effected that night at least rescuers would be able to get up to the pair even in difficult conditions the next day.

Events over the next hour moved swiftly.

Ron Small took off in the Squirrel with a load of rescue personnel. He landed them in fresh knee-deep snow on the Empress Shelf and then flew up to the summit ridge. To Ron the configuration of the snow slope seemed to have changed and he thought the bergschrund had collapsed on its occupants and he could see bodies lying out on the snow. He radioed that he was coming back and could Bert Youngman come out to the helicopter to meet him. The Search Headquarters was under virtual siege at this stage by reporters who sensed that something dramatic had happened.

Just as the Squirrel swung away from whatever had happened at Middle Peak Hotel the Iroquois came in to land at the advance base on the Empress Shelf with the rest of the rescue party. As the pilot put the machine into a hover in preparation for landing, the blades blew up drifts of the new snow. The pilot lost his horizon in the swirling whiteout, the tail plane hit the ground and the helicopter flipped on to its back, the tail plane and rotor hanging over the 1,000-foot drop to the lower Empress Shelf.

The park mountaineers burst out of the side of the stricken machine, followed by the Iroquois crew. Apart from some minor injuries no one was hurt. For Ron Small, hovering above, after two weeks of dawn-to-dusk standby and some very difficult mountain flying, this was getting to be the last straw. He had to leave the mystery of the Middle Peak bergschrund and now rescue the Iroquois crew. Daylight was fading fast and a southerly front was sweeping across the Mackenzie country. It was snowing heavily only twenty-five kilometres away from Mount Cook.

Inside the chill confines of Middle Peak Hotel Phil Doole was trying to keep a record of the passing time. It was the evening of Day 11:

Waiting. Watching mossy threads of spindrift overhead. The light of another dawn spreads into the tunnel. Waiting. Listening. Just the slightest shiver runs across the roof. Silence. Is it really calm outside . . .?

Stirring. Searching for the transistor radio amongst the clutter. The two RTs are kaput. Station 3ZA has the only steady signal, no surprise – it's a direct line of sight to the transmitter at Kumara, only 145 km [90 miles] north of Mount Cook. Familiar sounds of West Coast breakfast radio. Have a nice day. Sure, anytime. But our isolation is quickly blown away by Morning Report: a wrecked Iroquois lies on the Empress Shelf. What! We trade expletives and wait for the rest . . . thoughts zeroing in on people, mates, lives. Anxious, we want to know more from this noise invading our hole. No more . . .

Meanwhile, another drama was unfolding at Search Headquarters:

To take the pressure of reporters off his back, (they knew that Ron had reported something strange) Bert Youngman sent a member of his staff out the door to the press to say that despite appearances hope was not given up for the climbers. For instance, in cases of severe hypothermia even people who appeared clinically dead had been revived.

A reporter at the back of the group picked up on these words and raced off to ring his office with the dramatic news that after all the struggle the two mountaineers overdue on Mount Cook were "clinically dead". Even the news reader who had to read out the bulletin on TV looked dubious as he read the words but the mistake had been made and the news was broadcast around the country. The shaken parents and relatives tried to ring through for verification of the dreadful news but once again the phone lines to the small alpine village went into overload.

Darkness was nearly upon the scene and time had run out for a proper rescue attempt that night. Ron Small managed to make one flight back in after bringing out the Iroquois crew. Another drop bag went over the side to the entrance of the bergschrund and, unaware of all the drama the premature news of his demise was causing, a figure in a blue jacket strolled out of the cave, picked up the bag and disappeared again. The two bodies that Ron thought he had seen were empty drop bags that the conscientious pair had staked into the snow to mark their exact location.

Monday the 29th just had to be the day. The forecast at 4.00 am indicated the lowest wind speeds yet at 3,000 metres. At dawn the team on the Empress Shelf reported that everything above them was clear. They had finally snatched some sleep at 3.00 am after digging snow caves most of the night. They weren't digging just a shelter for themselves but a potential field hospital in case evacuation only got that far before becoming bogged down by the weather. Dr Price was there with a full medical kit including oxygen and a portable defibrillator.

The only problem was that everywhere on the east of the Main Divide there was a thick sheet of low cloud. It hugged the ground around the Mount Cook village and spread far out into the Mackenzie Country. The temperature at Mount Cook was 0°C and then it began to snow, fine above, atrocious below. The forecasters were predicting a break in the clouds but it wasn't appearing. The worst possible scenario was for the rescue to get under way and then for cloud to form around the machines as they were lifting people out. Ron Small had decided that after the previous night's events he needed some support from the people he knew well. Bill Black, the legendary bush pilot from the rugged Fiordland area, came through with his Squirrel and brought with him Rex Dovey who had taught Ron how to fly.

Back to Phil Doole at Middle Peak Hotel:

7.30 am Radio New Zealand news: Middle Peak Hotel has the lead: No mention of the wreck – that's old news. The Chief Ranger outlines today's rescue plan for the nation to digest. Better get ourselves organised, lad. Sounds like this could be it.

I find the overboots which arrived in the last airdrop, last night. Pull them on over cold socks. I read the name – borrowed gear. So was the transistor radio, I find out later. Long laces and lots of hooks, clumsy fingers. Quiet communication between us: some worry, some anticipation of the action. Wonder who'll be on the strop? Laces just tied and we hear the chopper. Gotta go.

Outside it's brilliant. The crisp air wakes a weary, troubled mind. An early-morning glow and the Tasman Sea glittering not so far away. The sun lets me feel warm.

A new RT comes down by rope. Calling Hotel-Whisky-Whisky draws no response; where's the chopper gone? On to the other channel, and it takes Search Control a little while to react. Put it all on hold, fight the worry trying to burst out. Asking the question: "Who copped it in the crash?" The answer comes unexpectedly from Lisle Irwin, senior ranger, back from vacation: "Everyone's OK, Phil." All right then. We're ready for a lift. Don't push it.

By 7.30 am the cloud in the Hooker Valley was still holding a ceiling of 2,700 metres and the decision was made to go. It was 3,200 metres out over the Tasman riverbed before the two Squirrels broke into sunlight and swung back towards the Hooker. A quick recce flight lowered another radio down to the bergschrund. Soon Phil's strong voice reported that he could be lifted out on his harness but that Mark should be moved in a stretcher.

Ron landed on the shelf and the strop system was set up, first developed by Canadian rescue teams. The helicopter takes off with the rescuer dangling twenty metres below, which enables him to be flown into tight locations with the helicopter hovering above. The sensation of flying this way is not unpleasant. It's similar to parachuting, usually lasts longer and there is no nasty thump at the end. So long as the pilot is doing his job.

The senior mountaineer, Don Bogie, had developed this system at Mount Cook along with Ron Small. It had been in use for two seasons but so far had been tried only with rescuers picking up bodies in dangerous locations. Now it was Bogie's opportunity to try it out on some climbers still very much alive.

Also as an aid for a quick pick-up, Bogie had adapted another Canadian modification of a European compact stretcher. The Bauman bag is a large nylon bag opening its full length with a series of attachment points that join it to the bottom of the helicopter strop. This simple bag can be carried on the rescuer's hip, quickly unpacked, the patient rolled in and attached to the strop with the helicopter hovering above. This way the rescuer doesn't have to detach from the strop and the helicopter spends the minimum time in the hover in a dangerous location.

So, with the cloud boiling up below them, a white wall of southerly snow showers on the horizon and the first sign of clouds already beginning to appear over the Caroline Face just above where Mark and Phil were trapped, they set to work.

Phil Doole again:

> Alone, back in our tunnel. Our hole is a mess of gear, empty gas canisters, unused food, and yellow snow. Gathering together the RTs. Leaving everything else behind, even my ice axe, when the chopper returns again.
>
> Smack on the shelf! Don unclips our harnesses and is gone. Alone again for a moment, body tuning to this new locale. Whisto crouches in the snow. A quiet grin from a face dark with stubble: "Gidday, man." Dull awareness of activity about the landing pad; proficiency typified by a line of safety pickets leading out to the wreck.

Don Bogie reported later:

> We landed on the Empress Shelf and set up the strop, tying each end of the two strands to the fixed bolts underneath the helicopter. I clipped my harness on to the other end and two minutes later was dangling in the – 20°C air over the bergschrund. Ron lowered me to the snow right at the entrance. Mark was in a sleeping bag about three metres inside so I asked Ron to give me more rope. I went inside and dragged Mark back to the entrance so that I could work on him in the open. Ron was hovering

about fifteen metres above as Phil came out of the cave to help me get Mark into the Bauman rescue bag. I checked all my attachments then the stretcher attachments before asking Ron to take off. We flew down and landed by the others on the shelf. I unclipped Mark and then returned up to Porter Col. This time I clipped Phil on to the strop directly by his harness. We were only on the ground fifteen to twenty seconds. As we landed by the others the cloud was starting to spill over the top of the mountain from the Tasman Glacier and around the West Ridge.

A last word from the joint proprietor of Middle Peak Hotel, now closed for the season:

Finally – slumped in the front passenger seat of HWW. They didn't let me walk; no one realising the damage was already done, long before. Fumbling again with the belt fastener, just like the last time. Chewing on Dick's liquorice, staring alternately at the instrument panel and Ron – talking to his headset – wondering what he is saying. Bill's out there somewhere, flying back-up in HMV. I remember Don told me that, coming down on the strop.

Snug, isolated in the machine, away from the mountain and the cold, watching the dials. A glance out through the windscreen. A jolt back to reality! Where are we going? Above Haast Ridge, spiralling down towards the Tasman Glacier, to find a way home under the wall of snow clouds. Stunned – realising then the incredible commitment these guys have made – my tears roll freely as Dick leans over with more liquorice. His grinning nod says Mark is OK too.

A month later on Christmas Eve both climbers had their frostbitten feet amputated. Five months later after learning to walk on their artificial legs, Mark Inglis was back at work at Mount Cook National Park Headquarters and Phil Doole left with a climbing team on an expedition to the Peruvian Andes. Ron Small was awarded the MBE for his part in this and many other rescues. Ken Joyce was later killed in a plane crash on the Tasman Glacier.

Rescues in the Grand Canyon

Hamish MacInnes, Tammie Keller, Tom Clausing

This great channel in the earth's crust, even impressive from space, is one of the wonders of the world. Surprisingly, its cultural history goes back a long way, 3,000–4,000 years. Now it is visited by up to three million tourists a year.

The Canyon is not noted for its good rock climbing, yet there is evidence that prehistoric man climbed here, not for pleasure or thrills, but probably for flints or while escaping from enemies. However, its verticality, white water and unrelenting heat, result in many technically difficult rescues which come under the wing of a friend of mine, Ken Phillips, Search and Rescue Controller of the Grand Canyon National Park. It is to Ken and his colleagues that I am indebted for this selection of rescues. These park rangers must be fairly unique in the fact that they go downhill to conduct their call-outs. The following call-outs are from various recent reports of the day to day rescue work of the Park Rangers. It is their task to look after those that get into trouble in this remarkable place.

Canyoneers Boat Flip

Grand Canyon National Park search and rescue personnel first started training with helicopter short haul technique (fixed rope attached beneath a helicopter for insertion or extractions) in September 1989. However as the summer of 1990 began they had not deployed the technique on an actual mission. On the afternoon of 16 June commercial boatman Ben Cannon of Canyoneers Inc. prepared his twenty-two passengers and crew, whom he was guiding on a two-week river trip, for the notorious

Crystal Rapids (River Mile 99), which is one of the two most difficult rapids on the Colorado River within Grand Canyon. Just as the thirty-eight-foot raft entered the top of the rapids, the outboard engine prop struck a rock and disabled the vessel, causing it to drift out of control. The flow of the river, close to 20,000 cubic feet per second, caused the five-ton vessel to career down through the rapids and it struck a cliff face on river left causing it to overturn on its side. Although the majority of the PFD (personal flotation device)-equipped passengers were thrown clear of the raft and drifted downstream, a few were trapped underneath the raft in the deck space between the enormous side tubes. The raft sped down the middle of the river and became stuck on a submerged group of boulders known as the Island

Meanwhile, high overhead, the pilot of a tour helicopter spotted the disabled raft and radioed his findings to the Grand Canyon Airport Control Tower, who immediately contacted the National Park Service. Rescue personnel quickly assembled at the South Rim Helibase within the park at the direction of Incident Commander, Mark Law. An initial helicopter flight was dispatched with National Park Service rangers aboard to conduct a size-up. As helicopter 210, a Bell 206-B Jet Ranger on year-round contract to the park, dropped into the Grand Canyon the sweltering 107° F (42°C) heat hit the rescuers at the river. There numerous onlookers stood on shore waiting with other boats to go through Crystal Rapids. A man stood on top of the overturned craft in the river and signalled to the hovering helicopter that there were others trapped beneath the raft.

The inaccessibility of the stranded raft in the 300-feet (90 metre) wide river channel, and the critical situation with the passengers in frigid 50°C water, made for a quick decision by Operations Chief, Ken Phillips. He resolved to deploy a short haul rescue. Rescuers landed at a beach helispot and began to re-rig the helicopter for this operation.

Two kayakers self-dispatched themselves from the shore and reached the raft, where they began rescue efforts. They relayed to the shore party with short range FM radios, "There are still another three people trapped." They were in an air pocket between the massive inflated tubes. A metal bow plate restricted them from swimming out from the front end of the raft. The kayakers eventually managed to rescue one person from beneath the raft. Meanwhile boatmen from the motorised rafts, which were positioned upstream, put themselves at the disposal of the rescue operation. An outfitted ranger, Albert DeLaGarza, was ferried as close as possible downstream of the accident scene, then he waded up through an eddy to reach the stranded raft. Meanwhile Park Ranger Brian Smith was sent downstream on yet another commercial motorised raft to search for the remaining missing passengers. All of them were located by Brian and Park Ranger Keith Lober within a distance of one and a half miles. They reported back that there was only one casualty, a leg injury.

During the re-rigging of the helicopter for short haul, however, there was an unanticipated problem. The extreme heat. The helicopter had been shut down to make the rigging process safer, but the engine couldn't be restarted until it cooled sufficiently. Rescuers stood by anxiously waiting for the temperature of the power unit to cool for a restart. Eventually it was a go situation, everything was readied and the pilot, Rick Carrick, with Ranger Chris Pergiel as spotter, took off for a power check over the accident. While attempting to hover over the moving water, Rick suddenly experienced the symptoms of spatial disorientation. Immediately he overcame this distraction by fixing on a stationary reference point on shore. The helicopter then returned and lifted Ranger Dave Ashe as an additional rescuer to the stranded raft. Once there, the remaining passengers, now suffering from hypothermia, were extracted and pulled up on the overturned craft. Going from the extreme of freezing water to the blasting heat triggered a rapid recovery of the victims. All the passengers, together with the rangers, were short hauled back to the helispot

During all this, an additional National Park Service contract helicopter, together with a US Forest Service helicopter, responded to the scene. Coordinated by Ranger Paul Crawford, they shuttled in rescuers and began transporting passengers from the raft back to the South Rim Helibase.

The complexity of this rescue can be measured in the use of multiple aircraft during a mass-casualty incident (MCI). Also, it was a first for the use of the short haul rescue technique at Grand Canyon National Park.

Bowers/Cottonwood Creek Rescue

On 6 July, 1996 two former frat brothers from Purdue University, twenty-six-year-old Todd Bowers and his companion Brandon Tipton, headed down the Grandview Trail on a day hike into Grand Canyon. Descending past the typical destination of Horseshoe Mesa, they reached the Tonto Plateau in Cottonwood Creek drainage, over midway down into the Canyon, in the searing midday heat.

Todd and Brandon drank through the last of their fluids between them, a single bottle of Powerade drink. The streambed of Cottonwood Creek lay bone dry, being an intermittent water source, which doesn't last into summer. Now confronted with the fate of no water, Todd urged Brandon to come with him, following Cottonwood Creek to the Colorado River for water. After a tense discussion the two hikers separated. Brandon headed up the trail toward the rim as Todd began an off-trail odyssey downstream in a desperate attempt to reach water. Less than one mile from the river Todd's progress was halted by a forty-five foot pour-off (dry waterfall). He began to traverse off the left side of the precipice, believing he could negotiate a climb back down to the creek bottom. At three o'clock, while attempting this exposed traverse, he slipped and fell thirty feet onto rocks. Todd desperately tried to stand, but found it impossible and crashed down again.

Brandon did not reach the trailhead at the rim until 8.20 pm, where he ran into a father and son who gave him water. That night he slept in the car and waited till nearly midday or 7 July at the trailhead. He then began searching other trailheads along the South Rim, when he eventually contacted a National Park Service ranger at 3.30 pm to report his companion overdue. Based upon the circumstances outlined in the initial report, a rescue was launched immediately. Forty-five minutes later Ranger Chuck Sypher, aboard NPS helicopter 210, spotted Todd lying motionless on a sloping boulder slab in Cottonwood Creek drainage. Chuck was dropped by the helicopter with NPS volunteer, Tim Vogelzang on a narrow saddle on a ridge jutting out from the base of the Tapeats Cliff. The hike from this landing zone to the casualty was rugged and exposed. Upon their arrival at 5.00 pm they found Todd Bowers beside a thirty-foot blood trail from above, with ashen grey dry skin and hot to touch.

Todd looked at Chuck through glassy eyes and from parched lips, covered with blood, slowly responded to Chuck's questions in short four-word sentences. Chuck and Tim stablised his injuries, rigged a sling around his pelvis to keep him from sliding down the rock slab and then initiated IV therapy to replace the fluid loss. The first litre was quickly infused and made little changes in his status. Starting his second and final IV bag of normal saline, Chuck knew that the need for backup personnel and supplies was critical. The heat was oppressive and Todd was now coughing up bright red blood. Chuck ran out of IV fluid before reinforcements arrived. Rather than remove the IV he had established, Chuck switched it to a saline lock, which is a plug on the IV catheter.

Initially the rescue seemed like it would be a simple operation with a quick short haul extraction from the site. Unfortunately, as communication problems got complicated, the initial strategy suddenly appeared more elusive. Prior to sunset an Arizona Department of Public Safety (DPS) Air Rescue helicopter (Bell Long Ranger) performed a reconnaissance flight over the accident site for a short haul mission. The confines of the area in a narrow gorge right at the base of a cliff-face, caused them to back off and relay that it was a "No go." At sunset, 7.48 pm, the heat finally began to ease and it was apparent that the patient would not get evacuated that night. Following another helicopter insertion at the small saddle helispot, Ranger/EMT-Intermediate Matt Vandzura arrived at 8.20 pm with oxygen, IV fluids and drinking water.

Ranger Tammie Keller (earlier)

I responded to the South Rim Helibase to assist with an ongoing SAR in the Cottonwood Creek Drainage. When I arrived a manned radio relay was being set up from the scene to Flagstaff by Chuck Sypher. Chuck was also asking for more man power and additional medical equipment. Ranger Nick Herring was Incident Commander at the time. This was a very dynamic incident in that the patient seemed to be deteriorating, it was extremely hot at the scene and a short haul rescue didn't seem to be an immediate option; it was late afternoon and we were running against daylight.

With a rescue plan developed, a switch was made in the role of Incident Commander, which was then taken over by Dan Oltrogge. Nick Herring and I boarded NPS helicopter 210 armed with backup EMS (Emergency Medical Services) equipment. I was critical of the ten additional litres of normal saline fluid asked for by Chuck Sypher at the scene. I couldn't imagine the need for such quantities of IV fluid for one patient. Herring and I were dropped at the saddle helispot west of Cottonwood Creek. We landed at what we refer to as "pumpkin time", which is sunset when helicopters must return to the South Rim Helibase and suspend flight operations. (Federal regulations prohibit NPS agency aircraft conducting flight operations thirty minutes after sunset.) Nick and I dropped our flight helmets and Nomex flightsuits as we gathered our supplies for the hike in. I took what I thought would be plenty of water. At the time I had over a gallon with me, and Nick was also carrying an equally burdensome amount. We began our descent over loose talus and steep terrain. We quickly lost available light and our progress slowed. We didn't reach the scene until 9.30 pm. Even at that late hour it was still hot in Cottonwood Canyon and there was absolutely no breeze.

Chuck was attending to Todd Bowers, the casualty, and had rigged a harness system that provided good immobilisation. He gave me a patient assessment, and then he and I took shifts through the night providing patient care. When I arrived, Todd was alert and oriented. He showed the signs and symptoms of dehydration with pain to his back and leg as well as leg cramps. He was now able to speak in full word sentences, but complained of a discomfort in his chest. He had clear lung sounds, but diminished on one side. Chuck and I discussed a probable pneumothorax (collapsed lung) and specifically monitored him for any deterioration in respiratory condition. Todd was moved from his perch on the rock slab and immobilised in a full-length vacuum mattress, referred to locally as a Germa. The insulating nature of the thick vacuum mattress in the stifling heat meant that we had to pour water on him to lower his temperature.

He asked for a drink which we gave him in increments to prevent vomiting. He was being hydrated with an IV of normal saline. As the night progressed he became more difficult. Chuck and I monitored him, considering the possibility that his mental status was becoming altered. He demanded more water and began to chant, "Water, water, I need water", over and over again. We explained to him that he was being re-hydrated with an IV and that we could only give him capfuls at a time to prevent vomiting. We also explained that two rescuers were currently making their way to the Colorado River to get more water. Most of this emphatic explaining was done by me I actually told him: "You should have considered your actions before you acted and you wouldn't be now injured on the rock begging for water."

He told me he wanted the "nice ranger" back, but remained alert, oriented, talkative, and occasionally argumentative.

About an hour after arrival on scene I began to show the symptoms of dehydration. Ranger Vandzura was also suffering from dehydration. It was necessary for both of us to receive IV therapy with an infusion of a litre of normal saline. The heat in the canyon continued to be above 100 degrees until just before daylight, when the temperatures finally fell to about 89 degrees. Due to the heat and the physical exertion required to access the patient, the rescuers were low on water. As mentioned, Rangers Herring and Vandzura made a trip, in the dark, to the Colorado River to get water. I had a gallon, but allowed myself to become dehydrated to the point that I couldn't tolerate water without vomiting. I mention this embarrassing point; my lack of personal responsibility, in the hope that others, acknowledging that they too may be susceptible to haste and lack of situational awareness. I was an experienced search and rescue member- I knew better.

The next morning several fresh waves resources were deployed from the South Rim involving a rescue plan that was quite unparalleled for Grand Canyon. Rescuers were shuttled by helicopter to a landing zone on a vestpocket beach along the river. This landing zone provided much better clearance than the precipitous saddle helispot utilised the day before. The tiny beach jutted out into the river from the base of the cliff, but it precluded any sort of upstream hike. A motorised inflatable raft was carried in by helicopter sling load and deployed at the improvised helispot. River Ranger Dave Desrosiers then shuttled rescuers upstream over a mile on his improvised "ferryboat". Helicopters shuttled wildland fire crew personnel to the river helispot and a raft journey upstream to Cottonwood Canyon. From the river's edge a steep talus slope had to be climbed in order to gain access into the mouth of Cottonwood Creek. Flowing downstream, Cottonwood Creek terminated at a sheer pour-off eighty feet above the river. The fire crew equipped with "brush tips" mounted on their chainsaws cut a path along the canyon bottom. The vegetation was so thick that it would have made a litter carry impassable. It was now early afternoon and the temperature in the canyon was beginning to rise. The original rescuers had now been in the canyon so long, that back up was sent in to assist with carrying the patient down the canyon.

Todd was carried in a litter to the confluence of the Cottonwood Creek and the Colorado River. As he was being evacuated, making progress out of the canyon, his spirits greatly improved. At the mouth of Cottonwood Creek he was transferred from the Stokes Litter to a Bauman Bag Stretcher for a short haul extraction. The mouth of the drainage was wider than the terrain at the accident site and Arizona DPS Air Rescue was able to maneuver carefully in for the short haul extraction. He was then airlifted downstream to the vestpocket helispot on the river. Here he was loaded aboard the DPS helicopter and flown to the Grand Canyon National Park Airport, where he was transferred again to a fixed wing air ambulance for a flight to Flagstaff.

It took the combined efforts of fifty NPS personnel, three helicopters and a fixed wing aircraft to complete the difficult rescue operation.

Todd recovered from his injuries and some years later he was recruited to take part in a preventative search and rescue (PSAR) video production and discuss his accident, edited with actual footage from the rescue. Many Grand Canyon hikers have actually learned to be more cautious through Todd Bower's personal tragedy.

Elves Chasm Rescue

River runners journeying down the Colorado River through Grand Canyon make frequent stops to hike up side drainages at some of the "attraction sites". Elves Chasm within Royal Arch Creek, located at River Mile 116, provides a lush oasis as water trickles past ferns and wildflowers in a deeply shaded, narrow gorge granting sanctuary from the relentless summer along the river. Tying up their boats at the boulder-strewn mouth, river runners have etched a popular route far up the drainage that involves daunting exposure to negotiate. The furthest regions of Royal Arch Creek are only attained by the most adventurous. Commercial guides typically limit the wandering of their passengers to the first few pools in the lower reaches of the canyon.

Paramedic Tom Clausing

On 17 October 1997 an experienced group of eight boaters on a twenty-one-day private river trip through the Grand Canyon stopped at Elves Chasm. Three of the group had been to the highest possible point in the side canyon accessed by an exposed, loose, two-stage cliff band about twenty-foot high that allows access to the last amphitheatre. It's a climb seldom done by parties, as its approach is well hidden and the rock is poor. One of the group, thirty-year-old "Susan" (not her real name), asked about the approach to the last amphitheatre but was discouraged by those who had been there, as it was dangerous. The party enjoyed the tranquillity at the dripping spring at the head of the second to last bowl. Unbeknown to the group, Susan climbed to the base of the loose wall and started up. Shortly after the peace and quiet was shattered by the crash of heavy rock fall in the direction of the last cliff band. Suddenly the party realised Susan was missing.

The boaters quickly scrambled up to the base of the wall to a fresh rock fall on the forty-foot scree slope and an unconscious Susan lying breathing in ragged gasps. She had a head injury and appeared to take on a pre-seizure posture, an ominous sign of traumatic brain swelling. This quickly resolved and her breathing became more regular as the rate of bleeding increased from a large, deep laceration at the posterior base of her skull. She remained unresponsive.

Faced with a friend in critical condition high in a steep, technical side canyon, the group quickly evolved into rescuers, dividing into three patient care providers, and four to return to the boats for rescue equipment. They didn't have radios – satellite telephone technology wasn't then readily available and ground-to-air emergency radios, although available for rent, were limited to line of sight – not much use in a deep canyon! The four headed back to the boats. It was going to take some time due to the difficulties, including various climbs. Meanwhile, Susan's injuries were taken care of with the basic equipment available at the accident scene. When the four who went to the boats arrived, by a stroke of good luck, another private river party pulled into the eddy at the mouth of Royal Arch Creek, and they asked them to contact any passing commercial river craft, with an emergency radio, to obtain assistance for the evacuation of Susan.

The four, now laden with equipment, climbed back up to join the others. When they arrived, the patient was assessed, properly bandaged and repositioned ready for transport. An improvised c-collar from a lifejacket was used to immobilise her cervical spine and a table, whose normal job was for riverside lunches, was deployed as a backboard/litter. She was stabilised on it with a collection of fleece clothing and numerous webbing cam straps used to rig the boats. Webbing was also used to improvise anchors, and rescue ropes for lowers on the descent. At the start, Susan started to vomit at fairly frequent intervals and remained unresponsive, unable to control her own airway. It seemed as if she would vomit just before she was lowered over the next drop. During this vulnerable lower, while she was unattended, suspended on the ropes, we thought that she was going to vomit again. We were lucky, she never once aspirated.

While the evacuation was underway, word of the accident had been relayed from the boat party, to a commercial river trip with an emergency radio. This group travelled down river to a wider spot in the canyon from where they were able to transmit on the universal distress frequency to a commercial airliner at high altitude. The distress call was then relayed to the LA Center

(Los Angeles Air Route Traffic Control Center) in Palmdale, CA and then passed on to the Grand Canyon National Park Communication Center.

Ranger Tammie Keller

We received a call for a fall at Elves Chasm at approximately 1515 hours. River Ranger Dave Desrosiers and I responded in NPS helicopter 210, a Bell Long Ranger. Jerry Bonner was the pilot. We flew along the Colorado River toward Elves Chasm, as we didn't have an exact location of the injured party. When we got to the junction of Royal Arch Creek and the Colorado River we had a difficult time finding a landing zone. Once on the ground, we made contact with some of the river party who told us that the patient had been moved to an area that they thought might be appropriate for a short haul. Ranger Desrosiers and I sifted through the EMS gear we had brought with us. We needed to travel light to the accident site. The nature of the call was a trauma, so we opted to leave the cardiac monitor behind and take the vacuum mattress for spinal immobilisation. Dave and I, assisted by members of the river party, began carrying technical. rope rescue equipment, EMS gear, oxygen as well as a Bauman Bag, which is a Helirescue stretcher constructed of Cordura employed for short haul missions.

I followed Ranger Desrosiers up Elves Chasm as he knew the route. This involved climbing, crawling and jumping, all with considerable exposure. It was beautiful but at the same time worrisome, since I expected we would have to bring the patient back down the same way. The slot canyon configuration of the area didn't look like it would allow for a helicopter short haul extraction. We climbed and passed equipment up in a neverending series of ledges and constrictions. Although the vacuum mattress was light, it was bulky and difficult to manoeuvre through narrow gaps in the rock. Dave and I made the climb to the patient in about forty minutes. The "golden hour" for this patient, which is the recommended time to be delivered to a trauma surgeon, had long since passed, a common problem in wilderness rescue.

When we reached them, Tom Clausing gave me a breakdown

of events. They had moved her to their present location. I began patient care with Tom's assistance, while Dave prepared for the short haul extraction.

Susan was incredibly well packaged and immobilised to her improvised backboard. Although the vacuum mattress had been lugged to the scene with great difficulty, it wasn't used. An IV of normal saline was started, utilising a pressure infusion system that allowed the IV to run at a set rate without someone holding it above the patient's heart. A blood glucose check of 70, which is below normal, was obtained. Susan had a Glasgow Coma Scale (GCS) of 6 post-accident, and by the time she was transported her GCS was 9.

Desrosiers, the pilot, suggested a reconnaissance flight of the area to check out the situation, as the canyon was both narrow and steep and to ensure a short haul rescue was feasible from the site. Helicopter 210 had repositioned onto the flat Tonto Plateau area above the Royal Arch Creek drainage. Meanwhile the Incident Commander had dispatched Classic Lifeguard Air Ambulance, a commercial air ambulance helicopter from Page, AZ, to rendezvous in the Canyon at the rescue helispot. An additional helicopter was deployed to transport a park ranger to a position on a high summit within the Canyon, where he could operate a radio relay back to the Incident Command Post at the South Rim Helibase.

Jerry Bonner, with Spotter Craig Letz in the aft cabin, completed the recon flight directly overhead the accident scene, carefully checking the helicopter power requirements and rotor clearance. Susan had experienced vomiting prior to my arrival, had a closed head injury and a GCS of 9. All factors that indicated she may not be able to maintain her own airway. Her gag reflex was present however and intubation was not attempted on site. Jerry radioed that the recon flight was successful and the short haul mission could be accomplished with an adequate power margin. The patient was packaged inside the Bauman Bag for the short haul extraction and I served as the litter attendant. Jerry Bonner skillfully took the helicopter down between the canyon walls, with the incredible ease he had deployed on hundreds of previous missions in the Grand Canyon. As he delivered the end of the 150-foot short haul line right to me with amazing precision, I clipped my harness, and the Bauman Bag to the line dangling beneath the helicopter. Right on cue Jerry carefully lifted us directly out of the gorge. Susan and I were flown nearly 3,000 feet up to the enormous improvised landing zone on the Tonto Plateau.

The patient had taken her fall at approximately 1230 hours, NPS rescuers were on scene at the patient's side at 1635 hours, and she was short hauled to a transfer point with Classic Lifeguard at approximately 1720 hours. Susan was then transported by Classic Lifeguard eighty-five air miles to Flagstaff Medical Center. Total time from the accident in the bottom of Grand Canyon to a neurologist in Flagstaff – six hours!

Postscript from Tom

Susan remained in a coma for a number of weeks and eventually regained consciousness before being transferred to a medical centre near her home in Seattle. It took almost two years, but she has regained function, learning all over how to speak and walk and drive and bicycle. She still has some difficulties related to her significant brain injury but is a healthy, happy individual and continues to make progress. I'm afraid if she had spent the night on the river unassisted, we would have lost her, but there's no way to be sure.

Undoubtedly with the onset of affordable satellite telephone technology calls for assistance will likely multiply beyond the bounds of our ability to respond. Many of these calls for help will be minor in nature and would be appropriately handled by the self-reliant wilderness traveller. There's no way back from our technological advances and some would argue they've gotten in the way of our enjoyment of remote places. I've pondered that thought in the past as one who is used to being a rescuer and not a recipient of such services. In the very near future, when somebody make an affordable satellite telephone the size of a pack of cigarettes, I don't suppose I'll consider it too deeply before I throw one in the bottom of my pack.

Winter Rescue on Mount Ararat

Tunç Findik

This is a modern tale of a mountain steeped in history, an extinct volcano possibly tramped by Noah and his four-legged friends. The flood threat has diminished for today's adventurers however, but the mountain presents other threats to the unwary intent on scaling its ancient heights.

A few years ago I was invited on a winter attempt on this ice-domed peak. Winter is now a popular season to make the ascent as, due to the low temperatures, the snow is in better condition, I was also told of an added winter safety bonus as the anti-personnel mines were covered in a deep insulating layer of snow, a legacy of the Kurdish problem. I understand that now this hazard no longer exists.

This chapter is an account of the emergence of official mountain rescue in Turkey, where remote region rescue presents logistic nightmares, and where dedicated mountaineers, mainly living in the big cities in the west, are the long-range rescuers They provide the manpower, with the backing of the military. These rescues by today's Samaritans, surely rival the tales of the Old Testament.

The great Mount Ararat is known as Agri Dagi in Turkey. Its summit (16,916 feet/5,137 metres) is perpetually sheathed in dazzling ice armour. This isolated mountain has always attracted climbers and adventurers. It has been the subject of many stories and legends throughout history, the most famous one being the claim that it is where Noah's Ark came to rest after the Flood. There have been numerous unsuccessful expeditions searching for its timbers. For climbers the mountain is a popular venue, a peak to bag – just like Mont Blanc in the golden age of alpinism.

The first recorded ascent of the mountain was made by Russian climber Friedrich Parrot in 1829. At the time of Parrot's ascent, the religious fanatics refused to believe he reached the top. Now many people have scaled Mount Ararat. Until 1989 and the fall of the Iron Curtain, the icy northern face of the mountain was very close to the USSR border and, being in such a sensitive area, it was generally off limits for climbers. Beginning in the early 1990s, terrorist conflict in eastern Turkey interrupted mountaineering on and around Ararat and, until recent times, the mountain was closed to climbing. However, in 1998, Ararat was reopened and, being the highest peak on Turkish territory, it has attracted huge numbers of climbers, both novice and experienced, like a powerful magnet. Until then, a full generation of Turkish climbers had grown up without being able to climb on the mountain. Unfortunately, when many people rush enthusiastically to a large mountain, accidents occur. The classic South Face route on Ararat is a high-altitude trek in summertime, just like the North Face of Aconcagua in South America. But in winter, it's a different ball game, the tables turn and the mountain becomes more dangerous and serious. Ararat is a peak which looks deceptively easy but it has its own arsenal of hazards, like violent fast-changing weather, severe thunderstorms at any time of the year, and ice and rockfalls, as well as hidden crevasses for good value.

In Turkey mountaineering is in its infancy and until the 1980s, mountain rescue was virtually non-existent. Add to this the great size and complicated terrain of the country, then the logistical problems of a rescue become enormous. Today, thanks to the development of a climbing community, rescue organisations like AKUT, an Istanbul-based rescue unit, and the helping hand of the Turkish armed forces, the mountain rescue set-up is much more effective both in quality and quantity. The main problem is that the rescuers (climbers) live generally in the big cities of Istanbul and Ankara situated in western Turkey. Therefore attempting a rescue in the mountains of eastern Turkey is time-consuming at best. In organising a rescue call-out the back-up of the Turkish military is indispensible with their transport planes, helicopters, supplies and manpower.

Before the advent of search and rescue organisations, climbers going to the Turkish hills and mountains did so at their own risk, unable to depend on any organised rescue, only on fellow climbers who happened to be in the area. Self-rescue and self-sufficiency were the name of the game. Around 1995 the first organised mountain rescue efforts were made by AKUT. Things got better with specialised training and more equipment was acquired.

After the Marmara earthquake of 1999, many organisations, including the Army's own rescue units, were established. Still, mountain rescue in the remote mountains of Turkey remains a logistical headache, but it's only a matter of time until regional SAR units are formed.

The following story illustrates such a long-distance rescue at a high altitude and it is remarkable how so many skilled climber/rescuers got to this remote mountain a thousand kilometres from their homes in a very short space of time.

At the beginning of March 2000 on a frigid but sunny day on Mount Ararat there was hardly a cloud in sight. The weather was typical for a high-pressure eastern Anatolian winter's day. Four climbers had pulled off a successful summit climb on this remote volcanic peak; that's to say that all went well until fate took a leading role – which cost one of the party his life.

The four alpinists, Nasuh Mahruki, Selcuk Kahveci, Kuvvet Lordoglu and Iskender Igdir, were all having specific winter climbing training as well as getting alpine experience. One of them, Nasuh Mahruki, was the first Turkish climber to summit both Mount Everest and the notorious K2 in the Karakoram, the second highest point on the planet, and reputedly the most dangerous. On this Mount Ararat climb they had established Camp 1 at an altitude of 3,200 metres. After a day resting and acclimatising, the team ascended to their assault bivouac site for the summit bid. This cold site was located on an exposed ridge at an altitude of 4,200 metres on the South Face of the mountain.

Mount Ararat is a gargantuan mass, it's a mountain with a very large base area like a voluminous bustle – the total circumference round this base is 100 kilometres. Approach to the mountain in winter, especially after a heavy snowfall, takes two days with big rucksacks. The mountain's easy lower slopes are strewn with black-grey volcanic rocks and a proliferation of scree fields. The peak itself has an enormously deep glacier cap (in some places seventy metres thick).

The northern, eastern and western upper slopes give moderate glacier climbs, whereas the classic route up the South Face of the mountain is much simpler and, up to an altitude of 4,850 metres it generally follows a footpath in summertime. Obviously the glacier cap which covers the upper and summit sections of the mountain has to be climbed to get to the top. Here comes the crunch. In winter this can sometimes be very dodgy due to a covering of very hard black-blue ice, created by the violent winter wind and cold at 5,000 metres. So, being the only technical difficulty of the climb on the classic route, one has to make a short and moderately angled ice climb here, especially in winter, but in summer this slope transforms to a snow hike and occasionally ascent teams fix a rope by using ice screws at this section to safeguard the descent.

The four climbers successfully reached the summit, and took in the fantastic view from the highest point in Turkey, but they had to pull themselves away and face the descent. They started down just after midday and for crossing the icefield they used the classic hip belay for security. Kuvvet slipped and fell. Iskender, while trying to arrest him, fell to his death down the southern gully. The other two climbers were pulled off their stances by the impetus of the fall but somehow managed to stop themselves by using their ice axes. This happened about midday and the survivors descended to search for Iskender as he had shot out of sight down the ice gully. They spent the rest of the day looking for him without success. As they had a mobile phone they used this and managed to report the accident.

Despite the vast distances involved and due to the fact that Ararat is an isolated peak, mobile phone communication is possible. Already, as darkness was falling, the wheels of a major rescue operation were turning over a thousand kilometres away.

News of the tragedy reached our rescue team shortly after dusk and preparations were immediately under way with a military transport plane scheduled to fly us to Kars, one of the larger cities in eastern Turkey. We had mustered a big party of rescuers from different organisations: AKUT and ORDOS, a volunteer rescue club, also individual climbers from Istanbul and Ankara. By midnight we landed successfully at Kars, despite an enveloping mist. Here road transport was waiting and we drove to the town of Dogubayazit which is situated to the south of the mountain. It was here after about two hours work that we finalised our rescue plan.

It was proposed that a large team of rescuers would try to reach the fallen climber on foot, and a smaller group would be dropped near the accident location by a military Blackhawk UH-60 helicopter. By the first hours of daylight, every rescuer moved up the mountain. For us a brief and turbulent flight resulted in a windy drop from the helicopter at an altitude of 3,600 metres. This was on the top of a flat shoulder on the icy South Face of Ararat. There were six of us in our party, with limited equipment, bivouac gear and food. As soon as possible we climbed to a higher position, closer to the area where we understood the fallen climber was.

There's always a risk in rising too quickly to altitude. However, we were all well acclimatised, except one of our rescue party who immediately got altitude sickness, caused by this sudden height gain from 1,100 metres to 3,600 metres, and realised that he would have to descend. The rest of us continued up in changing snow conditions: first, a long traverse on a deep wind-slabbed snowfield, then a tricky climb up powder snow, followed by loose and low-angled rocks. At a safe place around 4,000 metres we decided to stop and establish a bivouac. While Kursat Avci, my climbing partner, and I dug out a snow ledge for the tents, Yilmaz Sevgul, Ertugrul Melikoglu and Burak Akkurt continued upwards to try and locate Iskender.

It was cold, probably in the region of −25°C, but it had now turned into a bright sunny day, with hardly a breath of wind. Yet it wasn't until the sun was dipping on to the horizon, with the mountain transforming to a pinkish hue, that our friends returned. They had grim news: Yilmaz had located Iskender, but as he was trying to reach him on treacherous snow, he had fallen into a small hidden crevasse. He had injured his knee and had trouble even getting back to our bivouac. We now had a further casualty.

That night at our lofty camp it was bitterly cold but by dawn we had struggled into our freezing boots and shortly afterwards were joined by the other rescuers who had climbed up from base.

The southern glacier gully of Ararat is reminiscent of a glacier canyon. It has steep crumbly rock walls on both sides, a few big sérac barriers and many hidden crevasses. Generally it is moderately hard snow or ice climbing. In summertime this place can be a death trap with huge volcanic rocks falling from above, it's a case of running the gauntlet (with crampons), but in winter it's frozen solid due to the numbing cold of eastern Turkey, a cold which always seems worse in the centre of large land mass. We were now faced with negotiating this defile.

It was a cloudy windy day and visibility had deteriorated. Nevertheless, we were told that the helicopter was awaiting our radio call to pick up the body. We ascended within this gully for a few kilometres and as the terrain got steeper we had a council of war, just below the dangerous section. We decided that Kursat, Ertugrul and I would go up, find Iskender and prepare him for the helicopter pick-up. The rest of our group would meantime wait in a safe place, free from stonefall; from there they could come and give us back-up in case of complications.

Upon entering the narrow section of the glacier which by-passes the fifty-metre high sérac wall, we climbed a 45–50° hard snow gully which harboured several hidden crevasses, then ascended to a scree-covered glacier plateau. From here, we spotted our deceased friend Iskender at the foot of the yellow right wall of the canyon, at a height of about 4,600 metres.

We were all friends of his and were devastated that he had lost his life when he had so much to live for. From where we were we could see the full line of his fall of the day before. It was a slope of steep blue glacier ice, dotted here and there with rocks. I realised that once he picked up speed there was no possibility of him self-arresting on the steep stone-hard surface.

We got to him and secured him with perlon slings and a climbing rope which made it easier to lower him to a safer place, out of stonefall danger. We also called the helicopter, as well as our ground control, informing them of progress. In a short time we were ready for a pick-up, with, I must add, little confidence that the chopper would make it. The safe operational ceiling of a Sikorsky UH-60 helicopter is 3,000 metres. Where we waited in anticipation was at an altitude of 4,600m.

At this ceiling, the air is too thin to allow this class of helicopter to operate safely. To compound things, sinister black clouds were nudging the mountain and the wind was rising by the minute. Because Ararat is a massive bulk of a volcano rising from the flatlands it gets hammered by every storm going, as well as manufacturing its own particular brand!

Kursat belayed himself to a large rock alongside the casualty ready to clip Iskender onto a weighted line which had been lowered from the machine. The helicopter approached, slowly edging in as if expecting at any moment to be smashed against the slope by the wind. It was tricky flying, all the stops were out now. A fusillade of snow and ice particles violently hit us as the huge olive green Blackhawk inched slowly down and, after what seemed an eternity, hovered only four to five metres above us. The temperature plunged due to the downwash. We peered through this maelstrom of ice particles as Kursat tried to catch the snaking rope end. He got it, clipped Iskender on, and gave a thumbs-up signal. The roar of the powerful turbines increased and was deafening, reverberating from the ice. Then the body slowly rose suspended from the green monster.

The success of the operation was beyond all our expectations and with this came relief as the cyclone of arctic wind subsided. Our friend was on his way home. We watched sadly as the big aircraft sped away and down – down with its grim suspended load. It was a blessing that he had been lifted by the helicopter, for it would have been a traumatic task for us to have taken him down the long descent through séracs and across the scree fields.

We were both sad and happy; happy that we had completed the mission. We watched with relief as the Blackhawk sank smaller to the horizon until it was barely a speck. But we were sad as we had lost a good comrade and kindred spirit. We climbed down to the others, waiting patiently below, and under ominous skies and unrelenting blizzard we slogged back to our bivouac. That night, we ate the remains of our food.

The following day dawned bright but very windy and we were picked up by a military helicopter. From the fuselage windows we gazed back at that great icy mountain one last time. We were returning with an empty feeling. Later we were told that this had been the highest helicopter-assisted rescue in Turkey.

Peak of the White Stone

Hugh Morris, Richard Wigzel, Dafydd Morris,
Gareth Roberts, Duncan Tripp, Steve Hayward
and Bill Amos

The Gaelic name for the Peak of the White Stone is Sgurr nan Clach Geala. Perhaps for this account it should be called Peak of the White Hell for, on the 24 February 2001, a party of climbers were caught in an avalanche which swept into Alpha Gully. This outback, the Fannichs, is one of the most inaccessible areas of Britain, for there are no roads leading into the region other than a Land Rover track which, when not blocked by winter snow, takes one to Fannich Lodge, a hunting base on the apron of Loch Fannich. Another chapter in this book was enacted close to here, on An Teallach, just to the north-west, an equally wild place also popular with red deer and golden eagles and, of course, the ubiquitous climber.

The maps for the Fannichs are not that hot, in fact the prodigious Geala Buttresses are not marked and lie to the north of the summit, rising 800 feet above the broken lower rocks. These are a series of narrow buttresses of mica schist, numbered one to six running in a northerly direction. Between these rocky skyscrapers, in fact one is called Skyscraper Buttress, lie various gullies. These have been christened Alpha to Delta. Alpha Gully is one of the most popular (if a handful of ascents qualify it in the popularity stakes). This climb is not that difficult, but in certain winter conditions and in excessive snow it can be dangerous. Though the gully is only 400 feet high, a further 400 feet has to be ascended up an adjoining buttress to gain the top.

This mountain in these dangerous conditions can be the venue for a drama. It has all the necessary attributes; remoteness, bad weather, difficult access, especially in deep snow, and if an avalanche is scheduled, all is set for an action thriller.

We start this scenario from the viewpoint of five climbers, all friends: Dave, Hugh, Gareth and Richard from North Wales and Hugh's son Dafydd who lives in Inverness. This record of the accident is unique in the annals of mountain rescues as it depicts the climbers observations of the same avalanche from their individual perspectives, as well as their efforts to extricate and help each other at a time of great need. It was a traumatic experience for them all, which will be with them for the rest of their lives. Hugh Morris is a veterinary surgeon and, like his colleagues on this climb, is an experienced mountaineer. He starts this account.

Hugh

My fourth trip to Scotland this year and we all said *probably my last*! At fifty-eight I didn't feel over the hill. However it transpired that this prediction wasn't far out. Foot and Mouth had been diagnosed in a slaughterhouse in Essex and traced back to pigs in Newcastle, so I knew I was in for a long campaign after this weekend. But for now the portents were promising, with frost forecast and snow conditions had been good recently. As we drove north through Aviemore to Inverness we could feel the cold and see the gleam of snow. The prospect of just a few hours sleep didn't deter us; we knew Dafydd would be planning his usual, a start in the wee small hours. So it proved to be – porridge at 0400 hours, car park at 0630 hours, despite some snow on the road at Dirrie More. It was going to be an epic day in any event as this was part of Dafydd's plan to take us into all the remote climbing regions in Scotland. This objective was to climb Beta or Gamma Gully on Am Blachdaich of Sgurr nan Clach Geala. This had something for each of us; a trek through a beautiful wilderness, some steep ice, a great ridge finish and, apart from Dafydd, none of us had been to the crag before.

It was a slog to the frozen lochan – it felt every bit as far as it looked on the map. We congregated at the big boulder to change into dry clothes after the sweaty exertions of the past three plus hours and got our climbing gear out for the descent into the corrie.

The wind chill was now quite marked. Nevertheless it was still sunshine and showers and we could see the top of the cliff and the exit ridge to the summit. The weather forecast seemed to be spot on. When we got to the corrie edge a snow shower scuttled in which, coupled with spindrift, reduced visibility to the point where going over the edge was a step into the unknown. We down-climbed over the lip (no cornice) and were immediately in a calmer world.

The snow here was powdery on top and we all gathered on a rock knoll to review our strategy. Dave went off to find a suitable slope to test the snow for avalanche risk – the body of the slope seemed stable. The showers passed and we got a good look at our objective; the cliff and gullies looked good, with no cornices, but, despite Dave's snow test, we didn't like the look of the gully exit fans. With only five or six hours of daylight left, and as the wind could be a problem, we decided on Alpha Gully. Dafydd had climbed it before. We could see it and the exit looked straightforward, a broad rock-strewn ridge to the main summit arête. Not quite the hard day to satisfy the young tyro but a great mountaineering day out nonetheless.

At the foot of Alpha I tried to find a belay. There was nothing, but I managed to ram in my hammer as an anchor. Dafydd set off with my plea for a nut or a natural runner at the earliest. He shouted down that he was now on excellent névé and Dave, who had joined me, suggested that we should all rope together, alpine-style, to save time.

Suddenly there was a dull rumble, the ground seemed to shudder and I was enveloped in a choking cloud of buffeting powder snow which appeared to come from somewhere on my right when – *wham* – I seemed to be whipped off to my right straight into the inferno, then cartwheeled totally out of control over the cliff edge to be abruptly brought up short, on my feet, with both axes dangling at my feet and out into sunshine! My hand felt painful, but otherwise no damage.

The relief was short-lived, Richard was all right but had lost his gear and helmet. Gareth too seemed to be in difficulty. I could see blood on the snow below me and Richard said Dave was upside-down tight up under the cliff. I couldn't communicate with Dafydd. That was a worry. I yelled at Richard to move up a bit to relieve the tension on the rope

Richard

The avalanche began as spindrift but just kept building in strength. I was hunched over my axes to the right of Hugh and a few feet left of Gareth. It felt like being under a fast-flowing stream. I was just thinking that this was getting ridiculous when I was blasted off my stance, over the rocks which did Dave such damage, then off down the slope. I was going head first and backwards, not that I knew it at the time. Swimming wasn't an option! Trying to keep a gap by my mouth was all I could think about which is why I suddenly found myself lying on my back, arms flailing, looking at the sky and congratulating myself on digging myself out – which of course I hadn't as the rope had stopped me, though the snow continued down. Gingerly testing my limbs and my head (my helmet had vanished along with my axes), I heard Gareth moaning and, on righting myself, saw him behind me. But Dave was lying sixty metres away up the slope moaning, with tiny red snowballs rolling down the slope from him. He was tangled in the rope and looked in real trouble. Gareth and I sorted ourselves out as soon as possible but this was complicated by the rope, taut as piano wire, there was an icy slab in front of Gareth and a big cliff below him. I didn't feel inclined to untie from the rope and solo up and neither of us had prusik loops.

It was Dave who sustained the most severe injuries.

Dave

I heard a "swish" then boom – clouds of powder snow enveloped me. I watched with horror as Gareth, then Richard disappeared down the gully in the maelstrom. Then the strain on the rope hit me. For an instant my axes held but then I was catapulted off my stance down the gully, hitting a rock buttress below. Everything stopped, a deathly hush and then the pain hit me. I was hanging upside down, the upper rope was twisted tight round one of my legs and I was unable to move with the rope above and below taut as a bowstring. I felt I was slowly suffocating, being hard to breath with a collapsed lung, a broken nose and a mouth full of blood and the rope above and below dragging me apart. It seemed an age before Dafydd could move up to release some rope for Hugh and before Gareth could move up to release the tension on me.

Dafydd (*who had been leading*)

Heard a faint rumble and there was shouting from below; seconds later, before I had established the belay, I was ripped from my stance, and found myself hurtling backwards head first down the gully. The force was incredible and, as I found out later, it was the weight of my four companions falling which was pulling me. I can remember receiving heavy blows to my lower back and then "bang", I came to a sudden halt as the 9-mm rope held on my running belay. I came to rest upside down facing outwards, thankful that my rapid descent had come to an end. I'd fallen about ten to fifteen metres.

I found it difficult to right myself as the tight rope and the pain in my back were restricting my movements. The pull from the rope put more pressure on my back via my harness and every time I made a movement the force pulled me upwards towards the sling. I think that the rope in my rucksack saved me from more serious damage. I remember thinking it was a bloody good job I'd got that runner on.

I was concerned for the others and figured an avalanche of some sort had taken them away, but were they still alive, and if so what condition were they in? Communication was difficult because of the wind and I had no visual contact with any of them, but it was a great relief to finally hear their voices.

Hugh

To do anything I needed to bring the two ropes together on my harness but I just couldn't do it – I desperately needed some slack. I shouted, "Slack" and it started to come. What a relief! However that half a metre of slack did allow me to crane my neck over the edge and see Dave. His situation was obviously serious. He was upside down, one leg tightly tangled in the rope to me, with his head and the surrounding snow covered in blood. What was of more concern was that his groaning was subsiding and there was still no communication. Things were getting desperate.

Then relief, Dafydd was now upright and dug in with the tape runner still around the rock spike above. He down-climbed using the sling as protection and at my belay we were briefly able to ascertain that all sensory and motor functions were present in his extremities.

I assessed that Dave's injuries were life-threatening to the point of not surviving the night. His facial injury, although dramatic, with blood everywhere, was not the main issue. The problem was the apparently extensive damage to his chest, with shallow laboured breathing, whether from internal bleeding into the cavity or from pneumothorax was indeterminable. In any event, unless we could get help before dark, it would be irrelevant. He also had the clammy pallor of the deeply shocked and communicating with him was difficult.

Gareth's ankle injury was not a major problem in the immediate sense. My right wrist was painful but wasn't going to interfere with things. Thankfully Richard was unscathed, despite having fallen about seventy metres. Dafydd's back in the pelvic region was going numb but he still had full sensory and motor function and no pins and needles at his extremities and didn't appear to have sustained any other damage.

Gareth

I was very briefly aware of snow running like sand around my ice axe shaft, then I was off! I heard nothing other than hissing and a strange hollow "bong" as I went tumbling down. I felt no panic, no pain and remember no thought processes. When I stopped I was upside down just above a cliff and couldn't move. I eventually got my bearings, then almost killed myself. I'd lost my specs and heard Hugh and Richard calling for slack. In order to take the weight off Dave's rope, I shouted to Richard, "I'll untie" because I thought I was on the valley floor! Richard screamed, "Don't do it". I was in fact only a metre or two from a cliff edge. All I could see was what I thought was one gentle white slope, which turned out to be the snow-covered corrie a long way below.

I had lost a crampon and couldn't reach one of my ice axes, or Richard's, without untying. My ankle was damaged. I later found that my helmet head band had detached completely from the shell. This was what caused the strange noise.

It took me what seemed ages to climb up to Richard and Dave because of a small two-metre ice band. I found it hard and called for slack to ease the pressure on Dave. We got up to Dave where Hugh and Dafydd eventually joined us. Here we discussed the options and agreed that Hugh and Dafydd should go for help but none of us were then aware of the seriousness of Dafydd's condition.

Our present position was too steep, with no secure belay and in line of fire from above, and we were hopelessly exposed to the weather. There was a rock buttress some forty metres away, a little higher up and to the left with solid mountain above it, under which the wind had blown out a snow scoop. We had to cross a steep broad fan of soft snow to get there with high avalanche risk, but could see no alternative. It was not a trip I'd like to repeat.

Richard, Dave and I were now safely belayed under the rock buttress. Dave's traverse of the slope was painful to watch; he was very weak, slow and stopped frequently, but when I tried to help by taking his weight on the rope, he screamed. Richard was powerless to help; the slope wouldn't take the weight of two on the same spot. When Dave reached our ledge we made him as comfortable as possible with spare clothing and covered him in a plastic bag, then spent two hours digging a snow hole, but spindrift filled it almost as fast as we could dig.

Dave

It took all my strength to traverse the relatively short distance up and across to the belay. I was shocked, cold, wet and in pain. I knew that I could not get off the mountain under my own steam, let alone walk the long distance out in deep snow. I had to wait for rescue. Spindrift was blowing everywhere and it seemed to find all the chinks in our clothing, adding to our misery.

We now switch to the difficult mission of going for help.

Hugh

On the descent to the corrie we took the conscious decision to solo far apart for safety reasons. Luckily, no more snow came down our route, but it was a very hairy descent on frozen turf (the good bits), slippy snow-covered scree and small cliffs. Dafydd had no difficulty leading down to the valley floor. Once there he went ahead and had only gone a short distance, ploughing a metre deep furrow, when he fell into a hole. There was a cry of pain. After a repeat of this incident, I knew we were in trouble when he asked me to take over. The going was really difficult, not so much for the metre-deep snow, but because of the holes that I kept falling into, and also Dafydd if he strayed from my channel.

After about an hour of this we called a halt and discussed the situation. Dafydd assessed that we couldn't get to Fannich Lodge before dark. I knew that this meant Dave wouldn't get out alive. I then gave Dafydd the first dose of Brufen. I had my mobile but there was no signal. Dafydd knew from previous visits that the mobile would work from the top of Clach Geala, and as it turned out only from there.

It was a steep and exhausting climb to the summit and just five metres short of the top – bing – bing – bing – we had a signal! I called 112.

"Newcastle Emergency Centre." That threw me!

I said, "but I'm in north-west Scotland."

"Don't worry, sir. What is your problem?"

I gave full details and we were asked to remain at our MR (map reference), and to keep the phone on. Minutes later he called back to say a SAR helicopter was on its way, ETA less than half an hour. Could we stay at our MR and could we please confirm our MR?

A shower went through and the day cleared, though wind chill was high. Despite digging in behind some rocks, Dafydd couldn't remain on top of the ridge for long. I rang Newcastle again to inform them of the situation and was told to hang on five more minutes as the helicopter would be with us. We then heard it.

The winchman was lowered and when he established that we were part of the Alpha Gully group he asked for the MR for Dave and the others. We gave him this as concisely as possible. It appeared that they had a problem with fuel/weather/weight ratios. He told us he could only take one casavac, so who was that to be? Daf or Dave? I had a brief discussion with Dafydd. He was in poor shape, but I couldn't honestly say at that stage that his condition was life-threatening. The winchman said something like, "It's up to you it's your choice." We knew it had to be Dave.

Due to Dafydd's condition, I made clear to the winchman our plans for the route out, finally asking him to return for Dafydd if at all possible.

Duncan Tripp

202 Squadron, Royal Air Force, provides a twenty-four hour search and rescue service covering the UK from the Midlands of England to the north of Scotland, from the North Sea to the Atlantic Ocean, an area of approximately a quarter of a million square miles. The squadron is made up of three flights; Leconfield near Hull, Boulmer to the north of Newcastle and Lossiemouth near Elgin in the north-east of Scotland. Of the three flights Lossiemouth is the busiest with 250–300 jobs a year. The primary role and secondary role of the squadron is to provide SAR cover for military and civilian aircrew, the tertiary role is everything else.

The weather on 24 February 2001 was a classic mid-winter's day with unstable air moving in from the west giving heavy snow showers, squalls and strong gusts.

With my four colleagues, I arrived on the station at around 0830 hours to check over the first and second standby aircraft before we took over from the off-coming shift. The only difference for the crew on a Saturday is that there's little flying activity at RAF Lossiemouth, the base of the Tornado GR4 aircraft, therefore making it quieter with fewer people around. For us though, Saturday's a normal working day.

The crew on 24 February was, Squadron Leader Steve Hayward, a very experienced SAR pilot, captain and the Boss of the flight at Lossiemouth; Flight Lieutenant Rob Green, co-pilot, on his first flying tour and new to SAR; Flight Sergeant Dougie Cripps, radar/winch operator, like the Boss, a very experienced SAR operator, and finally myself, Flight Sergeant Duncan Tripp, relatively new to helicopter SAR but with experience on support helicopters and a former part time member of RAF Kinloss Mountain Rescue Team. In addition we were joined by two Scottish Ambulance Service paramedics from Aberdeen who wished to experience at first hand the work of the SAR flight.

After we had completed the handover brief at 0930 hours, the rest of the morning and afternoon was spent briefing the paramedics on our role and exchanging ideas. At around 1530 hours the scramble phone rang. It's a direct line to the Aeronautical Rescue Co-ordination Centre (ARCC) based at RAF Kinloss. When this phone rings, which sounds like a school bell, I'm sure, like any emergency service worker, it doesn't matter how often one hears it, the effect is to deposit half a pint of adrenalin into the body. The ops clerk picked up the phone and the first thing we wanted to know was it "wet or dry", was it a land or sea job, which will determine what we wear. At the same time he hit the scramble bell which calls everyone in the hangar into action, including the ground crew. Listening intently, the ops clerk shouted: "Mountain Job." Then he continued recording details as we got into our mountain kit and packed our immersion survival suits in case we diverted to a sea job. As we got ready the Ops Clerk wrote down and repeated what the ARCC was saying: Ordnance Survey 1:50 000 map sheet number and six-figure grid reference, casualty details, weather on scene and the MRT rendezvous point. We plotted the point, it was on Ben Nevis. The ground crew shift boss ran in. "Do you need additional fuel?"

"No thanks, it's on the Ben," replied the Boss.

Grabbing the maps and our equipment – mountain kit and immersion suits – the four of us and the two paramedics ran towards the aircraft waiting outside. The ground crew were already busy preparing the aircraft and, as we were now on a job, it had the call sign, Rescue 137.

We got Rescue 137 up and running and, with our checks complete, Rob transmitted on the radio to Air Traffic:

"Lossie Tower Rescue 137 request immediate take off."

"Rescue 137, Tower clear take off."

The flight from Lossiemouth to Ben Nevis normally takes forty-five to fifty-five minutes but because of the weather it was going to take sixty-five. However, about fifteen minutes into the flight, when Rescue 137 was near Inverness, we were contacted on the HF radio by the ARCC. They told us that a Royal Navy Sea King from RNAS *Gannet*, based at Prestwick, had just completed a job fifty miles south of Ben Nevis and was already in the area. There's considerable friendly rivalry and banter between ourselves, the ARCC and the Navy, so there were a few comments made on board Rescue 137 about the Navy and the ARCC. ARCC came off second best for giving the job to the Navy. As the aircraft turned to return homewards, another call came over the HF from ARCC.

"We have further tasking for you. Reports are sketchy. Five climbers were caught in an avalanche near Sgurr Mor in the Fannichs. Sheet 20 grid 193718. Initial reports are of two casualties, one with an ankle injury, the other a serious chest injury."

The weather forecast in the area was for scattered snow showers, cloud base 1,500 to 3,000 feet, with north westerly winds of thirty to forty knots with gusts of fifty to sixty. Now ARCC were the greatest thing since sliced bread! We plotted the new point. Dougie and I prepared our equipment. In addition to the usual items I put on the avalanche transceiver, also my ice axe, crampons, map and a hand-held GPS into which I put the casualty position. We then discussed escape routes, should I be left by Rescue 137. Dundonnell MRT had also been called out by the Police and were en route. This always gives me a warm feeling knowing that the MRT are there as back up and that if we are unable to do the job they can always be relied on to finish it.

We arrived on scene at around 1600 hours. Winds were thirty to forty knots, although it wasn't snowing at that time. We were obviously between showers with large black angry clouds looming out to the west. The mountains were covered in deep fresh snow. The grid we had been given was on the west side of a very large steep-sided corrie. With the winds coming from the west we would be in down draughting air.

Steve Hayward, the Boss, appears elsewhere in this book. Steve, though retired from the RAF is still in the air, now driving an air ambulance He relates the first part of his side of this story.

Steve Hayward

An initial sweep of the area failed to locate the climbers, but did reveal turbulent conditions, with significant down drafts in the corrie. Power to hover was likely to be an issue. A helicopter requires considerably more engine power than it does for forward flight and can reduce the power needed to stay over the same spot on the ground. Unfortunately if the conditions are turbulent, with the wind changing strength and direction, or tumbling on you from above, you easily find yourself with insufficient power to hover at all. If this situation comes upon you without warning as you are in a hover, life can become very exciting – very quickly. We decided to collect members of the MR from Dundonnell. This would give us the opportunity to drop off the two paramedics. We would trade this weight for a mix of increased hover performance and MRT personnel.

Duncan is a dedicated winchman as well as a climber, with a passion for the mountains. He continues.

Duncan Tripp

Just before we departed the scene we took advantage of a break in the weather to have a look along the top of the corrie edge. There were large overhanging double cornices, spectacular but you wouldn't want to be under one if it broke off. As we got to the top of the corrie, Dougie spotted two walkers. We were unsure if they were part of the five so I was winched down to find out whether they had been involved or had any information relevant to the incident. I was lowered down to the two men, both still wearing climbing harnesses, one with a two-foot tail of snapped rope. After speaking with them and ascertaining the position of their injured friends, we decided that David required immediate evacuation. They then advised me on their proposed route out to the main road.

Then I was winched up and Rescue 137 immediately moved to the grid position to search for the casualty and his two colleagues. By now it was 1615 hours the light was starting to fade and the snow showers increasing, and we were regretting not having taken the two survivors who may have been able to more accurately identify the position and we would have saved them the long walk off. After approximately ten minutes, with no sign of the three climbers, the crew elected to go and pick up MRT members from Dundonnell.

At Dundonnell we offloaded the two paramedics and the life rafts. To further increase our power margin by keeping Rescue 137 light, we elected to take just two MRT, Dave Neville and Donald MacRae, two top blokes.

Steve got the large machine airborne and headed once more for Clach Geala . . . He now gives his account of the next phase of the operation.

Steve Hayward

As Duncan has mentioned, conditions on the mountain were now very turbulent, with heavy snow showers. It was essential to get Duncan and the MRT to the casualties.

Once at the scene, and after a short search, Rob sighted three climbers at the base of a high rock buttress on a narrow ledge at 2000 feet. Conditions were extremely turbulent in the snow showers. We couldn't simply hover above them; delivering nine tons of screaming machinery with the associated downwash could easily trigger another avalanche, but we found an alternative winching area some 150 metres from and thirty metres below the casualty. It was a 40° boulder/snow slope. During the approach I asked Duncan, "Are you happy to be winched?"

Duncan Tripp

What Steve actually meant was, "We may not be able to get you out, so you're on your own." There was a strong possibility that I would have to make my own way off the mountain.

It wasn't an easy decision to make, to be severed from the umbilical safety of the winch cable. But given the casualty's condition, it was a gamble I was willing to take.

"Yes," I said, "I've got all the kit I need if you leave me!"

Dougie then checked my winching harness and my equipment, rucksack, GPS, crampons (fitted), ice axe to hand and the Main Response Bag, full of medical equipment. Just before I was winched we confirmed escape routes and plans. In the hover Rescue 137 was being tossed about. The air speed indicator was showing readings of between zero and forty knots and the torque gauge was showing power variations from 30–110 per cent.

Basically, because of the turbulence and to maintain a hover, the Boss was having to use virtually no power one second to full power plus the next, not a good situation to be in. It was taking all his skill to tame this beast!

Once I was on the ground, Steve took Rescue 137 away to do a circuit to give the crew a chance to relax and compose themselves before coming in again to drop off Dave and Donald. I always find it quite surreal when Rescue 137 flies away, one minute you're on a noisy rollercoaster from hell, the next you're in the relative peace and quiet of a Scottish mountain. However, no time to appreciate the peaks resplendent in their winter garb. To reach the casualties I had to cross a forty-metre snow slope which I assessed as potentially avalanche-prone, perhaps category 3 to 4 (medium to high – not to be messed around on). The snow was deep on a rock boulder base. To minimise the risk and the time spent on the slope, I went straight up to the bottom of the rock face as there was no way around it. Once there I moved up and along the base of this using my ice axe.

During this phase Rescue 137 made a second approach to lower Dave and Donald. Once this was done, Steve put down on the far side of the corrie, in line of sight, to conserve fuel. Dave and Donald followed my steps. Meantime I arrived at a point slightly higher and some ten metres from the casualty, but encountered a dangerous 60°–70° snow filled gully with obvious serious avalanche risk. From here I shouted to the three climbers through the howling wind and confirmed that two were OK. However, the third was having great difficulty breathing and could be seen sitting with his knees to his chest and in a lot of pain. At this point Dave and Donald joined me, we discussed our options. They agreed that the possibility of moving across the slope was just too risky without more climbing gear. They, like myself, had medical kit but no rope, slings, pegs or climbing hardware with which to get a decent anchor.

I got on to the radio and informed the crew that further man power would be required as we might have to set up a belay to lower the casualty and requested they bring crag kit, a stretcher and the 200-metre ropes.

To save time and to get to the casualty ASAP, I shouted across, "How much rope do you have?"

"About thirty metres of undamaged rope," was the reply.

My thoughts were that they could perhaps set up a belay and for one of them to come across. We could then set up a fixed rope across the gully.

With concern for the casualty mounting, his friends were asked to put this into operation; however as the rope was damaged, frozen and badly tangled it took ten minutes to sort out. This was frustrating; the temptation to move across the gully with a nasty drop below, and accept the risk, was over-whelming. Common sense prevailed. Whilst waiting, we dis-cussed the evacuation options.

The quickest solution would be to scoop and run by double stropping. This would involve winching the casualty with two strops, one over his head and under his arms, the other under his legs so he could be winched in the horizontal position. A fast extraction, but not good with a suspicion of spinal injury, as this casualty had.

The ideal scenario, considering his probable injuries, would be to get the stretcher up to his present position, then winch him. This however wasn't practicable, due to the time factor. Darkness was almost upon us. Also there was barely enough room for three to stand on that ledge, let alone prepare a stretcher.

Another possible solution would be to lower him 800 feet to a point where Rescue 137 could pick him up. This also had a time penalty. Getting the stretcher, gear and ropes up into this dangerous area, and then finding solid belays for the long lower wasn't viable. Also if Rescue 137 was unable to pick up the casualty from the bottom of the corrie, it was an eight-kilometre carry to Fannich Lodge, followed by a twelve-kilometre four by four vehicle track in deep snow to the nearest main road, with no guarantee that this track was driveable. This we estimated would take a further eight hours, giving a total delay of ten to twelve hours. With the casualties condition deteriorating, time was of the essence.

I must now introduce a further participant in this chain of events, Bill Amos. Bill is a friend of mine whose day job is as a microbiologist, but by inclination he is a mountaineer as well as Team Leader of the Dundonnell Mountain Rescue Team. The team's area is this vast empty quarter of the Scottish Highlands. With the understatement common to those in MR, he tells their side of the rescue.

Bill Amos

The most difficult call-outs include those in which there are more unknowns than certainties, where the map reference of the location and the description are not in agreement and where the choice of base location and best access route are debatable. The need for fast decisions and urgent action due to multiple casualties adds further confusion. As six of us stood waiting for Rescue 137 at Dundonnell I realised that this rescue had the lot, plus failing light, fresh snow and avalanche risk.

Other team members had been directed to the dam at Loch Droma on the Garve to Ullapool road, known locally as the Geerie. The bends and dips, much loved by summer motorcyclists, would be a challenge for those driving there in the snow. From that location, which lies to the north of the Fannichs, they might be able to drive about four kilometres up the track and then walk a further five kilometres towards the grid reference point given by one of the survivors by mobile phone. The caller said that he was in a party of five who had been avalanched in Alpha Gully on Sgurr nan glach Geala, a remote, but popular mountain, resulting in at least two being injured, one seriously. However, the grid reference was not that of Alpha Gully. He could not be in two places at the one time! The fact that he was near Sgurr Mor had also been mentioned by the police, adding yet more confusion. If the position was an error, the team members could continue on to the ramp that allows access to the gullies. Despite many attempts, we had been unable to make any further contact. We had to assume that they were all together at the gully but we did not know if they were near the top, back at the bottom or trapped somewhere in between.

I had stood on the summit of the mountain the day before, with climbing friends from Edinburgh. We had opted for a walk because we reckoned that due to the recent heavy snow showers few climbs would be in condition. It had been a long trudge to the summit and we had stayed well back from the double cornices that overhung the winter routes. Fresh snow and spindrift had billowed from the top, falling into the summit snowfield, below which lie most of the gullies, including Alpha.

In Dave, Donald, Colin (all MR emergency medical technicians), John and "Spanner" I had an experienced and strong climbing team. Every alternative had been discussed. It made sense for us all to get to the scene as soon as possible, find the climbers, sort out the casualties, and prepare for an evacuation. With luck, the helicopter might be able to lift off the injured. If that was not possible, it might be able to take in the remainder of the team; otherwise, they would have a difficult hike, followed by a traverse into the bottom of the gullies or, alternatively, a climb to the summit. Without a helicopter this could take three hours in the thick drifting snow; if we walked in from the west it would take about the same time.

As you know, Rescue 137 came in and picked up two of our team, Dave and Duncan, and in what seemed a short period of time radioed to request that we bring a 200-metre rope and belay gear when we were picked up. It appeared as if a long lower would be required. Minutes later, while on our way to the scene in Rescue 137, we were able to contact the others at Loch

Droma. Eleven more team members had gathered there; they were asked to wait for the return of Rescue 137 after it had refuelled. It was clear from the chat on the intercom that we were flying on the edge of the helicopter's capabilities; the flight reminded me of being in a small open boat in rough seas when you know you should be on dry land.

We were winched down on to the sloping ramp that lies below Alpha, Beta and Gamma Gullies. Below lay a rock band that prevents easy access from the floor of Choire Mhor. A few boulders peeped through the snow, providing us with something to hang on to. As we sorted ourselves out, I could see that there were only three climbers with Duncan at the bottom of Alpha Gully. Where were the other two climbers? In the gully? Below us? Or possibly, not even on the scene? Rescue 137 was sitting on the top of Meall nam Peithirean, waiting. But not for long.

At the accident scene things were moving slowly. Two of the three survivors on their snow ledge were busy sorting out the tangled rope. Then Gareth tied on and moved out across the gully. He made it, quite a feat considering the trauma of the accident and a damaged ankle. When he got across he discovered he had forgotten the gear, but Duncan and the others fashioned a belay with his two ice axes.

Duncan Tripp

Once Gareth was with us he was belayed whilst I used his ice axes, one in frozen turf and one in ice, to complete the fixed rope anchor. I then clipped on and crab-crawled across the slope using my own ice axe. Once with the casualty I was able to clip onto a fixed belay on the snow platform which was barely big enough for us to stand. Finally I had the chance to assess the casualty.

"Hello, I'm Duncan. What's your name?"

"David," he gasped.

During the assessment there was continuous spindrift pouring down on us like a waterfall from the buttress above and that, combined with the wind, made coms with both David and Rescue 137 difficult. David was sitting to his right side with his knees pulled up to his chest, his respiration's were fast and shallow and he had difficulty speaking.

As well as being slightly cyanotic, he had an obvious facial injury and was very cold and wet.

At this point Rescue 137 radioed to say they were getting short on fuel; time was critical as heavy snow showers were approaching and light was fading fast. The Boss came up on the radio.

"Duncan, we need to make a decision in the next two minutes."

He then explained that Rescue 137 would have to depart the scene for refuel at Inverness as fuel was now down to 100 lbs, or six minutes flying time above the bare minimum – what we called running on chicken fuel.

"Stand by," I said. One casualty had an ankle injury, but could walk. However David was in a life-threatening condition. The quickest way to get David out of there was with Rescue 137. I looked up at the near vertical rock; it would be close, but I reckoned that with enough winch cable out, the rotor blades would be just clear of the rock face. Our laid down limit is fifteen feet. However that can be reduced to five feet for immediate life-saving only. I think this fell into that category. We would have to use the double strop method with the possibility that we could exacerbate any spinal injury. I relayed the idea to Rescue 137. They said they would try. I explained the predicament to David and through gasps he agreed emphatically. "Let's get to hell out of here!" I shouted the plan across to Donald and Dave and asked them to remain on their side of the gully, the fewer people on the ledge the better.

Steve Hayward

Things were obviously bad. I took the Sea King back in the air and flew an approach towards the scene. Meantime Dougie got the strops on to the hook and, with Rob, ran through the winching checks.

As the high buttress was going to be close in on our left, it meant we would have to be quite high over the casualty in order to have enough clearance for the rotors. This was good in one way, the downwash was less likely to effect them. However, it meant that winching would take longer, also we would have to be very precise. The aircraft was attempting to dance around in the turbulence again as we came to hover over the party. Although I had plenty of references to maintain an accurate hover, I couldn't judge blade clearance to our left, so Rob had his eyes very much outside to ensure that close didn't turn into too close. Dougie now calmly guided me to the position he needed the aircraft in to allow him accurately to deliver the strops to Duncan. It was going well, the strops were almost in Duncan's outstretched hand – then life got complicated.

The Sea King has a system called Automatic Voice Alerting Device (AVAD), or Gladys as we affectionately call it. In the event of a system malfunction, as well as a warning caption, Gladys, in an insistent female voice, will call "Master caution", this is to draw your attention to something you might miss if you are busy – such as hovering a few feet from a cliff in turbulence with most of the winch cable deployed. When Gladys called "Master caution", my immediate thought was, Oh, for goodness sakes. This just wasn't our day!

Rob called out; "Intermediate trans chip caption."

This tells you that you have either got metallic debris in one of the gearboxes that transmits the drive to the tail rotor, or that the gearbox is overheating. So something very dramatic was about to happen. Of course, the caption could be spurious, the way you endeavour to check this is by pulling the relevant circuit breaker and resetting it. If the caption comes back on immediately, or later on the sortie, you must assume the caption is genuine and land as soon as possible. This means pick a suitable spot nearby and put the aircraft on the ground. Rob reset the circuit breaker, the caption returned immediately. I remembered that a friend of mine had encountered a similar situation and by the time he landed the aircraft – at night on the nearest oil rig – the gearbox had become so hot it had melted the rubber seals round the filler.

Dougie quickly asked, "What do you want to do, Steve? Are you happy to continue? The strops are almost down."

"Yes," I replied. You have no time to ponder the risk/benefit calculation at length, you must take a decision and make it instantly. Duncan had already said the casualty needed to be removed urgently and was prepared for the extra risks of winching straight from the scene.

"We'll stay and take them. As soon as they're clear of the ledge, let me know and I'll start flying away."

This would allow us to winch in Duncan and the casualty as we flew slowly round the corrie. Although Duncan would be slightly more exposed while we did this, it at least would give us the opportunity to carry out an emergency landing should something fail in the tail drive. If we had stayed where we were in the hover, up against the cliff, the usual procedure to give the winchman a clear lift, we would be very poorly placed if things failed. All this happened and was dealt with in ten to fifteen seconds.

Dougie was calling, "Winching in, two on, clear to move forward and right."

"Roger," I replied. "Fast as you can with winch in, Dougie." This was a statement of the blindingly obvious, which Dougie ribbed me about later.

Dave can still recall the intermittent view of the chopper high above alongside the buttress. "How it hung there, buffeted by the wind, with the rotors almost touching the cliff I'll never know. It must have been on the very edge of safety and these guys had gone beyond such parameters and were risking their lives for me. I shall never forget it."

For a moment let's go down the 175 feet of that slender steel cable to Duncan, and to a point in time a few moments earlier.

Duncan Tripp

Unknown to me, when the winch hook was almost within my grasp, the audio warning on Rescue 137 interrupted the concentration of the crew. Dougie accurately delivered the strops first time and I quickly had David rigged for lift. I then unclipped us both from the belay and we were winched clear of the rock buttress. The aircraft immediately started to move forward followed by a right-hand rapid descending turn. At this point Dougie banged the cable to let me know there was a problem.

This was a difficult decision for Steve. The helicopter was in possibly one of the most vulnerable of situations, with the rotors dangerously close to a thousand-foot face, severe turbulence and driven snow – running on chicken fuel and with a possible catastrophic gearbox failure. Duncan was soon to be enlightened.

Duncan Tripp

When I looked up again it suddenly struck me, inconceivably, Dougie had closed the cabin door. Alarmed, I realised that I wasn't actually looking at the starboard side, it was the port side of Rescue 137! The aircraft continued to fly away and descend. Once at the door, Dougie and I assisted David into the cabin. Dougie shouted that we had a hard latched Intermediate Gearbox caption. We were released from the winch hook and I plugged into the intercom.

David, who thought that the worst was over, was lifted and secured in a seat and told to adopt the crash position, which coincidentally was the most comfortable for him, and all loose kit was stowed. Dougie declared a MAYDAY on the HF, Rob declared one on the air traffic radio and I activated my Personnel Locator Beacon – well, if we were going down the whole world was going to know about it! Once all the immediate procedures were complete the crew faced a dilemma: the drills say with this type of emergency "Land as soon as possible." This had to be weighed up against the isolated hostile terrain, finding a suitable landing site and the very serious nature of David's condition. This was all rapidly discussed and the Boss elected to fly to the nearest road head, at the lowest safe height and speed to minimise the loading on the tail rotor.

During all this Hugh and Dafydd were engaged in their epic hike back to safety with Dafydd more seriously injured than had been realised. . . . Hugh re-lives the end game: "We set off down, but immediately Dafydd was in a hole – this time the pain was severe. We stopped and had some food and drink and some more Brufen. It was sunny now and the chopper went over and we assumed that Dave was on his way to safety."

Dafydd was relieved to get going again. "The weather had improved as we descended. In the back of my mind I hoped the chopper would return, but we ploughed on regardless. For me at least it was a struggle and for Hugh, breaking the trail, a seemingly endless treadmill. As we forced our way through the snow, I said, 'I bet Richard and Gareth will be shacked up in some cosy pub recuperating with a few pints in front of a roaring fire, the jammy swines.' I didn't realise they too were struggling in the terrible conditions."

Hugh and Dafydd reached their car at 2030 and were informed by the police that the helicopter had landed nearby and that Dave was now in hospital. Also that Gareth and Richard were with Bill Amos's group, still heading out to Fannich Lodge. Hugh suggested to the police that he would take Dafydd directly to Raigmore Hospital in Inverness.

Rescue 137 had managed to limp ten minutes and eighteen kilometres from the incident to a point just up from the main Achnasheen road and was safely shut down at 1810 hrs. Duncan now got to work to do everything possible for Dave and put him on max. flow oxygen. Steve was onto the ARCC, trying to get another helicopter to evacuate David, but it was a busy day. The estimate for an ambulance was thirty minutes. Meantime Dave was responding to Duncan's efforts. When the ambulance crew managed to get through the snow to the road below the emergency landing site Dave was supported sitting up on a stretcher, which made it very unstable. He was then moved to the ambulance which took a further twenty minutes due to the very rough ground. He was finally handed over to the Ambulance crew at 1930 hrs.

Bill Amos and the team were still a long way from home.

Bill Amos

We were oblivious of this crisis with Rescue 137 and our immediate concern was to get off the mountain. Conditions were deteriorating. Whilst we waited for the return of Rescue 137 we started to hunt around for gear placements which could be used to secure our present position, or as an anchor for an abseil to the corrie floor, provided that we could find a reasonable way down. We were soon joined by Dave and Donald, together with Gareth and Hugh. It was quickly agreed that waiting for a helicopter below a potential avalanche was not an option and that we needed to get out from our present position pronto! Colin and John had found a possible descent route and were digging out snow from behind a boulder that appeared to be frozen in position; it was the only belay available.

Gareth said that, despite his ankle injury, he would be OK for an abseil. A team member was paired up with him and Hugh so that, if there was a further avalanche, the avalanche transceiver worn by the team member would help the others to find both. It occurred to us all that the whole party could be buried, but these thoughts remained unspoken. It was an "interesting" descent over mixed conditions of ice, some rock, a few good bits of névé and a lot of soft snow which flowed down the gully, only to be blown back up, obscuring the route. We arrived on the corrie floor in darkness. There was still no sign of Rescue 137; they seemed to be taking a long time to refuel. We were on our own and in these conditions and with the amount of first aid equipment, ropes and gear that we were carrying, the five kilometre walk out to the track at Loch Fannich would be a trial. We knew our ordeal was not yet over, it was a long way home. Drifting snow crowded the beams of our headlamps.

Richard

I struggled through sometimes chest-deep snow, weighed down by the remainder of the ropes and gear I was carrying because of Gareth's damaged ankle. I was kept going by the humour of the rescue team and the image of Dafydd and Hugh sitting in a pub replaying the day's events over several sharpeners.

Bill Amos

Stopping only to help each other when we plunged in up to the waist and sometimes up to the armpits. By 9.00 pm we were getting pretty exhausted and it was a welcome relief to pull the ten-man bothy bag over ourselves and sit down on our laden sacks for a brew and something to eat. A bothy bag is like a lightweight tent without poles or a ground sheet. It's anchored by sitting on the bottom wall. It can be a lifesaver.

We had a look at Gareth's ankle and bound a SAM splint round his boot and up his leg for support. Whilst still in the comfort of the bothy bag, we picked up transmissions from the team Land Rover, which had nine team members on board. They had figured out that we would head out by Fannich Lodge. We eventually established contact and asked them to request a second four-wheel drive vehicle from the police. Spirits lifted, we headed off towards the track that runs westwards from Fannich Lodge and within an hour saw the welcoming sight of head torches moving up to meet us. We exchanged our sacks for their lighter loads and were soon down at the track where we were greeted by Robert, a police sergeant from Dingwall and Ruaraidh Matheson, the keeper from Fannich Lodge, each with a four-wheel drive vehicle.

Fannich Lodge lies about twelve kilometres from the nearest public road at Lochluichart, where we learned that Rescue 137 had made an emergency landing. The final five kilometres to the lodge is a rough track, cut into the hillside above Loch Fannich. On many previous searches, we had asked Ruaraidh to help, even if only to turn on a few outside lights and on the occasional visits team members had been treated as welcome guests. As we crowded out the kitchen on that wild winter's night, Ruaraidh, his wife and two children rose to the occasion, handing out home-made soup, bread, tea and a small dram to wash it down. With thirteen people in the Land Rover and the rest in the Police vehicle, we bade farewell to the Matheson family and headed down the track. Ruaraidh had been surprised that anybody had managed to make it up to the lodge that night and here we were, driving down, after even more snow had fallen.

The six of us who had left from Dundonnell arrived back at Dave's bunkhouse at 4.00 am. As we went into the lounge, we agreed that after the departure of Rescue 137, it had been an old-fashioned rescue, where the calibre of the people you are with is what really matters. We had all been very much reliant on each other. We decided that it might as well end in the old-fashioned way. I sneaked into the bedroom where my climbing friends lay sleeping, pinched a bottle of whisky and just as quietly left. On the way through to the lounge I picked up six glasses, opened the bottle and threw the top in the bin.

Dafydd – a postscript

Sitting in my climbing clothes and boots in the corridor of the overworked A&E Department at Raigmore Hospital my thoughts drifted to the others, Dave in particular, as we had no idea what state he was in. The place was full of Saturday night drunken casualties giving the nursing staff a hard time as they tried to help them. The next thing was I collapsed on to the floor – one way to grab attention!

I woke up slowly on a trolley to find nurses trying to get my boots and salopettes off as they wheeled me into a cubicle. Doctors came and went and, after some brief examinations, said that I should get my clothes on and I could go home.

Somewhat surprised, but in no real state to argue, I thought fine I'll get dressed and go, which is what I tried to do, and then – bang – I collapsed again. I was put into a room on the ground floor where this time I managed to black out in the toilet whilst having a pee. Fortunately my father, Hugh, and a couple of nurses came to my aid. I remember thinking as I came round on the floor with my head by the toilet, I hope they wash the floors in this place.

Subsequently, following the diagnosis of internal bleeding in the form of a serious pelvic haematoma, I was put on to a ward with some long-term cancer patients and a chap who wanted his manhood straightened, which provided some light-hearted entertainment for the rest of us on the fourth floor which, ironically, had a superb panoramic view of the Fannichs in their winter splendour.

Dave was in the High Dependency Unit just down the corridor and I was keen to see him but it took a couple of days before I was able to take my bags of blood for a short walk to Dave's room. This was the first time I'd seen him since Alpha Gully. He looked battered and bruised; the chest injuries had resulted in a pneumothorax, seriously life-threatening at the time but treatable in hospital. His head injuries were fortunately all superficial, though his face did seem to be a different shape and colour from a few days before!

I learned that the A&E consultant who saw him on arrival estimated that, given the injuries and with no intervention, he may not have survived for a further two to three hours, given his condition.

Acknowledgments and Sources

I would like to thank all contributors to this book. Their stories were often difficult to tell where past traumas were relived and recorded in black and white. I apologise for harassing them with deadlines when they had more rewarding things to do, such as rescue the less fortunate or go on expeditions.

The majority of the contributions from rescuers and rescued in this volume were originally commissioned for my earlier books, *High Drama* (Hodder & Stoughton, 1980) and *The Price of Adventure* (Hodder & Stoughton, 1987). A couple of these pieces developed out of climbing magazine articles, others became articles or were later incorporated into books. "Lucky Joe", for example, later developed into Joe Simpson's award-winning bestseller *Touching the Void*.

Later versions of "We Recover the Bodies of our Comrades" and "The Matterhorn and the Bergschrund" by Ludwig Gramminger appear in Hans Steinbichler's biography, *Ludwig Gramminger: das Gerettete Leben*.

"Shibboleth" by Andrew Fraser first appeared in the *Edinburgh University Mountaineering Club Journal* of 1959.

"A Cauldron of Wind" is reprinted in Markus Burkard's book, *Mein Flugbuch*.

"Buried on Mount Cook" is included in Karen Gazley's book, *My Everest*.

"Not a Place for People" by Pete Sinclair is excerpted from his *The Last Innocent Americans*.

"Self-help on the Ogre" by Doug Scott has appeared in part in *Mountain* magazine and in *Games Climbers Play* compiled by Ken Wilson.

"Windy Mountain Epic" by Alison Osius appears in her biography of Hugh Herr, *Second Ascent*.

I am grateful to Blyth Wright for last minute translations, Dawn McNiven, the Press Officer of RAF Kinloss, and my editor, Margaret Body, who has checked all my literary body bags.

Hamish MacInnes
Glencoe